Teach Yourself VISUALLY™

Access® 2010

Visual

by Faithe Wempen

Wiley Publishing, Inc.

Teach Yourself VISUALLY™ Access® 2010

Published by
Wiley Publishing, Inc.
10475 Crosspoint Boulevard
Indianapolis, IN 46256

www.wiley.com

Published simultaneously in Canada

Library of Congress Control Number: 2010923552

ISBN: 978-0-470-57765-3

Manufactured in the United States of America

10 9 8 7 6 5 4 3 2 1

Trademark Acknowledgments

Disclaimer

In order to get this information to you in a timely manner, this book was based on a pre-release version of Microsoft Office 2010. There may be some minor changes between the screenshots in this book and what you see on your desktop. As always, Microsoft has the final word on how programs look and function; if you have any questions or see any discrepancies, consult the online help for further information about the software.

Contact Us

For general information on our other products and services please contact our Customer Care Department within the U.S. at 877-762-2974, outside the U.S. at 317-572-3993 or fax 317-572-4002.

For technical support please visit www.wiley.com/techsupport.

WILEY

Wiley Publishing, Inc.

Sales

Contact Wiley
at (877) 762-2974 or
fax (317) 572-4002.

Credits

Executive Editor
Jody Lefevere

Project Editor
Christopher Stolle

Technical Editor
Joyce Nielsen

Copy Editor
Marylouise Wiack

Editorial Director
Robyn Siesky

Business Manager
Amy Knies

Senior Marketing Manager
Sandy Smith

Vice President and Executive Group Publisher
Richard Swadley

Vice President and Executive Publisher
Barry Pruett

Project Coordinator
Lynsey Stanford

Graphics and Production Specialists
Carrie A. Cesavice
Andrea Hornberger
Jennifer Mayberry
Mark Pinto

Quality Control Technician
Jessica Kramer

Proofreading and Indexing
Shannon Ramsey
Johnna VanHoose Dinse

Screen Artist
Jill Proll

Illustrators
Rhonda David-Burroughs
Cheryl Grubbs

About the Author

Faithe Wempen, M.A., is a Microsoft Office Specialist Master Instructor and the author of over 100 books on computer hardware and software, including the *PowerPoint 2010 Bible, Microsoft Office 2010 for Seniors for Dummies,* and *A+ Certification Workbook for Dummies.*

Faithe is currently an adjunct instructor of computer information technology at IUPUI, where she teaches PC hardware and software architecture and A+ certification. Her online courses for corporate clients, including Hewlett Packard, Sony, and CNET, have educated over a quarter of a million students all over the world.

Author's Acknowledgments

Thanks to my wonderful team of editors at Wiley for another job well done, including Jody Lefevere, Christopher Stolle, Marylouise Wiack, and Joyce Nielsen.

How to Use This Book

Who This Book Is For

This book is for the reader who has never used this particular technology or software application. It is also for readers who want to expand their knowledge.

The Conventions in This Book

1 Steps

This book uses a step-by-step format to guide you easily through each task. Numbered steps are actions you must do; bulleted steps clarify a point, step, or optional feature; and indented steps give you the result of the action.

2 Notes

Notes give additional information — special conditions that may occur during an operation, a situation that you want to avoid, or a cross-reference to a related area of the book.

3 Icons and Buttons

Icons and buttons show you exactly what you need to click to perform a step.

4 Tips

Tips offer additional information, including warnings and shortcuts.

5 Bold

Bold type shows command names, options, or text or numbers you must type.

6 Italics

Italic type introduces and defines a new term.

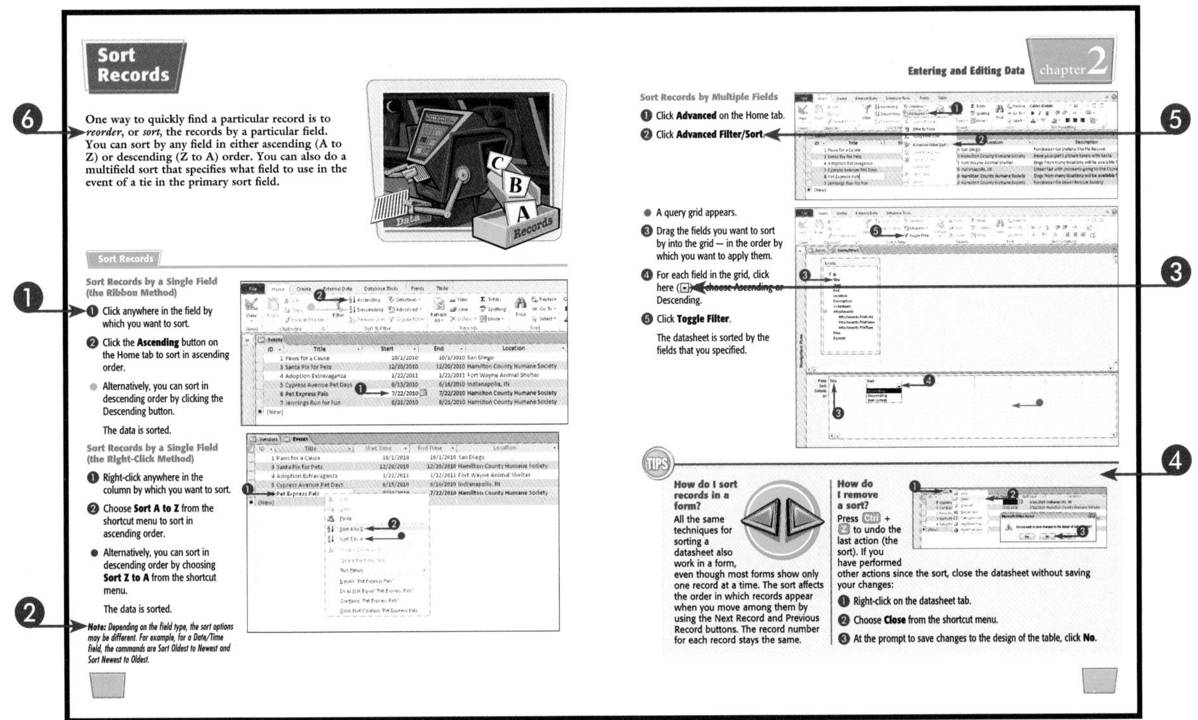

Sort Records

One way to quickly find a particular record is to *reorder*, or *sort*, the records by a particular field. You can sort by any field in either ascending (A to Z) or descending (Z to A) order. You can also do a multifield sort that specifies what field to use in the event of a tie in the primary sort field.

Sort Records

Sort Records by a Single Field (the Ribbon Method)

1 Click anywhere in the field by which you want to sort.

2 Click the **Ascending** button on the Home tab to sort in ascending order.

- Alternatively, you can sort in descending order by clicking the Descending button.

The data is sorted.

Sort Records by a Single Field (the Right-Click Method)

1 Right-click anywhere in the column by which you want to sort.

2 Choose **Sort A to Z** from the shortcut menu to sort in ascending order.

- Alternatively, you can sort in descending order by choosing **Sort Z to A** from the shortcut menu.

The data is sorted.

Note: Depending on the field type, the sort options may be different. For example, for a Date/Time field, the commands are Sort Oldest to Newest and Sort Newest to Oldest.

Entering and Editing Data chapter 2

Sort Records by Multiple Fields

1 Click **Advanced** on the Home tab.

2 Click **Advanced Filter/Sort**.

- A query grid appears.

3 Drag the fields you want to sort by into the grid — in the order by which you want to apply them.

4 For each field in the grid, click here ( ) to choose Ascending or Descending.

5 Click **Toggle Filter**.

The datasheet is sorted by the fields that you specified.

TIPS

How do I sort records in a form?

All the same techniques for sorting a datasheet also work in a form, even though most forms show only one record at a time. The sort affects the order in which records appear when you move among them by using the Next Record and Previous Record buttons. The record number for each record stays the same.

How do I remove a sort?

Press Ctrl + Z to undo the last action (the sort). If you have performed other actions since the sort, close the datasheet without saving your changes:

1 Right-click on the datasheet tab.

2 Choose **Close** from the shortcut menu.

3 At the prompt to save changes to the design of the table, click **No**.

Table of Contents

Getting Started with Access 2010

chapter 2

Entering and Editing Data

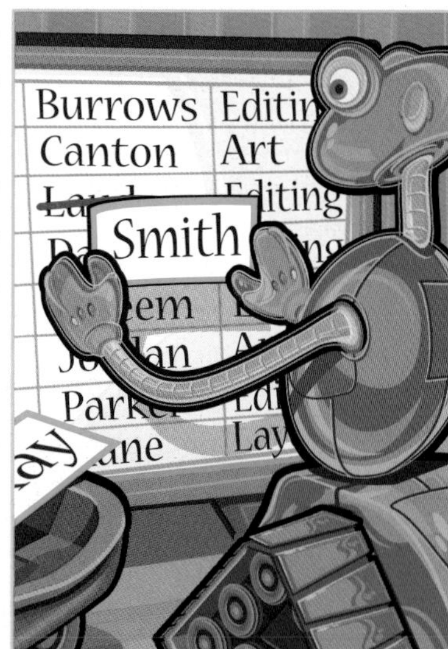

Working with Tables

Working with Fields

Table of Contents

chapter 5 Working with Relationships and Lookups

chapter 6 Finding and Filtering Data

chapter 7 Creating Simple Queries

chapter 8 Creating More Complex Queries

Table of Contents

chapter 9 Creating Forms

chapter 10 Modifying and Formatting Forms

Creating and Formatting Reports

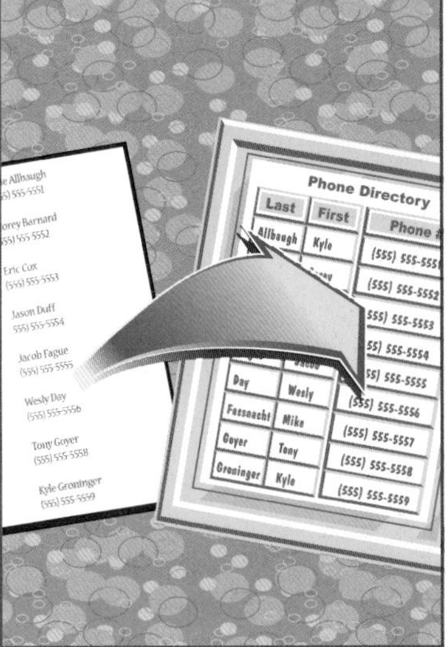

Table of Contents

chapter 12 Grouping and Summarizing Data

chapter 13 Creating Mailing Labels

chapter 14 Creating Charts

chapter 15 Working with External Data

Table of Contents

Performing a Mail Merge with Microsoft Word

Maintaining a Database

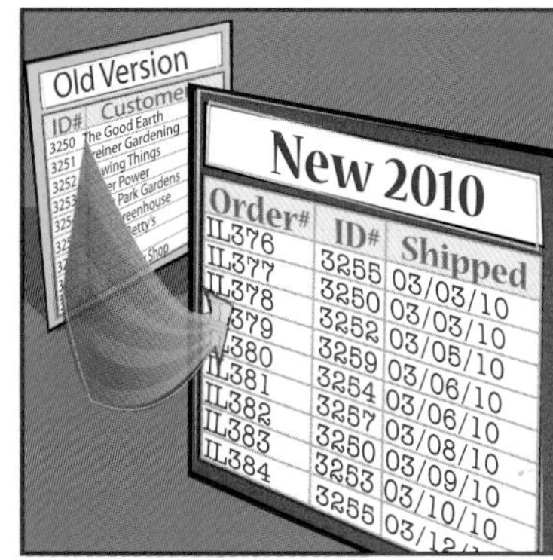

CHAPTER 1

Getting Started with Access 2010

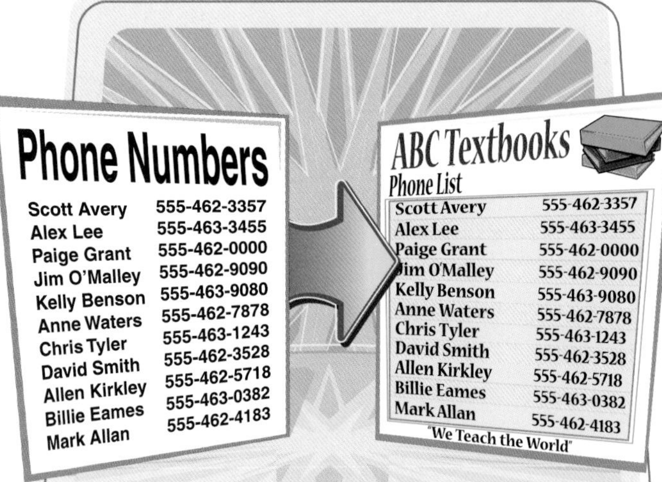

Are you new to Access or upgrading to the latest version? This chapter explains how to create a database as well as how to navigate through the new-and-improved Microsoft Office Access 2010 interface.

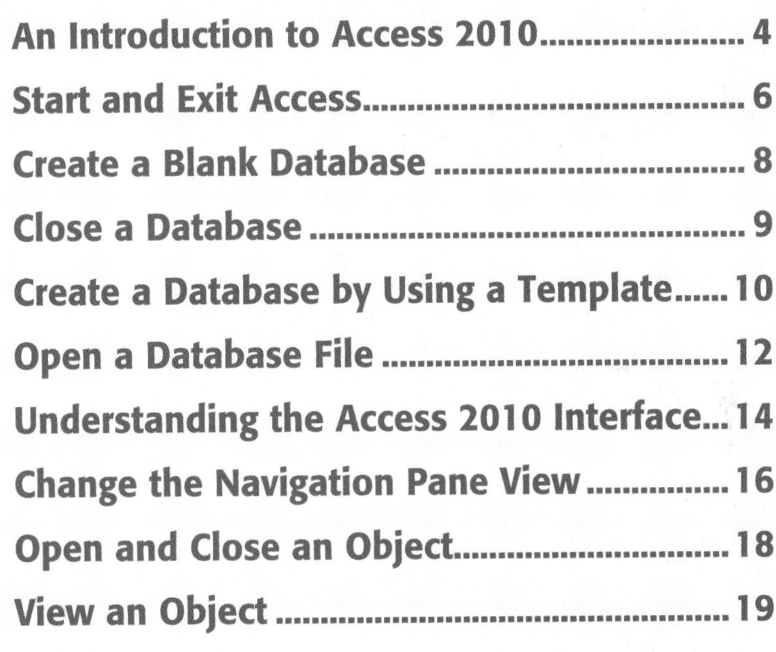

An Introduction to Access 2010

Microsoft Access 2010 is a program for creating databases to store business or personal data. You can use Access to create, retrieve, and manage large or small collections of information.

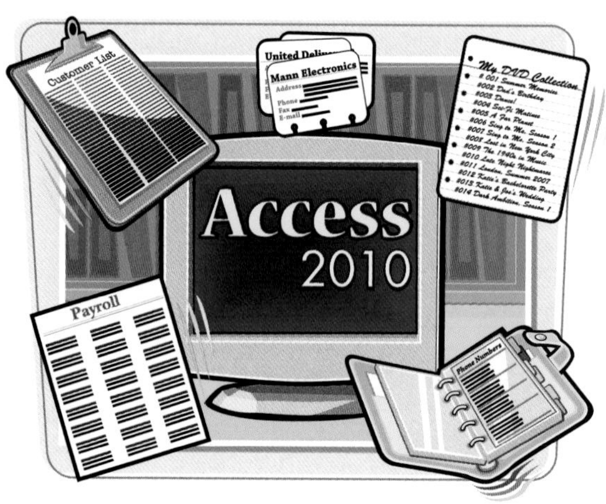

Relational Databases

Microsoft Access creates *relational databases* — that is, databases that can contain multiple tables with links between them. For example, a business may have a Customers table for storing customer contact information and an Orders table for storing information about orders placed. Each customer in the Customers table has a unique ID, and each order in the Orders table references a specific customer ID.

Tables, Records, and Fields

In Access, data is stored in *tables*, and each individual entry in the table is called a *record*. For example, in a Customers table, the information about each customer is a separate record. Each record is composed of one or more *fields* that contain individual pieces of data. For example, customer fields may include Name, Address, City, State, and Zip Code.

Datasheets and Forms

By default, each table appears as a spreadsheet grid called a *datasheet.* You can type directly into a datasheet. To make data entry more convenient, some people choose to create on-screen *forms,* which are like dialog boxes that prompt for field entries. An attractively formatted form is easier and more pleasant to use to enter new records than a plain datasheet.

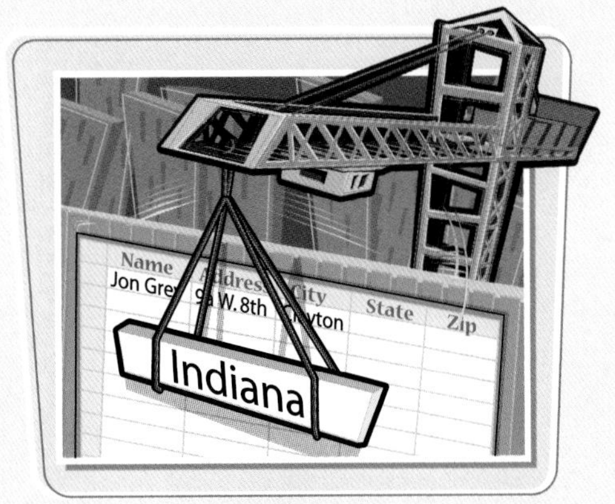

Filters and Queries

It is often useful to display a filtered view of a table. You can filter a table to show only certain records, only certain fields, or both. You can run a one-time filter or you can create a *query,* which is like a saved filter. Queries also enable you to combine data from multiple related tables into a single datasheet of results.

Reports

Tables and query results appear in plain datasheets, which are not very attractive when printed. Reports present data from tables and queries in an attractive, customizable format — complete with titles, headers and footers, and even logos and graphics.

Start and Exit Access

Before you can create or open a database file, you must first start Access. Access starts with the File menu open and the New command selected. From here, you can create a new database or open an existing one. When you are finished working with Access, you should exit the program.

Start and Exit Access

Start Access

1. Click **Start**.
2. Click **All Programs**.
3. Click **Microsoft Office**.
4. Click **Microsoft Access 2010**.

The Access program window opens.

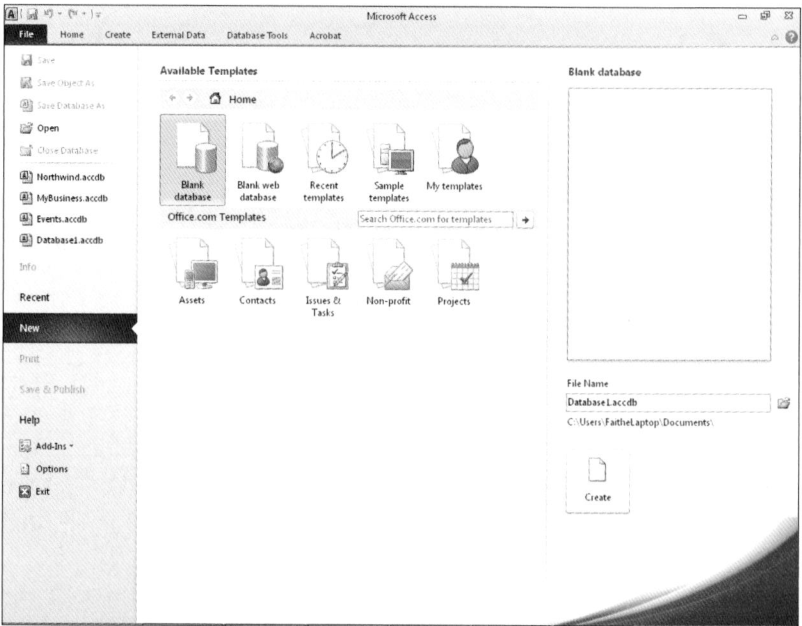

Exit Access by Using the Close Button

1. Click the **Close** button (☒).

   Access closes, returning you to your desktop view.

Exit Access by Using the File Menu

1. Click **File**.
2. Click **Exit**.

   Access closes, returning you to your desktop view.

How is the File tab different from the tabs?

The File tab in Access 2010 opens a menu, with commands arranged vertically. Each command displays different options. It is equivalent to the Office button's menu in Access 2007.

- To open the File menu, click the **File** tab.
- To close the File menu, click any other tab (Home, for example).

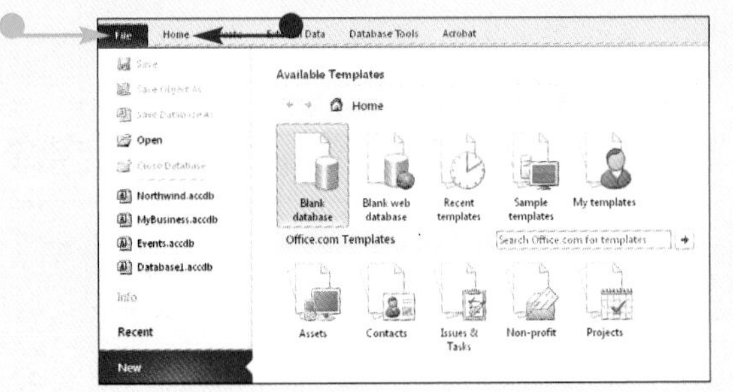

Create a Blank Database

A blank database contains only a single blank table and no other database objects, such as queries or forms. It provides the freedom to create exactly the objects that you want for your project.

Create a Blank Database

1. Click **File**.
2. Click **New**.
3. Click **Blank Database**.
4. Type a file name for the database.
5. Click **Create**.

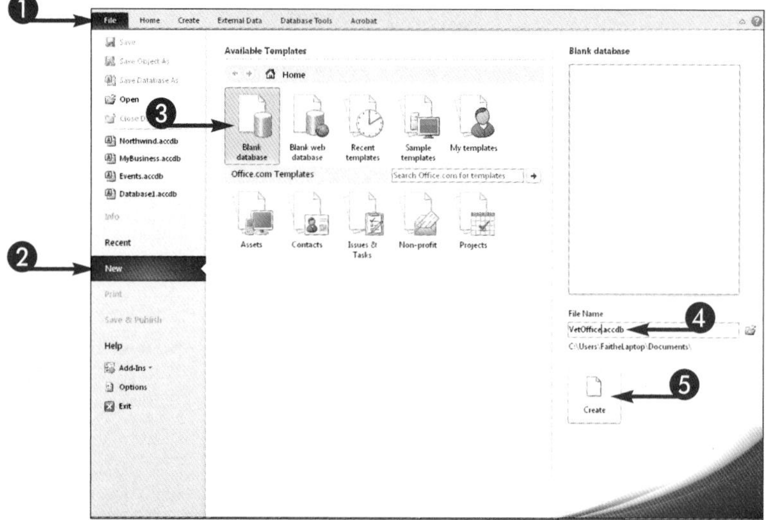

- A new database opens, with a new blank table started.

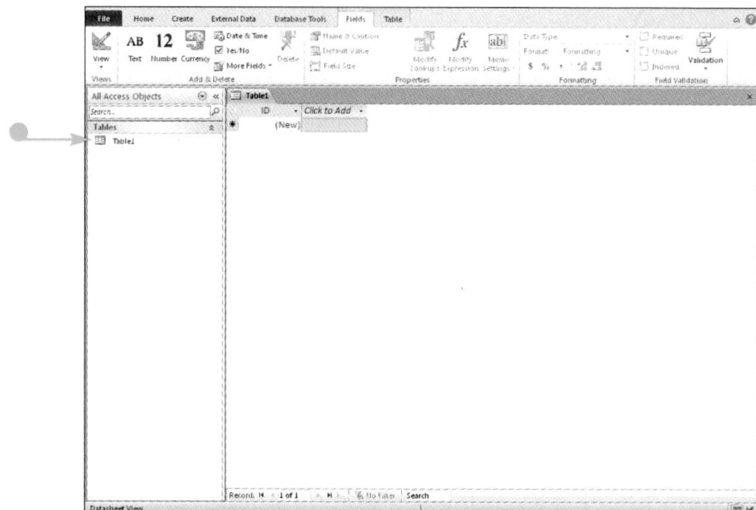

Close a Database

You can close a database without closing Access 2010 itself. Multiple databases can be open at once, each in its own copy of the application, but closing a database when you are finished with it frees up your computer's memory.

Close a Database

1. Click **File**.

   The File menu opens.

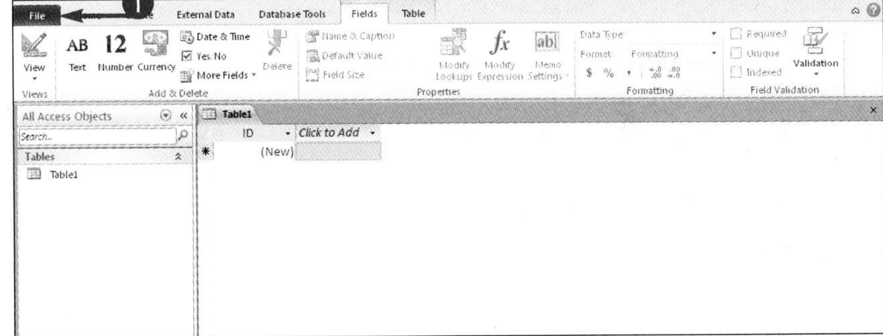

2. Click **Close Database**.

   The File menu stays open, and the New command becomes selected.

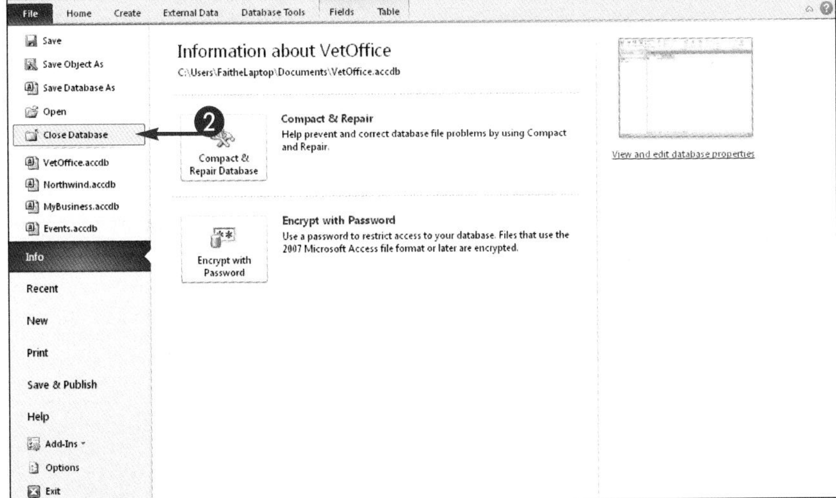

Create a Database by Using a Template

You can create a new database based on a template. Templates provide a jumpstart in creating a database by supplying tables, forms, and queries that you are likely to need.

Create a Database by Using a Template

1. Click **File**.
2. Click **New**.
3. Click the template category that you want.

- Sample templates are Microsoft-supplied templates stored on your hard disk.
- Office Online Templates are available from the Internet if you are connected.

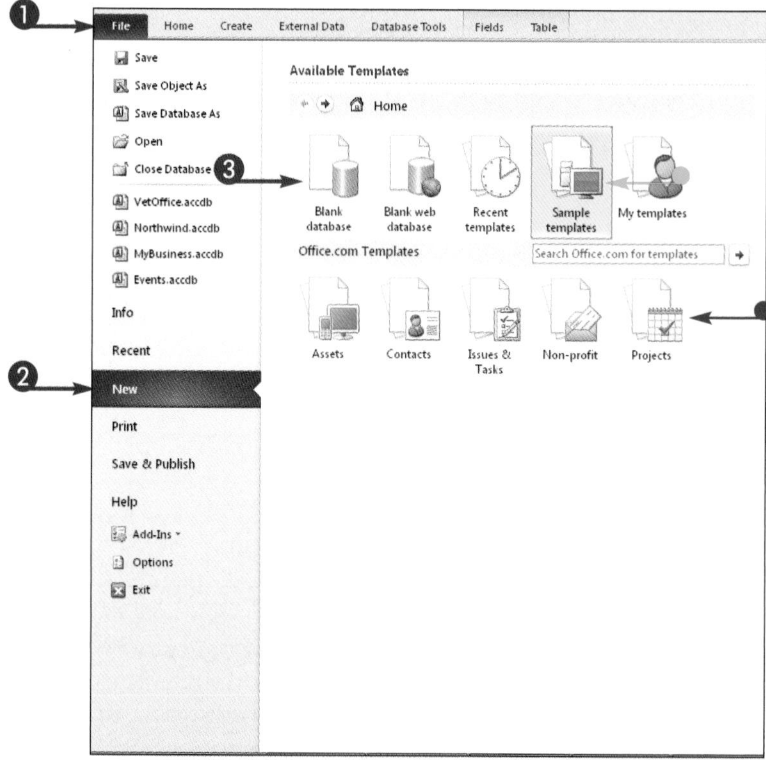

4. Click the template that best matches your needs.

Note: *Under Sample Templates is a Northwind Traders template, which provides sample data and many objects. This database is used for many of the examples in this book.*

- The screen for the template category that you chose appears on the right.

5. Type a name for the database file or accept the default name.

6. Click **Download**.

Note: *If you chose a template stored on your local hard drive, the button name in step* ***6*** *is Create.*

- If you chose an online template, it is downloaded from the Internet.
- A form opens. Its appearance depends on the template that you chose.

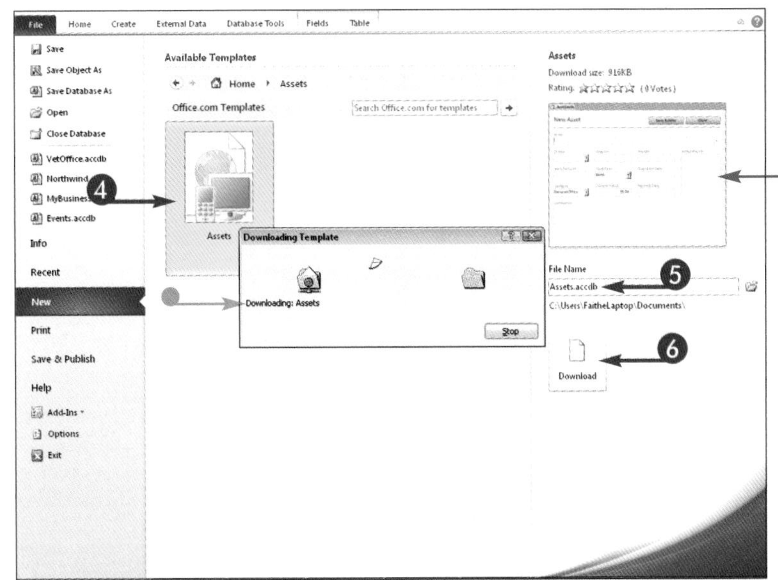

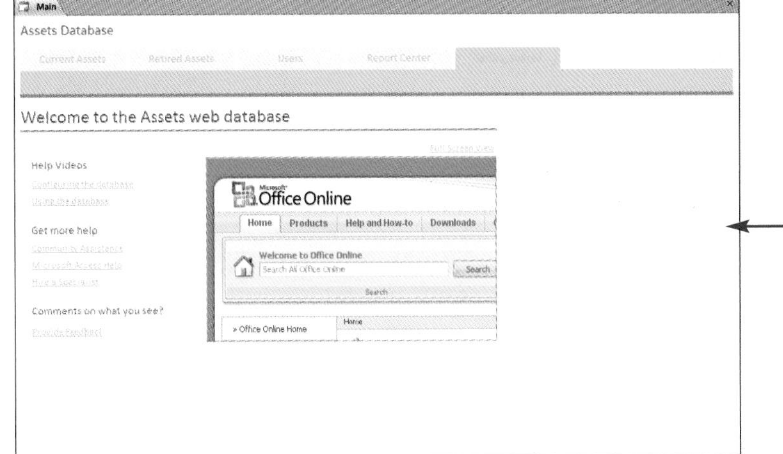

TIP

What do I do if a Welcome or Getting Started tab or window appears in the new database?

Just follow the prompts that appear. Depending on the template, there may be instructions to read, a video to play, or Web hyperlinks to explore.

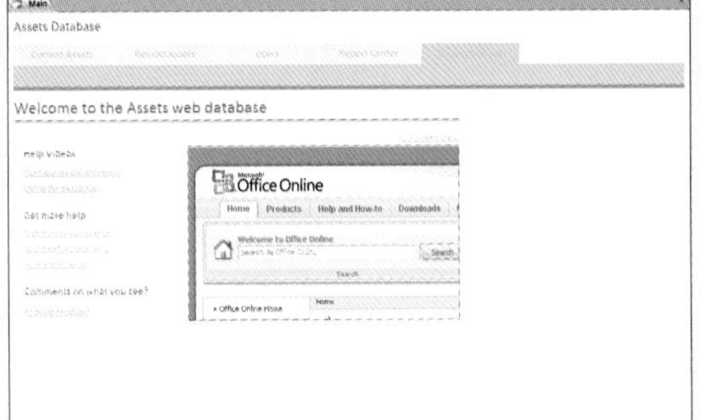

Open a Database File

You can open a database that you previously created to continue developing its structure, typing data in it, or analyzing its data. Database files can be stored on a local hard drive or on a network or SharePoint server.

Open a Database File

Browse for and Open a Database File

1. Click **File**.
2. Click **Recent**.

- If the desired file appears in the Recent Databases list, click it — and you're done. Otherwise, proceed to the next step.

3. Click **Open**.

***Note:** You can also press Ctrl + O instead of performing steps **1** and **2**.*

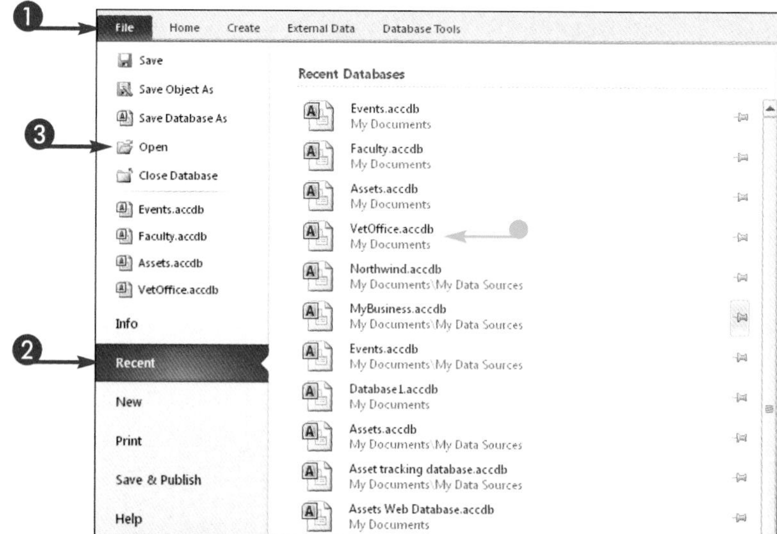

The Open dialog box opens.

- If necessary, you can navigate to a different location.

4. Click the name of the file that you want to open.
5. Click **Open**.

The database file opens.

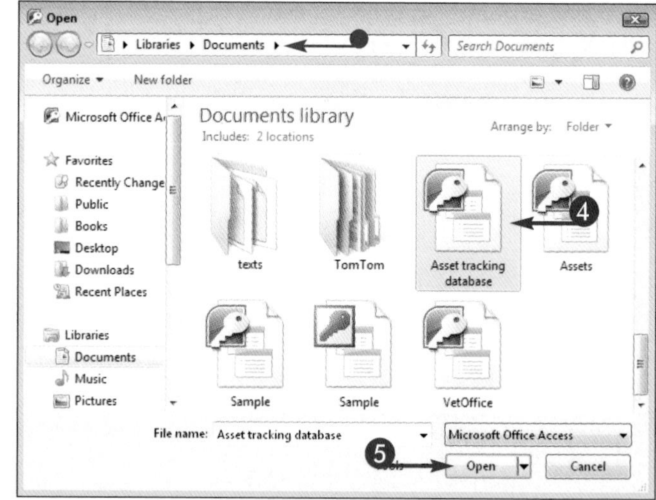

If a Security Warning Message Bar Appears

- Click **Enable Content**.

  The message bar closes and the content is enabled.

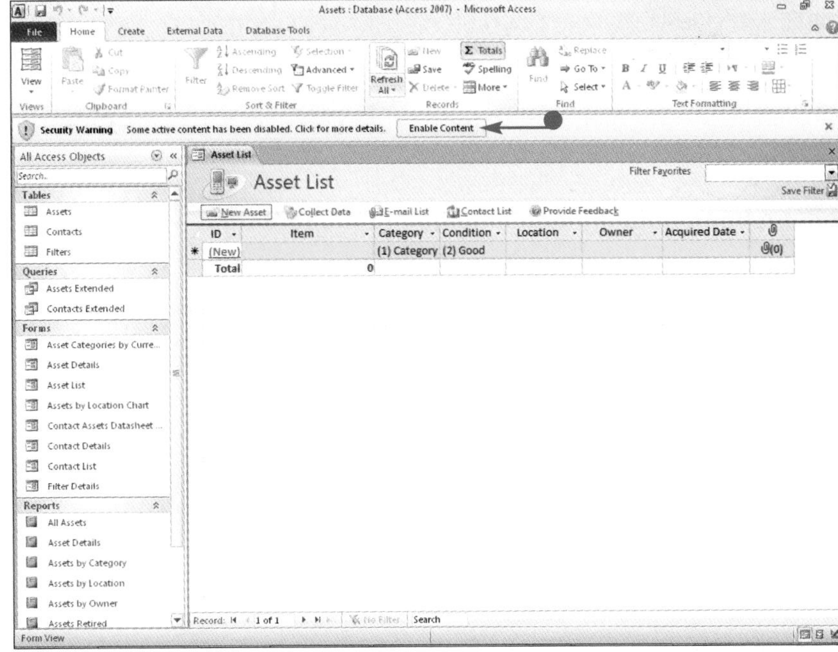

Why does the Security Warning message bar appear?

A security warning appears when you are opening a database that is stored in a location that is not trusted, such as a file you received as an e-mail attachment, or when opening a file that contains macros (sets of recorded actions). The message implies that the file contains dangerous content, but that is not necessarily so; even a blank database can trigger this warning.

How can I prevent the security alert from appearing?

After the first time you click **Enable Content** for a document that contains macros, the warning will not reappear for that document. If the warning pertains to an untrusted location rather than a document with macros, you can prevent the security alert by adding the location to your Trusted Locations list. To do this, see Chapter 17.

Understanding the Access 2010 Interface

Access 2010 has a user interface consistent with those of other Office 2010 applications, including Word and Excel. It contains tabs, a multiple-tabbed Ribbon, and a status bar.

Understanding the Access 2010 Interface

- File displays a menu of database commands.
- Tabs contain buttons and other controls for working with data.
- The Ribbon displays and organizes tabs.
- Groups organize controls into sections within tabs.
- Clicking this icon opens a dialog box related to the group.
- The Record selector displays the current record number and allows you to navigate to other records.

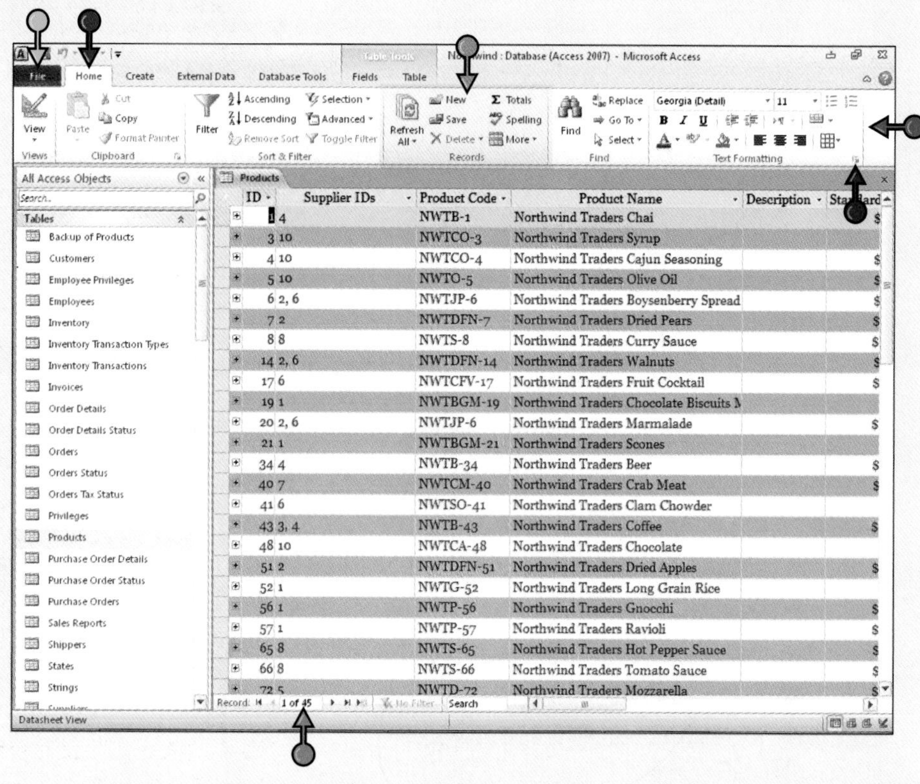

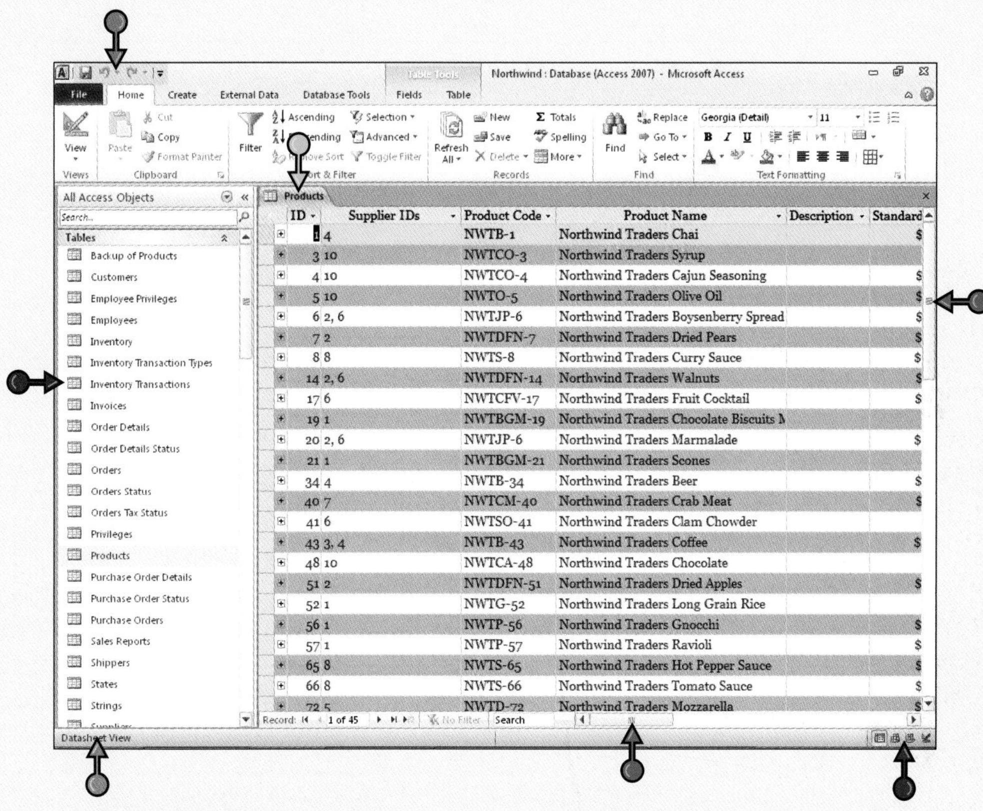

- Object tabs provide access to all open database objects, such as tables, reports, and forms.
- The Navigation pane lists all available database objects.
- The scroll bars scroll through a datasheet.
- The status bar displays information about the current object or view.
- View buttons switch between various views of the selected object. The buttons are different depending on what type of object is active. Hover over a button to find out which view each button represents.
- The Quick Access Toolbar provides shortcuts to commonly used features. This toolbar is customizable.

Change the Navigation Pane View

The Navigation pane allows you to view and manage database objects, such as tables, queries, reports, and forms. You can display or hide the Navigation pane as well as change the way it sorts and lists objects.

Change the Navigation Pane View

Display the Navigation Pane

1. If the Navigation pane is hidden, click this button (»).

   The Navigation pane appears.

Hide the Navigation Pane

1. If the Navigation pane is displayed, click this button («).

   The Navigation pane disappears.

Adjust the Size of the Navigation Pane

1. Drag the border to the left or right (↖ changes to ⇔).

- A black line shows the new position for the border.

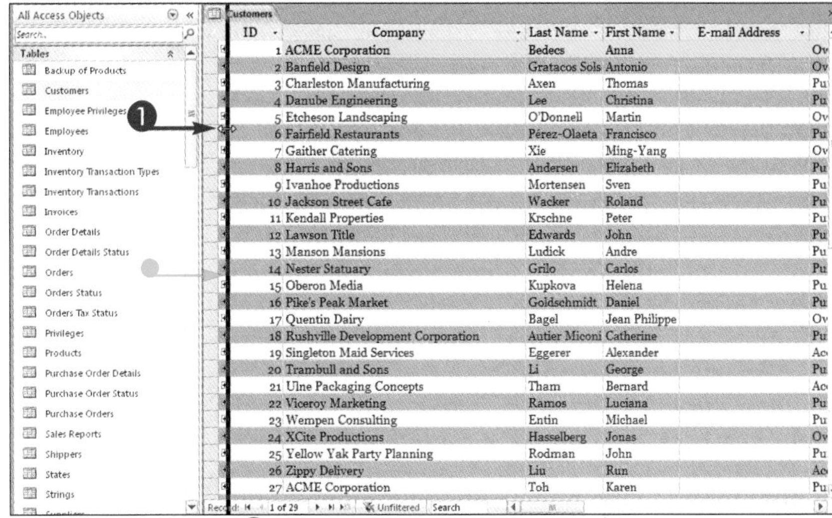

Change the Way Objects Are Displayed

1. Click this arrow (⊙).

   A menu of object options opens.

2. Click the way that you want to view the object list.

- You can also filter the list to show only a certain type of object.
- You can choose **All Access Objects** to return to the full list after filtering.

What are some other ways to display and hide the Navigation pane?

Pressing F11 toggles the Navigation pane on and off. You can also click **Navigation Pane** along the left edge of the screen when it is hidden to display it. Another way to hide it is to double-click the divider line between the Navigation pane and the main window when it is displayed.

What are those blue bars in the Navigation pane?

Those are category headings. You can expand or collapse a category by clicking its bar.

Open and Close an Object

You can open any available database object from the Navigation pane. The object appears in the main window to the right of the Navigation pane; from there, you can work with its content.

Open and Close an Object

Open an Object

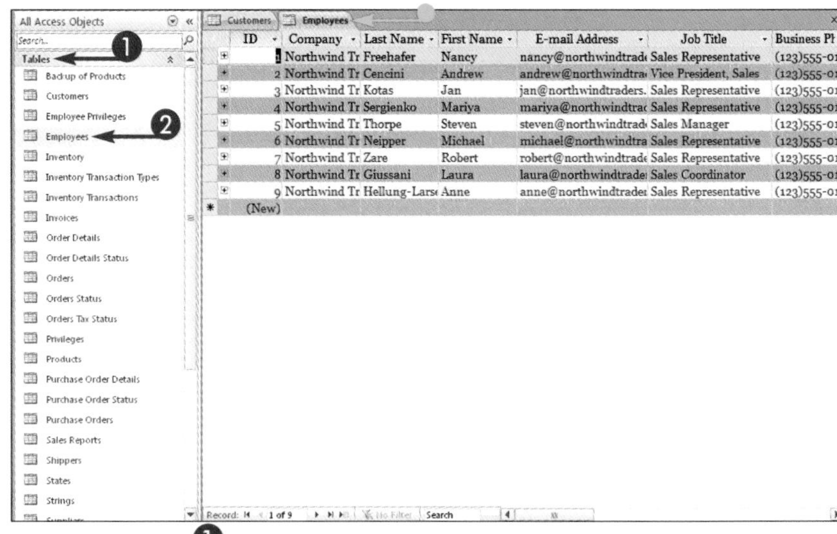

1. If necessary, click a category to expand it.
2. Double-click the object.

- To switch among open objects, click the tab of the object that you want.

Close an Object

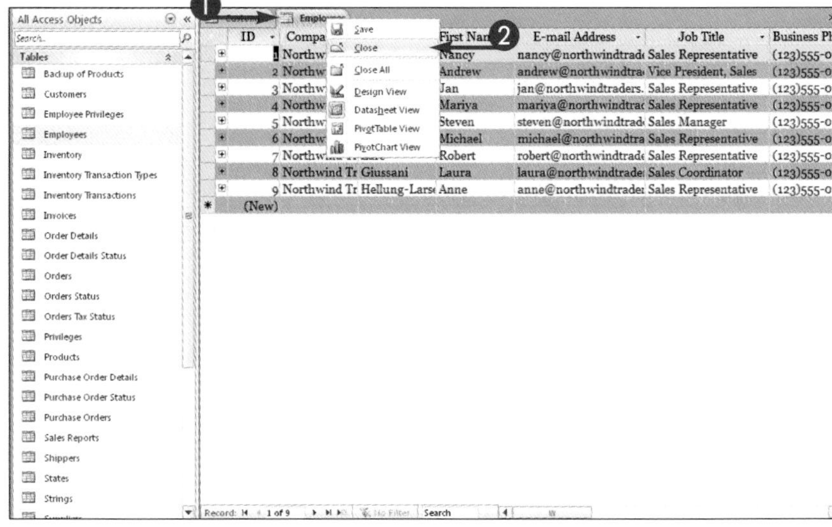

1. Right-click on the object's tab.

   A shortcut menu opens.

2. Choose **Close** from the shortcut menu.

   The object closes.

View an Object

You can display objects in different views. The available views depend on the object type but usually include a view for using the object, such as the Datasheet view, and a view for modifying the object, such as Design view.

View an Object

Select a View from a Menu

1. Right-click on an open object's tab.

   A shortcut menu opens.

2. Choose the view that you want from the shortcut menu.

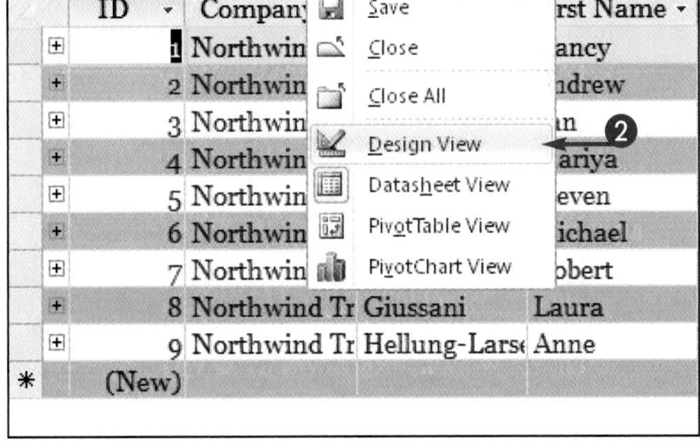

Select a View by Using the View Buttons

1. Click the button for the view that you want.

***Note:** The buttons that are available change depending on the object type.*

- To determine which view a button represents, you can point to it to see a screen tip.

CHAPTER

Entering and Editing Data

Entering data into a database is one of the most common activities that Access users perform. This chapter explains how to enter data into existing database tables and how to edit, sort, and view the data that you have entered.

Enter New Records

You can enter records either into a datasheet (in a row-and-column spreadsheet format) or into a form. A *datasheet* enables you to see records that have already been entered, whereas a *form* enables you to concentrate on one record at a time.

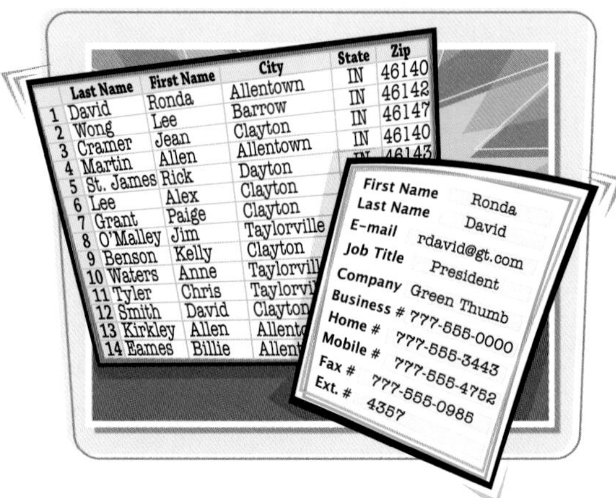

Enter New Records

Enter a Record into a Datasheet

1. In the Navigation pane, double-click the datasheet.

   The datasheet opens.

2. If there is already data in the table, click the **New Record** button (▶✱).

   The insertion point moves to the first field in the first empty row.

3. If the first field contains (New), press Tab to move past it.

Note: *A field that contains (New) is an AutoNumber field, and Access will fill it in.*

4. Type an entry in the selected field.
5. Press Tab to move to the next field.

- Some fields have special selectors that you can use to make an entry, such as a calendar.

6. Repeat steps **4** and **5** until all fields have been filled in for that record.

- The next row in the datasheet becomes active when you press Tab at the last (rightmost) field in a row.

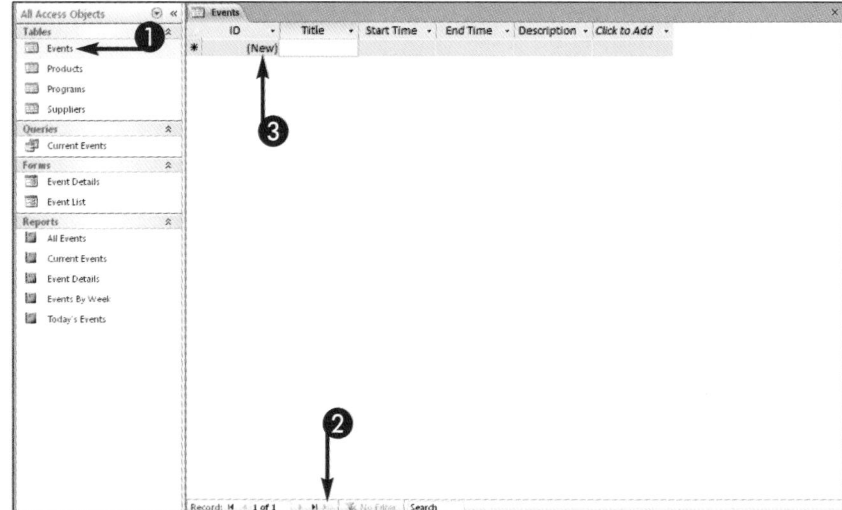

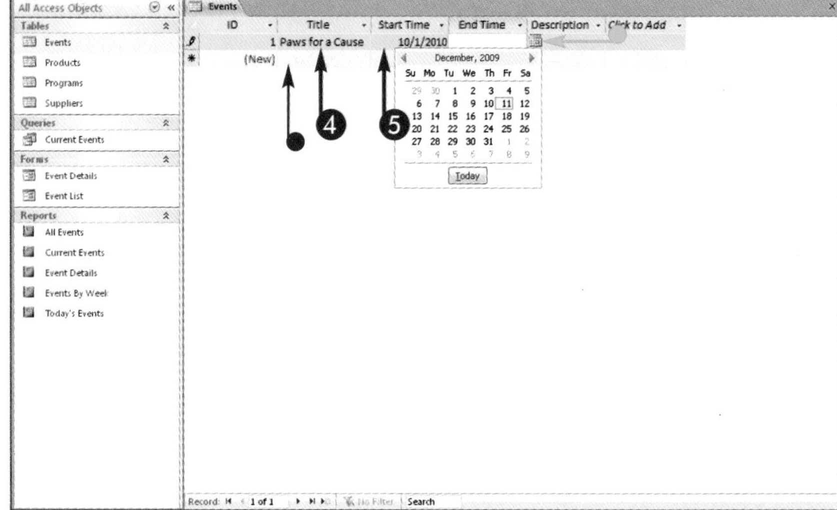

Enter a Record into a Form

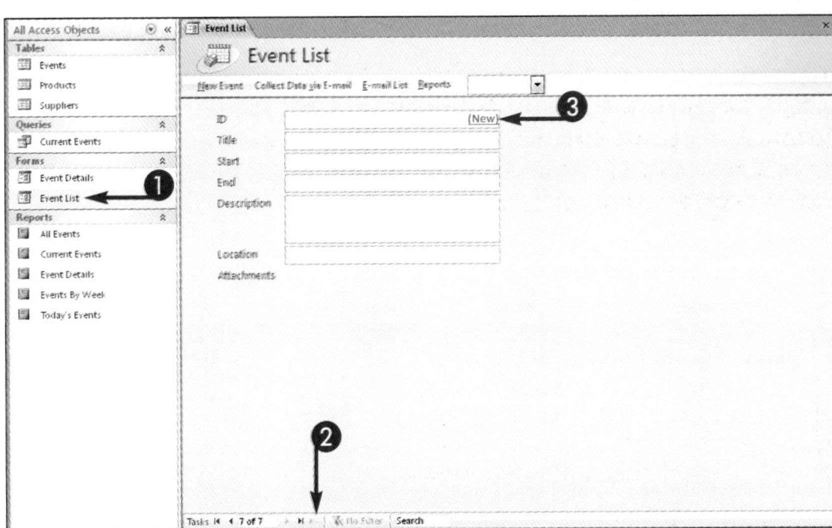

1. In the Navigation pane, double-click the form.

   The form opens.

2. If an existing record appears in the form, click the **New Record** button (▶).

   The form clears, ready for a new record.

3. If the first field contains (New), press Tab to move past it.

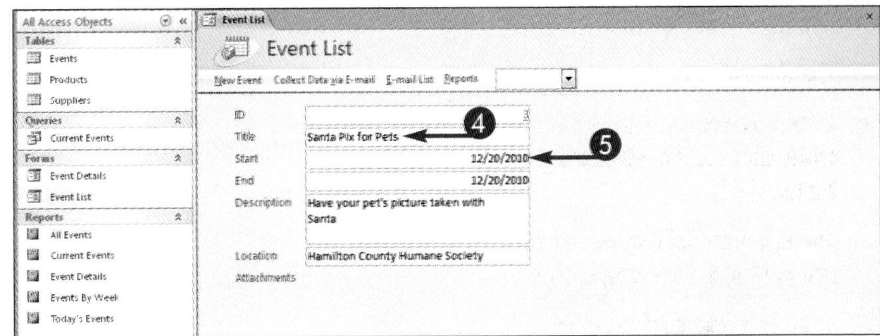

4. Type an entry in the selected field.

5. Press Tab to move to the next field.

6. Repeat steps **4** and **5** until all fields have been filled in for that record.

   The form clears, and a new record begins when you press Tab at the last field on the form.

Can I skip certain fields?

Yes. Just press Tab to move past a field without entering anything in it. If the field is set up to require an entry, however, Access does not let you continue past it without typing something. In Chapter 4, you learn how to specify whether a field is required.

Do I have to complete the fields in the given order?

No. You can click to move the insertion point to any field. You may want to do that to skip several fields. You can also start a new record early, without moving through all the fields, by clicking ▶. In a datasheet, you can also press the ↓ key to move down to the next row to start a new record.

Navigate between Records

After entering several records into a table, you may want to revisit one of them, either to make changes or to simply review the data that you have entered. The same controls for navigation appear on both datasheets and forms.

Navigate between Records

- Move the insertion point to any field in any record by clicking there.
- Click here (⏮) to jump to the first record.
- Click here (◀) to go to the previous record or press the ↑ key once.
- Type a record number here to jump to that record.
- Click here (▶) to go to the next record or press the ↓ key once.
- Click here (⏭) to jump to the last record.
- Click here (▶*) to start a new record.
- Use the scroll bars to see other fields or records.

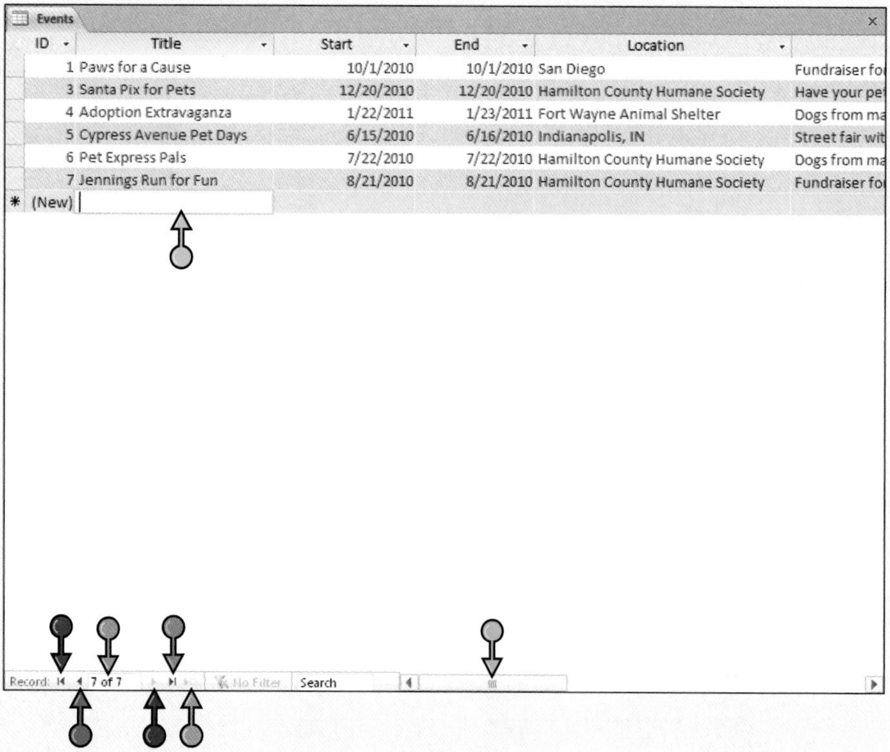

Events

ID	Title	Start	End	Location	
1	Paws for a Cause	10/1/2010	10/1/2010	San Diego	Fundraiser fo
3	Santa Pix for Pets	12/20/2010	12/20/2010	Hamilton County Humane Society	Have your pe
4	Adoption Extravaganza	1/22/2011	1/23/2011	Fort Wayne Animal Shelter	Dogs from ma
5	Cypress Avenue Pet Days	6/15/2010	6/16/2010	Indianapolis, IN	Street fair wit
6	Pet Express Pals	7/22/2010	7/22/2010	Hamilton County Humane Society	Dogs from ma
7	Jennings Run for Fun	8/21/2010	8/21/2010	Hamilton County Humane Society	Fundraiser fo
(New)					

Record: 7 of 7 No Filter Search

Edit Records

You can edit database records from either a datasheet or a form. After redisplaying the record that you want, you can move the insertion point to the field to be edited and make a change or delete the field entry entirely.

Edit Records

Edit the Content of a Field

1. Click in the field where you want the insertion point to be placed.
   - You can press Delete to remove a single character to the right of the insertion point.
   - You can press Backspace to remove a single character to the left of the insertion point.
2. Type your new text.

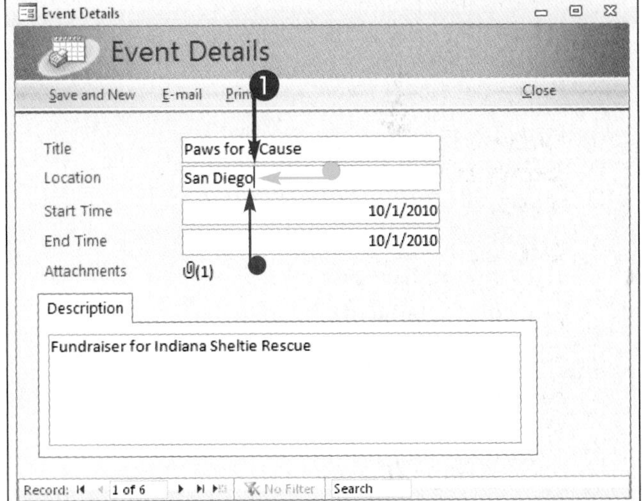

Delete the Existing Entry in a Field

1. Drag across an entry to select it.

   Alternatively, you can press Tab to move to the next field and select its content.
2. Press the Delete key.

   The selected text is deleted.

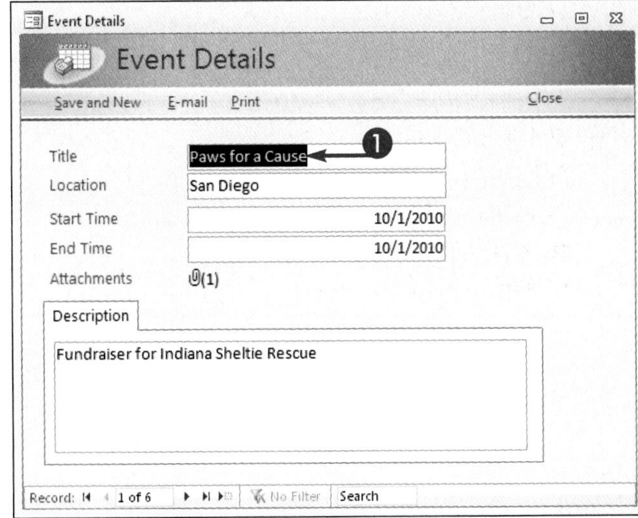

Attach Files to Records

In Access 2010, you can use attachment fields to attach files from other programs to individual records. For example, you may store an employee's résumé with his or her personnel record. A single record can have multiple attached files.

Attach Files to Records

❶ Double-click an attachment field.

Note: *Attachments can be placed only in attachment fields. To learn how to set a field's type to attachment, see Chapter 4.*

- In a datasheet, an attachment field is indicated by a paper clip (📎). The number in parentheses is the current number of attachments that the field holds.

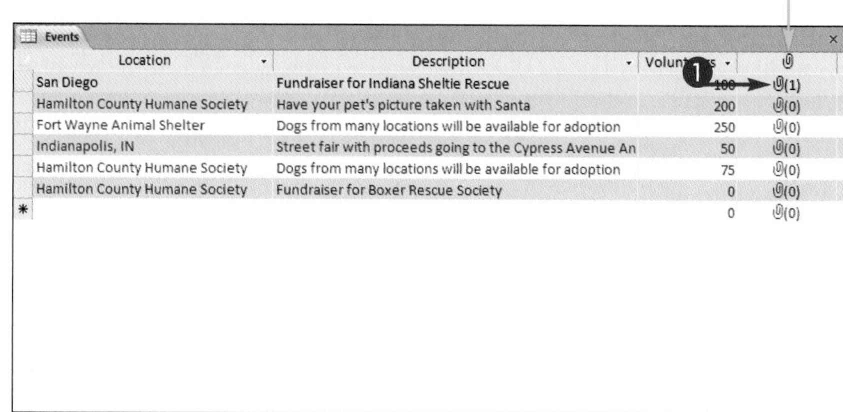

The Attachments dialog box opens.

❷ Click **Add**.

The Choose File dialog box opens.

3. Navigate to the folder or drive where the file is stored.

Note: *Windows 7 is shown here, and Windows Vista looks very similar. If you have Windows XP, the dialog box uses Windows XP–style navigation controls instead.*

4. Click the name of the file that you want to attach.

5. Click **Open**.

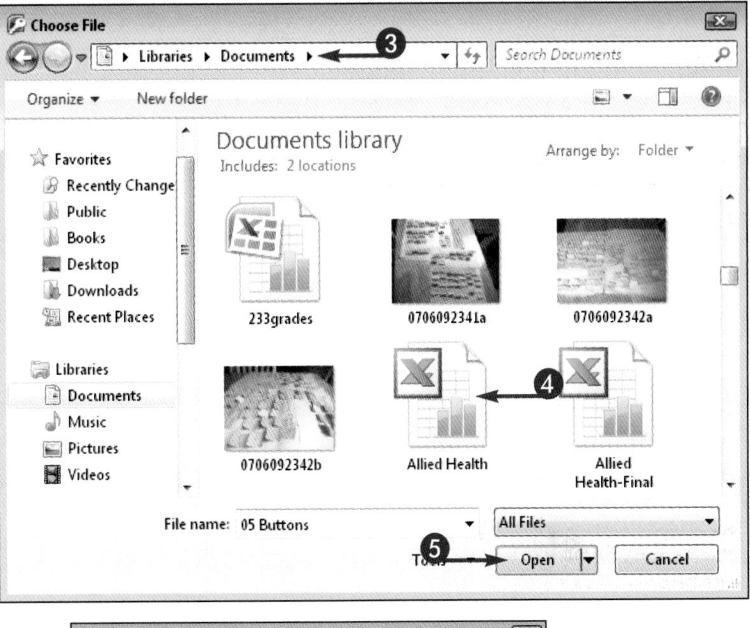

- The file is added to the list of files in the Attachments dialog box.

You can repeat steps **2** to **5** to attach more files if necessary.

6. Click **OK**.

The file is attached to the record and a (1) appears on the attachment icon.

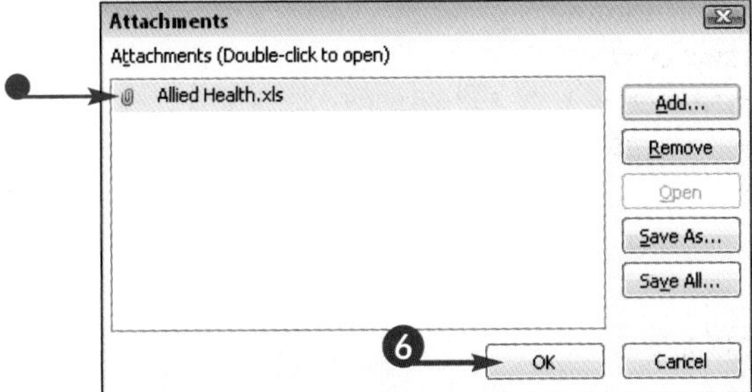

Can I attach files from a form instead of a datasheet?

Yes. In a form, double-click the Attachment icon (●) to open the Attachments dialog box.

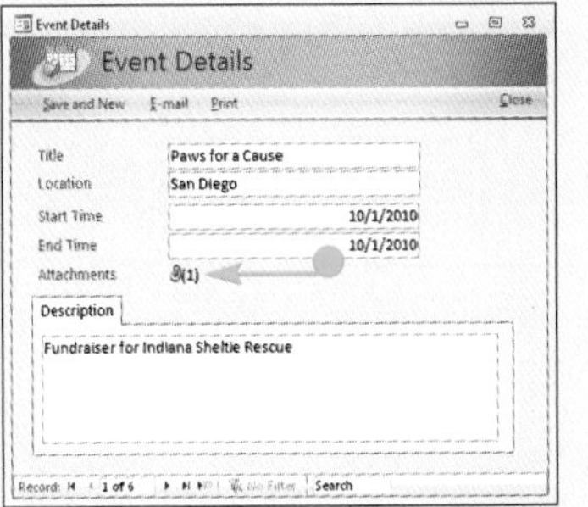

Open, Save, and Remove File Attachments

After you have attached files to a record, you can open those files and review them at any time. You can also save them as separate files outside of Access or remove them from Access.

Open, Save, and Remove File Attachments

Open an Attached File in Its Native Program

1. Double-click the attachment field that contains the attachment.

   The Attachments dialog box opens.

2. Double-click the attachment.

   The attachment opens in its native program.

- Alternatively, you can click the attachment and then click **Open**.

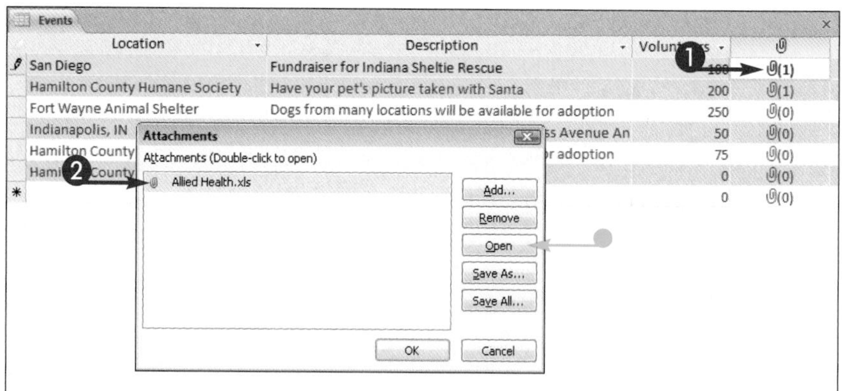

Save an Attachment Outside Access

1. Double-click the attachment field that contains the attachment.

   The Attachments dialog box opens.

2. Click the attachment.
3. Click **Save As**.

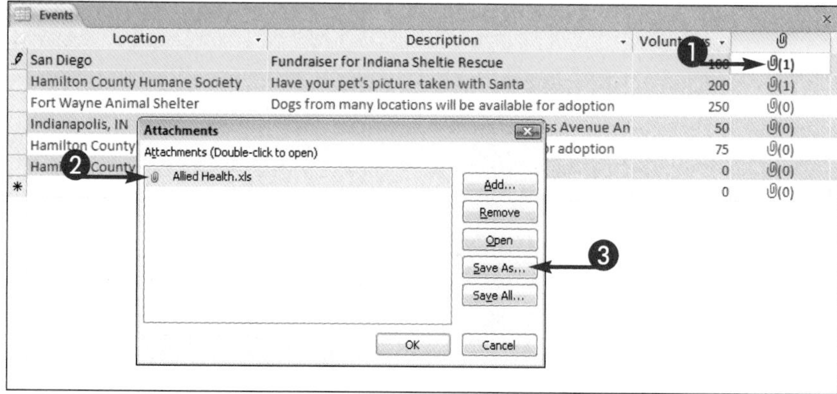

The Save Attachment dialog box opens.

4 Navigate to the folder or drive in which you want to store the file.

***Note:** If you have Windows XP, the dialog box uses Windows XP–style navigation controls instead of the type shown here.*

- You can change the name in the File name field.

5 Click **Save**.

6 Click **OK** in the Attachments dialog box.

The Attachments dialog box closes.

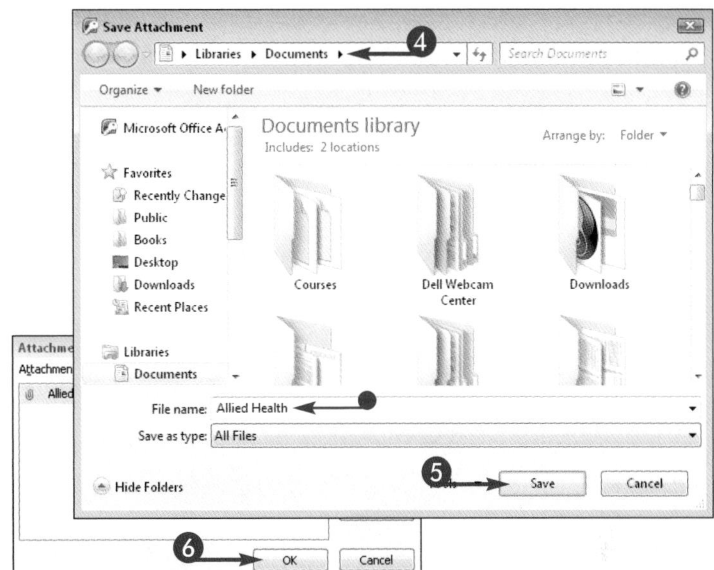

Remove an Attachment

1 Double-click the attachment field that contains the attachment.

The Attachments dialog box opens.

2 Click the attachment.

3 Click **Remove**.

The attachment is removed from the list.

4 Click **OK**.

The dialog box closes.

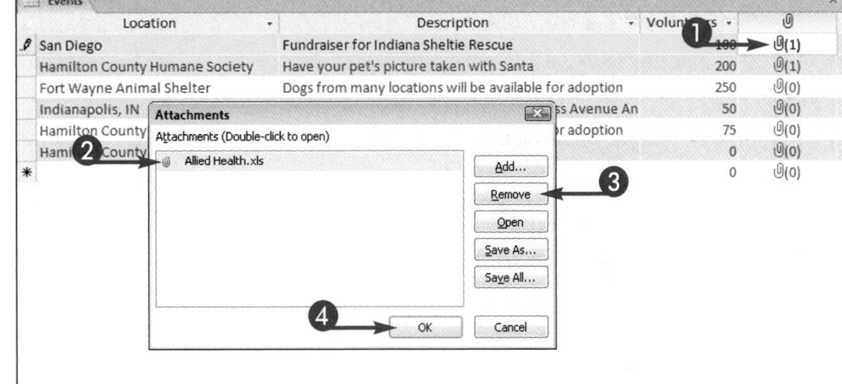

Are there any disadvantages to using attachments?

Yes. Each attachment is embedded in the Access database, so each one increases the size of the Access file. Access compresses attachment files when possible, but they still greatly add to the file size.

What are my options if I do not want to use attachments?

Instead of attaching related documents, you can hyperlink to them. Set up a field's type as Hyperlink (see Chapter 4) and then create a link to the original file rather than embedding the whole file into the database. The only disadvantage of this method is that if the original file is moved, you must update the link in Access. In addition, if you send the Access file to someone else, you must also make sure you send the hyperlinked files.

Insert an OLE Object

You can use the object linking and embedding (OLE) field type to store data files of various types. An OLE field has one advantage over an attachment field: It can maintain a dynamic link to the original copy so the version in Access updates automatically.

To insert objects, you must set the field up as an OLE data type; you learn how to do this in Chapter 4.

Insert an OLE Object

1. Right-click on a field that has the OLE data type.
2. Choose **Insert Object** from the shortcut menu.

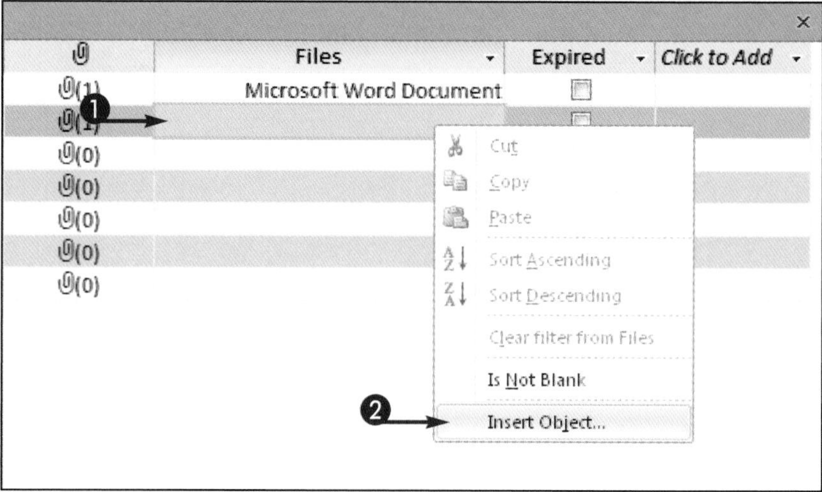

The Microsoft Access dialog box opens.

3. Click the **Create from File** radio button (◎ changes to ◉).
4. Click **Browse**.

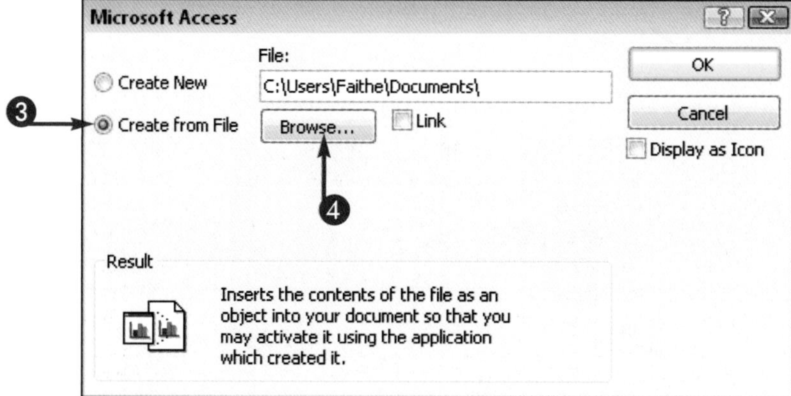

The Browse dialog box opens.

5 Navigate to the folder or drive containing the file you want to embed.

6 Click the file.

7 Click **OK**.

The Browse dialog box closes.

- If you want to create a link, click the **Link** check box in the Microsoft Access dialog box (☐ changes to ☑).

Note: *If you create a link, the copy in Access is updated when the original updates; otherwise, no link is maintained between the copies.*

8 Click **OK**.

The field shows the type of file that you chose.

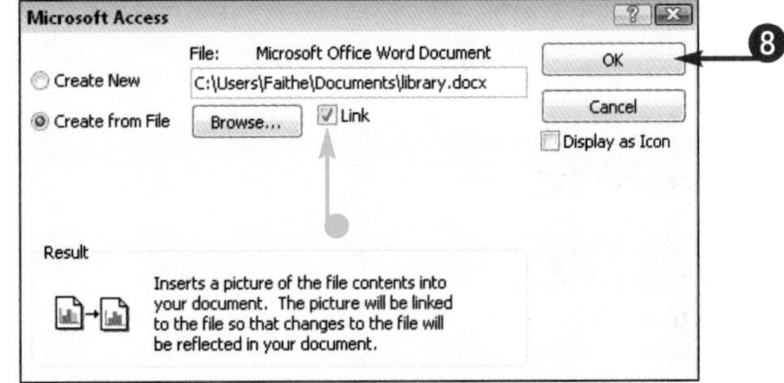

TIPS

What does the Create New option do?

Create New lets you create a new embedded object by using virtually any program on your computer. After you click **Create New**, a list of object types appears. Click the type that you want and then click **OK**.

Why would I want to use the Display as Icon option?

That option is primarily for use in other programs, not Access. In Access, in Datasheet view, the OLE content appears with the text name of the file type, regardless of whether this check box is selected.

Open, Edit, and Remove OLE Objects

After inserting a file into an OLE field, you can open it for editing. If it is linked, the original opens; otherwise, the copy embedded in Access opens. You can then edit the file. You can also remove an OLE object from the field. This deletes the embedded copy in Access but does not delete the original file.

Open, Edit, and Remove OLE Objects

Open and Edit a File in an OLE Field

1. Double-click a field containing an OLE object.

   The object opens in the application that is associated with its type.

2. Make any changes needed to the file.

3. Click the **Close** button (⊠) in the OLE object's application window to close it.

4. Click **Save** to confirm the changes you made.

   The object closes, and the changes are saved.

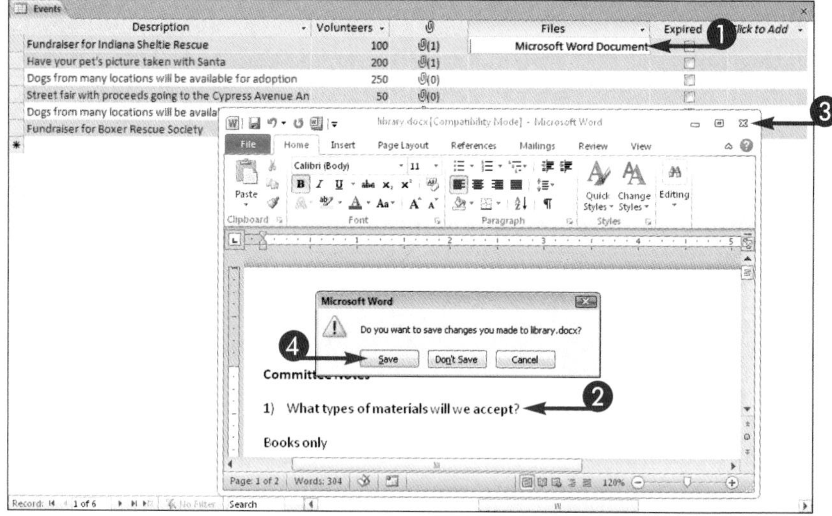

Remove an OLE Object from a Field

1. Click the field containing the object.

2. On the Home tab, click **Delete**.

   You can also press the Delete key on the keyboard.

   The OLE object is removed from that record.

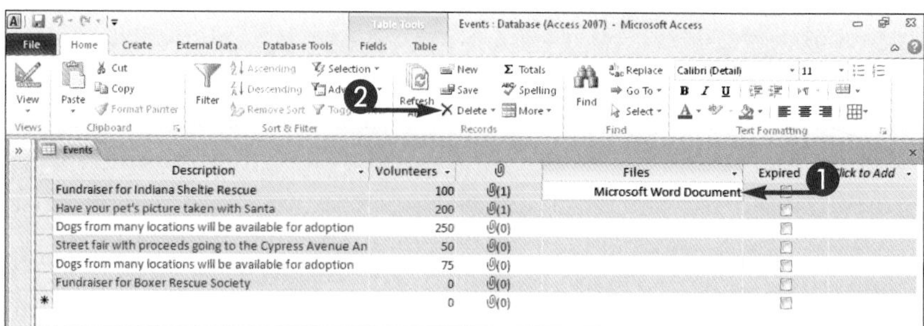

Enter Data in a Multivalued Field

A new feature in Access 2010 is the ability to store multiple values in a single field. Instead of typing in the field, you open a list and then click a check box next to each value.

To enter multiple values, the field must be set up with the Lookup Wizard to accept multiple values; you learn how to do this in Chapter 5.

Enter Data in a Multivalued Field

1. Click in a field that supports multiple values.
2. Click here to open the menu.
3. Click the check box next to each value you want to select (☐ changes to ☑).
4. To enter a new value, click here (📝).

   The Edit List Items dialog box opens.
5. Click in the list box and then type a new value.

Note: Place each new value on a separate line.

- You can click here (▾) to select a default value.

6. Click **OK**.

   The new value appears the next time you open the menu.

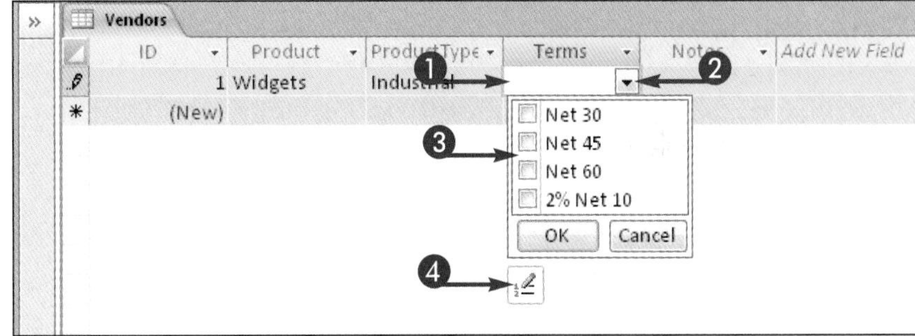

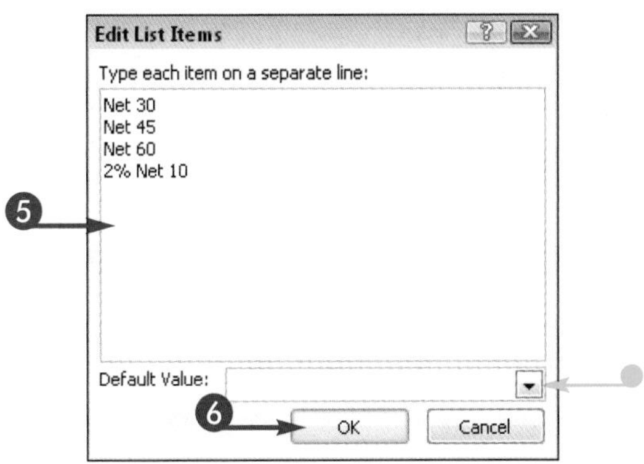

Delete Records

You can delete records either individually or in groups. Deleted records are gone permanently; there is no retrieving them, so delete with care.

Delete Records

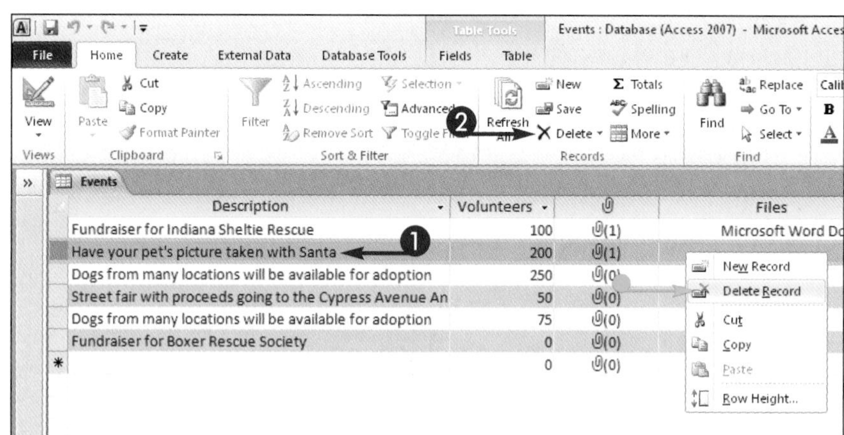

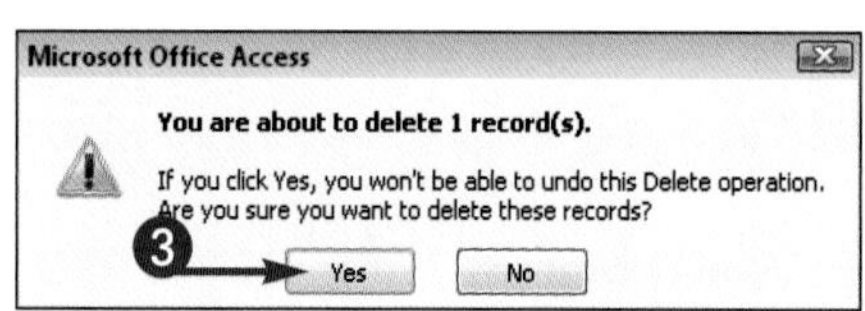

1. Click the record selector box to the left of the record to select it.

   To select multiple contiguous records, click the first one and then press and hold down the Shift key as you click the last one.

2. Click **Delete** on the Home tab.

- You can also right-click on the record and then choose **Delete Record** from the shortcut menu.

  You can also press the Delete key on the keyboard.

  A dialog box opens, asking you to confirm the deletion.

3. Click **Yes**.

   The record or records are deleted.

Resize Datasheet Columns and Rows

You can adjust the sizes of the columns in a datasheet to better display the data. For example, you may want to widen a column that contains long field entries so that all the entries are visible. You can also adjust the row height to create more space between records.

Resize Datasheet Columns and Rows

Change a Column's Width

1. Position the mouse pointer in the heading area — to the right of the column you want to adjust.

   The mouse pointer (⇖) changes to a double-headed arrow (↔).

2. Drag to the left or right to adjust the width of the column.

- A vertical line appears, showing what the new width will be.

3. Release the mouse button when the column is at the desired width.

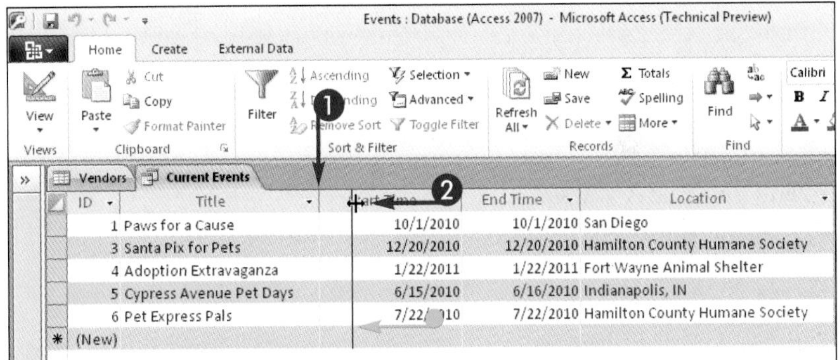

Change the Height for All Rows

1. Position the mouse pointer to the left of the records — on the divider between any two rows.

   The mouse pointer (⇖) changes to a double-headed arrow (↕).

Note: *All rows will be changed equally; you cannot adjust one row separately from the others.*

2. Drag up or down to adjust the row height.

- A horizontal line appears, showing what the new height will be.

3. Release the mouse button when the row is at the desired height.

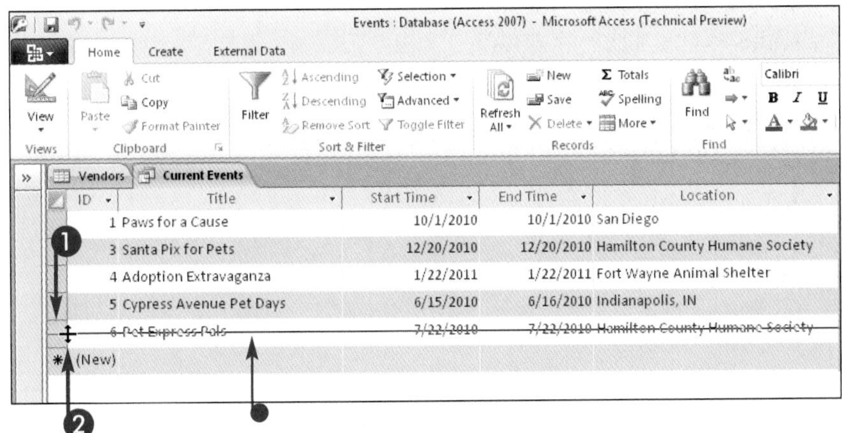

Sort Records

One way to quickly find a particular record is to *reorder*, or *sort*, the records by a particular field. You can sort by any field in either ascending (A to Z) or descending (Z to A) order. You can also do a multifield sort that specifies what field to use in the event of a tie in the primary sort field.

Sort Records

Sort Records by a Single Field (the Ribbon Method)

1. Click anywhere in the field by which you want to sort.
2. Click the **Ascending** button on the Home tab to sort in ascending order.

- Alternatively, you can sort in descending order by clicking the Descending button.

The data is sorted.

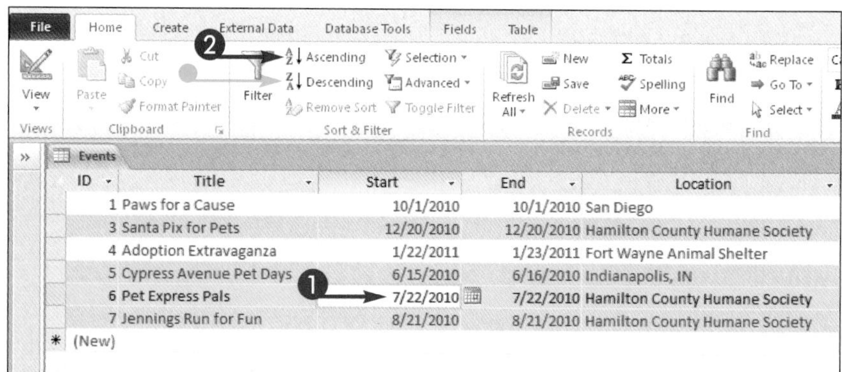

Sort Records by a Single Field (the Right-Click Method)

1. Right-click anywhere in the column by which you want to sort.
2. Choose **Sort A to Z** from the shortcut menu to sort in ascending order.

- Alternatively, you can sort in descending order by choosing **Sort Z to A** from the shortcut menu.

The data is sorted.

Note: Depending on the field type, the sort options may be different. For example, for a Date/Time field, the commands are Sort Oldest to Newest and Sort Newest to Oldest.

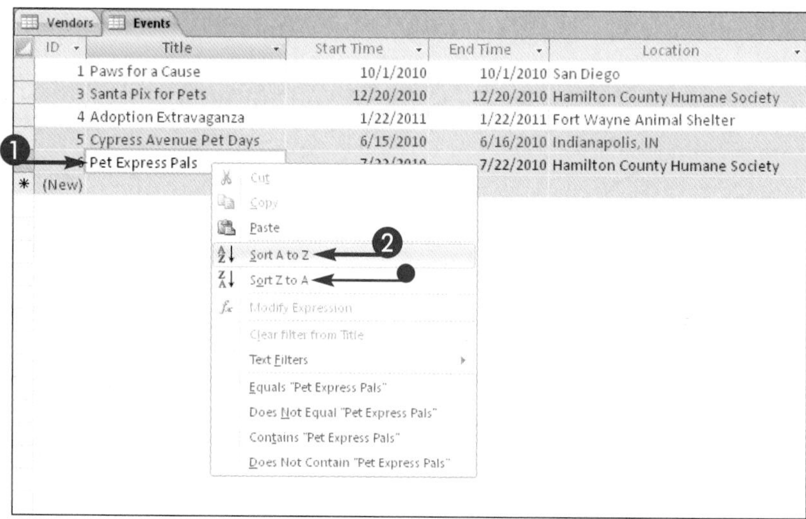

Sort Records by Multiple Fields

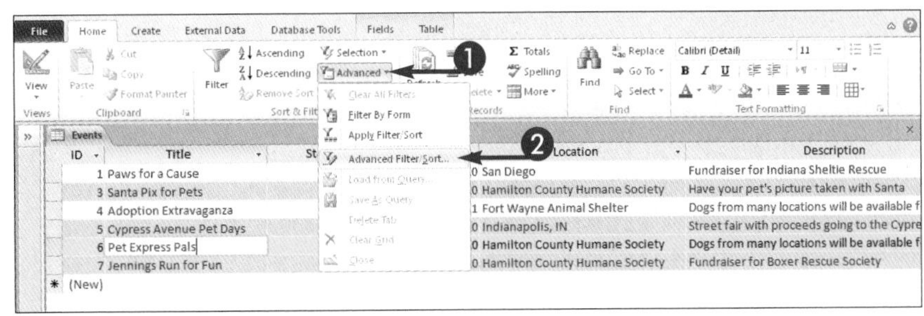

1. Click **Advanced** on the Home tab.
2. Click **Advanced Filter/Sort.**

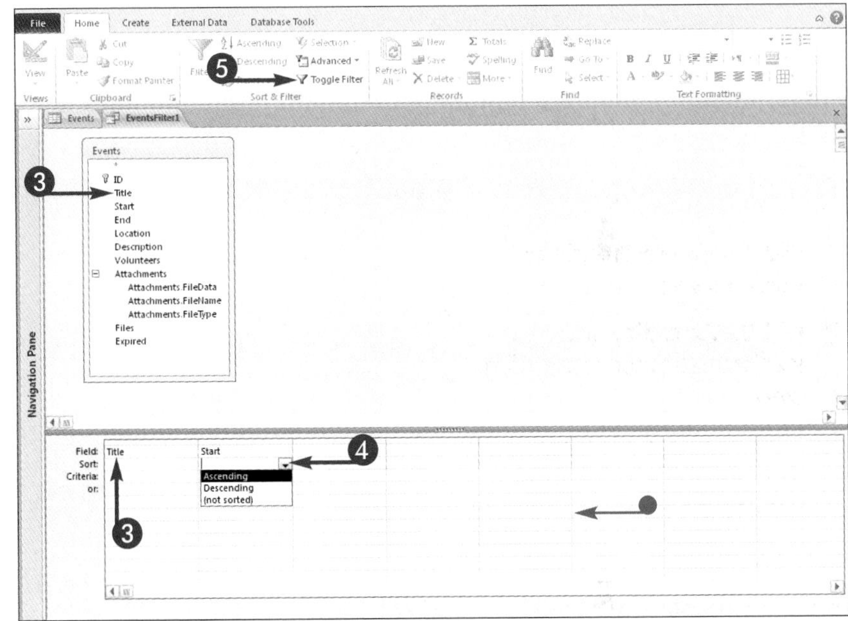

- A query grid appears.

3. Drag the fields you want to sort by into the grid — in the order by which you want to apply them.
4. For each field in the grid, click here (▾) to choose Ascending or Descending.
5. Click **Toggle Filter**.

   The datasheet is sorted by the fields that you specified.

TIPS

How do I sort records in a form?

All the same techniques for sorting a datasheet also work in a form, even though most forms show only one record at a time. The sort affects the order in which records appear when you move among them by using the Next Record and Previous Record buttons. The record number for each record stays the same.

How do I remove a sort?

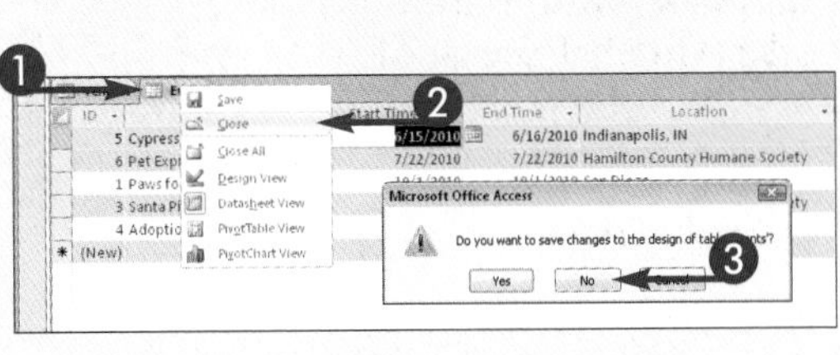

Press Ctrl + Z to undo the last action (the sort). If you have performed other actions since the sort, close the datasheet without saving your changes:

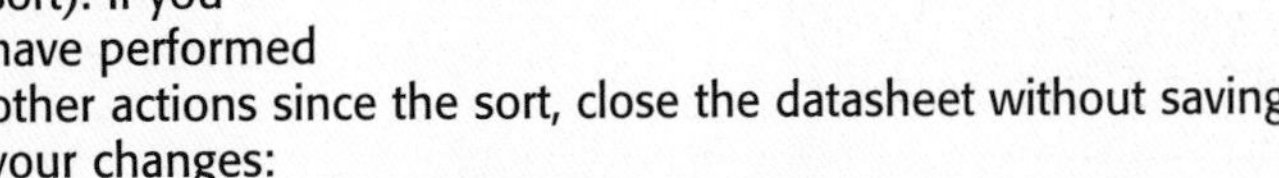

1. Right-click on the datasheet tab.
2. Choose **Close** from the shortcut menu.
3. At the prompt to save changes to the design of the table, click **No**.

Display Summary Statistics

One reason why people create reports and queries is to extract summary statistics about data, such as the sum or average of the values in certain fields. In Access 2010, you can display such information directly on the datasheet — without having to create a query or report.

Display Summary Statistics

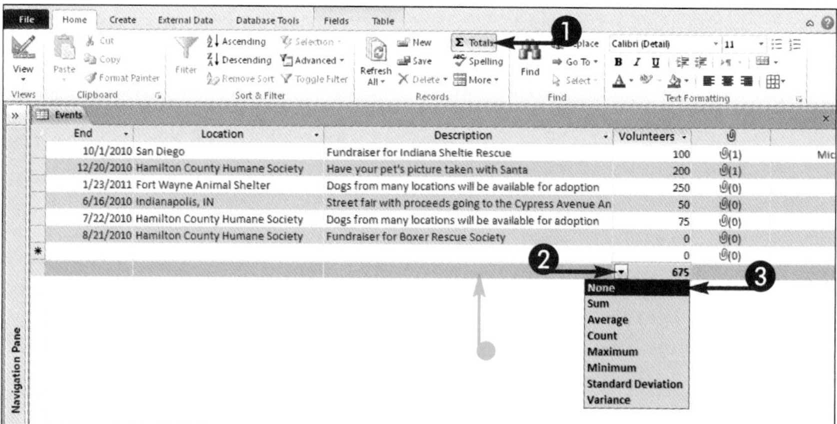

1. Click **Totals** on the Home tab.

- The Total row appears below the records.

2. Click here (▾) to see the available choices for the Total row.
3. Choose a statistic from the drop-down menu.

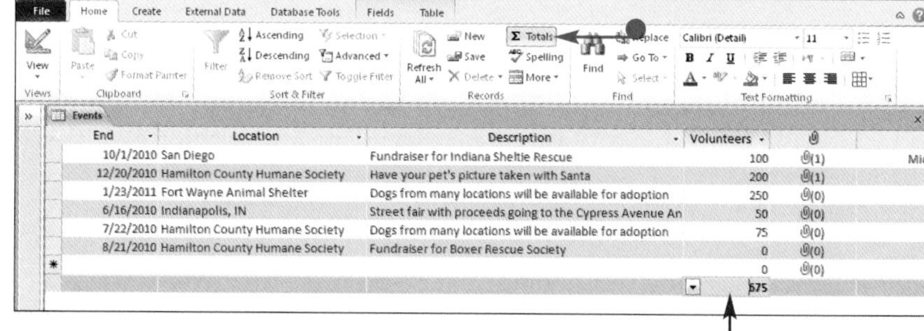

- The information appears in the Total row.

4. Repeat steps **2** and **3** for each additional field for which you want to display a statistic.

- To hide the Total row, you can click **Totals**.

Print a Datasheet or Form

You can print a quick copy of a datasheet or form at any time.

Printed datasheets and forms are not formatted for printing. They are useful for examining data, but you will probably want to create reports for more attractive printouts to distribute to others.

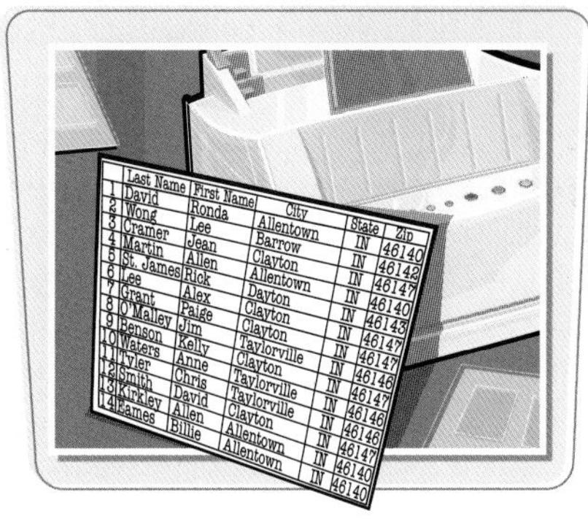

Print a Datasheet or Form

1. To print only certain records, select them.

   To select multiple contiguous records, click the first one and then press and hold down the Shift key as you click the last one.

2. Click **File**.

   The File menu opens.

3. Click **Print**.
4. Click **Print**.

   The Print dialog box opens.

- You can click here to select a different printer.
- You can click here to enter a page range to print only certain pages (◎ changes to ◉).
- You can click here to print only the selected record(s) (◎ changes to ◉).
- You can type a number here to print multiple copies.

   Click **OK**.

5. The datasheet or form prints.

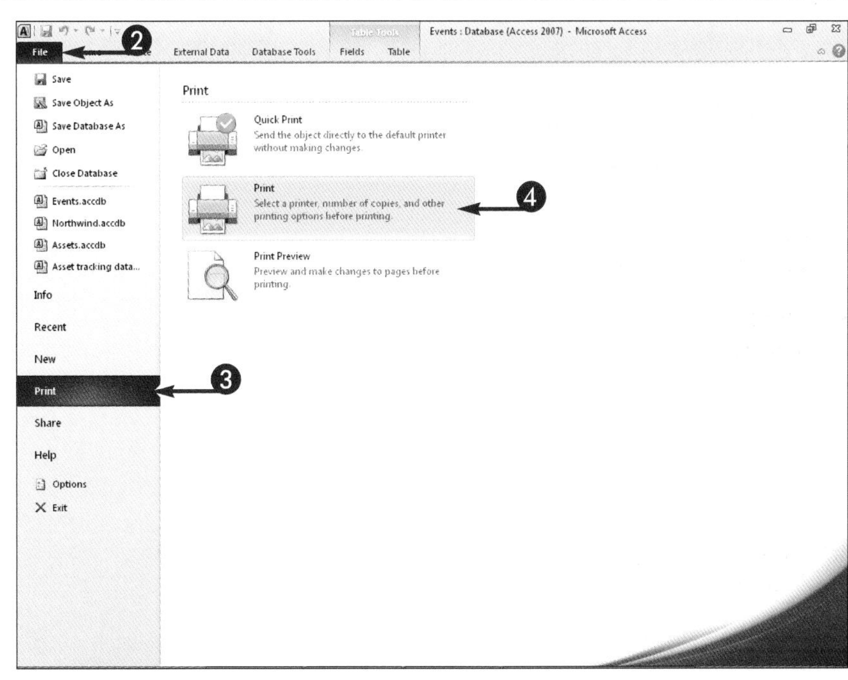

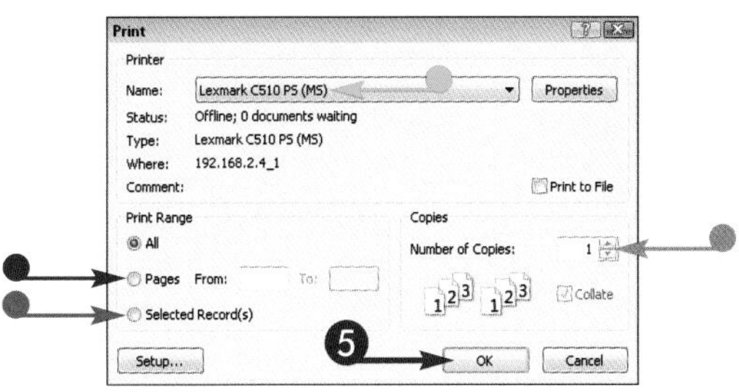

CHAPTER

3

Working with Tables

Tables are the foundation of any database. A table's structure defines the fields and their properties and specifies how data should be entered. In this chapter, you learn how to create and manage tables.

Plan Effective Tables

As a database designer, you have the opportunity to create tables in your database that match your storage needs. You can create tables based on templates that Access provides or you can create your own tables. Before creating the tables, however, you should spend some time thinking about what type of data each table should contain.

Plan Effective Tables

Choose One Purpose per Table

Each table should have a single, well-defined purpose. For example, a table may store customer contact information, product inventory, or personnel records. Do not worry that the information you need to work with is stored in different tables because you can easily create queries and reports that summarize and combine data from any number of tables.

Avoid Redundant Data Entry

Combining multiple purposes in a single table results in needless duplication and increases the chance of data-entry error. For example, suppose that your Orders table also contained fields for the customer's shipping address. Every time a repeat customer placed an order, you would need to re-enter the shipping address. By placing customer shipping information in a separate Customers table, you eliminate the duplication.

Plan for Relationships

Think about how tables will be related. For example, the Orders and Customers tables may be related to display a list of all the orders placed by a certain customer. You could also relate the Employees and Orders tables to display a list of orders taken by certain employees. It may be helpful to draw a diagram to envision the relationships needed.

Decide on the Fields to Use

If you think you may need to sort or filter by a certain type of information, then make it a separate field. For example, to sort a Customers table by last name, you need separate fields for First Name and Last Name. And if you ever plan on addressing your customers with Mr., Ms., or Miss, you need a field that contains that prefix.

Plan to Differentiate between Records

In most tables, at least one field should be unique to each record to differentiate between them. For example, the Customers table may have a unique Customer ID field. You could then use the number to refer to that customer in relationship to other tables. For example, each order could be positively matched with a particular customer by using a customer ID.

Create a Table in Datasheet View

You can create a table from Datasheet view, adding new fields simply by typing the field names into the column-heading placeholders. This method works well when you need a quick table consisting of just a few fields.

Create a Table in Datasheet View

1. Click the **Create** tab.
2. Click **Table**.

   A new datasheet opens with an ID field and a Click to Add placeholder.
3. Click the **Click to Add** placeholder.

   A menu of field types appears.
4. Click the desired field type.

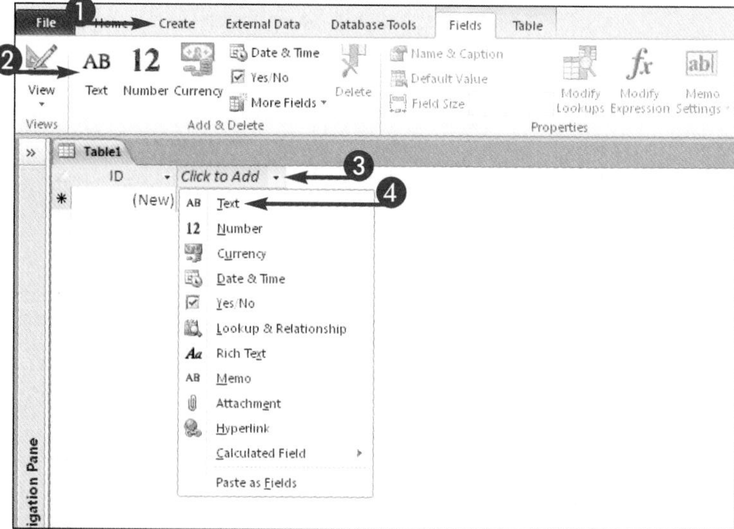

5. Type the name for the new field.
6. Press Enter to accept the field name.

   The menu of field types opens in the blank column to the right so you can create another new field if needed.
7. Repeat steps **4** to **6** as needed to finish entering field names.

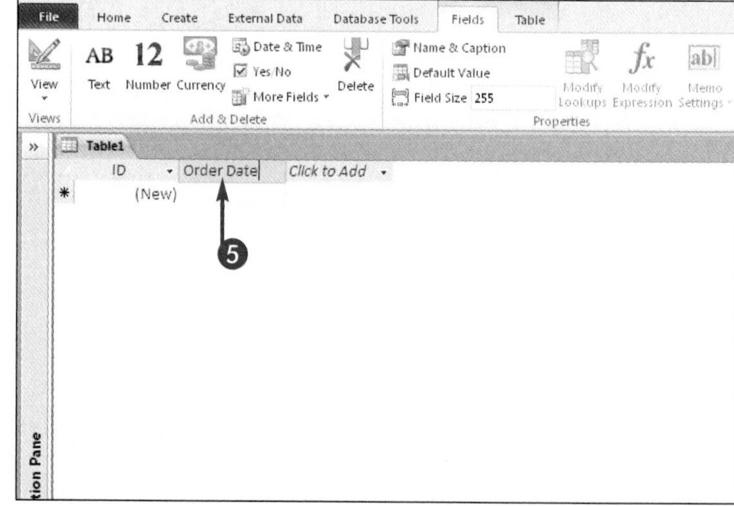

Save a Table

After creating a new table, you must save the table to make it a permanent part of the database. When you save a table, you give it a name that will help you remember its purpose.

Save a Table

1. Right-click on the table's tab.
2. Click **Save**.

- You can also click the **Save** button (💾) on the Quick Access Toolbar.

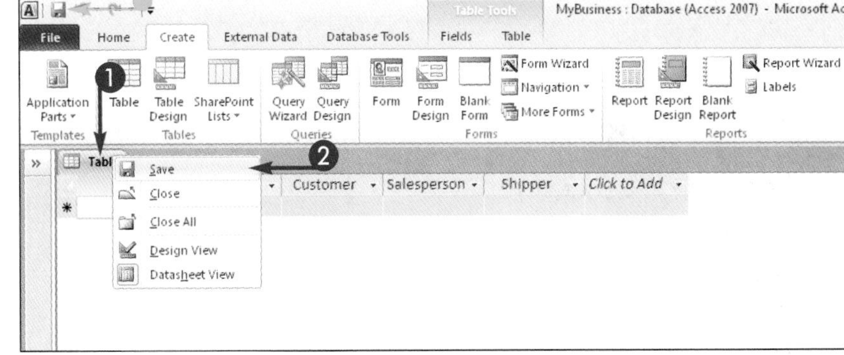

The Save As dialog box opens.

3. Type a name for the table.

***Note:** Access allows table names to include spaces, but you should avoid using spaces to make the names easier to refer to in some types of queries. Use an underscore symbol instead.*

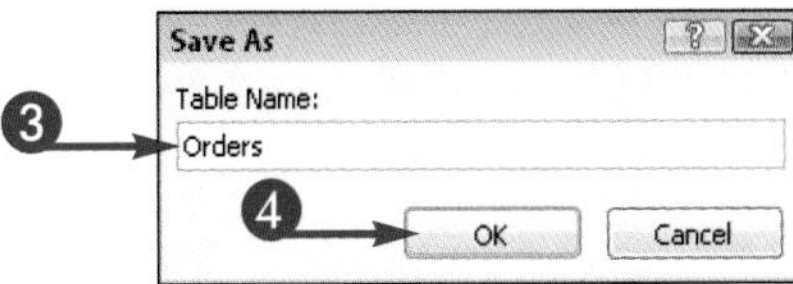

4. Click **OK**.

- The table remains open, and its new name appears on its tab.

You can either leave the table open to work with it or you can close it. To close the table, right-click on its tab and then choose Close.

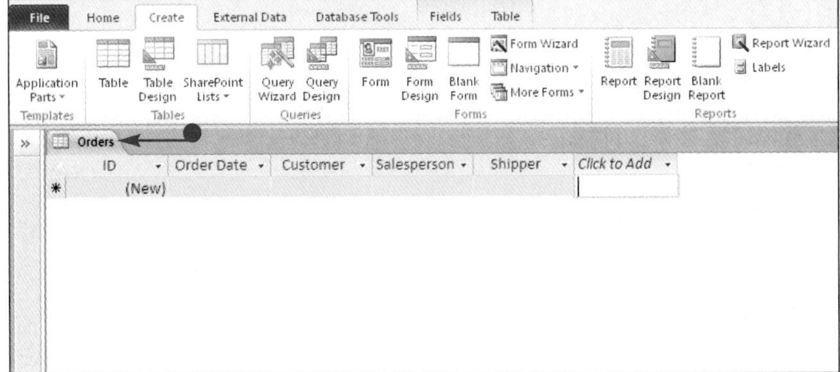

Create a Table in Design View

You can construct a table in Design view to get the exact fields that you want. In Design view, you can create and arrange fields, specify field types and properties, and enter field descriptions.

Chapter 4 covers modifying a table in Design view in more detail.

Create a Table in Design View

❶ Click the **Create** tab.

❷ Click **Table Design**.

Design view opens with a new table started.

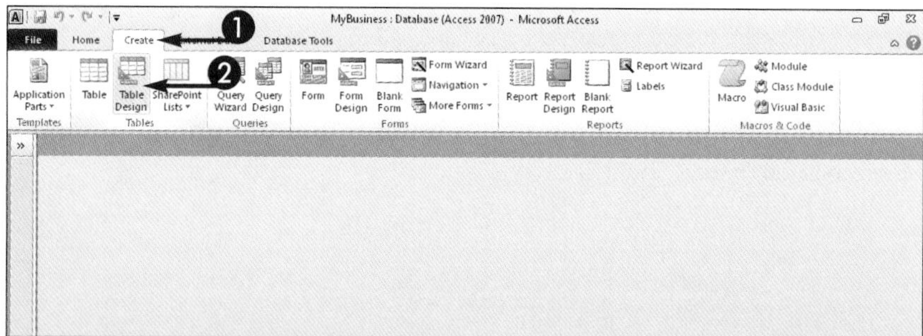

❸ Click in the first empty cell beneath Field Name and type a field name.

Note: *It is good design practice to begin with an ID field that will contain a unique value for each record.*

❹ Press Tab to move to the Data Type column.

A (▾) appears in the Data Type column.

❺ Click here (▾) to select a data type.

For a detailed explanation of data types, see the section "Understanding Data Types."

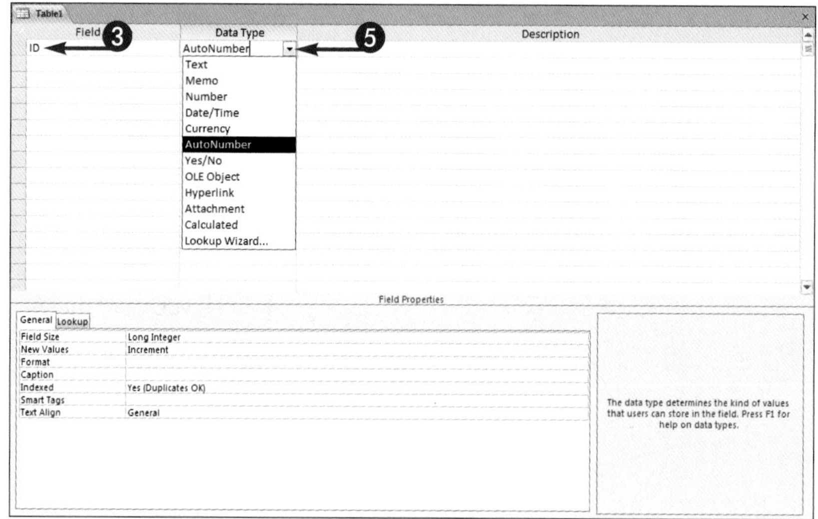

- You can click in the Description column to type a description for the field.

Note: *Descriptions are only necessary if the purpose of the field is not obvious from its name.*

Field Name	Data Type	Description
ID	AutoNumber	This field is filled in automatically

6. Repeat steps **3** to **5** to create additional fields as needed.

Note: *See the section "Set the Primary or Composite Key" to set up the primary key for the table.*

Save your changes to the table and then close it.

Note: *For more, see the section "Save a Table."*

Field Name	Data Type	Description
ID	AutoNumber	This field is filled in automatically
Vendor	Text	Company name
ContactPerson	Text	
Address1	Text	
Address2	Text	
City	Text	
State	Text	
ZIP	Text	Please use 9-digit ZIP code if available
Country	Text	
ProductType	Text	
Terms	Text	For example, Net 30 or 2% Net 10
Notes	Memo	
Attachments	Attachment	Attach any correspondence here

Is it always necessary to start with an ID field?

You should have one field that contains unique data for each record, but it does not have to be named ID. If you have your own numbering scheme for this unique field, set the data type to accommodate it. But if you do not already have a scheme, use AutoNumber to save some time.

Why can I not use spaces in the field names?

You can use spaces if you want, but it makes it harder to refer to the fields when you create functions and write complex query specifications. It is better to get into the habit of not using spaces. You can simulate spaces by using the underscore character. You can also specify a caption for the field, as explained in Chapter 4.

Open a Table in Design View

To modify a table, you work in Design view. If you do not already have the table open in Design view, then you can go directly into Design view from the Navigation pane or if the table is already open in some other view, you can switch from that view to Design view.

Open a Table in Design View

When the Table Is Not Open

1. In the Navigation pane, right-click on the table.
2. Choose **Design View** from the shortcut menu.

   The table opens in Design view.

When the Table Is Open in Another View

1. Right-click on the open table's tab.
2. Choose **Design View** from the shortcut menu.

   The table opens in Design view.

- You can also click here to choose **Design View**.

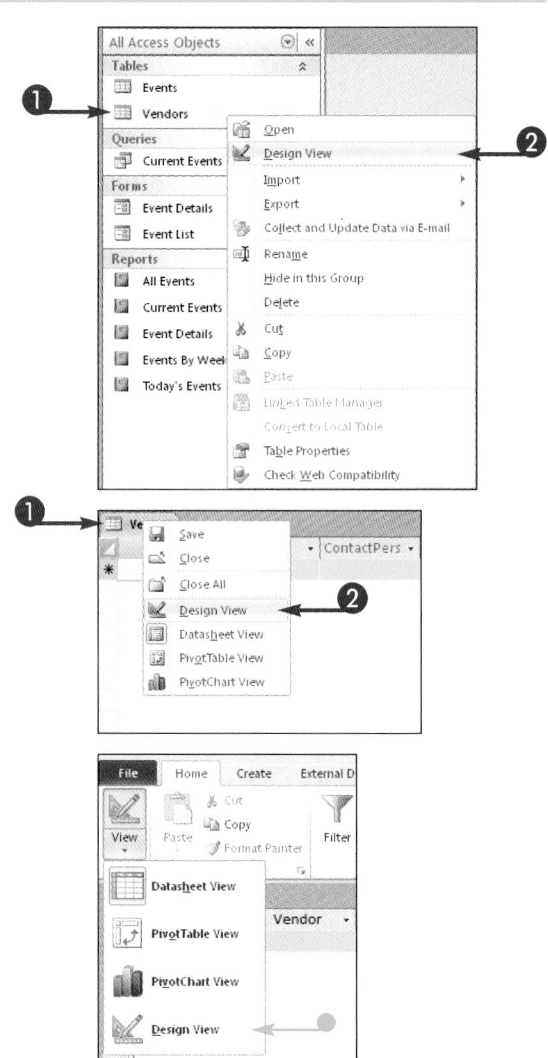

Rearrange Fields

You can change the order in which fields appear in a table. The field order in Design view from top to bottom corresponds to the order in a datasheet from left to right. Field order also determines the default positioning of fields on forms and reports.

Rearrange Fields

❶ Click the selector to the left of the field name.

Note: *To move multiple contiguous fields, click the first one, press and hold down* Shift*, and then click the last one.*

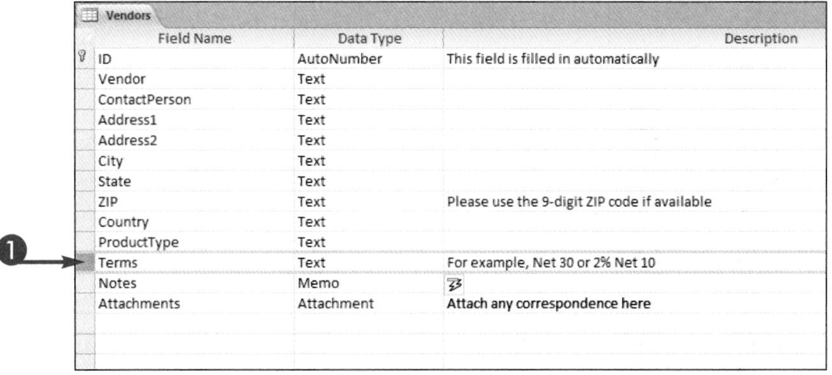

Vendors

Field Name	Data Type	Description
ID	AutoNumber	This field is filled in automatically
Vendor	Text	
ContactPerson	Text	
Address1	Text	
Address2	Text	
City	Text	
State	Text	
ZIP	Text	Please use the 9-digit ZIP code if available
Country	Text	
ProductType	Text	
Terms	Text	For example, Net 30 or 2% Net 10
Notes	Memo	
Attachments	Attachment	Attach any correspondence here

❷ With the mouse pointer on the selector, drag up or down to move the field.

- A horizontal line shows where the field is going.

❸ Repeat steps **1** and **2** to move other fields as needed.

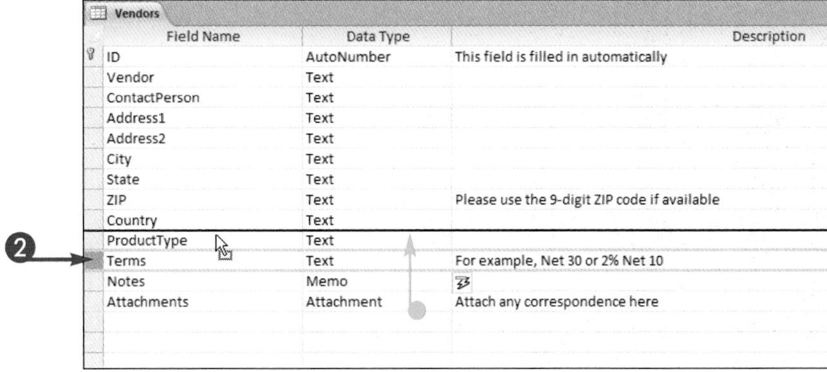

Vendors

Field Name	Data Type	Description
ID	AutoNumber	This field is filled in automatically
Vendor	Text	
ContactPerson	Text	
Address1	Text	
Address2	Text	
City	Text	
State	Text	
ZIP	Text	Please use the 9-digit ZIP code if available
Country	Text	
ProductType	Text	
Terms	Text	For example, Net 30 or 2% Net 10
Notes	Memo	
Attachments	Attachment	Attach any correspondence here

Insert and Delete Fields

You can insert new fields into a field list, and you can remove existing fields from that list.

You can add a field at the bottom of the field list and then move it to the position that you want. However, it is easier to insert a new blank row directly where you want it in the field list.

Insert and Delete Fields

Insert a Field

1. Click the field that the new field should appear above.
2. On the Design tab, click **Insert Rows**.
   - A new row appears in the grid — above the one you selected.
3. Type a field name and choose a field type as you would normally.

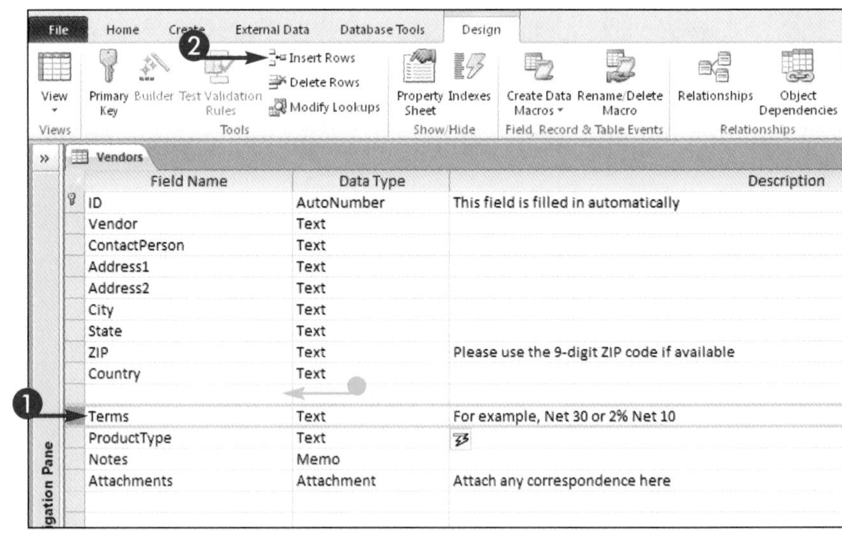

Delete a Field

1. Click the field that you want to delete.

***Note:** To delete multiple contiguous fields, click the first one, press and hold down Shift, and then click the last one.*

2. On the Design tab, click **Delete Rows**.

   The row is deleted, along with any data that the fields contained.

***Note:** If you make a mistake, press Ctrl + Z to undo the deletion.*

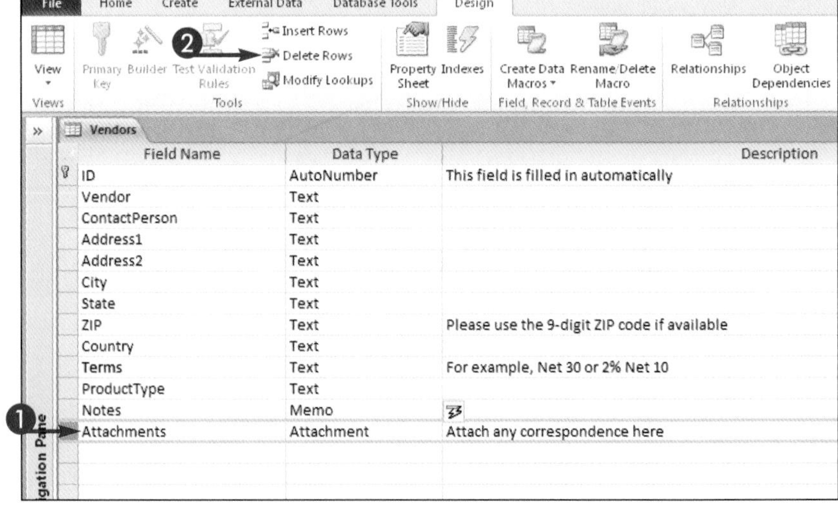

Understanding Data Types

Each field has a data type that defines what you can store in it. Data entry is restricted to valid entries for the type you choose, which helps to prevent data-entry errors. For example, you cannot enter letters in a field set to Number, and you must enter valid dates or times in a Date/Time field.

The choice of data type also affects the other properties available for the field, as you will see later in this chapter.

Data Types

This table lists the available data types in Access 2010 and explains possible uses for each one.

Data Type	*Used For*	*Notes*
Text	Text and numbers	This is a general-purpose field containing any data. It has a limit of 255 characters and cannot be used for numeric calculation. Use this type for numeric entries that will not have calculations performed on them, such as telephone numbers and ZIP codes.
Memo	Text and numbers	This type has a limit of 63,999 characters. In the Access 2010 file format, it can hold rich text with formatting. There are some limitations on usage in formulas and functions.
Number	Numbers only	This type offers a flexible field size of 1, 2, 4, 8, or 16 bytes. It can also hold symbols used as helpers for numbers, such as decimal points and commas.
Date/Time	Numbers representing dates or times	This type stores dates and times as 8-byte numbers. It only stores numbers representing valid dates and times.
Currency	Numbers representing currency values	This type stores currency values as 8-byte numbers. Even though the field might only show two decimal places depending on formatting, it keeps track of up to four places to prevent rounding off.
AutoNumber	Automatically generated numbering for each record	This type stores Access-generated values as 4-byte numbers.
Yes/No	Boolean data	The value -1 represents Yes, and the value 0 represents No, but the field can be formatted to display values as True/False, On/Off, or Yes/No.
OLE Object	Embedded OLE objects	Use this type when you need to attach external documents in a backward-compatible database or when you need OLE linkage.
Hyperlink	A text address representing an external source	You can link to Web sites, e-mail addresses, files on your computer, files on a LAN, or virtually any other location.
Attachment	Any supported file type	This type works only in Access 2007 and Access 2010 databases. You can attach data files from word-processing programs, spreadsheets, graphic editing programs, and so on.
Lookup Wizard	Varies	Depending on the usage, this type creates either a lookup list from data that you specify or a lookup list from the values in another table. It can also be used to set up multivalued lists.
Calculated	The result of a calculation performed on one or more other fields	This field type is new in Access 2010. You can use it to create calculated fields directly in a table; in earlier versions, you could create calculated fields only in queries.

Change a Field's Data Type

You can change a field's data type to better represent what you plan to store in it.

It is easiest to set field types before you enter data into the table, but you can change the field type at any time. Any existing data that violates the rules of the new data type is deleted, but Access warns you before deleting it.

Change a Field's Data Type

❶ In Design view, click here (▼) to open the Data Type list for the field.

❷ Click the new type.

The type changes in the Data Type column.

❸ Click **Save** (💾) on the Quick Access Toolbar to save the changes to the table.

You can also press Ctrl + S.

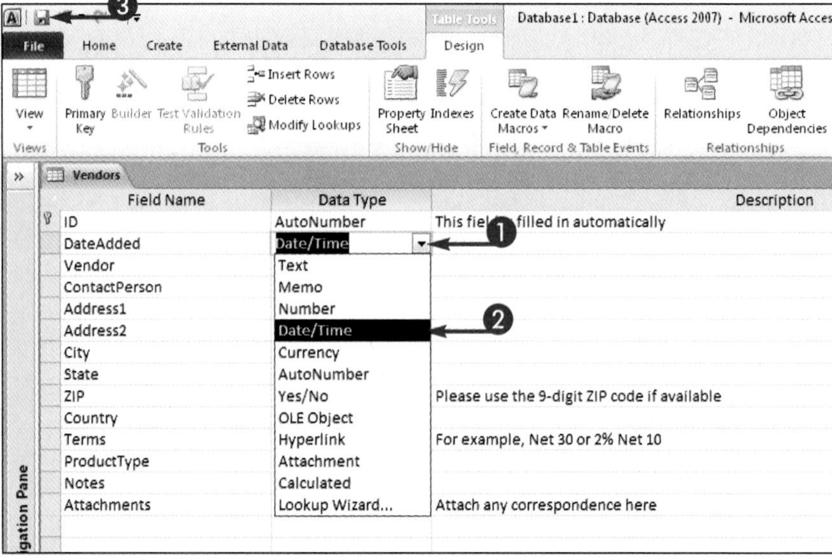

If the existing data violates the rules of the new data type, a warning message appears.

***Note:** Even though the warning may say that records were deleted, they have not actually been deleted at this point; you can still change your mind.*

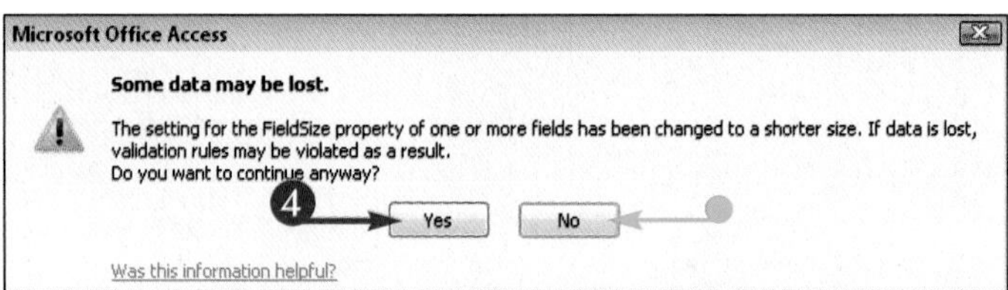

❹ Click **Yes** to allow the deletion of records that violate the new field type's rules.

● You can also click **No** to abandon the change.

Understanding Primary and Composite Keys

The *primary key* is the field by which each record will be uniquely identified and by which relationships between tables can be created. A table usually has only one primary key. When a unique combination of two or more fields' values forms the primary key, it is called a *composite key.*

Understanding Primary and Composite Keys

Which Field?

Traditionally, the first field in the table is the primary key. Using this convention makes it easy to browse and sort records by this field. However, you may use any field you like for it. You can use an AutoNumber field to allow Access to assign numbering for you or you can use a Number or Text field. The only limitation is that the field must contain a unique value for each record. The primary key field cannot be left blank nor can it duplicate the value of another record.

Composite Keys

In rare cases, a single field may not uniquely identify each record. For example, suppose you have a table that records which students have taken which classes. It contains two fields: StudentID and ClassID. Neither of those fields is unique for each record, but the combination of the two is unique for each record. In those situations, you may need to set a multifield primary key (also called a *composite key)*, in which each record must have a unique combination of entries in those fields.

Set the Primary or Composite Key

It is fairly simple to set a primary or composite key. A primary or composite key is not required for every table, but it is highly recommended.

If you try to save or close a table without a primary or composite key, Access displays a warning dialog box.

Set the Primary or Composite Key

Set a Single Primary Key

❶ In Design view, click in the row for the field that you want to set as the primary key.

❷ Click **Primary Key**.

● A key symbol (🔑) appears to the left of the field.

Note: *The Primary Key symbol is an on/off toggle; you can click it to remove it.*

File Home Create External Data Database Tools Design

View | Primary Key | Builder | Test Validation Rules | Insert Rows | Delete Rows | Modify Lookups | Property Sheet | Indexes | Create Data Macros | Rename/Delete Macro | Relationships | Object Dependencies

Views | Tools | Show/Hide | Field, Record & Table Events | Relationships

Vendors

Field Name	Data Type	Description
ID	AutoNumber	This field is filled in automatically
DateAdded	Date/Time	
Vendor	Text	
ContactPerson	Text	
Address1	Text	
Address2	Text	
City	Text	
State	Text	
ZIP	Text	Please use the 9-digit ZIP code if available
Country	Text	
Terms	Text	For example, Net 30 or 2% Net 10
ProductType	Text	
Notes	Memo	
Attachments	Attachment	Attach any correspondence here

Set a Multifield (Composite) Key

❶ In Design view, click to the left of the first field that you want to include.

❷ Press and hold down Ctrl and then click to the left of additional fields that you want to include.

❸ Click **Primary Key**.

A key symbol (🔑) appears to the left of each of the chosen fields.

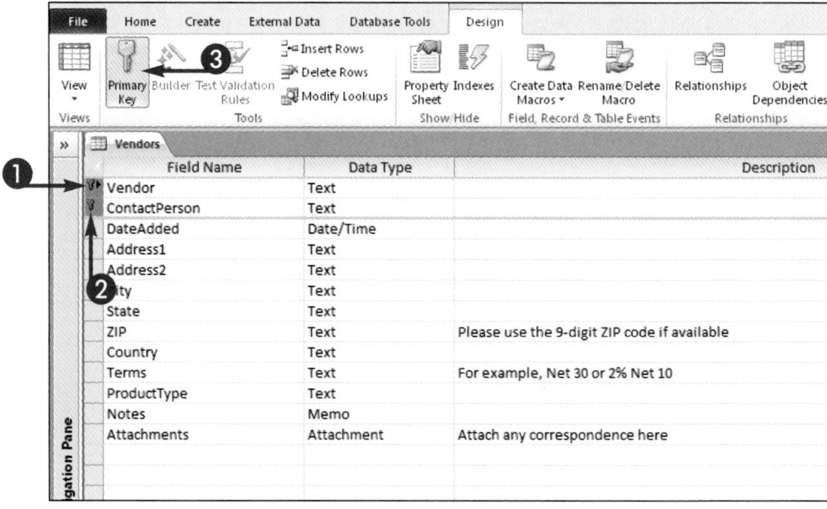

Rename a Table

You can rename a table at any time. Access automatically updates all references to the table throughout the database, so any forms, reports, or queries based on that table continue to work. The table must be closed in order for you to rename it.

Rename a Table

1. In the Navigation pane, right-click on the table name.
2. Choose **Rename** from the shortcut menu.

   The table name appears in Edit mode.

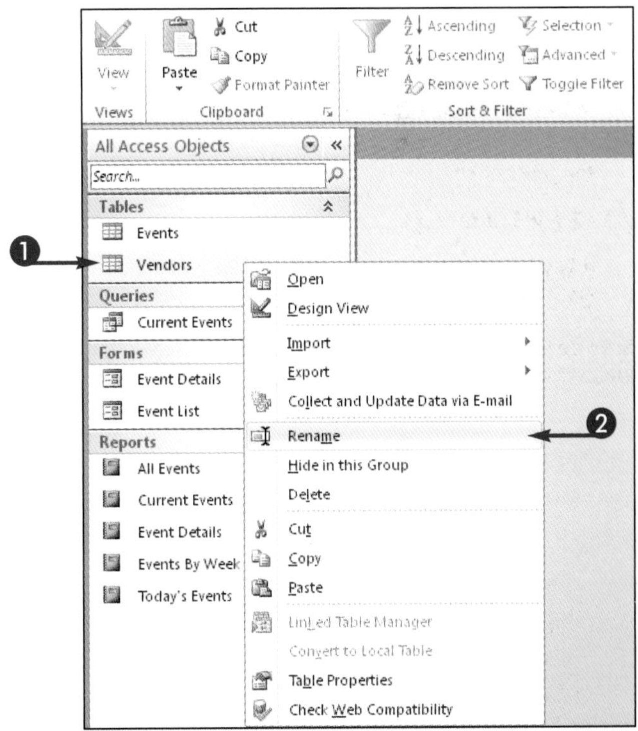

3. Edit the name as needed.

   You can use the Backspace and Delete keys to delete one character to the left or right of the insertion point, respectively.
4. Press Enter or click away from the table name to accept the new name.

- The new name appears on the table.

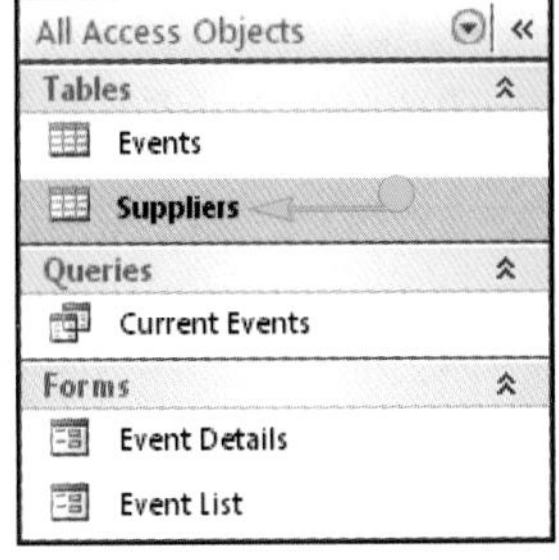

Delete a Table

You can delete any table from your database — even tables that contain records. Be careful not to delete anything that you need to keep because it is not possible to undo a table deletion.

Delete a Table

1. Right-click on the table name.
2. Choose **Delete** from the shortcut menu.

- You can also click **Delete** on the Home tab.

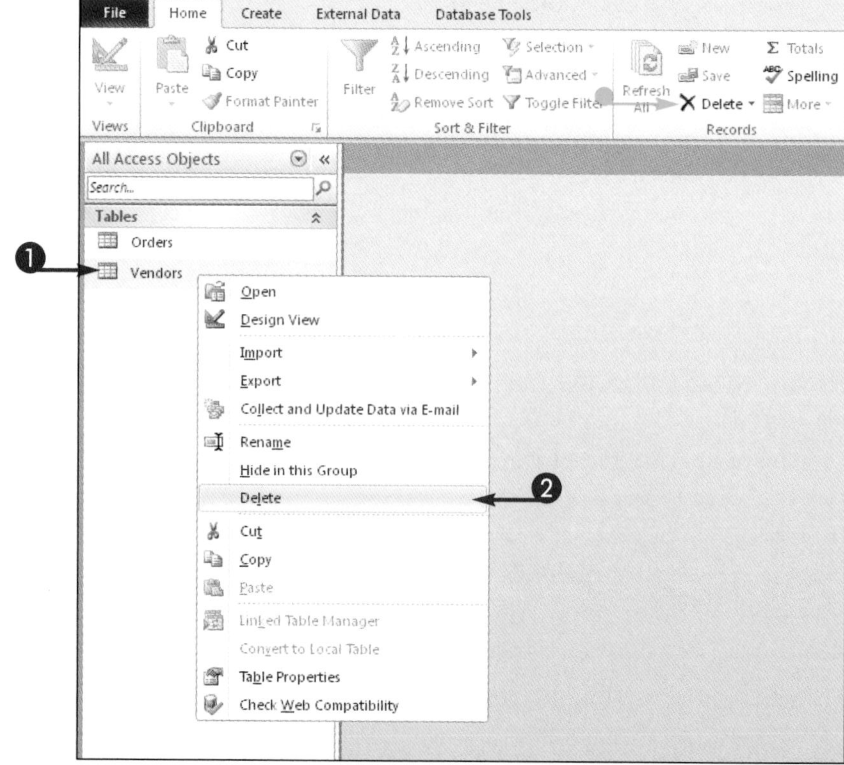

A confirmation dialog box opens.

3. Click **Yes**.

The table is deleted.

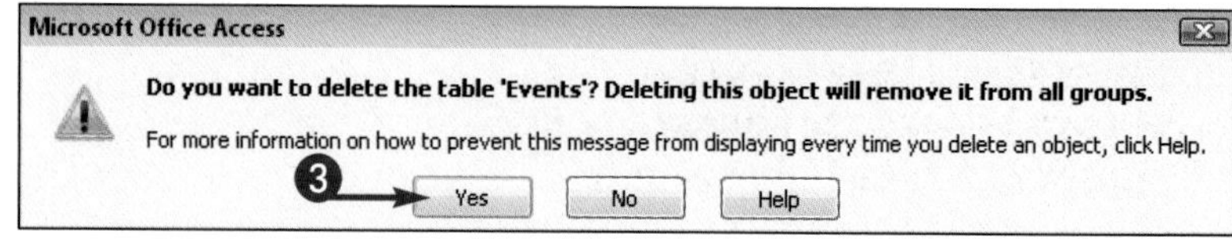

Copy a Table

When you need to have two or more tables with the same or similar fields, you can save time by creating one table and then copying it to create the other one. After creating the copy, you can make any minor changes needed to differentiate it from the original.

Copy a Table

1. In the Navigation pane, right-click on the original table.
2. Choose **Copy** from the shortcut menu.

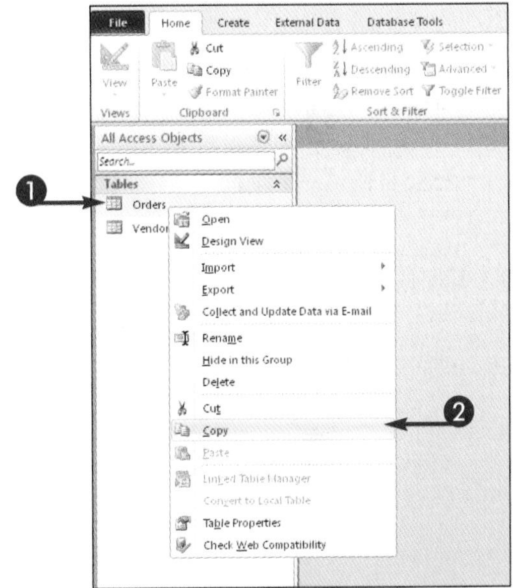

3. Right-click on an empty area of the Navigation pane.
4. Choose **Paste** from the shortcut menu.

   The Paste Table As dialog box opens.
5. Type a name for the copy, replacing the default name.

   - Optionally, you can copy only the structure by clicking the **Structure Only** radio button (◎ changes to ◉).

Note: *If you do not select Structure Only, the copy will also contain all the data.*

6. Click **OK**.

   The copy of the table appears in the Navigation pane.

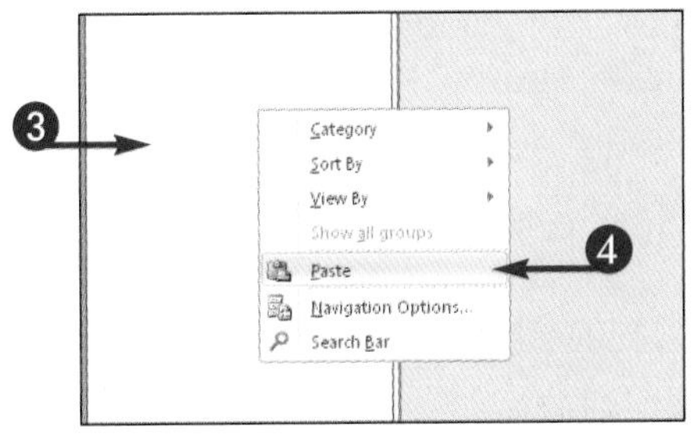

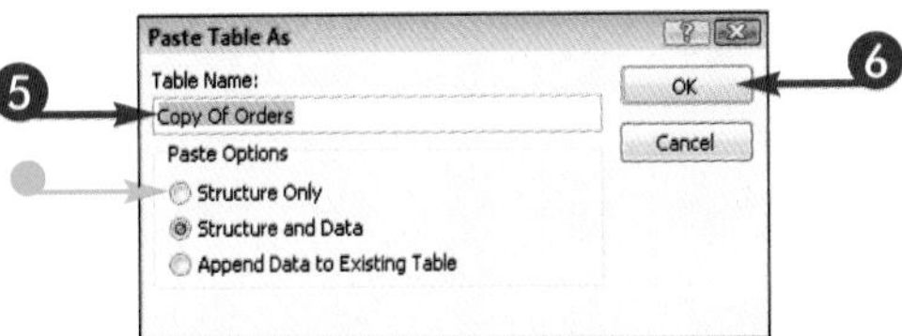

Working with Fields

Each table consists of one or more fields. In this chapter, you will learn how to set field properties, and you will create input masks and validation rules to reduce data-entry errors.

Understanding Field Properties

Each field has a set of properties that defines and controls it. These properties include basics such as its size and format as well as rules for making entries, such as specifying whether an entry is required or restricting an entry to certain values.

Properties pane
When a field is selected in Design view, its properties appear in the lower pane.

General tab
The General tab contains most of the properties you will work with.

Lookup tab
The Lookup tab is primarily for setting up lookup lists.

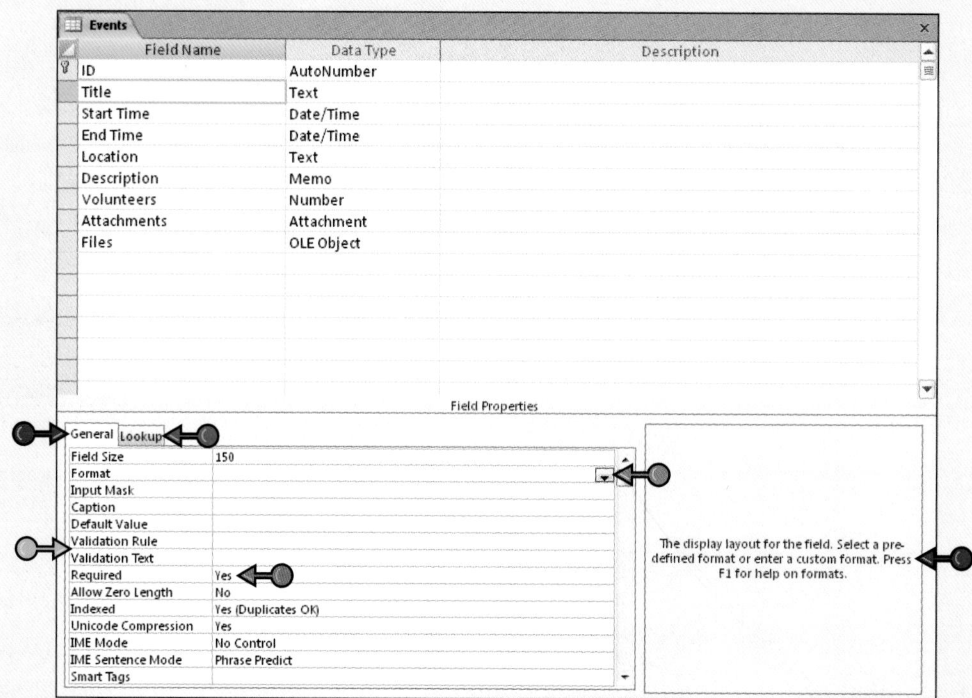

Drop-down lists
Some properties have drop-down lists from which you can make a selection; click the arrow (▾) to open the list. Other fields have Builder buttons (...), which open a dialog box that guides you through the process of building an entry.

Property information
When the insertion point is in a property's box, information about that property appears here.

Yes/No properties
Some properties represent yes/no questions; these are typically already filled in with default values.

Understanding Field Sizes

Each field has a size that limits the amount of data you can store in it. There are different ways of expressing the field size depending on the type of field.

The following table lists the specifications for the data types for which Field Size is a configurable setting. Many field types do not allow you to set a field size. For a numeric field, the advantage of choosing a field size that takes up fewer bytes is that it results in a smaller database file. The file size difference becomes more apparent the more records the table contains.

Field Type	*Default Size*	*Notes*
Text	255 characters	You can specify any number of characters from 0 to 255. Each character occupies 1 byte of disk space.
Number	Long Integer	The choice of number format determines the number of bytes used to store it: **Byte:** Integers from 0 to 255 (1 byte) **Integer:** Integers from -32,767 to +32,767 (2 bytes) **Long Integer:** Integers from -2,147,483,648 to +2,147,483,647 (4 bytes) **Single:** Integers from -3.4 × 1038 to +3.4 × 1038 and up to 7 significant digits (4 bytes) **Double:** Floating-point numbers from -1.797 × 10308 to +1.797 × 10308 and up to 15 significant digits (8 bytes) **Replication ID:** A globally unique identifier (GUID), such as a randomly generated ID number (16 bytes) **Decimal:** Integers with a defined decimal precision with values between -10^{28} and $+10^{28}$. The default precision is zero, and the default number of decimal places displayed is 18.
AutoNumber	Long Integer	The same as Number, except there are only two choices: Long Integer or Replication ID

Change a Field Size

Setting a field's size as small as possible — while still accommodating all entries — keeps the database file small. The difference in file size becomes more pronounced as more records are stored in a file.

Change a Field Size

For the Text Data Type

1. In Design view, click in the field you want to change.

   The properties for that field appear.

2. Click in the Field Size row on the General tab.

3. Type a new field size.

Note: *Field size for a text field is expressed as a number of characters.*

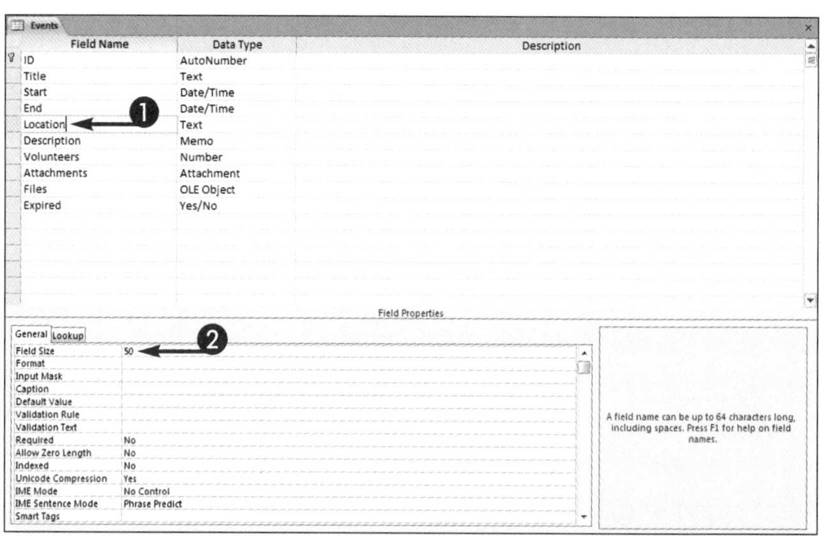

For the Number Data Type

1. In Design view, click in the field you want to change.

   The properties for that field appear.

2. Click in the Field Size row.

   A drop-down menu arrow (▾) appears on the row.

3. Click here (▾) to choose the field size that you want.

Note: *For a numeric field, size is expressed as a number type. See the section "Understanding Field Properties" for more.*

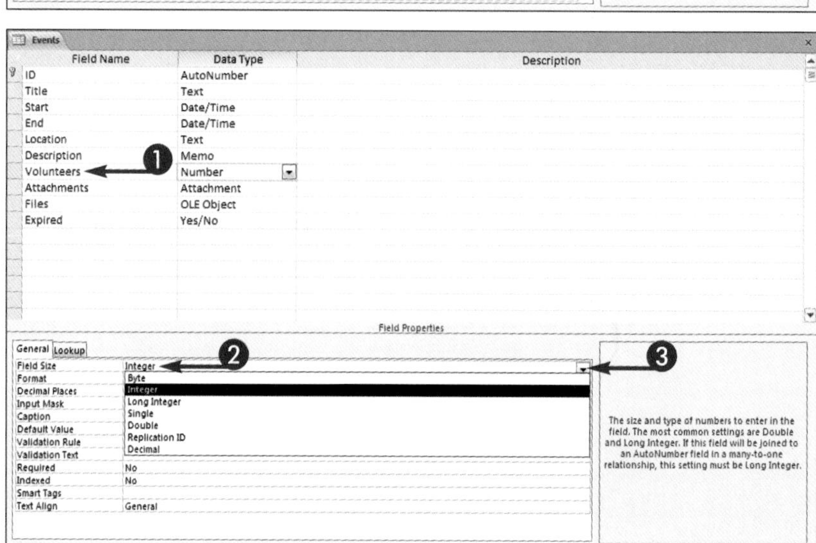

Set a Field Caption

You can specify captions for fields that are different from their actual names. For example, if you have a field called LastName, you can set up its caption to appear as "Last Name" with a space between the words.

Captions appear in datasheet headings and on labels in forms and reports.

Set a Field Caption

1. In Design view, click in the field you want to change.

   The properties for that field appear.

2. Click here to type a caption.

Note: *The caption can include spaces and symbols and can have up to 255 characters.*

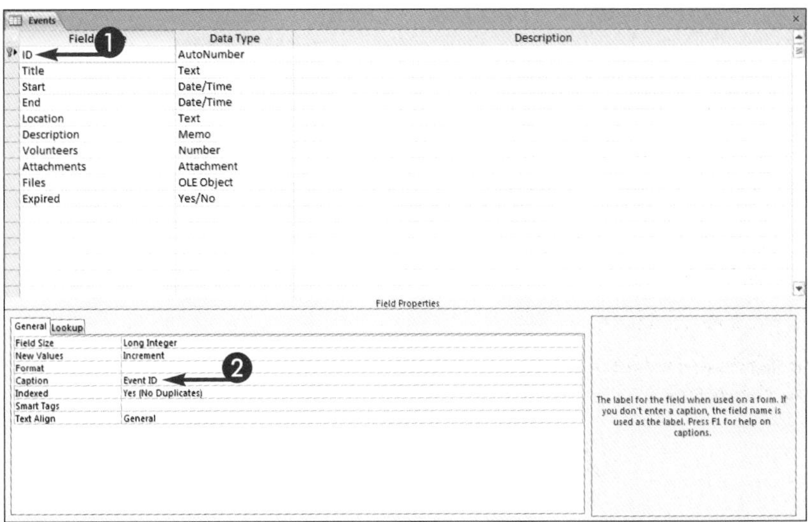

- When you display the table's datasheet, the field's caption appears as its column heading.

Note: *To check the caption in a datasheet, click the* ***Save*** *button ( ) to save it and then switch to Datasheet view.*

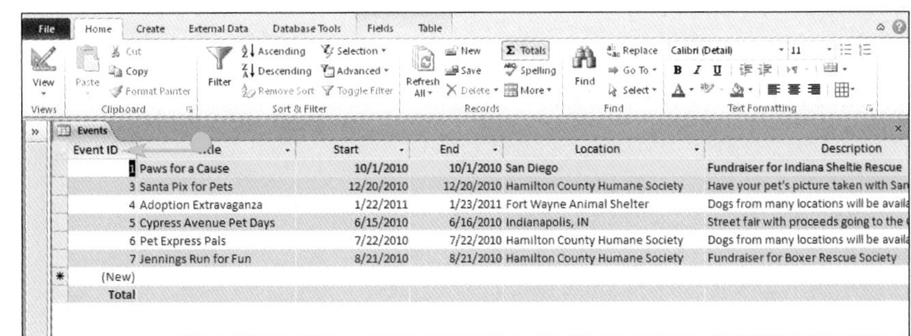

Set a Field's Format

A field's format determines how its data will be displayed. You can change a field's format to update its appearance in datasheets, forms, and reports.

The field format is most significant for fields that store data numerically, such as Number, Currency, Date/Time, and Yes/No.

Set a Field's Format

1. In Design view, click in the field you want to change.

   The properties for that field appear.

2. Click in the Format row.

   A drop-down menu arrow (▾) appears on the row.

3. Click here (▾) to choose the format that you want.

- For a Number or AutoNumber field, the choices represent different number types, such as General, Currency, and Percentage.

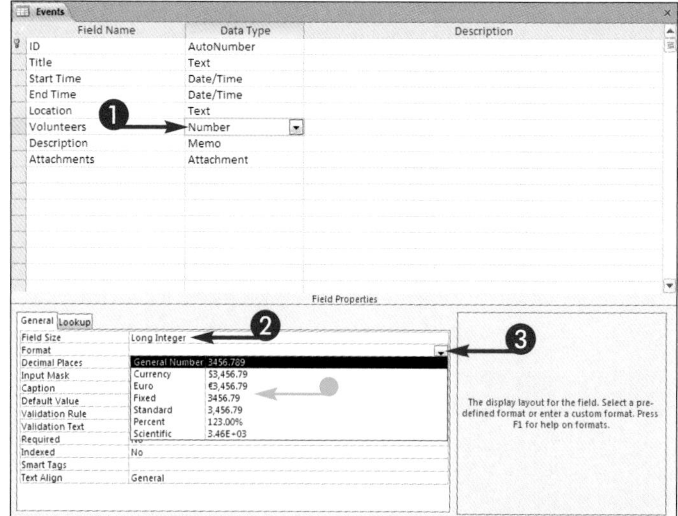

- For Date/Time data types, the choices appear as date/time formats.

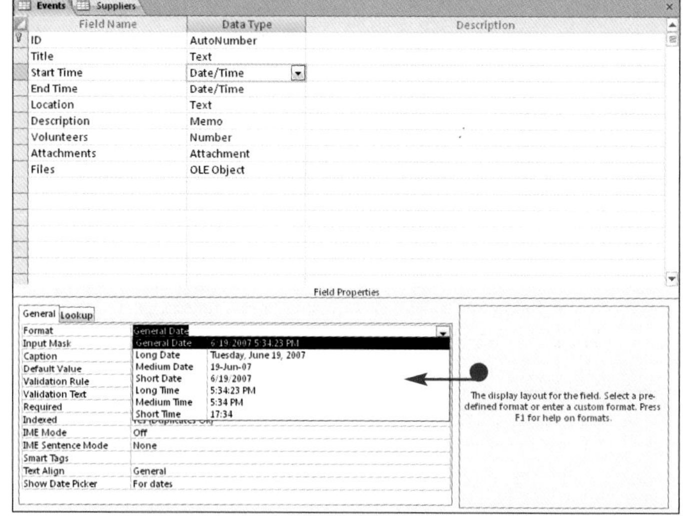

- For Yes/No fields, the choices appear as ways of expressing yes or no.

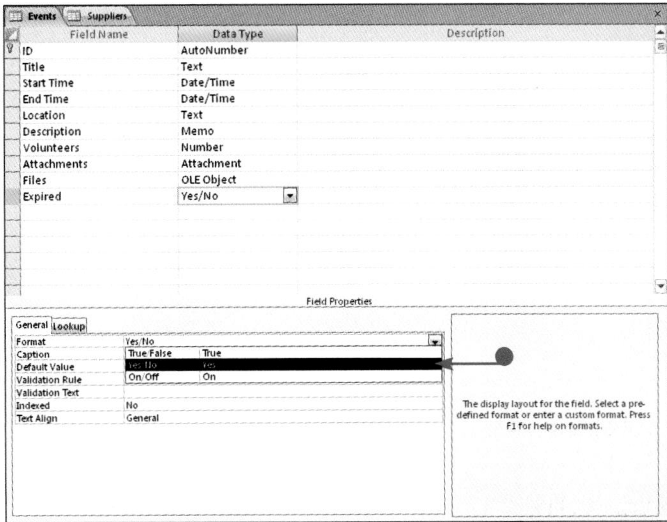

- For a Calculated field, all the choices from all the other field types are available because Access cannot automatically determine what type of data it will hold.

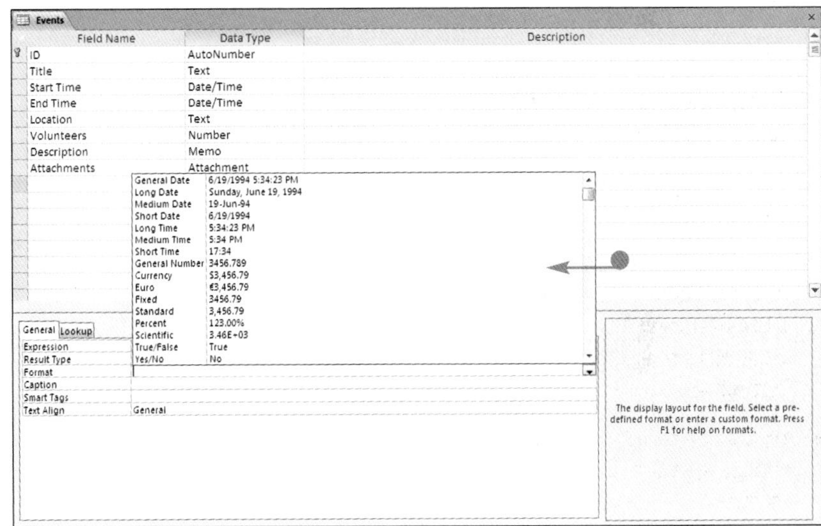

TIP

Why do some fields have a blank list for Format?

Certain field types have no preset formats. These include Text, Memo, and Hyperlink.

Set a Default Value

You can speed up data entry for fields that usually contain the same value by making that value the default. For example, if 90% of your clients pay by credit card, you can make Credit Card the default value in the PaymentType field.

Set a Default Value

1. In Design view, click in the field you want to change.

   The properties for that field appear.

2. Click here to type a default value.

***Note:** When you move away from the text box, Access automatically adds quotation marks around what you typed if the field type is Text.*

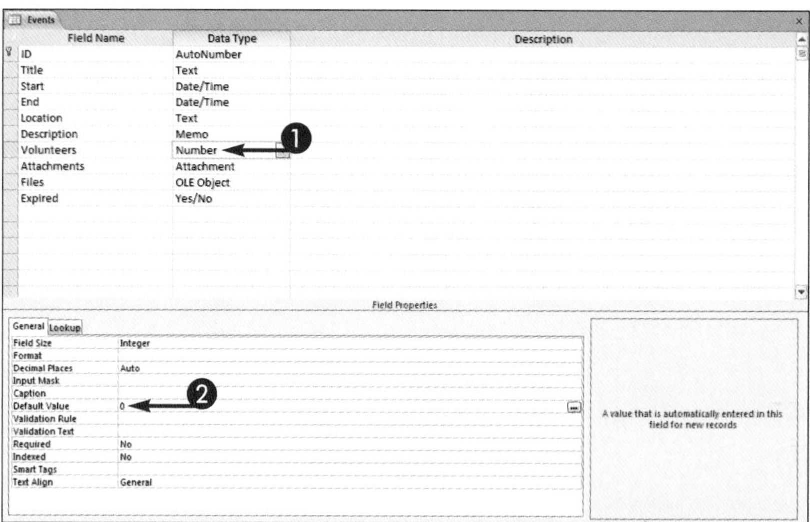

- When you display the table's datasheet, the default value appears in new records.

***Note:** The default value does not automatically populate existing records.*

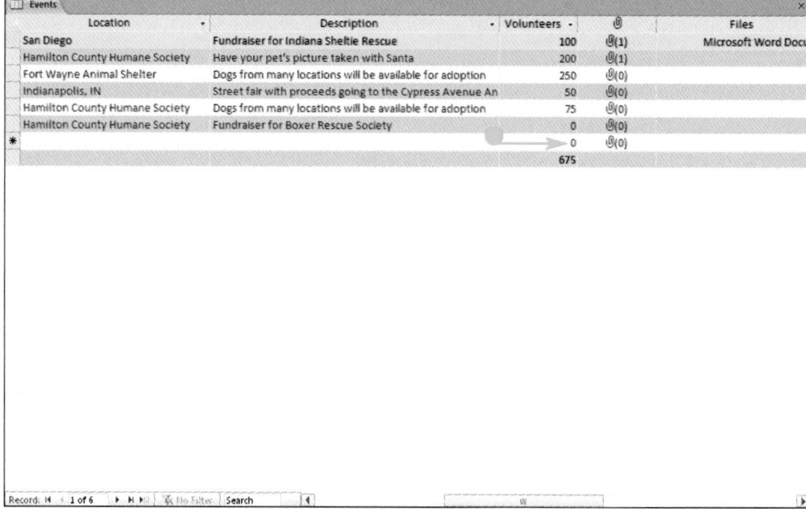

Make a Field Required

The primary key field is always required for each record in a database, but you can also make other fields required without changing the primary key setting. When a field is required, Access does not enable users to skip it during data entry.

Make a Field Required

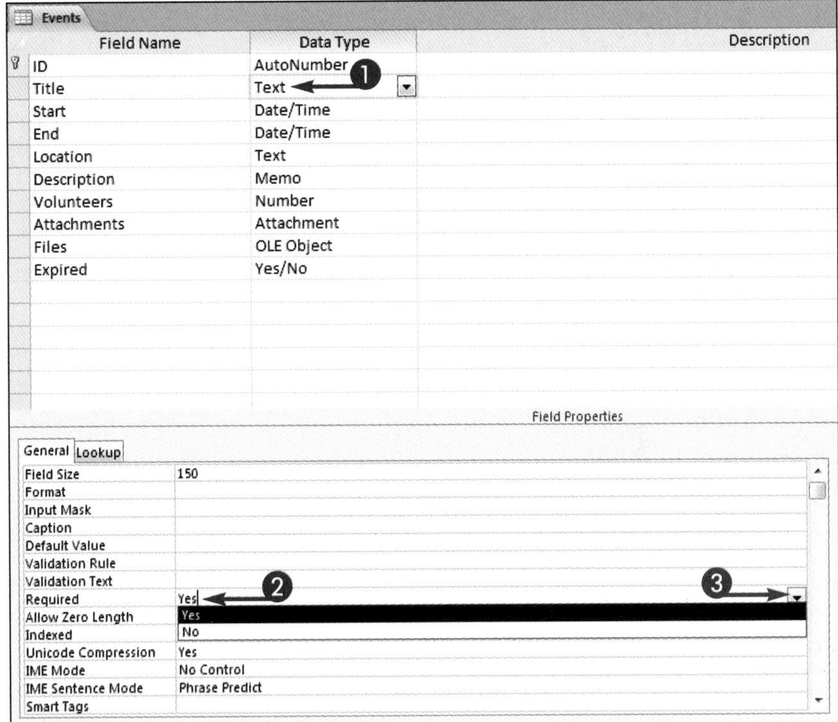

1. In Design view, click in the field you want to change.

   The properties for that field appear.

2. Click in the Required row.

   A drop-down menu arrow (▾) appears.

3. Click here (▾) to choose **Yes**.

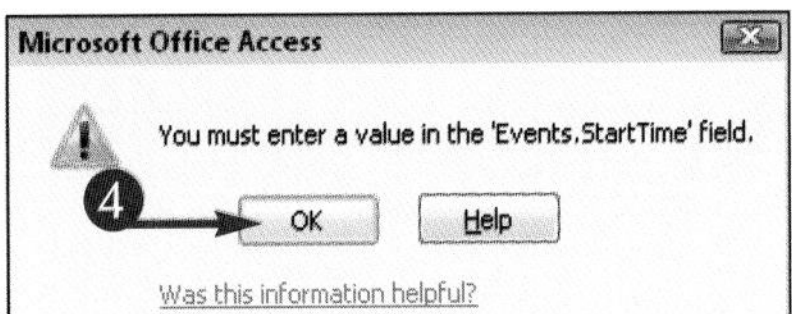

When you enter a new record in the table, a warning appears if you do not enter a value in a required field.

4. Click **OK** to clear the error and then type a value in the required field.

Index a Field

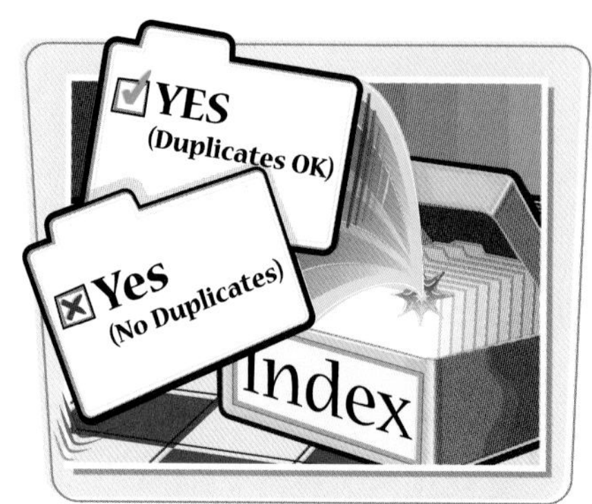

When you perform searches on a database that contains many records, a delay can occur as Access searches. To minimize searching delays, you can set certain fields to be automatically indexed. Searches based on those fields will take place more quickly.

The two types of indexing are Yes (Duplicates OK) and Yes (No Duplicates). The latter has the side effect of forcing each record to have a unique value for that field, as with the primary key field.

Index a Field

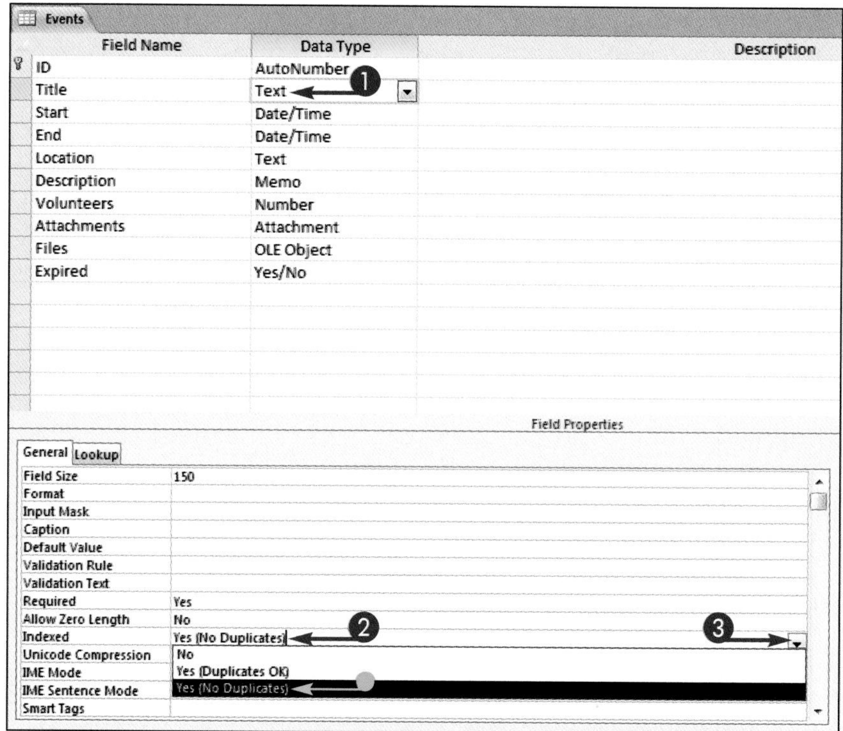

1. In Design view, click in the field you want to change.

   The properties for that field appear.

2. Click in the Indexed row.

   A drop-down menu arrow (▾) appears.

3. Click here (▾) to choose **Yes (Duplicates OK)**.

   This sets the field to be indexed without forcing entries in it to be unique.

- You can choose **Yes (No Duplicates)** if you prefer that records have unique entries for that field.

  If you chose **Yes (No Duplicates)** and you then try to enter an identical value for two records, an error message appears.

- Click **OK** to clear the message and then correct the error.

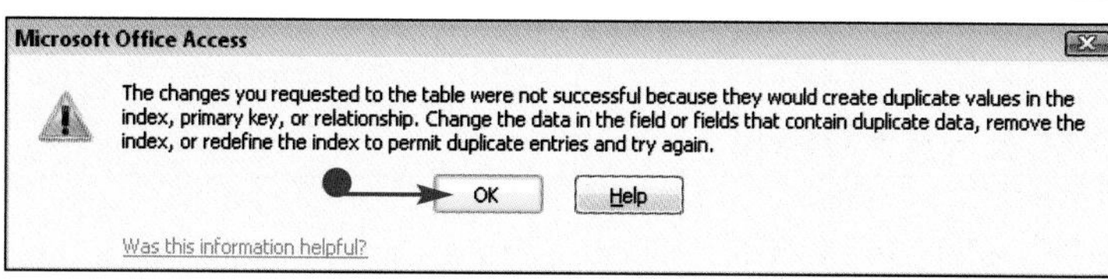

Apply Smart Tags

You can turn on smart tags for a field to make it easier to cross-reference data between the Access database and Microsoft Outlook (or another personal information and e-mail program) and the Web.

Apply Smart Tags

1. In Design view, click in the field you want to change.

   The properties for that field appear.

2. Click in the Smart Tags row.
3. Click the ⋯ that appears.

   The Smart Tags dialog box opens.

4. Click the check box for the type of smart tags you want to use (☐ changes to ☑).
5. Click **OK**.

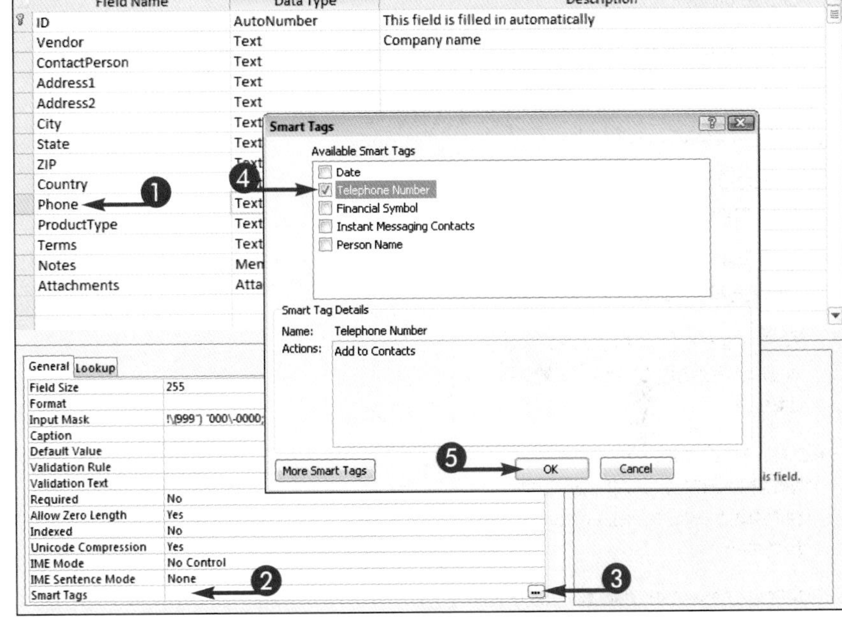

When working in a datasheet, a Smart Tag icon (ⓘ) appears next to a tag-enabled field when it is selected.

- You can click the **Smart Tag** icon (ⓘ) to see a menu of activities and then click the desired activity.

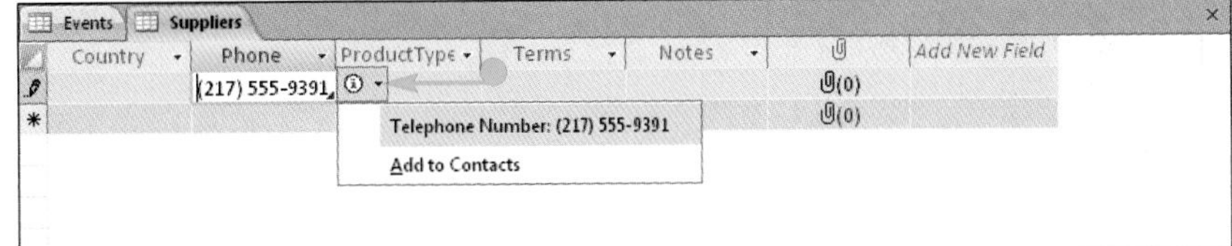

Create an Input Mask

You can create an input mask to help minimize data-entry errors. Input masks provide a template for entering data into a field, such as providing dashes between the parts of a phone number and parentheses around the first three numbers, like this: (317) 555-1298.

You can use one of the Access input masks as it is or you can customize it.

Create an Input Mask

1. In Design view, click the **Save** button (💾) to save any changes you have made.
2. Click in the field you want to change.

   The properties for that field appear.
3. Click in the Input Mask row.
4. Click the [...] that appears.

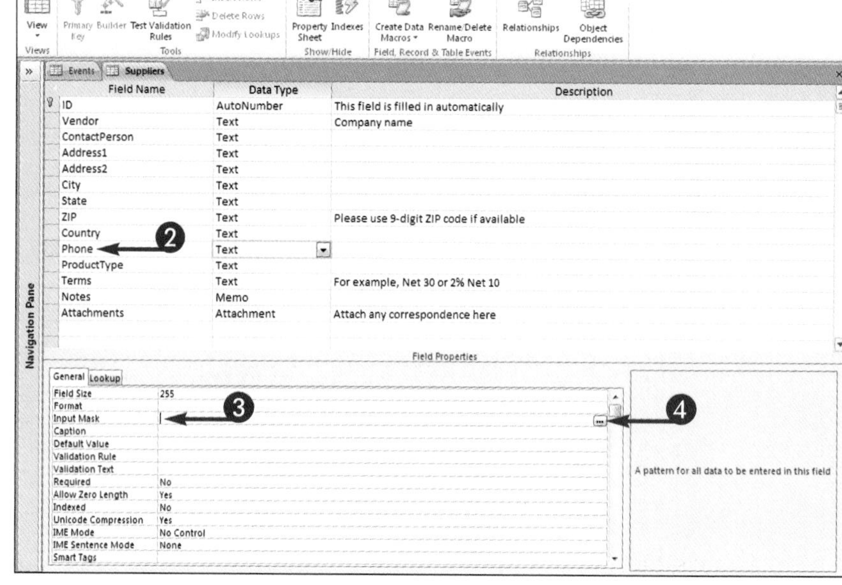

The Input Mask Wizard opens.

5. Click the type of input mask that you want.
   - To try the mask, you can click in the Try It box and then type a sample entry.
6. Click **Next** to customize the mask.
   - If you do not want to customize the mask, click **Finish**.

7 Modify the input mask's code if you want to.

8 Click here (▾) to select a different placeholder character if necessary.

- To try the mask, you can click in the Try It box and then type a sample entry.

9 Click **Next**.

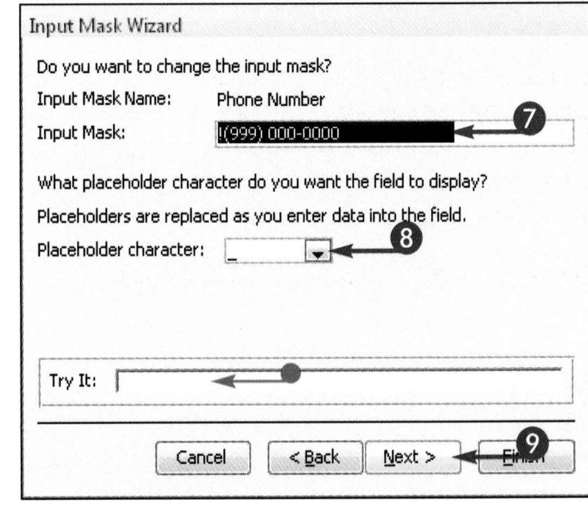

10 Click a radio button to specify how you want the data to be stored (◎ changes to ◉).

***Note:** This makes no difference unless you plan to export the data; your choice here determines how it looks when exported.*

11 Click **Finish**.

The input mask code appears in the Input Mask row in the field's properties.

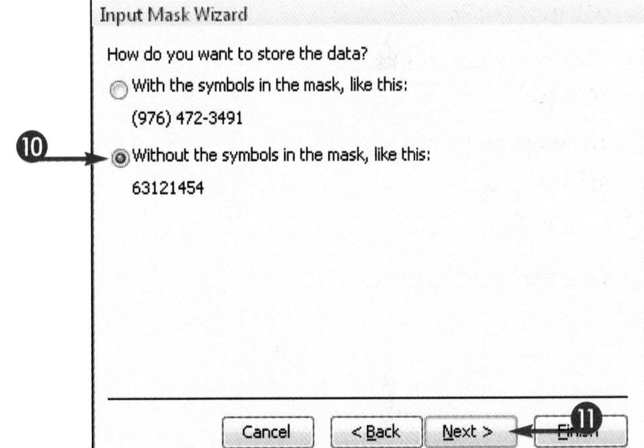

How do I create a custom input mask?

Input masks use characters to represent the types of data they will accept. This table shows the most commonly used characters. For more characters, look up "Input Mask Character Reference" in Access Help.

Character	Use
0	Single digit, required
9	Single digit, optional
#	A digit, space, plus sign, or minus sign
L	Single letter, required
?	Single letter, optional
A	Single letter or number, required
A	Single letter or number, optional
&	Any character or a space, required
C	Any character or a space, optional

Create a Validation Rule

Input masks help users enter the proper number and type of characters, but they cannot restrict the field to certain entries based on logic.

You can construct a validation rule that forces a field entry to meet a logical test of its validity. For example, you can make sure that negative numbers cannot be entered into a numeric field. You can also create validation text, which is a custom message that appears when the rule is violated.

Create a Validation Rule

1. In Design view, click in the field you want to change.

   The properties for that field appear.

2. Click in the Validation Rule row.
3. Click the ... that appears.

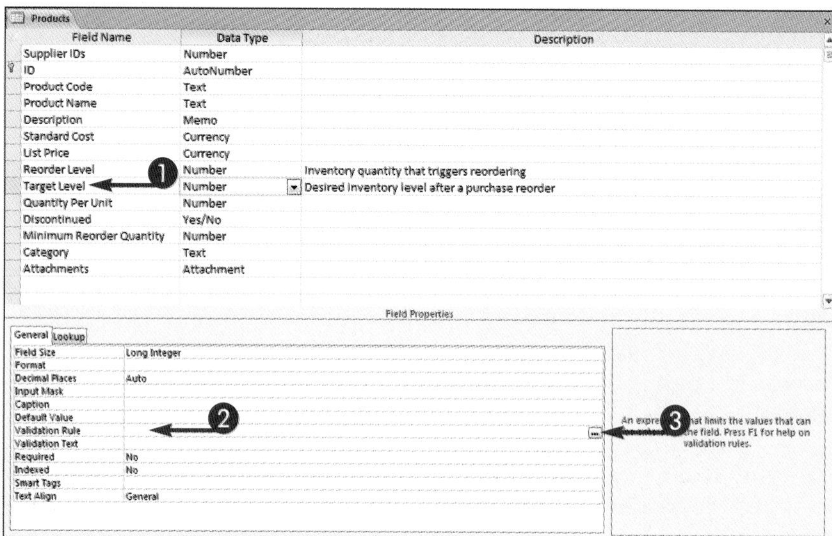

The Expression Builder dialog box opens.

4. Enter the expression that represents the criteria you want to specify.
5. Click **OK**.

***Note:** You could have simply typed the validation rule into the row and skipped steps **3** to **5**, but the Expression Builder's tools can be useful for complex expressions.*

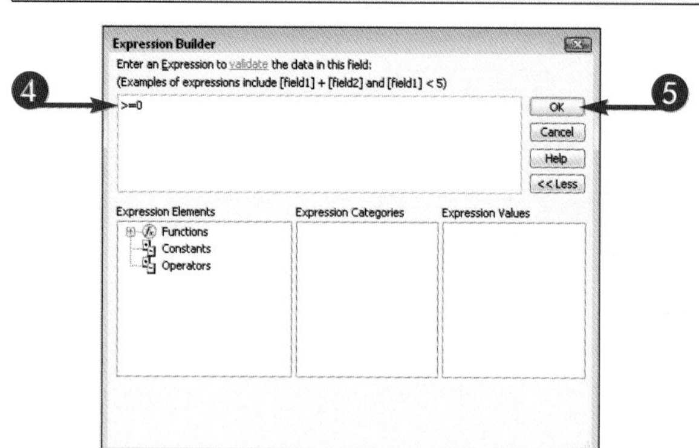

- The validation rule appears in the Validation Rule row.

6. Click here to type the text for the error message.

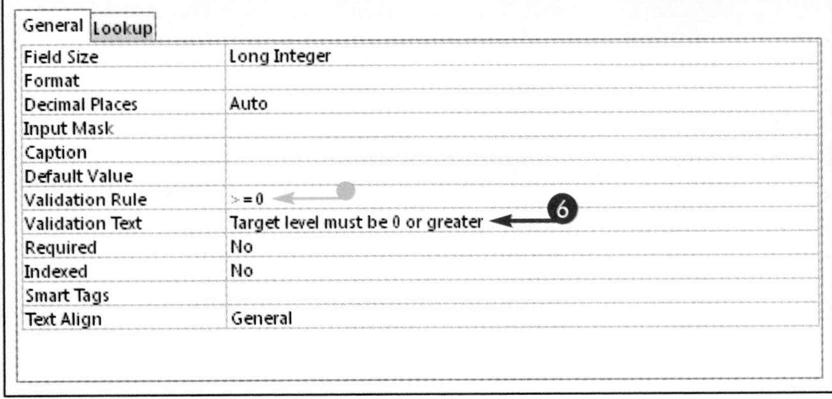

When the rule is violated, a custom error message appears, containing the text you specified in the Validation Text row.

7. Click **OK** and then retype the field entry.

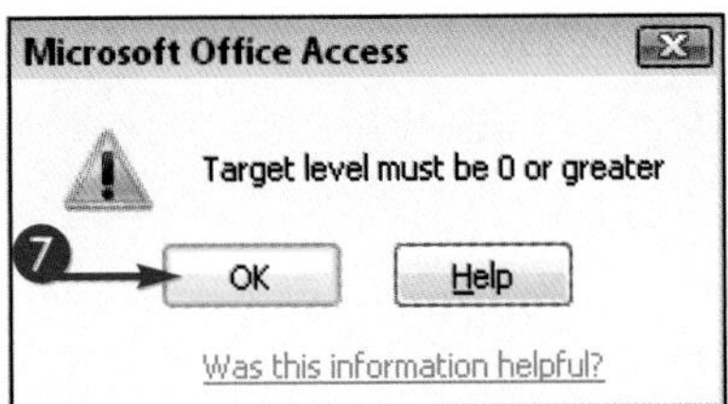

How do I use the Expression Builder?

The Expression Builder can guide you in determining the correct syntax for an expression. There are many types of expression content available, including functions, constants, and operators. For example, to enter the expression from the preceding steps (>=0) you would do the following:

1. Click **Operators**.
2. Click **Comparison**.
3. Double-click **>=**.

   The >= characters appear in the expression at the top of the dialog box.

4. Type **0**.
5. Click **OK**.

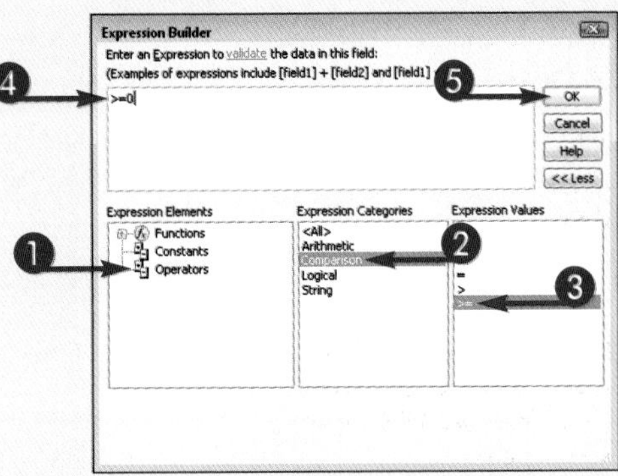

Create a Record-Level Validation Rule

You can construct a record-level validation rule to create validation conditions that involve more than one field.

For example, in an Employees table, you could make sure that the Hire date is before the Separation date because an employee cannot quit before being hired.

Create a Record-Level Validation Rule

1. In Design view, click **Property Sheet**.

   The Property Sheet for the entire table appears.

2. Click in the Validation Rule box to type the expression.

3. Click here to type the error message text.

4. Click **Test Validation Rules**.

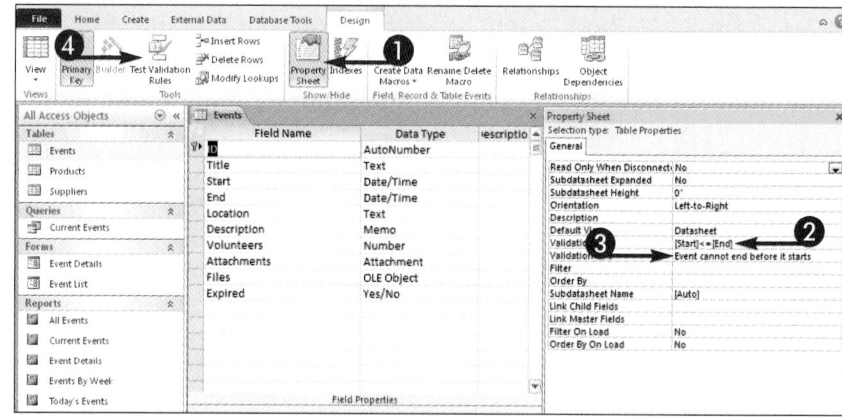

If the table contains data already, then a warning appears that the data must be checked.

- Click **Yes**.

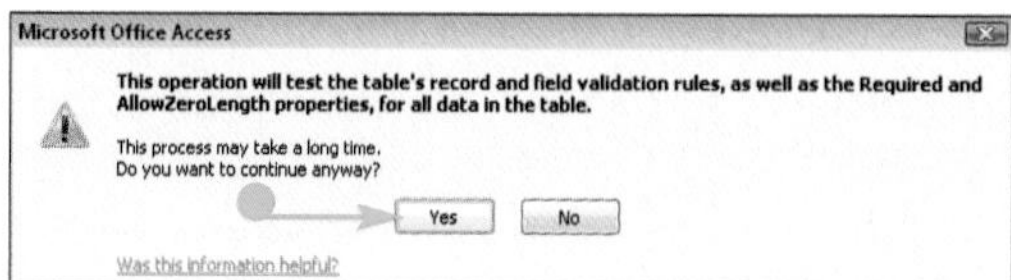

If the table has not been saved, a prompt appears to save it.

- Click **Yes**.

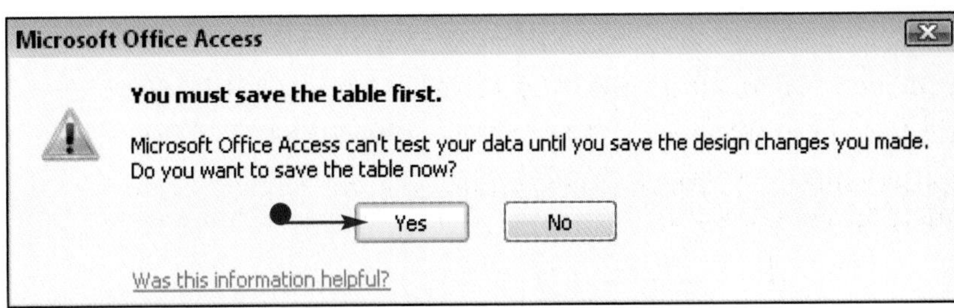

If existing data violates the new rule, then another warning appears. You can either keep the new rule or change it if this happens.

- Click **Yes** to keep the new rule, even if some existing data violates it.
- You can also click **No** to go back to the previous rule (if any).

A confirmation dialog box opens.

- Click **OK**.

The check is complete.

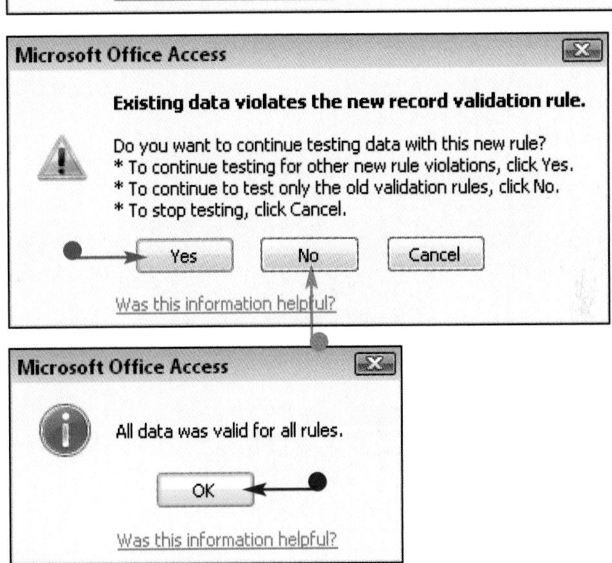

How do I construct a validation rule that contains field names?

You can type field names directly into an expression by enclosing them in square brackets: [StartDate].

What happens to existing data that violates the validation rule?

Nothing happens to it; it is allowed to continue to exist. However, new records will not be permitted to violate the rule, and if you ever edit the record that violates the rule, you will not be able to save changes to it until you fix the violation.

CHAPTER

5

Working with Relationships and Lookups

Relational databases are powerful because they can contain multiple related tables. You can create relationships between tables directly in the Relationships window or you can create relationships by building lookups that populate a field in one table with values from another table.

Understanding Relationships

You can connect tables by creating *relationships* between them based on a common field that they share. These relationships make it possible to create forms, queries, and reports that include fields from multiple tables.

Common Fields

For a relationship to exist between two tables, they must have a common field. For example, the Customers table may have a CustomerID field, and the Orders table may also have a CustomerID field. The two tables could be joined, or *related,* by that field. The field type must be the same in both tables for a relationship to exist. One exception is that an AutoNumber field can be related to a Number field.

The Primary Key and Foreign Key

In most relationships, the primary key field in one table is related to a field in the other table that is *not* its primary key. In one table, the field contains unique values, whereas in the other table, it does not. The related field in the other table is called the *foreign key.* For example, in the Customers table, each record has a unique CustomerID field, but in the Orders table, two different orders may have the same CustomerID.

Referential Integrity

Relationships can optionally be set to *enforce referential integrity.* This prevents the foreign key field from containing values that do not appear in the primary key field. For example, in the Orders table, a CustomerID value could not be entered that had no valid corresponding entry in the Customers table. This would prevent users from entering orders for nonexistent customers.

Cascade Update

When referential integrity is enabled, you can also enable Cascade Update and Cascade Delete. With Cascade Update, when a primary key entry changes, the foreign key entry in the related table also changes. For example, if a customer's CustomerID changes in the Customers table, all the orders in the Orders table reflect the new ID number.

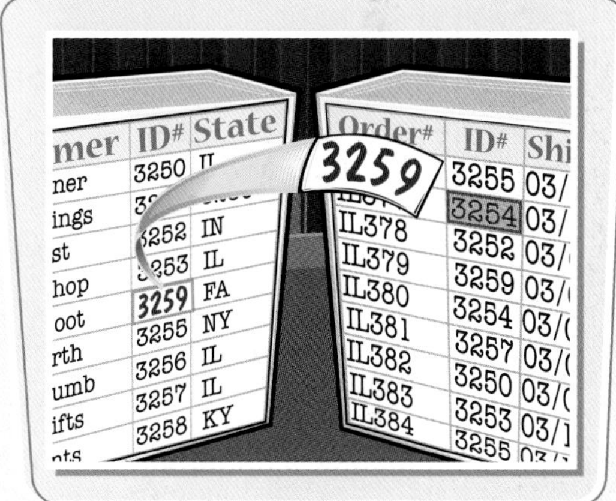

Cascade Delete

With Cascade Delete, when a record is deleted from the table containing the primary key part of the relationship, all corresponding records in the table containing the foreign key are deleted. For example, if a customer's record is deleted from the Customers table, then all of that customer's orders are deleted from the Orders table. Use this feature with caution.

Create a Relationship between Two Tables

Relationships are created and managed in a special database view called *the Relationships window*. You can create relationships between tables from this window by dragging a field from one table onto a field from another table.

Create a Relationship between Two Tables

Open Relationships View

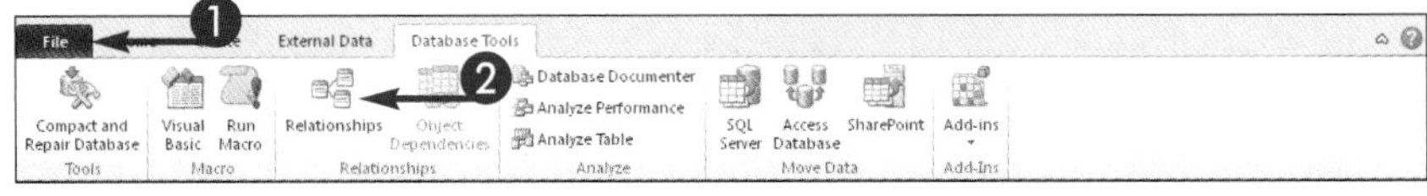

1. Click the **Database Tools** tab.

   The File menu opens.

2. Click **Relationships**.

   The Relationships window opens. It there are not any relationships yet in the database, the Show Table dialog box also opens.

Add Tables to the Relationships Window

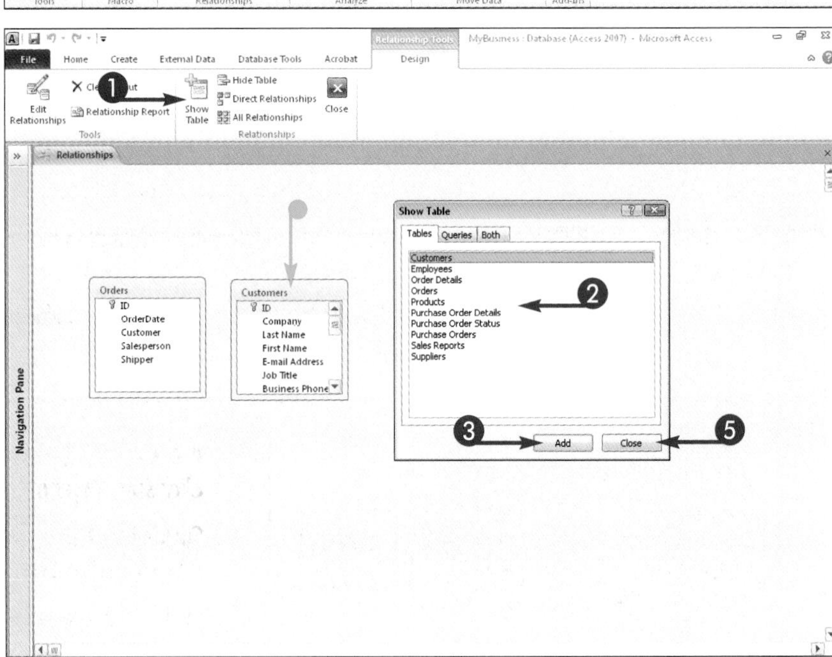

1. If the Show Table dialog box is not already open, click **Show Table**.
2. Click a table you want to add to the Relationships window.
3. Click **Add**.

Note: *You can double-click the table instead of following steps* ***2*** *and* ***3****.*

- The table appears in the Relationships window.

4. Repeat steps **2** and **3** as needed to add more tables.
5. Click **Close**.

Create a Relationship

1. Click the primary key field you want to be associated with a field in another table.
2. Drag and drop the primary key field onto the associated field in the other table.
3. Click the **Enforce Referential Integrity** check box if desired (☐ changes to ☑).
4. If you clicked the Enforce Referential Integrity check box in step **3**, you can do either or both of the following:
   - Click the **Cascade Update Related Fields** check box (☐ changes to ☑).
   - Click the **Cascade Delete Related Records** check box (☐ changes to ☑).
5. Click **Create**.

A connector appears between the two fields.

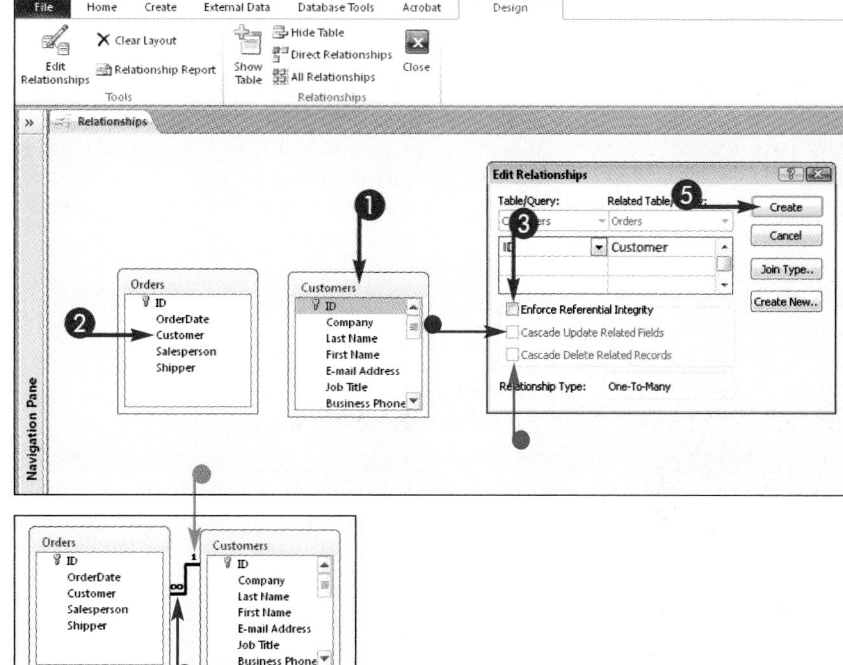

- On the "1" side, each record contains a unique entry for the joined field.
- On the "Many" (∞) side, multiple records can have the same value for the joined field.

Note: *If you did not enforce referential integrity, a plain line appears with no symbols on it.*

What is a join type?

A join type dictates what happens in a query or another combined view when there are records in one table that do not have a corresponding entry in the other table. The default join type is to include only records where the joined fields from both tables are equal.

How do I change the join type?

1. Click **Join Type** in the Edit Relationships dialog box.
2. Click a join type radio button (◎ changes to ◉) in the Join Properties dialog box.
3. Click **OK** in the Join Properties dialog box.
4. Click **OK** in the Edit Relationships dialog box.

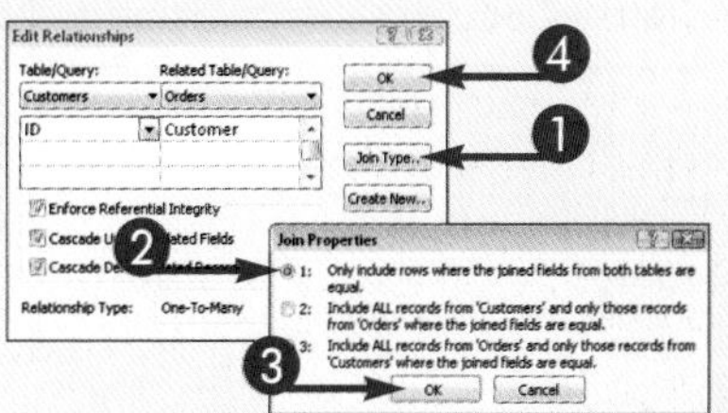

Edit a Relationship

You can change your mind about the nature of a relationship after creating it. For example, you may choose to change the referential integrity options or the join type.

Edit a Relationship

1. In the Relationships window, double-click the connector between two tables.

   The Edit Relationships dialog box opens.

2. Click or deselect the **Enforce Referential Integrity** check box (☐ changes to ☑).
3. If the Enforce Referential Integrity check box is clicked, you can do either or both of the following:

- Click or deselect the **Cascade Update Related Fields** check box.
- Click or deselect the **Cascade Delete Related Records** check box (☐ changes to ☑).

4. Click **OK**.

   The relationship is changed according to the option that you chose.

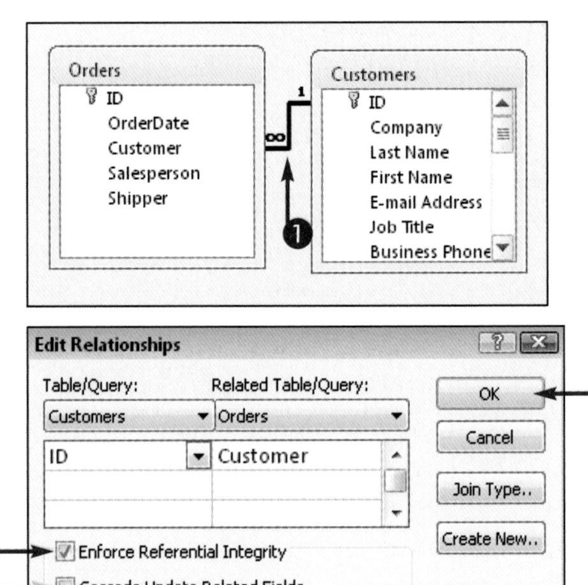

Remove a Relationship

You can remove the relationship between tables. For example, this may be necessary in order to create a lookup (because the Lookup Wizard likes to create its own relationships) or in order to change the data type for one of the fields.

Remove a Relationship

1. In the Relationships window, right-click on the line between the two tables.
2. Click **Delete**.

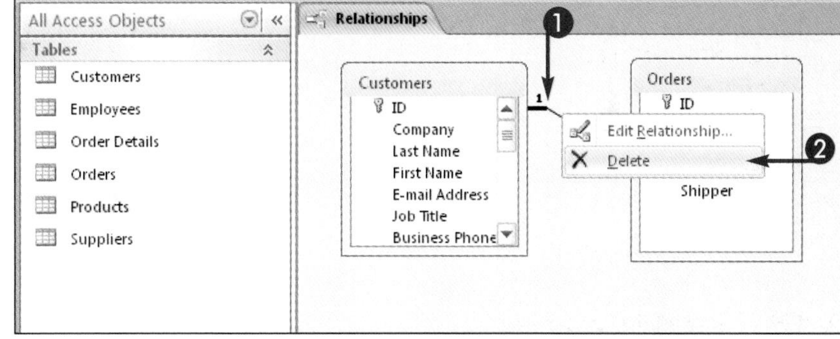

A confirmation dialog box opens.

3. Click **Yes**.

The relationship line is removed.

Note: *You cannot undo a relationship deletion. You must re-create the relationship if you want it back.*

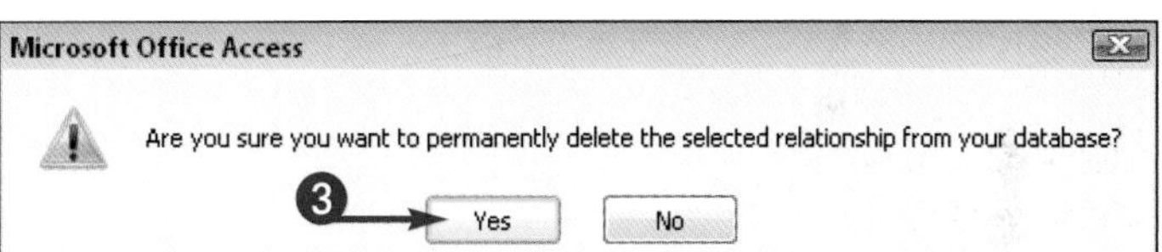

Arrange the Relationships Window

As you create more relationships and larger databases, the connector lines between tables may be difficult to see because of overlap. You can move the tables around in the Relationships window, and you can also resize the window for each table.

Arrange the Relationships Window

Move a Table in the Relationships Window

1. Click and drag a table's title bar to a new location.

   The relationship lines stay connected.

- If you need more room, you can use the scroll bars to scroll down or across.

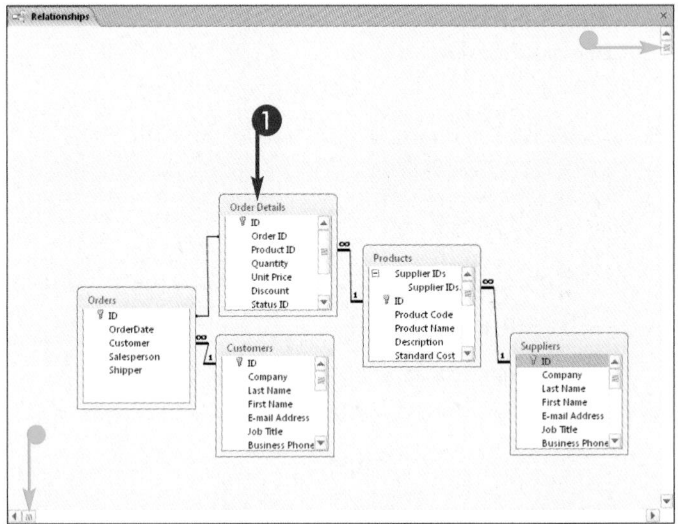

Resize a Table's Field List

1. Position the mouse pointer at the bottom of a table's field list and then click and drag up or down to shrink or enlarge the list box (⇖ changes to ⇕).

   You can also click and drag a field list's side border to expand the box horizontally or drag the lower right corner to expand in both directions.

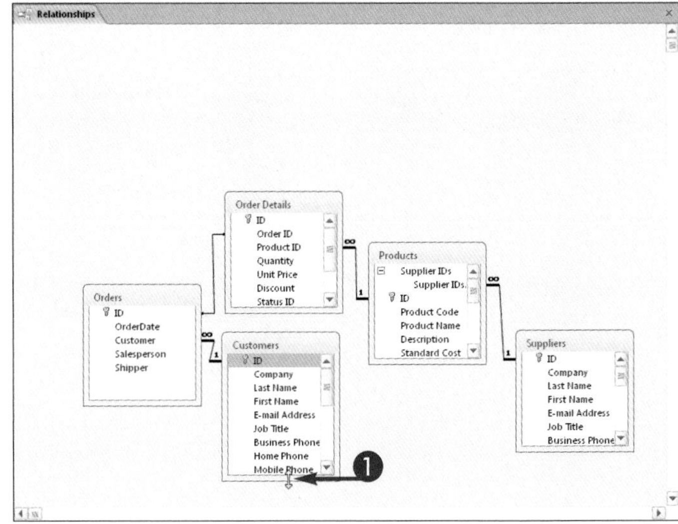

Print a Relationship Report

As you work on your database, you may find it useful to have a printed copy of the Relationships window to. You can get a printout by creating a relationship report.

Print a Relationship Report

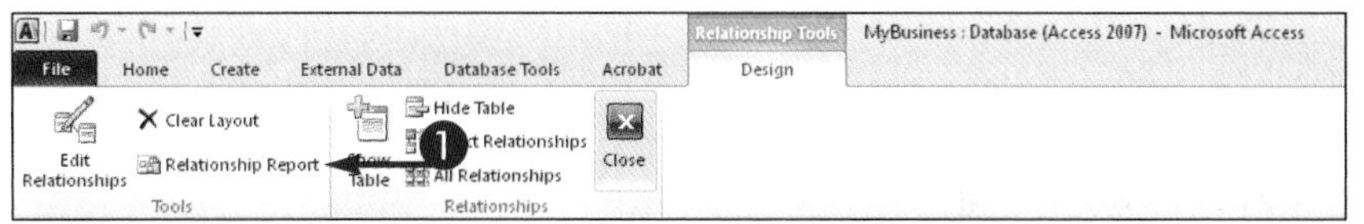

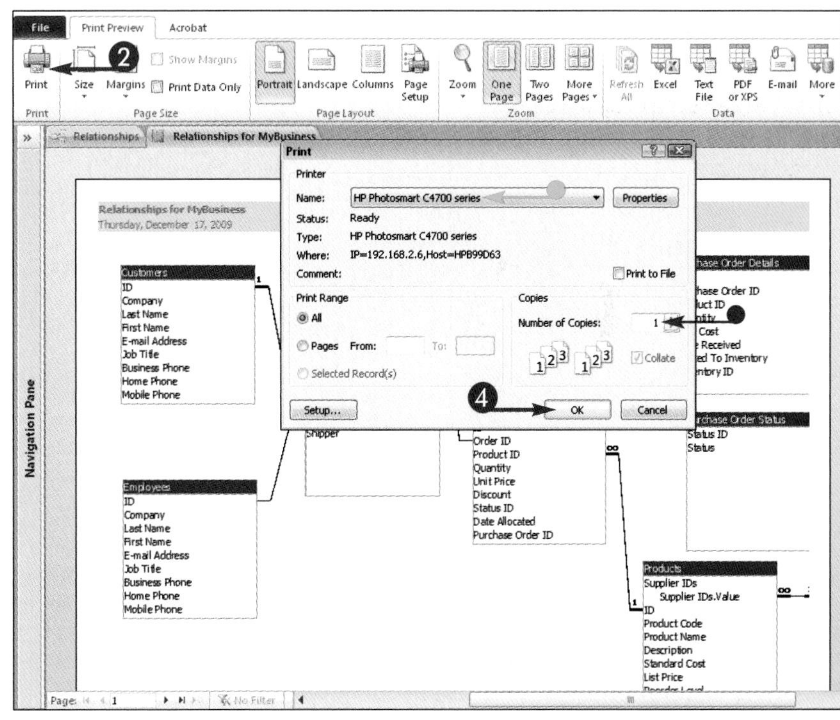

1. On the Design tab, click **Relationship Report**.

   A printable version of the Relationships window appears in Print Preview.

2. Click **Print**.

   The Print dialog box opens.

3. Set any printing options if needed:

   - You can click here to choose a different printer.
   - You can click here to increase the number of copies.

4. Click **OK**.

   The report prints out.

View Object Dependencies

You can view an object's dependencies from the Object Dependencies task pane. This is easier than trying to decipher the relationships in the Relationships window in a very complex database.

The Relationships window does not need to be open for you to view object dependencies.

View Object Dependencies

1. If you are in the Relationships window, click **Close** to exit.
2. In the Navigation pane, click an object you want to examine.

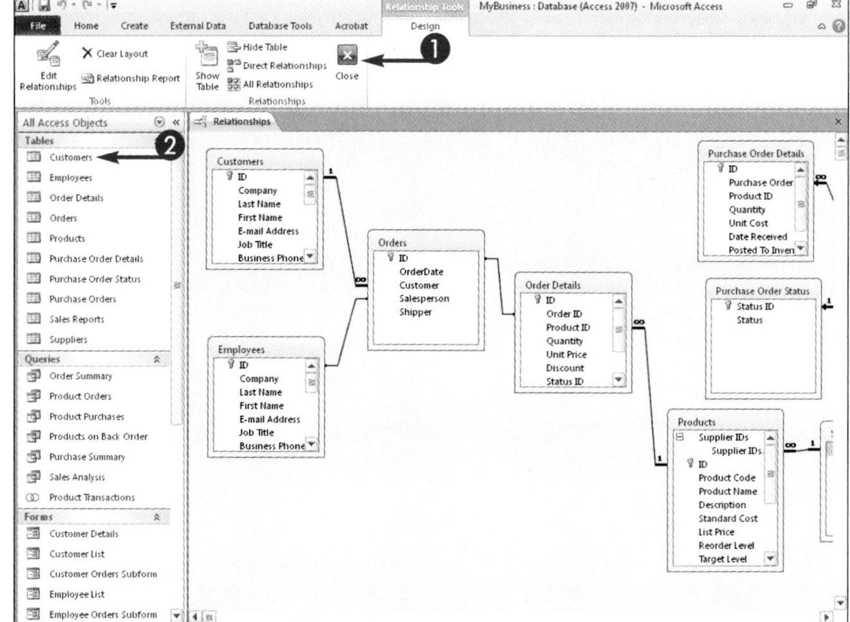

3. Click the **Database Tools**.
4. Click **Object Dependencies**.

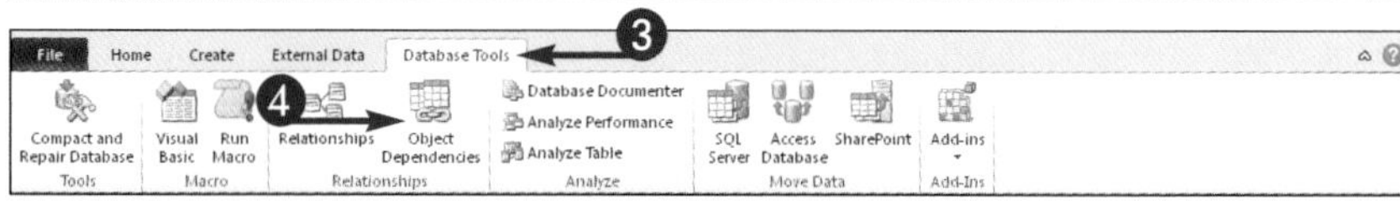

The Object Dependencies task pane opens.

6 Click a type of dependency to view:

- Click here to see objects that depend on the chosen object.
- Click here to see objects that the chosen object depends on.
- If any queries, forms, or reports are based on the table, they appear here.

7 Click a plus sign (⊞) next to an object to view its own dependencies.

The object's dependencies appear.

- If any of those dependencies have plus signs (⊞) next to them, you can also click them to expand them.

8 Click here (☒) to close the task pane when finished.

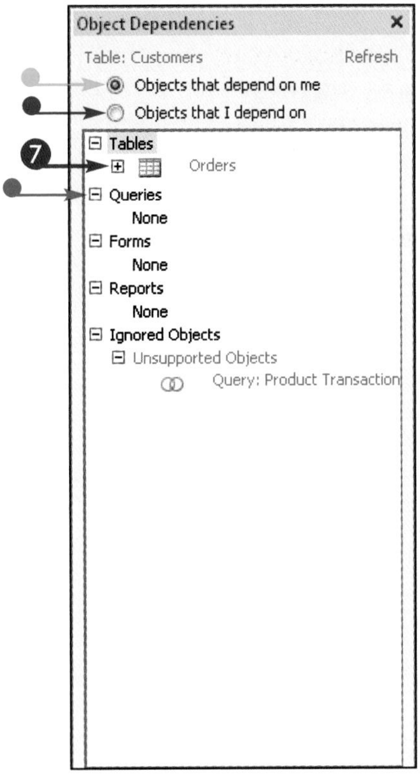

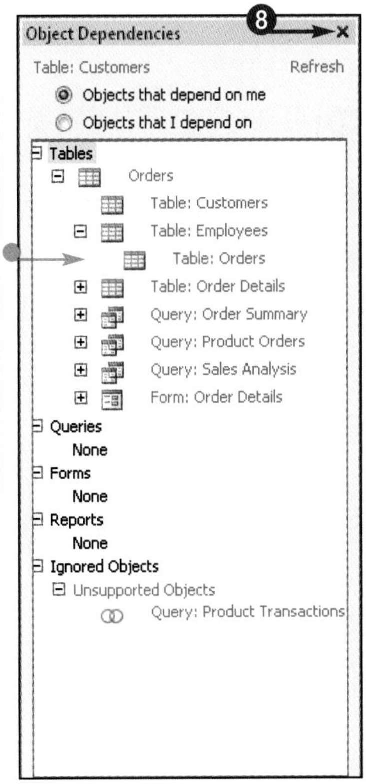

Why would I need to view object dependencies?
In a complex database, almost every object depends on some other object. Very rarely would a table stand alone. Therefore, you should not delete an object until you understand what other objects will be affected by that deletion. For example, if you delete a table, a form based on it will be orphaned.

Is there any way to see all the dependencies for all objects at once?
Yes. Use the Database Documenter feature to do this. For more, see the section "Document the Database."

Document the Database

You can use the Database Documenter feature to generate a full report about a database, including all the details about each object and its relationships and dependencies.

This report is useful to provide to another database designer to help him or her understand the structure of the database.

Document the Database

1. Click the **Database Tools** tab.
2. Click **Database Documenter**.

   The Documenter dialog box opens.
3. Click the **All Object Types** tab.
4. Click the check boxes for each object you want to include (☐ changes to ☑).
   - You can click Select All to select all objects.
   - To include the database's properties, click here.
   - To include the Relationships diagram, click here.
5. Click **OK**.

   The information appears in a report in Print Preview.

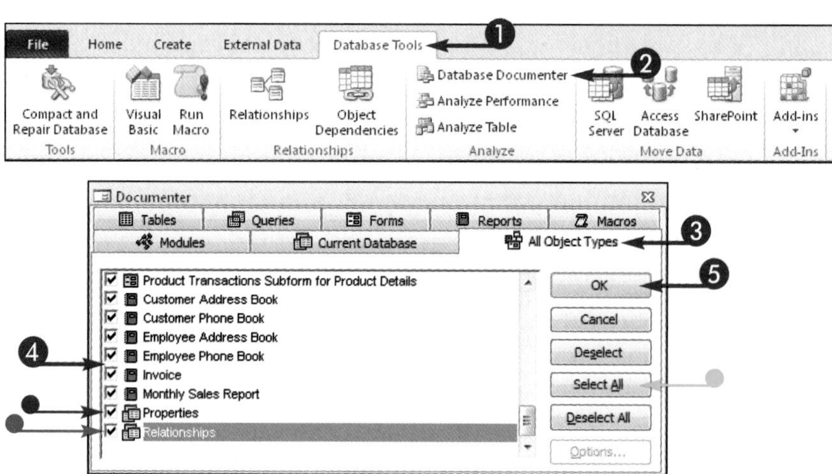

6 To zoom in on the report, click it.

You can click again to zoom out.

- You can also drag the Zoom slider (⍗) to change the zoom level.

7 Click **Print**.

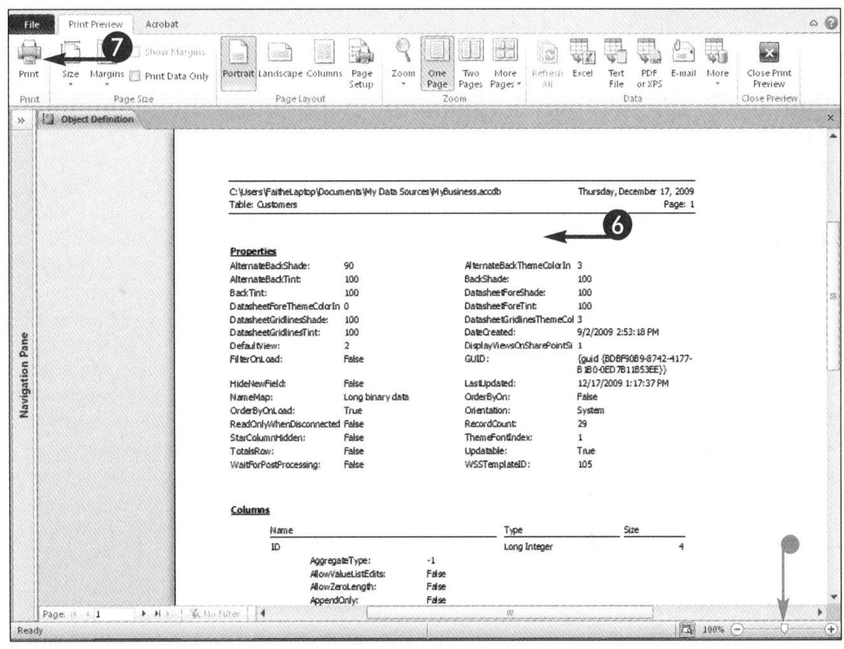

The Print dialog box opens.

8 Set any printing options if needed:

- Click here to choose a different printer.
- Click here to increase the number of copies.

9 Click **OK**.

The report prints out.

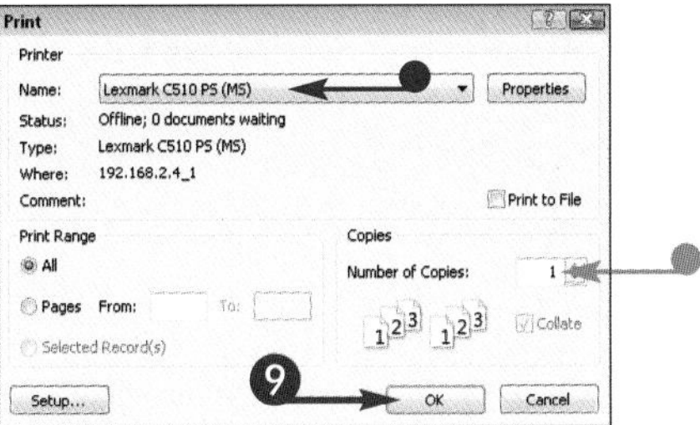

How do I get out of Print Preview?

1 Click **Close Print Preview** on the Print Preview tab to go back to working with the database.

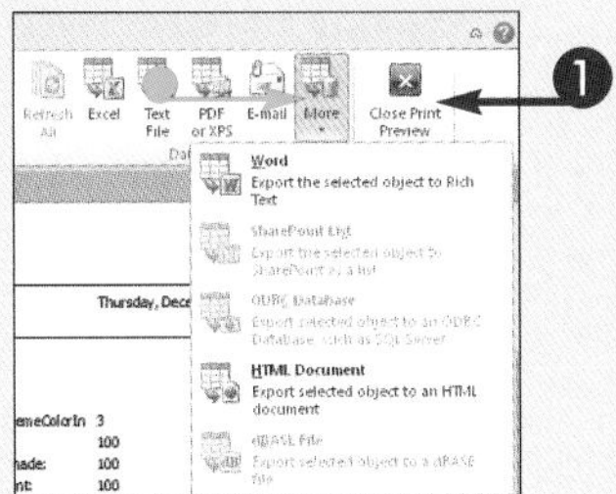

Can I export the report to another program instead of printing it?

Yes. On the Print Preview tab, in the Data group, there are several buttons for exporting to various formats.

- For additional formats, click **More** and then choose a format from the menu.

Understanding Lookups

A *lookup* is a relationship between a certain field in a table and either a list of items from another table or a manually created list.

Users entering new records can use the lookup to select from a list rather than having to type an entry in the field. This reduces data-entry errors and makes data entry more intuitive.

Relationships Based on Numbers

Relationships between tables often work best when they are based on numeric values. For example, the CustomerID in the Customers table may be a number, so the related Customer field in the Orders table would also need to be a number. But when a user is entering a new order, he or she probably does not know the customer's ID number without looking it up.

Lookups Match Numbers to Names

A lookup cross-references the related table and displays "friendly" fields that help users find the right record. For example, you could set up a lookup for the Customer field in the Orders table so users could choose from a list of customer first and last names and be shielded from the customer ID numbers.

Lookups Based on Tables

To set up a table lookup, change the data type for the field to Lookup and then use the Lookup Wizard to specify the source table. You do not need to set up the relationship between the tables beforehand.

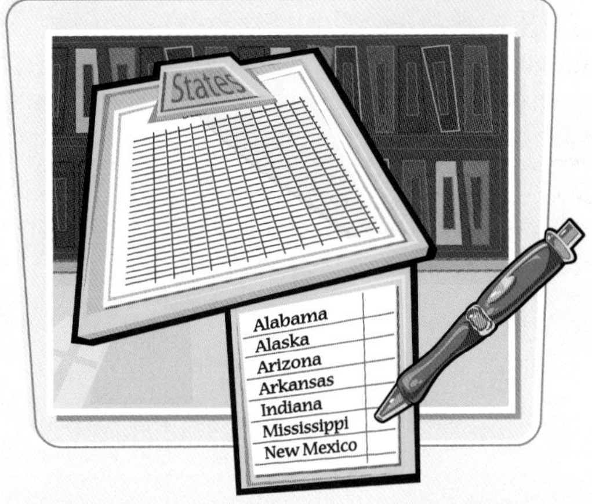

Lookups Based on Existing Relationships

If you have an existing relationship established between the table containing the field and the table containing the lookup list, you may encounter an error in creating the lookup if the Lookup Wizard wants to create a different kind of relationship than what exists already. The quickest way to solve this problem is to delete the existing relationship and then allow the Lookup Wizard to re-create it.

Lookups Based on Lists That You Type

If the number of entries to appear in the drop-down list is small or if it will never or seldom change, it may be unnecessary to put the entries in a separate table. In such cases, you may prefer to create a lookup based on entries that you set up yourself. The Lookup Wizard can also create this type of lookup and can prompt you for the entries to use.

Create a Table for Use as a Field Lookup

If the values you want for your lookup list already exist in another table, you can use them. But if they do not, you need to construct a new table for the values. Lookup tables are typically very simple, consisting of only one or two fields.

Follow the steps in this section only if the data for the list does not exist already in another table.

Create a Table for Use as a Field Lookup

1. Click the **Create** tab.
2. Click **Table Design**.

A new table opens in Design view.

3. Type a name that describes the list.

Note: *The name does not need to exactly match the field in the other table that will be looking up from it.*

4. Set the data type as appropriate.

Note: *Text is usually an appropriate data type.*

5. Click **Primary Key**.

- A key (🔑) appears next to the field, indicating that it is the primary key.

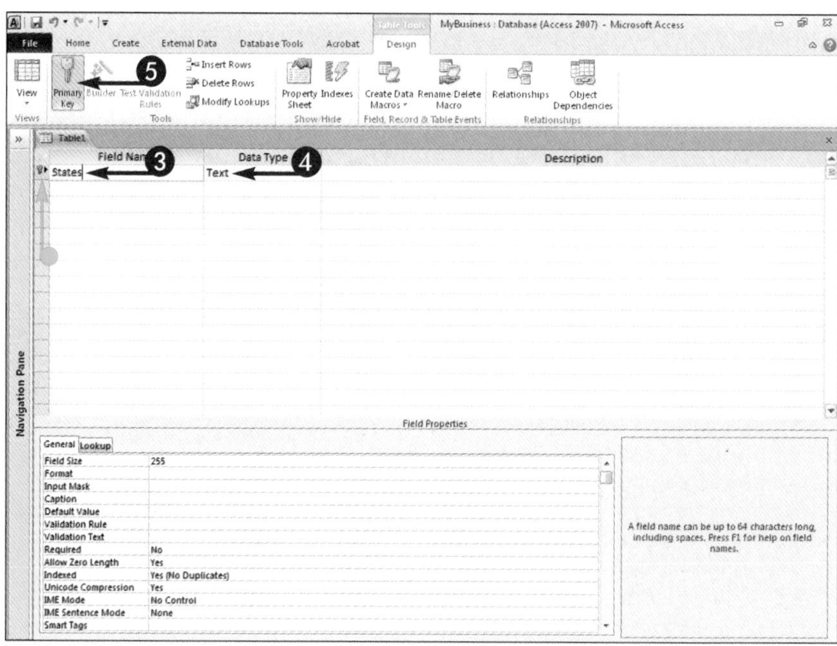

6 Click the **Save** button (💾).

The Save As dialog box opens.

7 Type a name for the lookup table.

8 Click **OK**.

9 Click **View**.

The view switches to the Datasheet view.

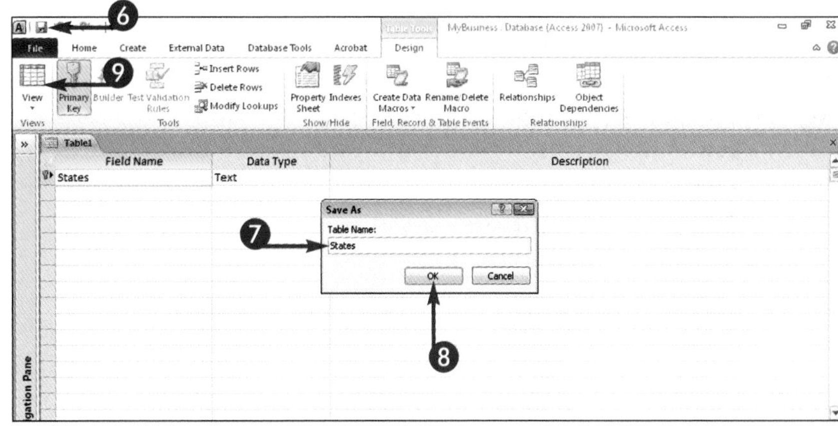

10 Type the records into the table.

***Note:** It does not matter what order you enter them in because you can specify a sort order when you set up the lookup.*

11 Right-click on the table's tab.

12 Click **Close**.

The table closes.

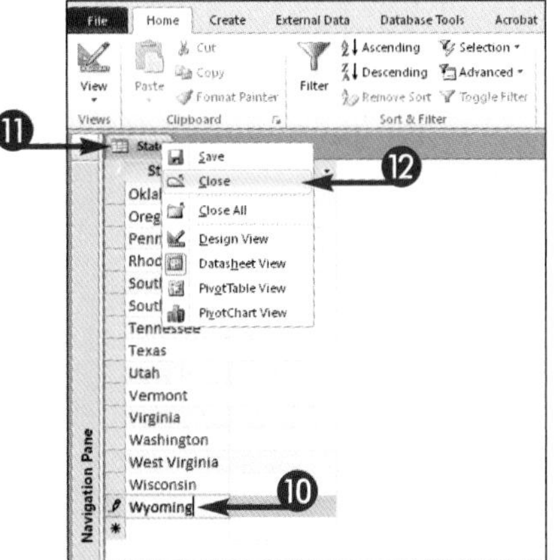

Why go to the trouble of creating a table?

A table makes editing the lookup list later much more convenient. With a lookup that consists of manually entered values, the only way to edit the values is through the field's properties in Design view, which can be inconvenient. A lookup table can also be reused for multiple lookups in different tables.

Does the lookup table have to have a primary key defined?

No. That is not necessary. However, assigning a primary key for every table is considered good housekeeping practice in a database. In addition, setting a field as a primary key is a good way to ensure that it contains no duplicate values.

Create a Field Lookup Based on a Table

You can create a lookup for a field that references the values in another table. When the user enters data for that field, instead of the ordinary text box, a drop-down menu appears, containing the values from the lookup. If the values in that other table change, the values in the lookup also change.

Create a Field Lookup Based on a Table

1. In Design view, click in the Data Type column for the field for which you want to use the lookup, click the drop-down arrow (▾) to open the menu, and then click **Lookup Wizard**.

***Note:** Make sure you are working in the table and field that should use the lookup, not the table containing the lookup values.*

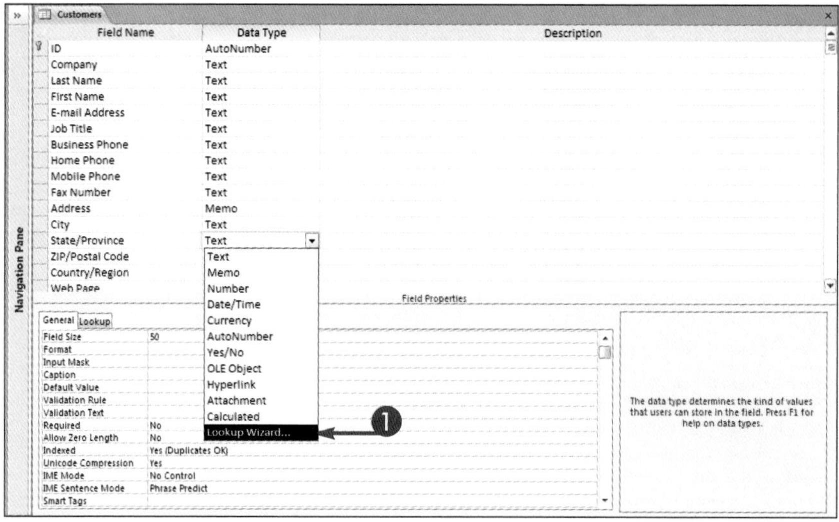

The Lookup Wizard opens.

2. Click **Next**.

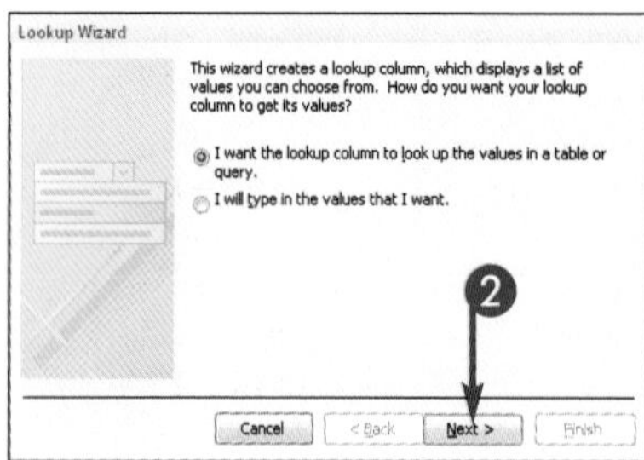

❸ Click the table that contains the lookup values.

***Note:** This can be a table that you created specifically for the lookup or an existing table that serves other purposes in the database.*

❹ Click **Next**.

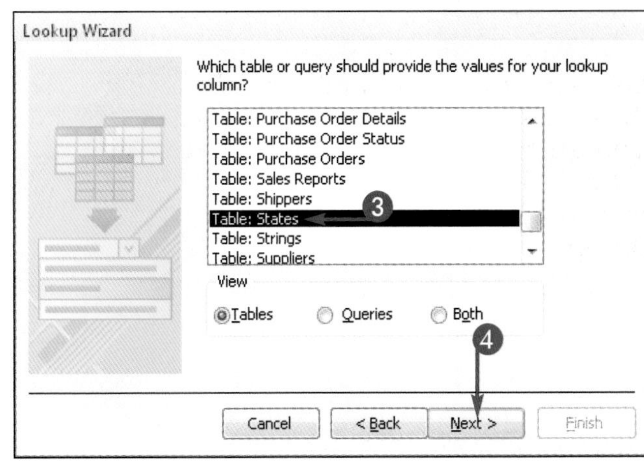

❺ Click the field containing the values.

❻ Click the **Add Field** button (>).

The field moves to the Selected Fields list.

❼ If there are other fields in the table that you want to appear in the lookup list, repeat steps **5** and **6** to add them.

***Note:** Access adds the primary key field automatically if you do not explicitly choose it.*

❽ Click **Next**.

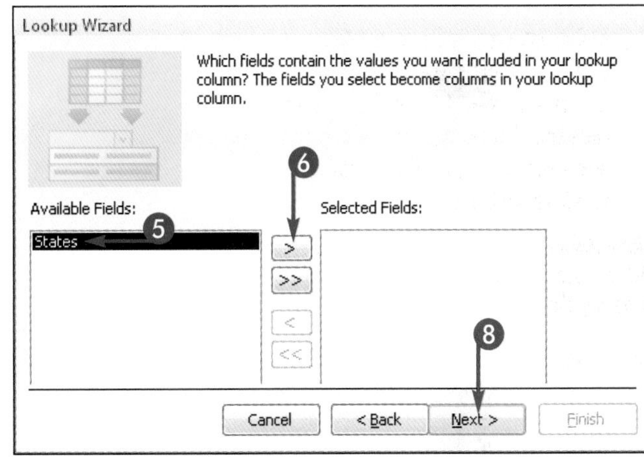

Can I use a query instead of a table?

Yes. A query is a sorted or filtered version of a table or a combination of tables. When two or more tables have relationships between them, you can create queries that join the data from them into a single datasheet. That way, you can use data from multiple tables as if the data resided together in a single object. For access to any queries, click **Queries** (●) (◎ changes to ◉).

Can I set up lookups without using the wizard?

Yes. You can use the Lookup tab in the field's Properties, placing a SQL (structured query language) statement in the Row Source box (●). You will probably not want to create lookups that way, but you might use the boxes on the Lookup tab to make minor changes to a lookup without having to completely re-create it.

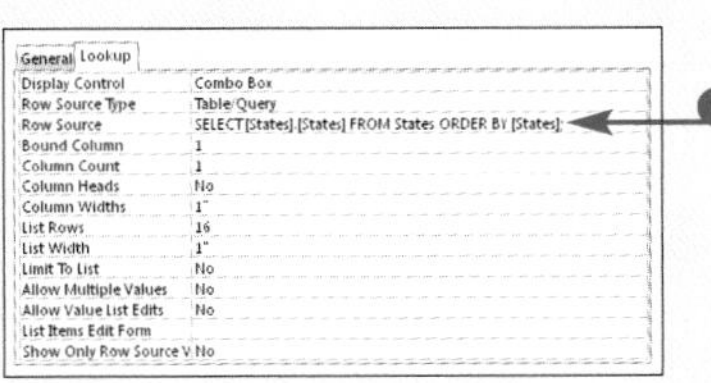

General	Lookup
Display Control	Combo Box
Row Source Type	Table/Query
Row Source	SELECT [States].[States] FROM States ORDER BY [States];
Bound Column	1
Column Count	1
Column Heads	No
Column Widths	1"
List Rows	16
List Width	1"
Limit To List	No
Allow Multiple Values	No
Allow Value List Edits	No
List Items Edit Form	
Show Only Row Source V	No

continued

Create a Field Lookup Based on a Table *(continued)*

You can sort the list as part of the lookup specification. This can be useful if you want the list to appear in the lookup in a different order in one usage than in another. The lookup table's records need not have been entered in any particular order because the values can be sorted later.

Create a Field Lookup Based on a Table *(continued)*

9. If you want to sort the list, click here (▾) to choose the field name.

***Note:** The default sort order is Ascending.*

10. If you want to toggle the default sort order to Descending, click **Ascending**.
11. If there are other fields that you want to sort by, repeat steps **9** and **10**.
12. Click **Next**.

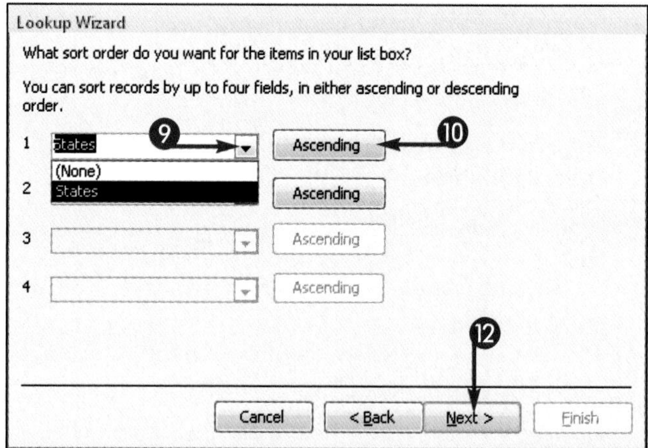

13. If you want to change the column width for the lookup list, drag the right edge.

    You can also double-click the right edge to automatically fit the column to the current contents.
14. Click **Next**.

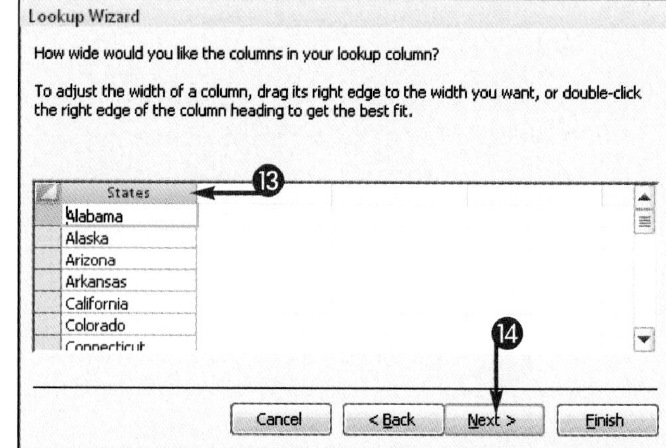

15 You can modify the label assigned to the field.

By default, the wizard uses the field name as the label.

16 Click **Finish**.

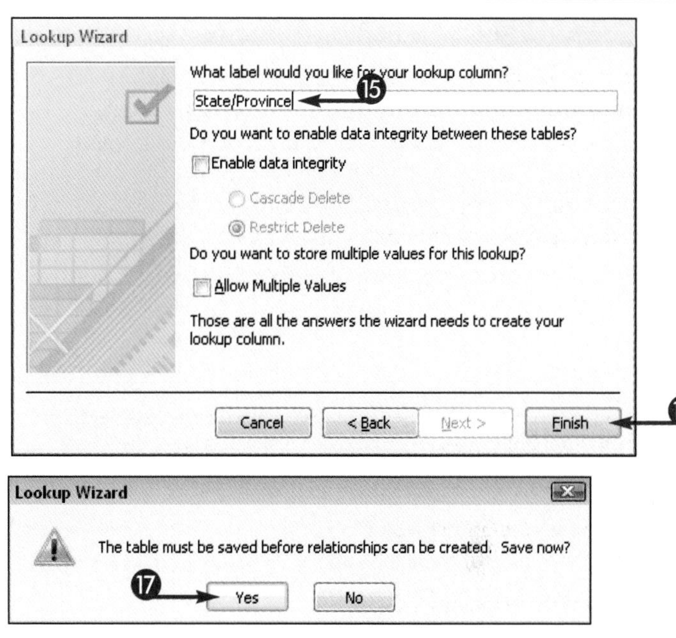

A prompt appears, asking you to save the table.

17 Click **Yes**.

The lookup is created. You can examine the lookup settings on the Lookup tab of the field's properties.

Lookup Wizard

The table must be saved before relationships can be created. Save now?

17 Yes No

How can I make changes to the lookup?

To make small changes, use the Lookup tab in the field's properties. If you need to re-create the lookup, you first need to delete the relationship that the Lookup Wizard created:

1. From the Relationships window, click and drag the lookup table into the layout if it is not already there.
2. Click the line between the lookup table and the other table.
3. Press Delete.
4. Click **Yes** to confirm.

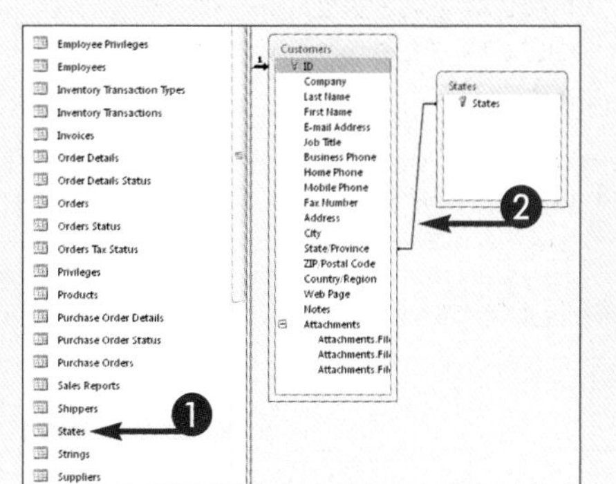

Create a Field Lookup with Values That You Specify

If the list from which you want users to choose for a field is fairly short and will not change frequently, you may prefer to create a lookup based on values that you enter into the Lookup Wizard. This creates a makeshift lookup table that exists only in the Lookup properties for the field. If you need to edit the list, you can make the changes from the properties.

Create a Field Lookup with Values That You Specify

1. In Design view, click in the Data Type column for the field for which you want to use the lookup, click the drop-down arrow (▾) to open the menu, and then click **Lookup Wizard**.

Note: *Make sure that you are working in the table and field that should use the lookup, not the table containing the lookup values.*

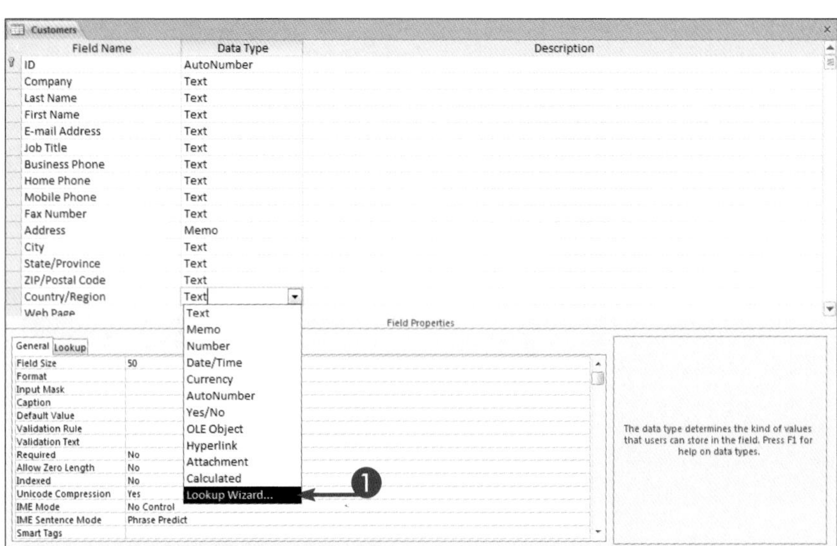

The Lookup Wizard opens.

2. Click the **I will type in the values that I want** radio button (◎ changes to ◉).
3. Click **Next**.

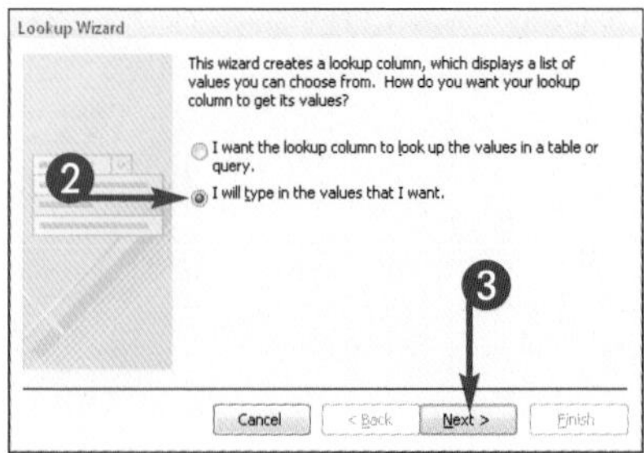

4. Type the values that you want to display in the lookup list.

Note: *It is common to use a single column. Use multiple columns only if a single column cannot adequately represent the values.*

5. Click **Next**.

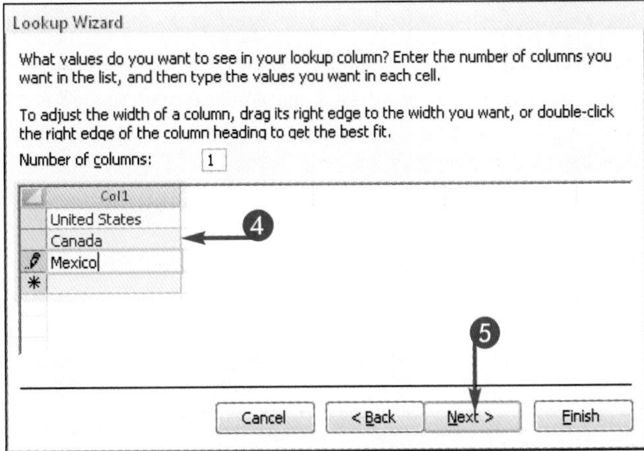

6. You can modify the label assigned to the field.

   By default, the wizard uses the field name as the label.

7. Click **Finish**.

   The lookup is created. You can examine the lookup settings on the Lookup tab of the field's properties.

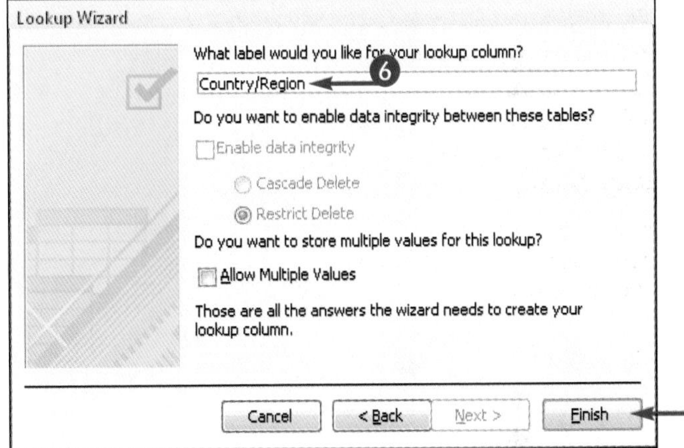

How can I change the values on the list?

On the Lookup tab of the field's properties, the Row Source box contains the values you specified for the list, each one in quotation marks, separated by semicolons.

- If you need to modify the list, type your changes directly into that text box, making sure you keep the correct syntax with the quotation marks and semicolons.

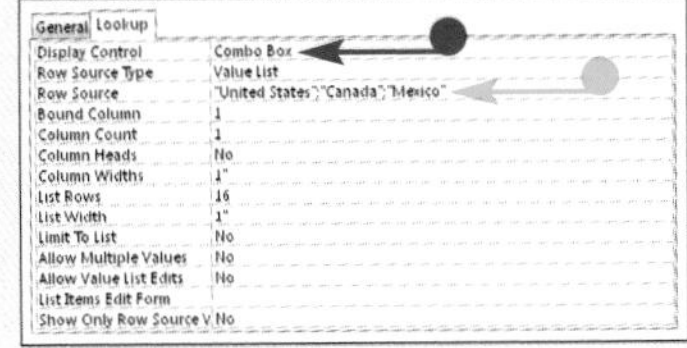

Are users limited to only the values on my list?

No. The default display control is a combo box, which also enables users to enter their own values.

- If you want to restrict users to your values only, open the Display Control property's list and then choose List Box.

Set Up a Multivalued Field

A multivalued field can store more than one value. For example, if you have a certain product that comes in three colors, you can use a multivalue Color field rather than have three separate records for that product in the table.

Creating a multivalued field is the same as creating any other lookup, except for the last option in the wizard.

Set Up a Multivalued Field

1. Follow steps **1** to **15** in the section "Create a Field Lookup Based on a Table."

   You can also follow steps **1** to **6** in the section "Create a Field Lookup with Values That You Specify."

2. Click the **Allow Multiple Values** check box (☐ changes to ☑).
3. Click **Finish**.

   A warning appears about changing the field to store multiple values.

4. Click **Yes**.

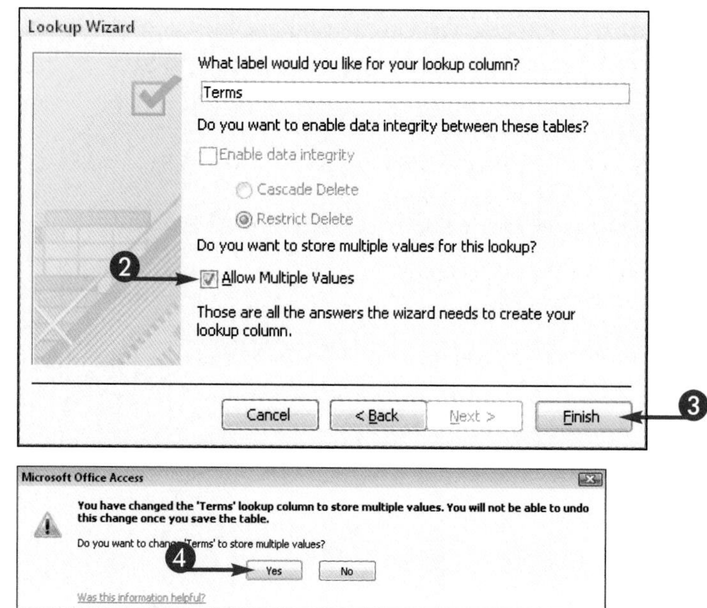

5. Click **View** to switch to the Datasheet view.

   A prompt appears, asking you to save the table.

6. Click **Yes**.

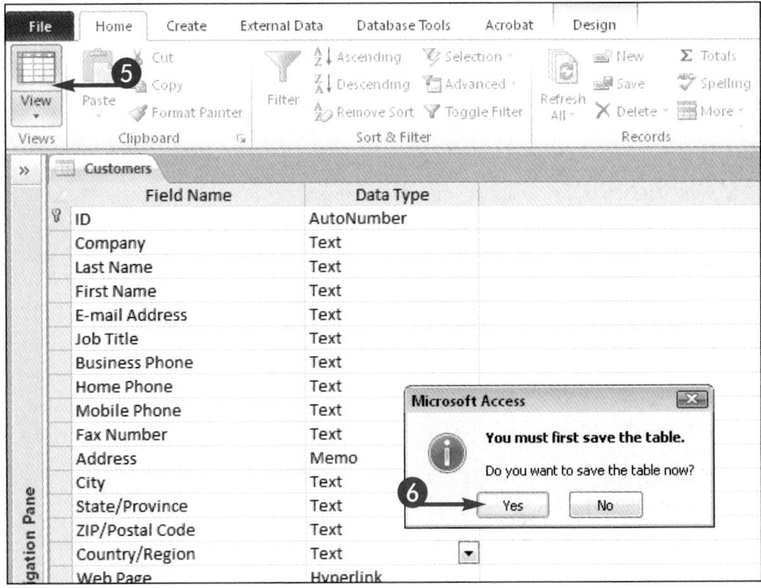

- The lookup is created and is displayed with multiple values allowed in the chosen field.

Note: *See Chapter 2 for more on entering values into a multivalued field.*

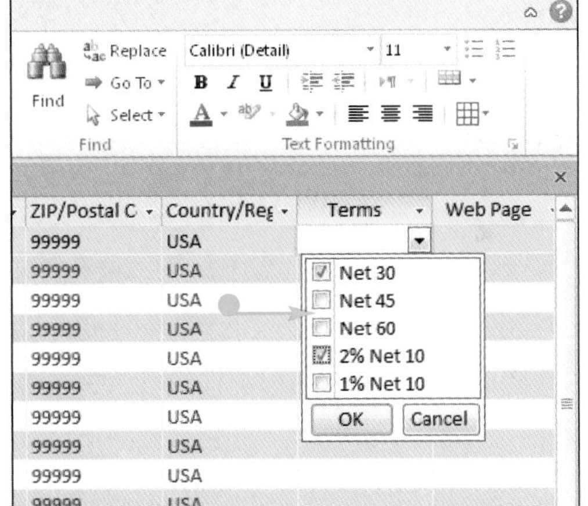

What are the drawbacks to using a multivalued field?

Multivalued fields are incompatible with Access versions 2003 and earlier. You cannot save a database in an earlier format if it includes multivalued fields, which may be an issue if you later need to share your data file with someone who only has the earlier version. Furthermore, you cannot convert a field from multivalue to single-value; you have to delete it completely to make the database compatible, and you lose all the data that was stored in that field for the entire table.

CHAPTER

Finding and Filtering Data

Access 2010 provides many ways of locating individual data records within your database. In Chapter 2, you learned about sorting a datasheet—one of the simplest methods of looking something up. In this chapter, you learn about two other ways to search for data: using the Find feature to find a text string and using the Filter feature to show only records that match criteria you specify.

Understanding Find and Replace

Find and Replace is a single feature with two parts. On the Find tab, you can find text strings within records. On the Replace tab, you can do the same thing, except you can also replace the found data with some other text that you specify.

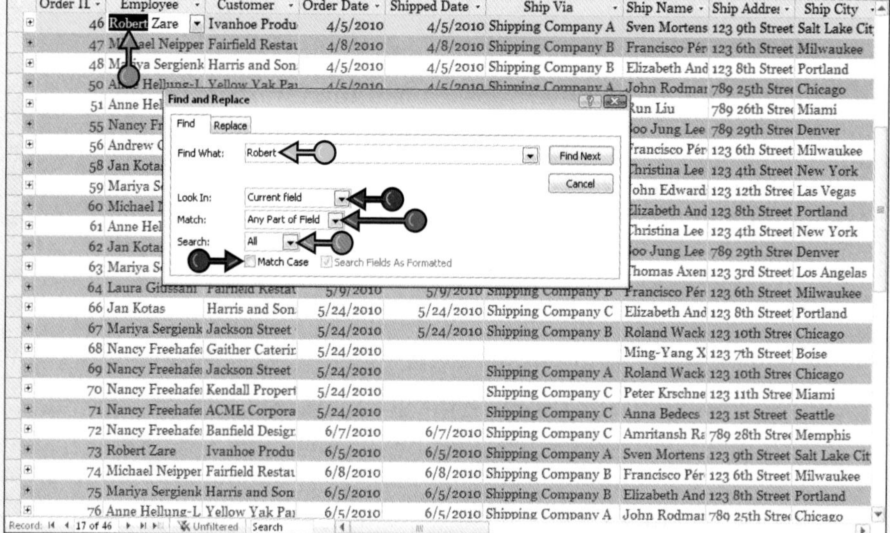

- **Find What**
  You can specify a text string or numeric value that you want to find.
- **Look In**
  You can limit the search to a certain field.
- **Match**
  You can look for exact matches of the whole field or partial matches.
- **Search**
  You can search above or below the currently selected record.
- **Match Case**
  You can choose whether the search is case-sensitive.
- **Found String**
  The found string is highlighted in the datasheet.

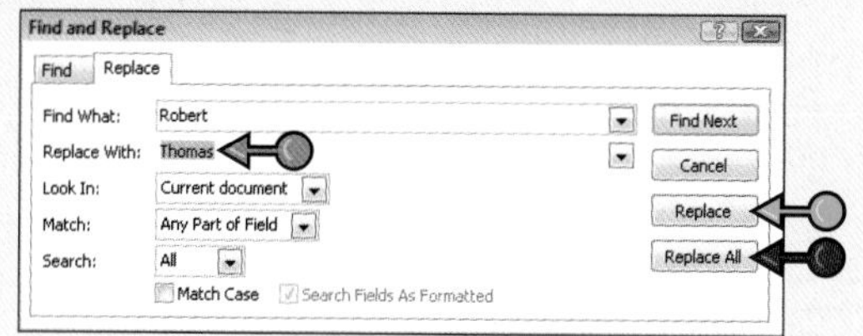

- **Replace With**
  The Replace tab has a Replace With text field, in which you can enter the replacement string.
- **Replace button**
  You can click Replace to replace one instance of what you are searching for and move to the next instance.
- **Replace All button**
  You can click Replace All to do a global replace. Be cautious about doing so; it might replace more than you intended.

Find Data by Using Find and Replace

You can use the Find feature to locate a text string or numeric value within any field in a datasheet. You can search in one particular field or you can expand the search to include all fields.

Find Data by Using Find and Replace

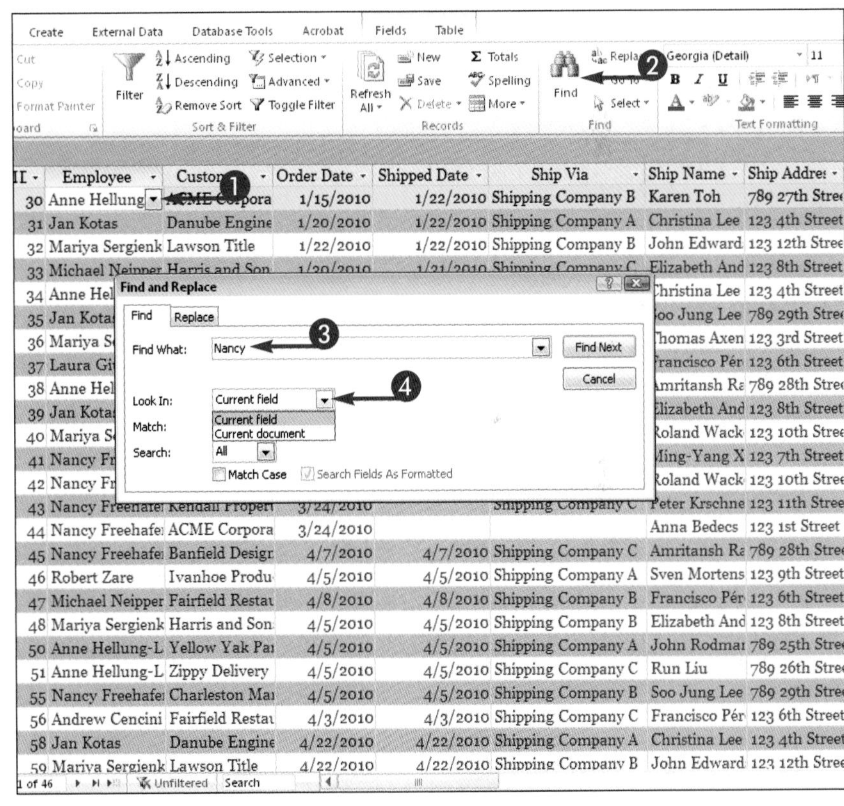

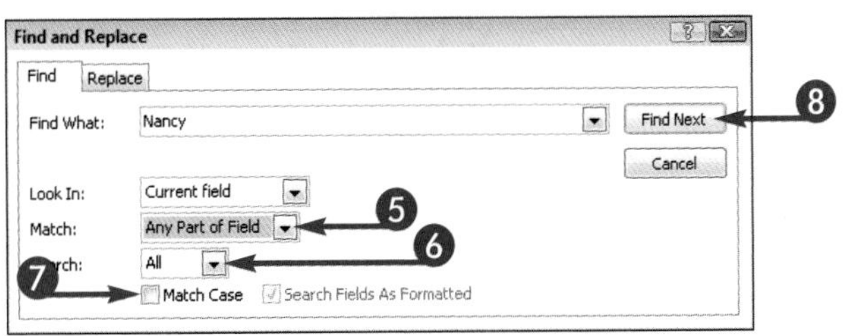

1. If you plan to limit the search to only one field, click in that field's column — in any row.
2. On the Home tab, click **Find**.

   The Find and Replace dialog box opens, with the Find tab displayed.
3. Type the text you want to find.
4. Click here (▾) to choose either **Current Field** or **Current Document**.
5. Click here (▾) to choose what you want to match.

Note: *The choices are Any Part of Field, Start of Field, and Whole Field.*

6. Click here (▾) to choose **Up** or **Down** if you want to limit the search to one direction.
7. You can click here to make the search case-sensitive (☐ changes to ☑).
8. Click **Find Next**.

   The datasheet view jumps to the first instance and highlights it.
9. Click **Find Next** to find the next instance.
10. Continue clicking **Find Next** until the instance you want is found.

Replace Data by Using Find and Replace

You can take the Find operation one step further by replacing the found value with other text that you specify. For example, if you find out that Robert prefers to be known as Bob, a replace operation can easily make the change.

Replace Data by Using Find and Replace

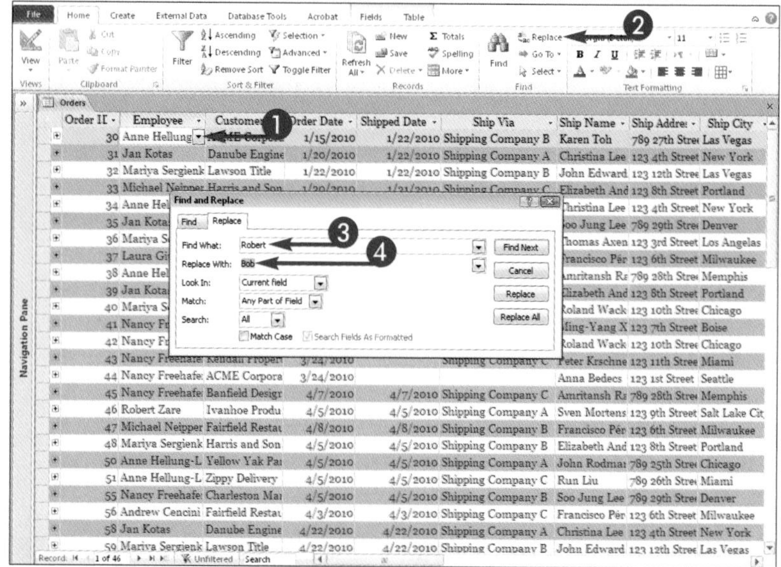

1. If you plan to limit the replacement to only one field, click in that field's column — in any row.
2. On the Home tab, click **Replace**.

   The Find and Replace dialog box opens, with the Replace tab displayed.

3. Type the text you want to find.
4. Type the text you want to substitute for the found text.

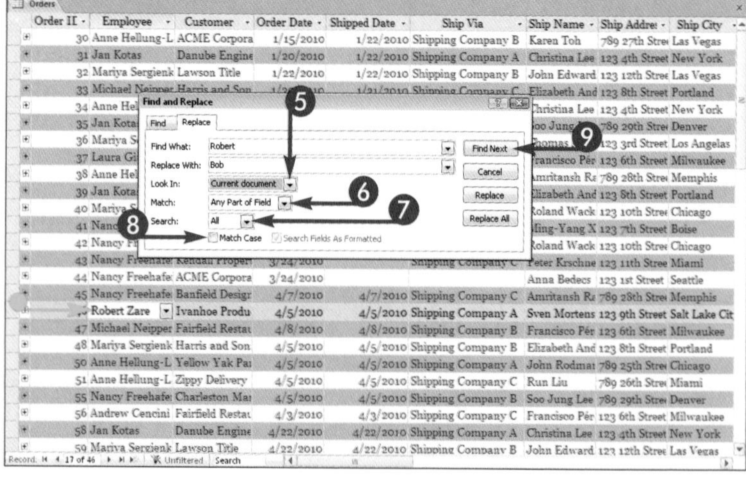

5. Click here (▼) to choose either **Current Field** or **Current Document.**
6. Click here (▼) to choose what you want to match.

Note: *The choices are Any Part of Field, Start of Field, and Whole Field.*

7. Click here (▼) to choose **Up** or **Down** if you want to limit the search to one direction.
8. You can click here to make the search case-sensitive (☐ changes to ☑).
9. Click **Find Next**.

- The datasheet view jumps to the first instance and highlights it.

❿ Click **Replace**.

- If you do not want to replace that instance, you can click **Find Next** to bypass it.
- The next instance of the text is highlighted.

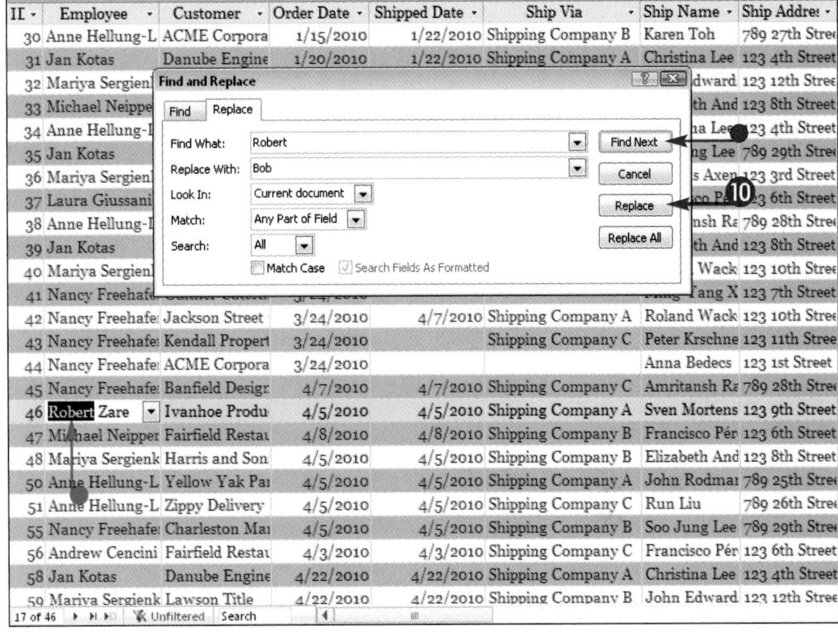

⓫ Continue clicking **Replace** or **Find Next** until a message appears that says Access has finished searching the records.

⓬ Click **OK**.

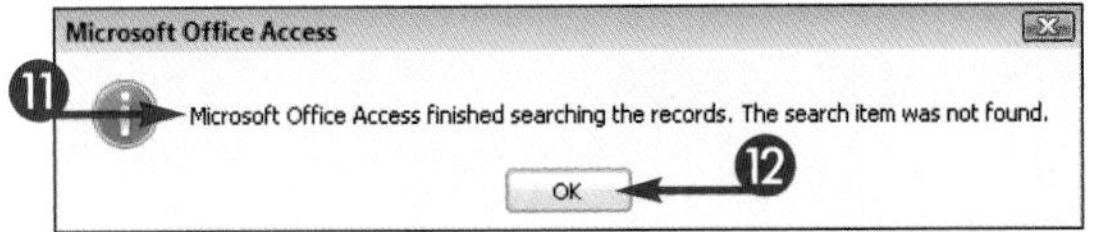

How can I replace all instances at once?

- Instead of clicking **Replace**, click **Replace All**. Be careful, however, that you do not make any unintentional replacements. For example, even though Robert prefers to be called Bob, his e-mail address might still call him Robert; a global replace operation would change the e-mail address and make it incorrect.

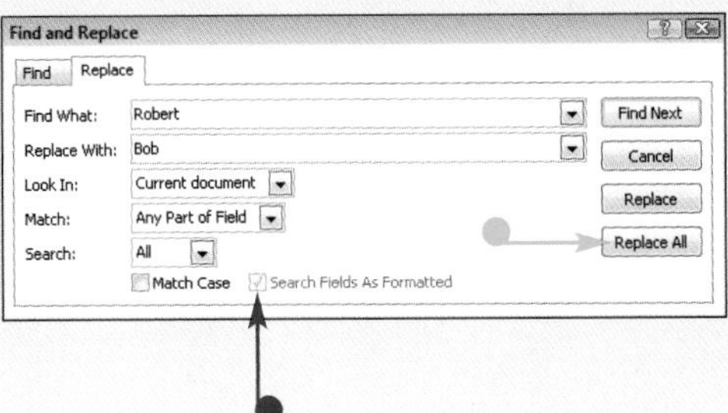

What is the Search Fields as Formatted check box, and why is it unavailable?

- If a field's Text Format property is set to Rich Text (in Design view), the field can hold formatting as well as text. For such fields, you can search for strings formatted a certain way. By default, most fields are plain text, so this check box is not available.

Filter to Show Only Blank or Nonblank Entries

One of the most common filter operations is to filter for records that are either blank or nonblank for a particular field. For example, you may want to find all customers for whom the Email Address field is nonblank so you can send an e-mail announcement.

Filter to Show Only Blank or Nonblank Entries

Apply the Filter

1. Click in the column for the field you want to search — in a row where that field is blank.
2. On the Home tab, click **Selection**.
3. Click **Equals Blank** to show only blank entries.

- Alternatively, click **Does Not Equal Blank** to show only nonblank entries.

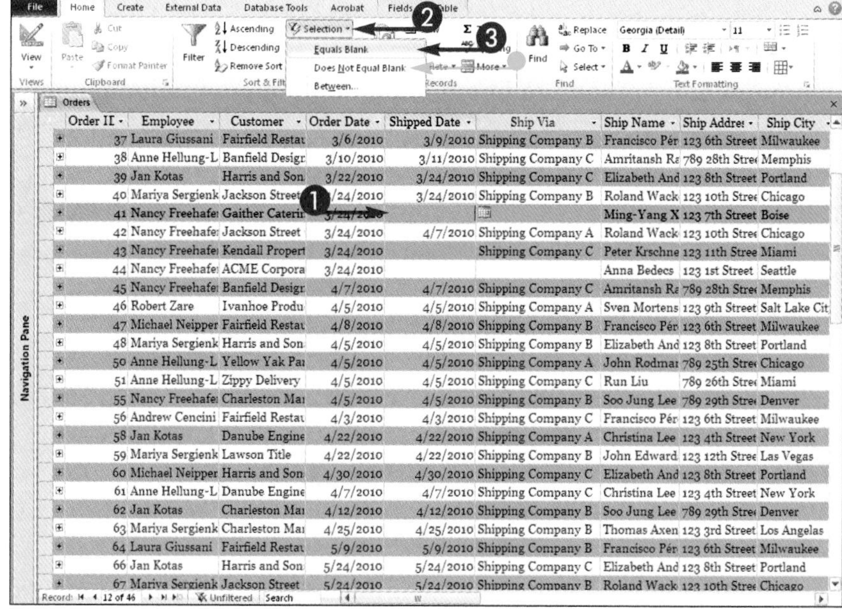

- Records that do not match the specification are temporarily hidden.

Remove the Filter

1. Click **Toggle Filter**.

   The filter is removed.

***Note:** To reapply the same filter, click **Toggle Filter** again.*

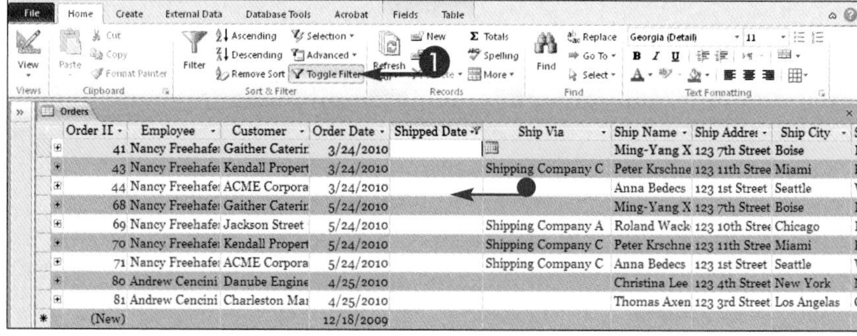

Filter by Selection

You can filter not only for blank versus nonblank entries but also for any specific value in any field. For example, you may want to find all the customers who work for a certain company or all the people with a certain job title.

Filter by Selection

1. Click in a field that contains the value for which you want to filter.

Note: For example, to filter for Owner in the Job Title field, you would click any instance of "Owner."

2. On the Home tab, click **Selection**.
3. Click the option that you want.

Note: The Equals options look only for entries matching the entire field. The Contains options look for the specified entry as any part of the field.

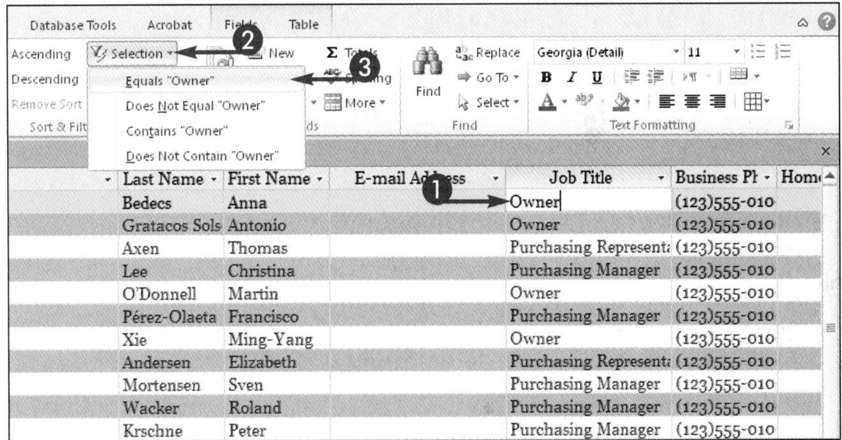

- Only records that match the filter are displayed.

4. Click **Toggle Filter** to remove the filter when finished.

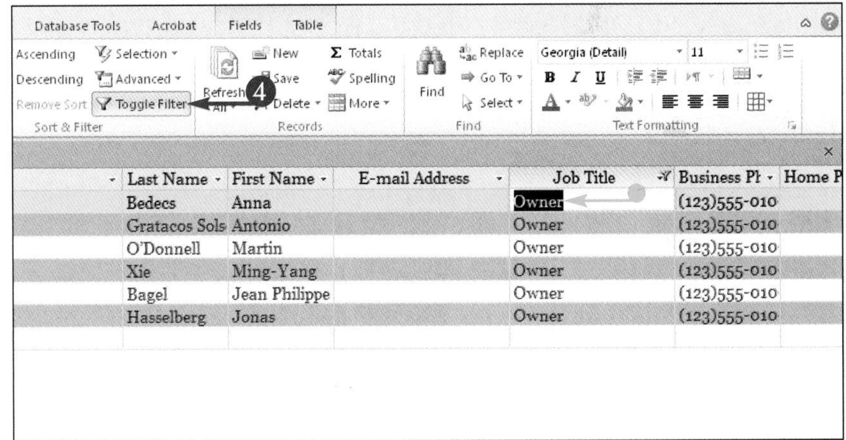

Filter for Multiple Values

Filter by Selection works well, but it finds only one value. For example, you cannot set it to find people with job titles of either "Owner" or "CEO."

To filter for multiple values, you can use the Filter button on the Datasheet tab. It opens a floating pane that contains check boxes for each value in that field, and you can select multiple values for which to filter.

Filter for Multiple Values

1. Click in the column for the field you want to filter.

Note: You can click in any row; it need not be a row containing a value you want to include.

2. On the Home tab, click **Filter**.

- You can also click the arrow (▾) to the right of the field.

A Filter pane appears below the selected field.

3. Deselect the check box next to any value that you do not want to include (☑ changes to ☐).
4. Click **OK**.

- The list is filtered to show only the values that you chose.

5. Click **Toggle Filter** to remove the filter when finished.

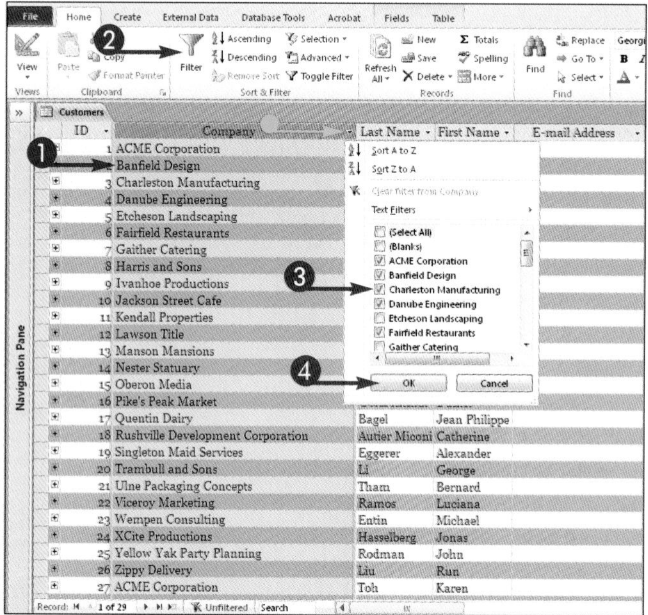

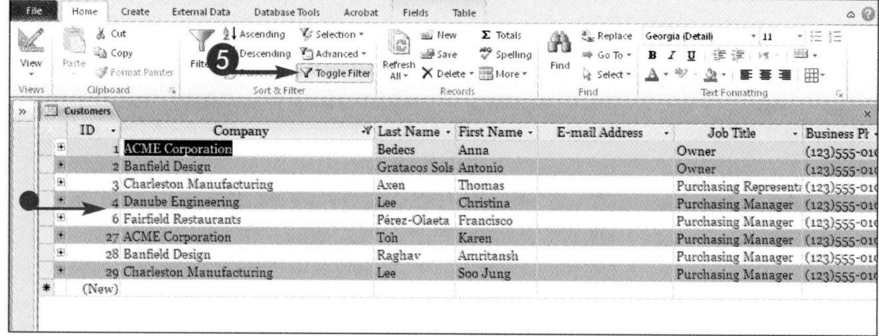

Using Text Filters

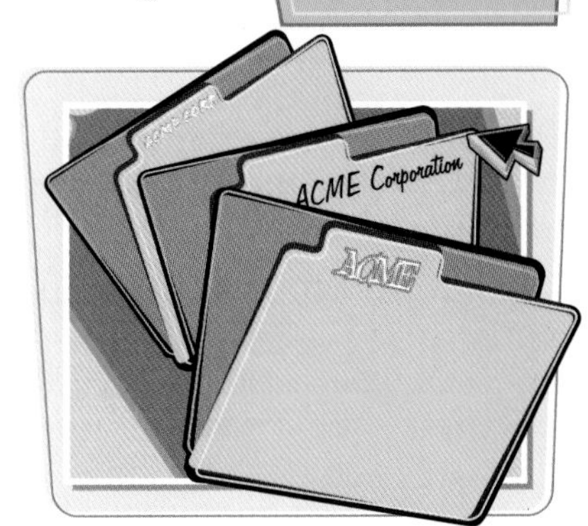

Access provides a special set of filters for working with text values. These filters take into account that text strings often contain more than just the searched-for value.

For example, if different people entered the records, the same company may be listed as "ACME," "The ACME Corporation," or "ACME Corp." You can use a text filter to find all forms of the name.

Using Text Filters

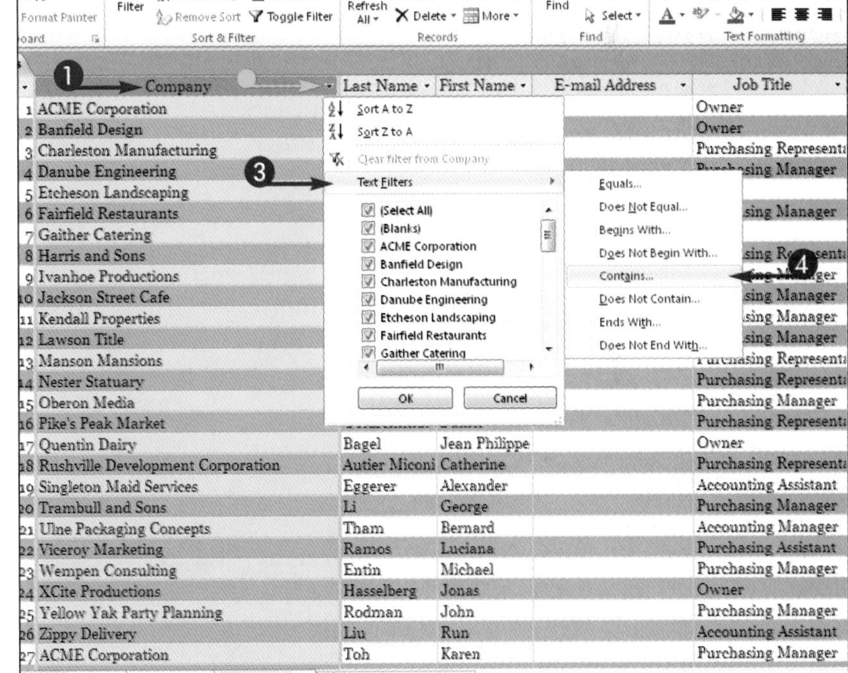

1. Click in the column for the field you want to filter.

Note: You can click in any row; it need not be a row containing a value you want to include.

2. Click **Filter**.

- You can also click the arrow (▾) to the right of the field.

A Filter pane appears below the selected field.

3. Click **Text Filters**.
4. Click the text filter you want to apply.

Note: For example, to find all records that contain a certain text string, you can choose Contains.

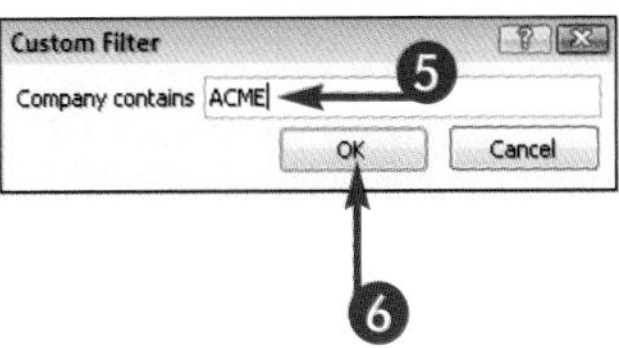

The Custom Filter dialog box opens.

5. Type the text string for the filter.
6. Click **OK**.

The filter is applied.

*Note: You can remove the filter by clicking **Toggle Filter**, the same as with any other filter.*

Filter by Form

Filtering by form enables you to filter by multiple fields and specify criteria for as many fields as you like.

When you filter by form, you can combine the criteria by using AND, OR, or a combination of the two. An AND combination finds records where both criteria are met; an OR combination finds records where at least one criterion is met.

Filter by Form

Using AND

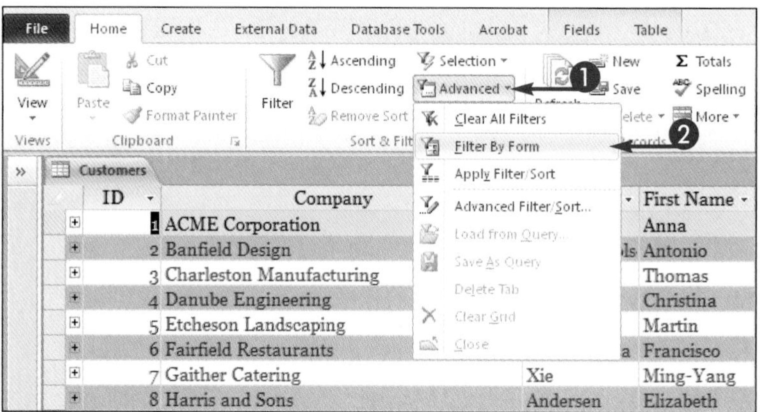

1. On the Home tab, click **Advanced**.
2. Click **Filter By Form**.

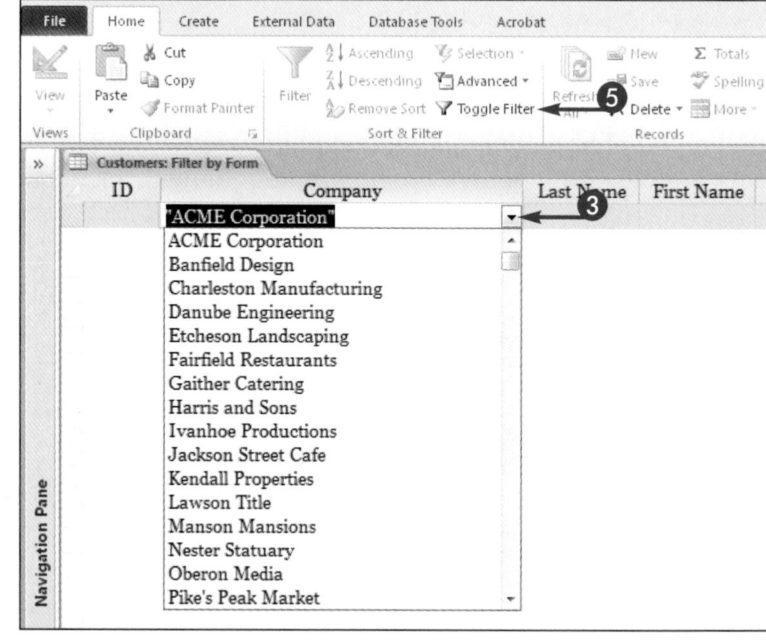

A Filter by Form sheet opens.

***Note:** If you previously performed a filter operation, the existing filter specification may appear. Delete any unwanted criteria.*

3. Click here (▾) to open the list for a field to choose the value that you want.
4. Repeat step **3** for other fields as needed.
5. Click **Toggle Filter**.

The filter results are displayed.

Using OR

1. On the Home tab, click **Advanced**.
2. Click **Filter By Form**.

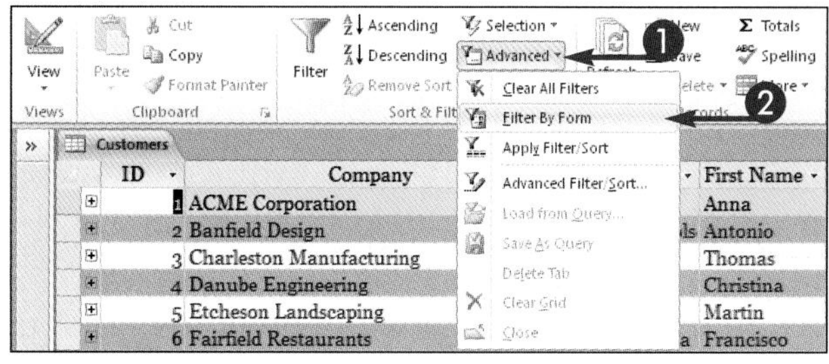

A Filter by Form sheet opens.

Note: *If you previously performed a filter operation, the existing filter specification may appear. Delete any unwanted criteria.*

3. Click here (▾) to open the list for a field to choose the value that you want.
4. Click the **Or** tab.

   A blank Filter by Form page opens.

5. Repeat step **3** to select another criterion.

Note: *Each page represents a separate criterion. Records are included that match the criteria on any page.*

6. Click **Toggle Filter** to apply the filter.

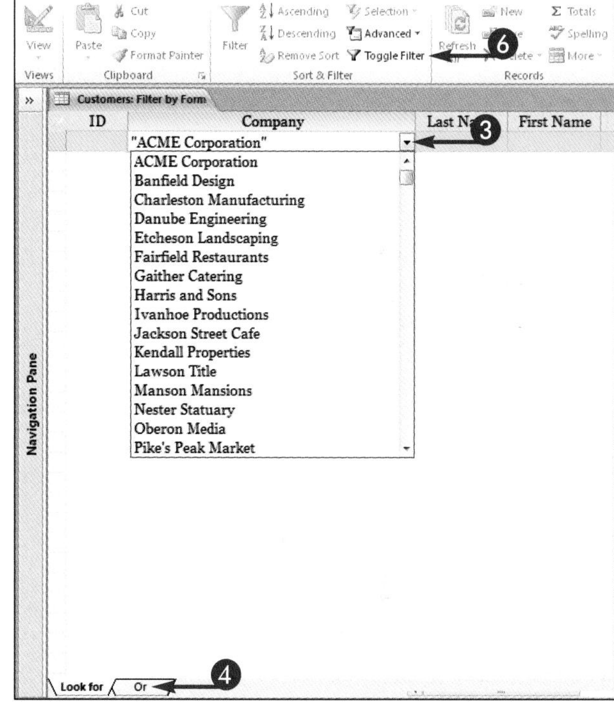

Why are there already criteria in the form?

If you previously performed a filter operation, the last filter that you ran appears in the form — for your convenience. Delete it from the form if you do not want it.

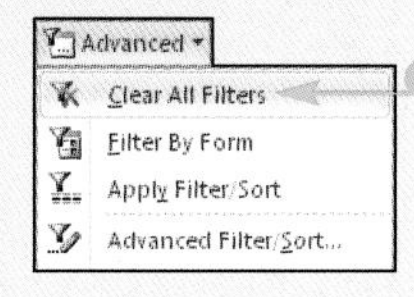

- Another way to clear all old criteria is to click the **Advanced** button (from the datasheet, not from the Filter by Form page) and then click **Clear All Filters**. If the Clear All Filters command is not available, there are no previously used filters to clear.

Is there an easier way to set up OR conditions for the same field?

Yes. You can manually type in a specification for a field. For example, if you want records where the Company field is either "ACME Corporation" or "Colvin Enterprises," you could click in the Company box and type **"ACME Corporation" OR "Colvin Enterprises."** Make sure that you include the quotation marks and the word OR. You can string together many OR statements for a single field. The Or tab is needed only if the Or condition involves multiple fields.

Save a Filter As a Query

You can save a Filter by Form filter as a query so you can rerun it later without having to set it up again. When you save a filter, a new query is created as a new object in the database. It works just like the queries you learn to create and modify in upcoming chapters.

Save a Filter As a Query

Save the Filter

1. Create a filter and then display it in Filter by Form.

Note: See the section "Filter by Form" for help if needed. Do not apply the filter yet.

2. On the Home tab, click **Advanced**.
3. Click **Save As Query**.

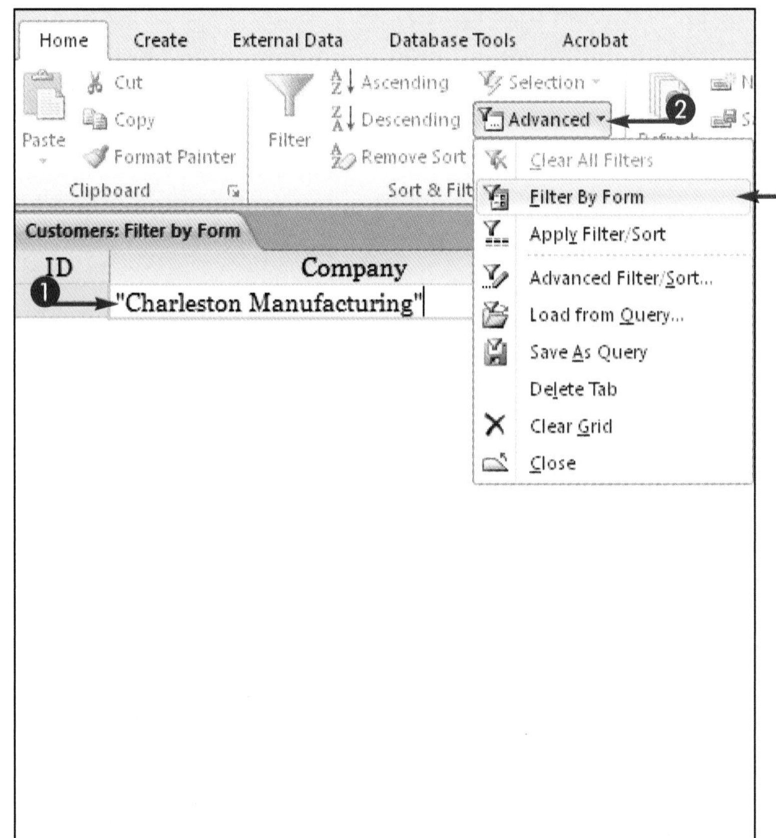

The Save As Query dialog box opens.

4. Type a name for the query.
5. Click **OK**.

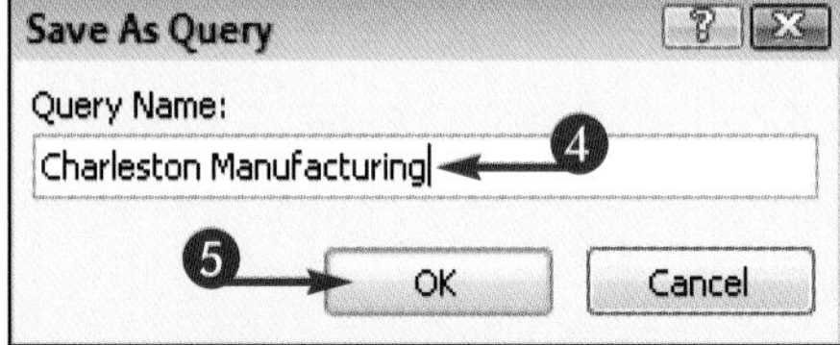

6 Right-click on the **Filter by Form** tab.

7 Click **Close**.

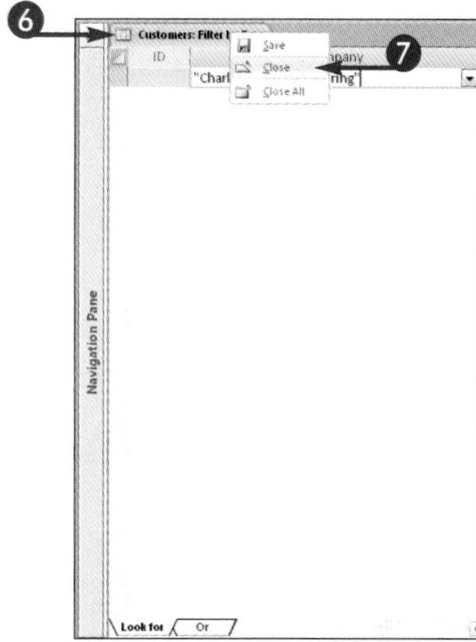

Run the Saved Filter

1 In the Objects list, double-click the query (filter) that you saved.

- The results open in a new datasheet.

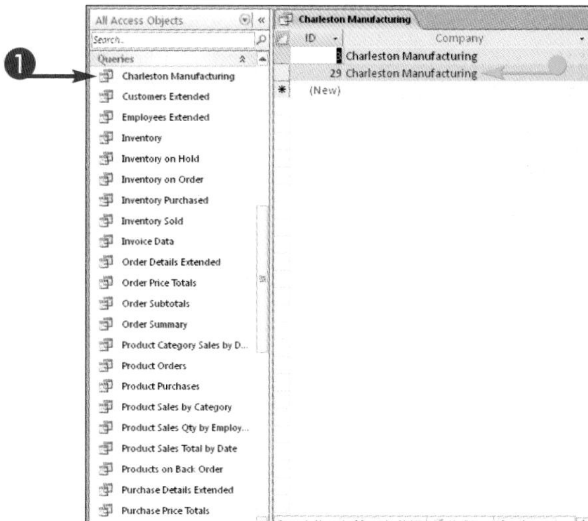

What is the difference between a filter and a query?

A filter is not saved. If you want to reapply it later, you must set it up from scratch. On the other hand, a query is saved, allowing you to reuse it. A query is also more versatile than a filter. A query can include a filter, but it can also include one or more sort levels, data from multiple tables, and input prompts.

CHAPTER 7

Creating Simple Queries

Queries enable you to save specifications for sort/filter operations as reusable objects. They are the backbone of any data retrieval system and enable users to quickly pull the needed information from large tables. In this chapter, you will learn how to create simple, effective queries that sort and filter the data from one or more tables.

Understanding Queries

Queries are like costumes that tables wear. They display the data from the table in some modified way, such as sorted by a certain field or filtered to show certain values in a field. In Design view, a query appears as a grid at the bottom of the window, into which you drag fields from the table or tables.

When you run a query, the results appear in Datasheet view, just like a table.

Tables
A query can pull fields from more than one table, provided they have a relationship between them.

Field lists
Each table's complete field list appears in a separate window.

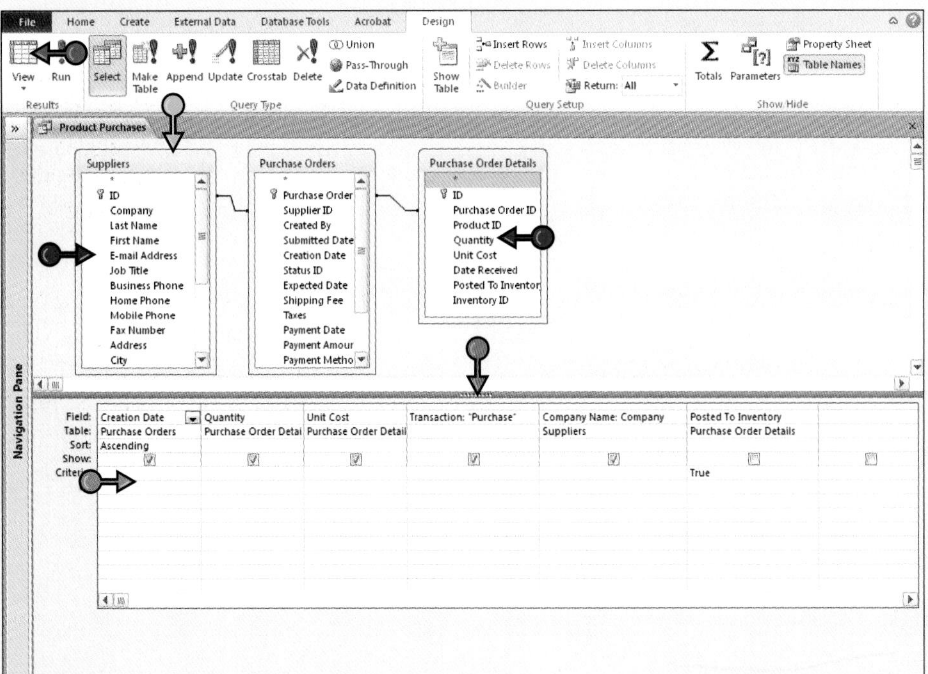

View button
To run the query, click **View**.

QBE grid
This grid, called the Query By Example (QBE) grid, contains the fields chosen to be in the query — one field per column.

Add a field
To add a field to the QBE grid, double-click it in the field list or drag it to the grid.

Select a field
To select a column on the grid, click the thin bar above the field.

Field
The Field row shows the field name.

Table
The Table row shows what table the field came from.

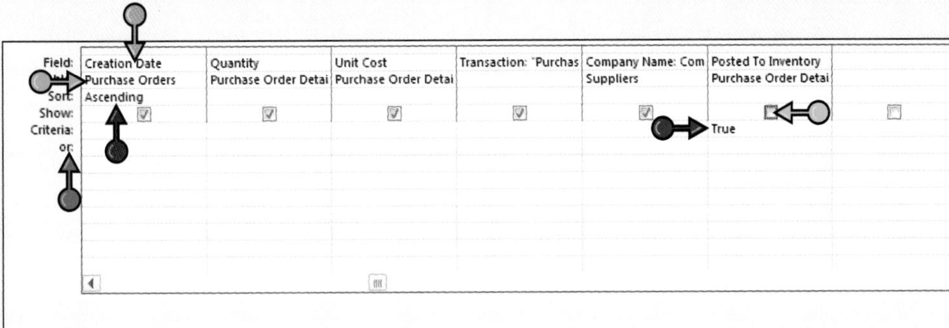

Sort
The Sort row indicates the field(s) by which the results should be sorted.

Show
A field can be omitted from the results by deselecting its check box.

Criteria
The Criteria rows hold any filters you want to apply.

Or
Additional criteria can be entered in the Or row.

Create a Query with the Simple Query Wizard

You can use the Simple Query Wizard to create a query that pulls only certain fields from one or more tables and shows them sorted in a certain order. It provides an easy way for a beginner to get started with queries.

You cannot use this wizard to set up any filtering.

Create a Query with the Simple Query Wizard

1. On the Create tab, click **Query Wizard**.

   The New Query dialog box opens.

2. Click **Simple Query Wizard**.
3. Click **OK**.

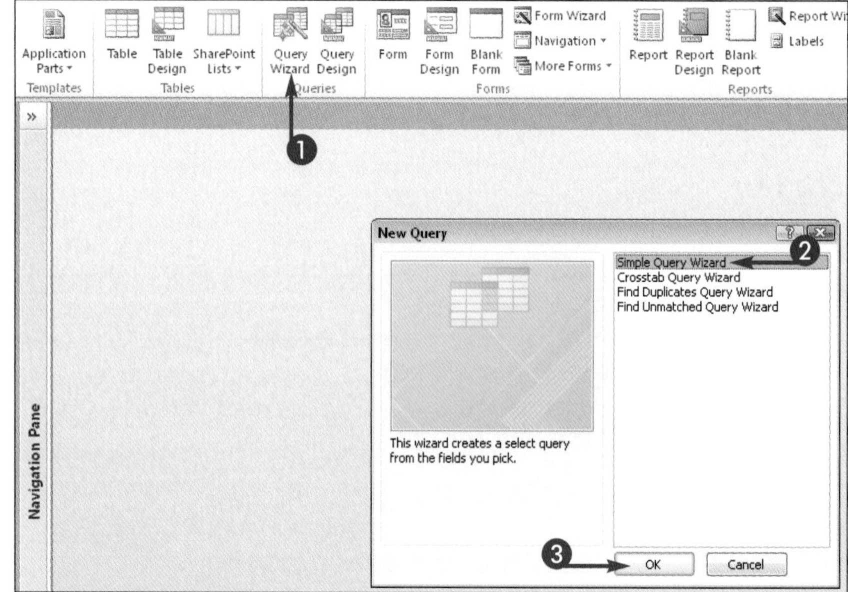

   The Simple Query Wizard opens.

4. Click here (▾) to choose the table (or other query) from which you want to select fields.
5. Click a field.
6. Click here (>) to move the field to the Selected Fields list.

- You can also click here (>>) to move all the fields at once.

7. Repeat steps **5** and **6** to pull more fields from the same table or query.
8. If needed, repeat steps **4** to **7** to pull fields from another table or query.
9. Click **Next**.

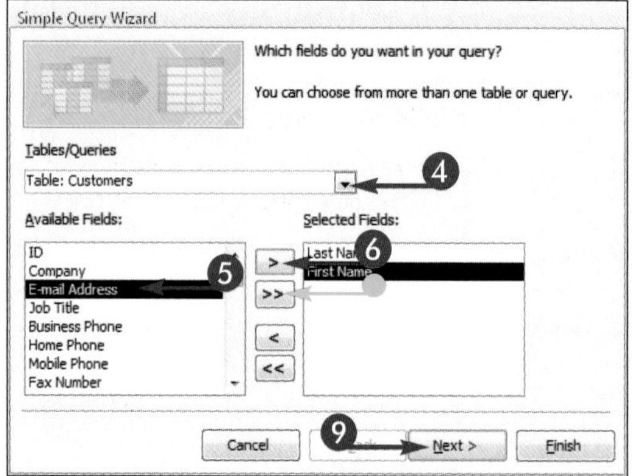

⑩ If you selected at least one numeric field, a prompt appears for a detail or summary query. Leave Detail selected for a query that includes all records.

- Alternatively, you can select Summary to summarize the data rather than show every record (◎ changes to ◉).

Note: *This screen does not appear if you did not select any numeric fields in step **5**. You will learn about summary queries later.*

⑪ Click **Next**.

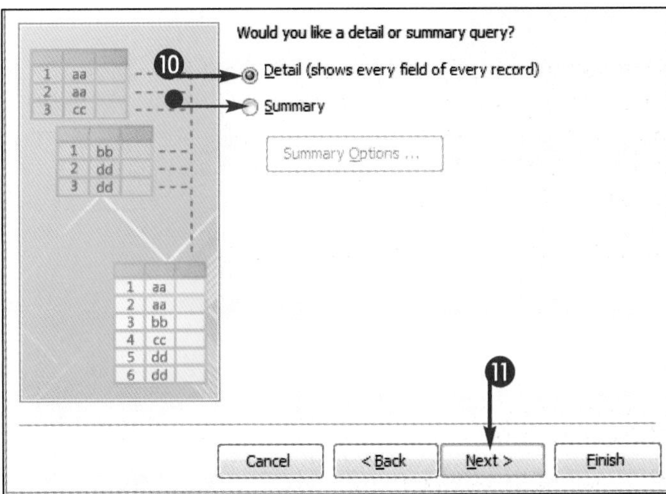

⑫ Type a name for the query, replacing the default name.

⑬ Click **Finish**.

The query results appear in a datasheet.

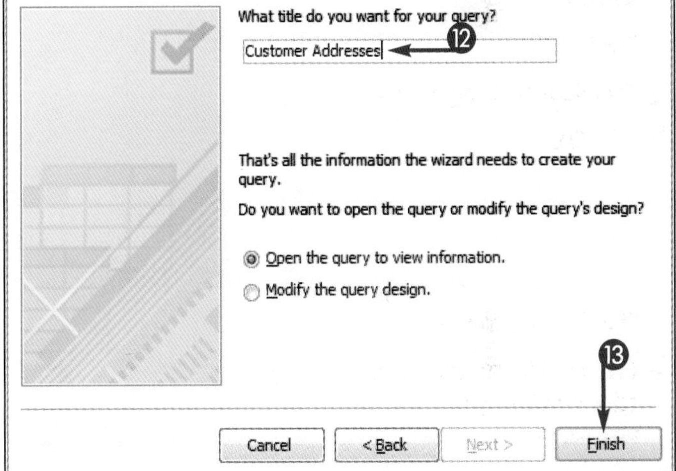

Can I use fields from any combination of tables?

No. The tables you use in a query must be directly related — that is, related with a connecting line between them, not related via some other table that they both connect to individually. If they are related only via another table, you must also include at least one field from the connector table to help Access find the relationship.

What are those other queries in the New Query dialog box used for?

They are for several types of special-purpose queries that are difficult to set up manually:

- A Crosstab query summarizes and groups data in a two-dimensional grid.
- A Find Duplicates query locates records that have the same value in a specified field or fields.
- A Find Unmatched query locates records in one table that have no corresponding entry in a related table. For example, you could find customers who have no orders.

Start a New Query in Query Design View

To create a query that has the full range of capabilities, including filtering, you must work in Query Design view. You can start a new query in Query Design view and then add the exact tables and fields to it that you want.

Start a New Query in Query Design View

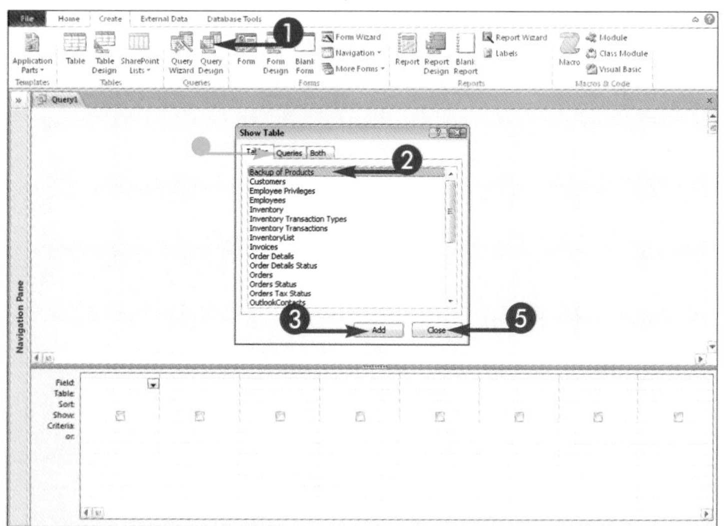

1. On the Create tab, click **Query Design**.

   A new query design window opens, and the Show Table dialog box opens.

2. Click a table that you want to include in the query.

- You can also click the **Queries** tab to choose a query to use as a table. This allows you to base one query on another.

3. Click **Add**.

4. Repeat steps **2** and **3** to add more tables.

5. Click **Close**.

   The selected tables (or queries) appear as field lists in the top part of the window.

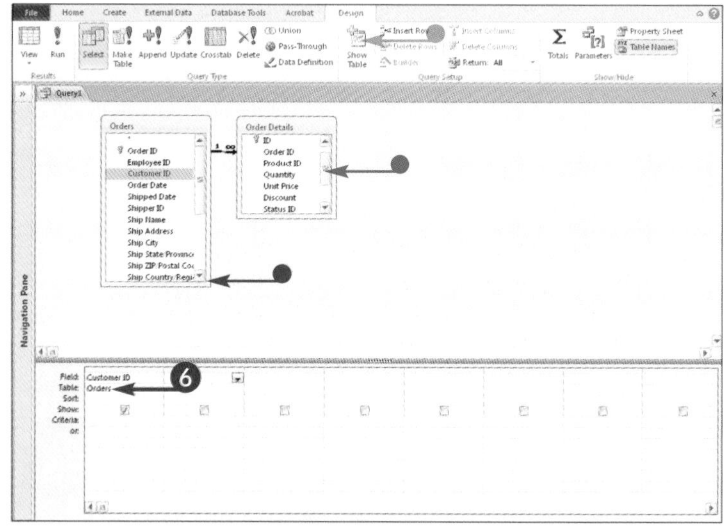

- You can drag the edge of a field list to enlarge the box.
- You can scroll through a field list, but it is sometimes more convenient if you can see more of the fields at once.

6. Drag a field into the first empty column in the query grid.

   You can also double-click a field name to place it in the grid.

   If you need to add another table, you can drag it into the top part of the query window from the Objects list.

- You can also click **Show Table** on the Design tab to reopen the Show Table dialog box to add another table or query.

7 Drag more fields into the grid as needed.

***Note:** The fields can come from different tables as long as the tables are related.*

8 Click **View** to check the query results in Datasheet view.

The results appear in a datasheet.

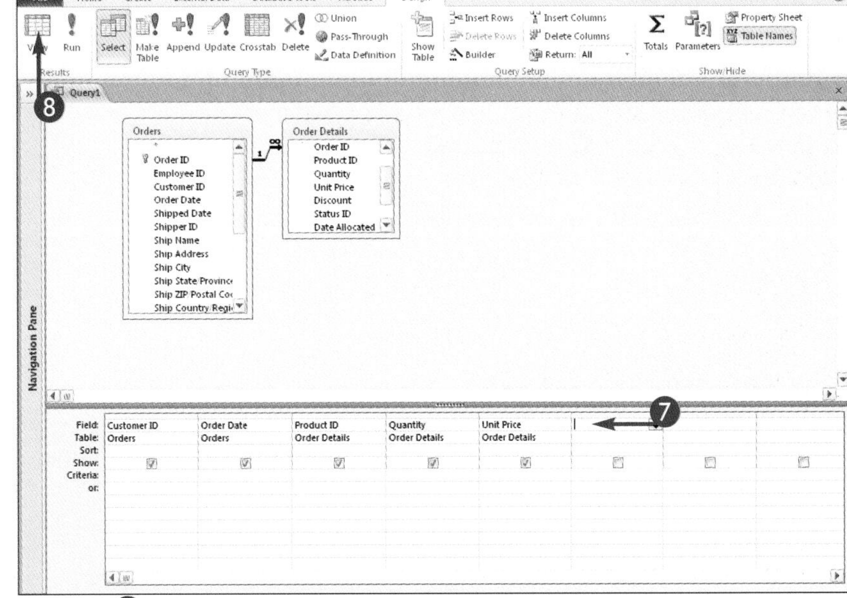

9 Click the **Save** button (💾).

The Save As dialog box opens.

10 Type a name for the query, replacing the placeholder name.

11 Click **OK**.

The query is saved.

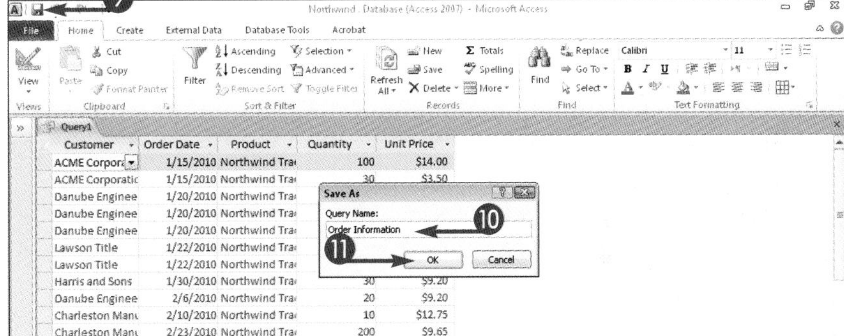

What is the Run button used for?

Some types of queries perform permanent actions on the data in the table. In such queries, there is a difference between previewing the results in Datasheet view and actually running the query. That is why there are two buttons: View and Run. For the type of query that you create in this section, though, the two buttons do the same thing.

Run

What if the query results are not what I wanted?

Rather than saving your work (steps **9** to **11**), click the **View** button on the Home tab to return to Query Design view. Make any changes as needed and then preview your work in the datasheet again.

Insert, Arrange, and Remove Query Fields

When you double-click a field to add it to a query, it appears in the first empty column. If you want to insert it somewhere else, you must use a different procedure. You can also rearrange fields after placing them in the grid and remove any fields that you added by mistake.

Insert, Arrange, and Remove Query Fields

Insert a Field in a Specific Position

1. In Query Design view, click at the top of a field's column to select the field that the new column should appear to the left of.
2. Click **Insert Columns**.

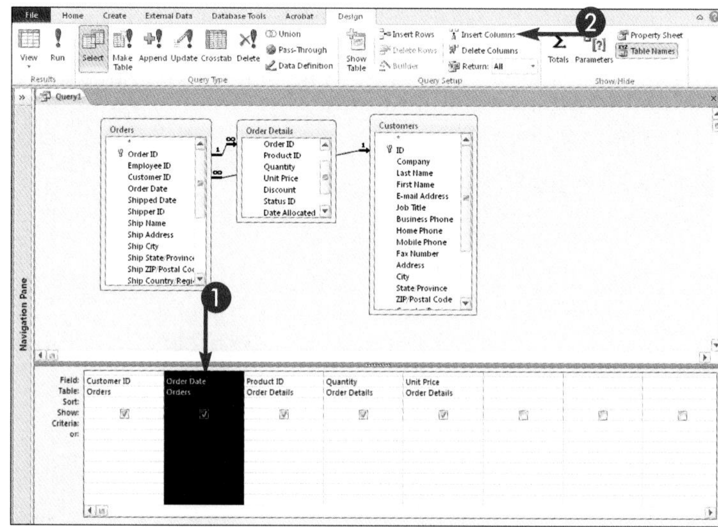

- A new blank column appears.

3. Drag the new field into the blank column.

***Note:** As a shortcut, instead of inserting the column, you can simply drag the new field on top of an existing one; a new column is automatically created to the left of it.*

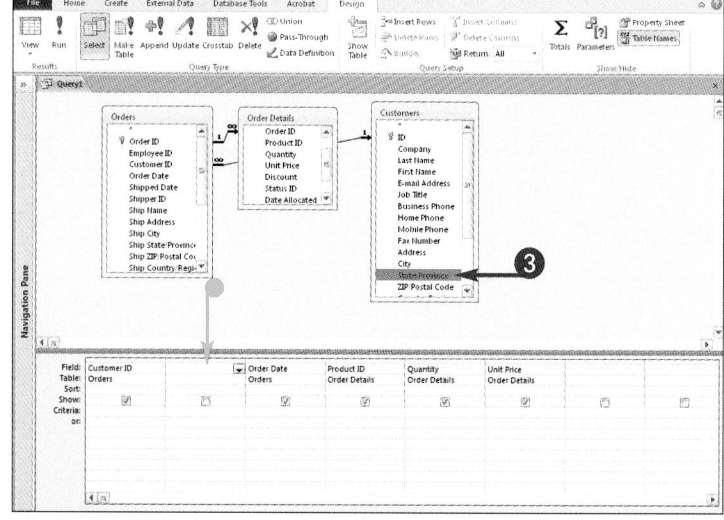

Remove a Field

1. Click the top of a field's column to select it.
2. Click **Delete Columns**.

   Alternatively, you can press Delete.

   The field is removed from the grid.

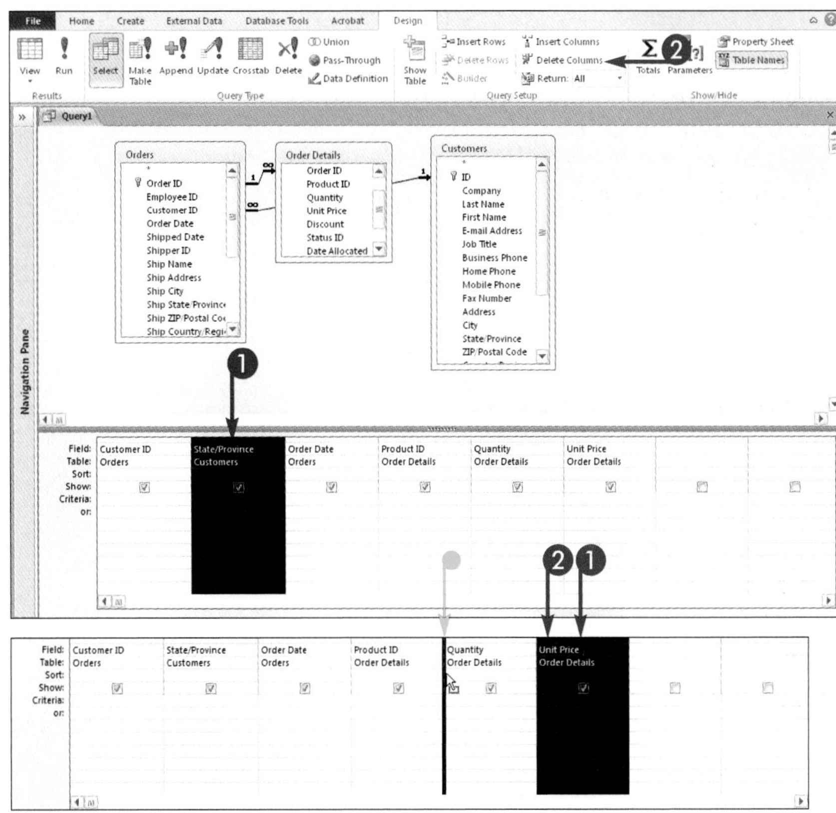

Move a Field

1. Click the top of a field's column to select it.
2. Drag the bar above the field left or right to move it.

- A black line shows where the field is being dragged.

When you release the mouse button, the field moves to the new location.

How do I remove a table's field list from Query Design view?

To remove a table's field list:

1. Right-click on the title of the field list.
2. Click **Remove Table**.

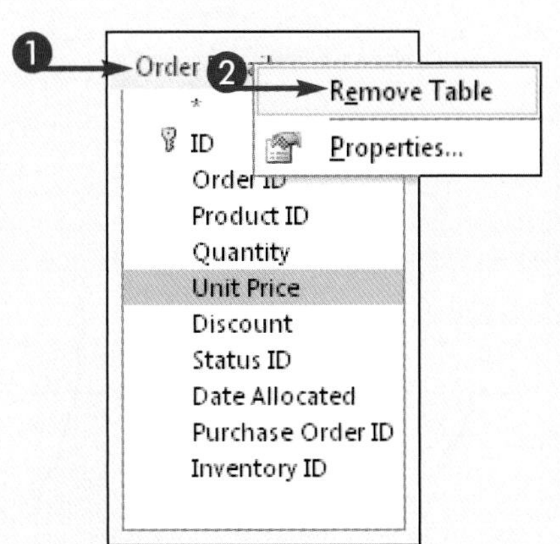

What happens if I remove a table that has fields in use in the query grid?

Those fields are deleted from the grid. Adding the table back again does not automatically restore them in the grid; you must manually add the fields.

Set Field Sorting

You can set a query to sort the results alphabetically by a certain field, either in ascending or descending order.

You can specify sorting for more than one field if you like. Access prioritizes them from left to right in the grid. The leftmost field that has a sort order set will take precedence; other sorts will operate only in the event of a tie.

Set Field Sorting

1. In Query Design view, click here (▾) to open the drop-down list in the Sort row.
2. Click **Ascending** for an A to Z sort.

- You can also click **Descending** for a Z to A sort.
- To turn off field sorting, choose **(not sorted)**.

3. Repeat steps **1** and **2** for other fields if needed.
4. Click **View** to check your work.

The results appear sorted by the chosen field(s).

You can return to Query Design view by clicking **View** again.

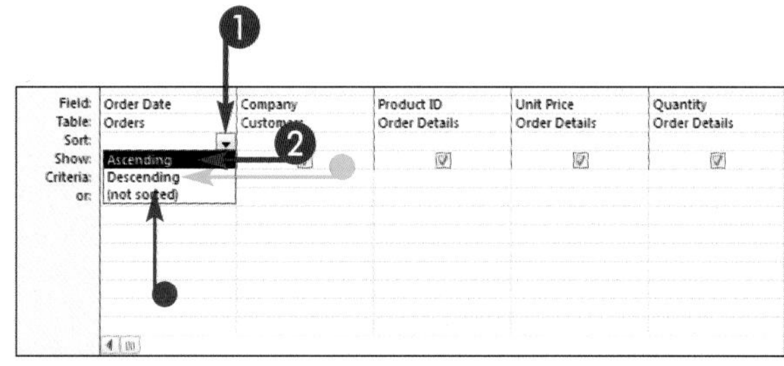

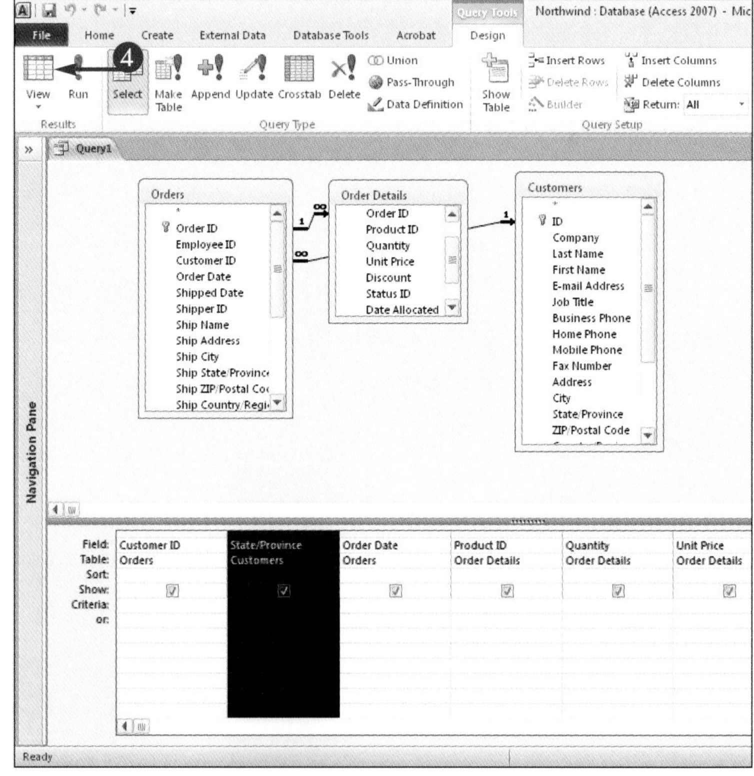

Add an Alias to a Query Field

Field names do not have to appear in the query results as their actual names. For example, perhaps you want the Product Name field to appear simply as "Product" or you want the Quantity field to appear as "Qty."

To change the wording of the column heading in the query results, you can create an alias for the field.

Add an Alias to a Query Field

1. In Query Design view, click at the beginning of the field name in the Field row and then type the alias, followed by a colon (:).
2. Repeat step **1** for other fields if needed.

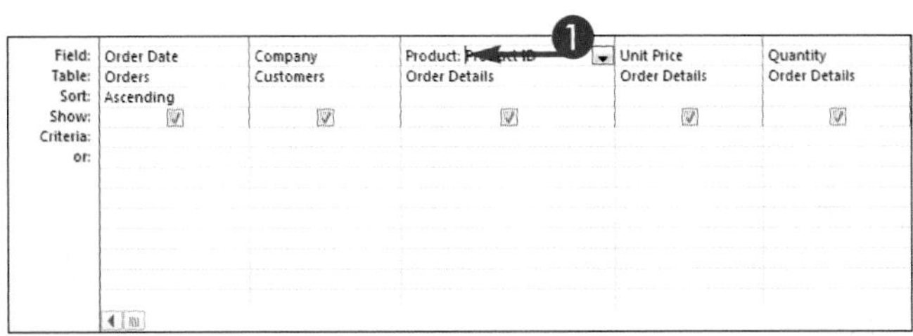

3. Click **View** to preview the change in a datasheet.

- The datasheet column(s) appear with the alias(es).
- You can return to Query Design view by clicking **View**.

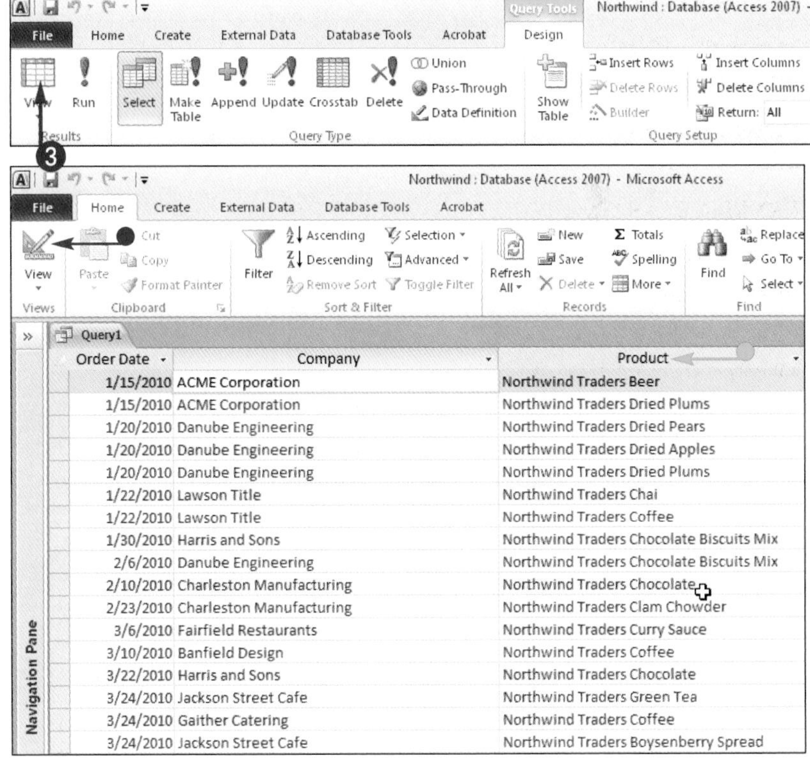

Understanding Criteria

To filter the query results, you can create criteria. *Criteria* are specifications that dictate which records will be included. For example, you may include only customers in a certain range of ZIP codes or only people who have placed orders in the last 12 months.

Numeric Criteria

You can specify a fixed numeric value as a criterion for a number field. Type the number directly into the Criteria row in the grid. You do not need quotation marks or any special formatting for it. Access interprets dates as numbers too. When using a date, enter hash symbols around it: #12/15/2010#. If you forget the hash marks, Access usually adds them for you.

Text Criteria

You can specify a text string as a criterion. It can contain multiple words, including punctuation and spacing, but you must enclose it in quotation marks. For example, to set a Customer field's criterion to John Doe, type **"John Doe"** in the Criteria row. If you forget the marks, Access usually adds them for you.

Criteria Ranges

It is often useful to specify a range of values for a criterion instead of one specific value. You can accomplish this with comparison operators and special keywords.

Use	*Description*	*Example*
<	Less than	<30
<=	Less than or equal to	<=#1/1/10#
>	Greater than	>100
>=	Greater than or equal to	>=50
<>	Not equal to	<>"Denver"
Like	Matches a pattern of characters	Like "Denver"
And	Matches two or more conditions	>5 And <10
Or	Matches any condition	"CO" Or "CA"
Between ... And	Matches values in a range	Between #1/1/10# And #1/15/10#
In	Selects from a list of values	In ("NM", "NY", "NJ")
Is Null	Includes the record only if the field is empty	Is Null
Is Not Null	Includes the record only if the field is not empty	Is Not Null
*	Wildcard, substituting for any characters	462*
?	Wildcard, substituting for a single character	462??

Filter a Query for a Specific Value

The simplest type of criterion is one in which you are specifying a single value. Only records containing that value in that field are included in the results.

Filter a Query for a Specific Value

Filter a Query for a Numeric Value

1. In Query Design view in the Criteria row, type the value you want to filter.

Note: *If the value is a date, enclose it in hash marks: #12/15/2010#.*

2. Click **View** to check your work.

Note: *If you enter criteria for more than one field, only records that match both criteria are included in the results. Multicriteria queries are covered later in this chapter.*

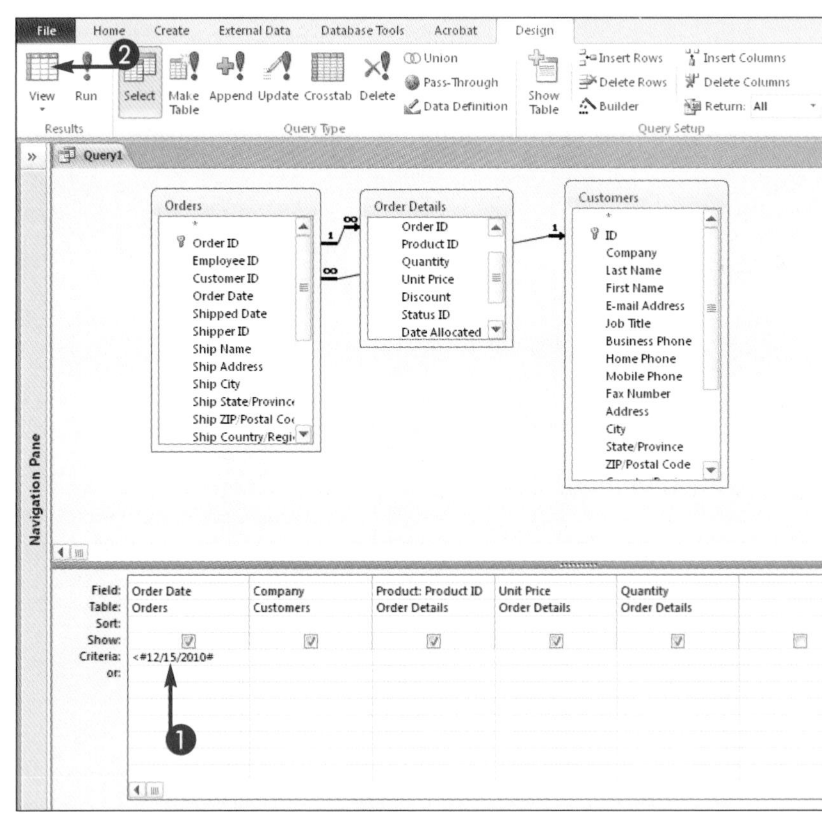

Filter a Query for a Text String

1. In the Criteria row, type the text string you want to filter, enclosed in quotation marks.

Note: *If you forget the quotation marks, Access usually adds them for you.*

Note: *If you are not sure of the entire text string, use a wildcard, as in the table in the preceding section. For example, "ACME*" finds ACME, ACME Corp., and Acme Corporation.*

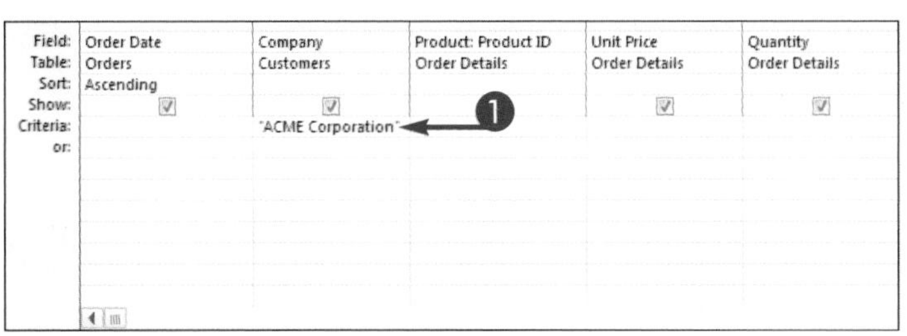

Specify a Range of Values

You can specify ranges of values in criteria by using comparison operators. A table of available operators appears in the section "Understanding Criteria."

Comparison operators work with all kinds of criteria (text, dates, numbers, and so on).

Specify a Range of Values

Use a Greater-Than or Less-Than Range

1. In the Criteria row, type the comparison operator that you want to use:

   > greater than

   < less than

   >= greater than or equal to

   <= less than or equal to

   = equals

2. Type the value to which you want to compare it.

Note: *The value can be a number, date, or text string. Remember to enclose text strings in quotation marks.*

Product: Product ID	Unit Price	Quantity
Order Details	Order Details	Order Details
		>10

Use a Between Range

1. In the Criteria row, type **Between** and then add a space.
2. Type the lower value in the range and then add a space.
3. Type **And** and then add a space.
4. Type the higher value in the range.

Product: Product ID	Unit Price	Quantity
Order Details	Order Details	Order Details
		Between 1 and 10

Specify a List of Values

You can create a list of values to use for a criterion. Records will be included in the results that have any of the values on the list.

There are two ways to create a list of values. You can separate each value with the word *Or* or you can use the *In* keyword and then place the values in parentheses as a group.

Specify a List of Values

Create a List by Using *Or*

1. In the Criteria row, type the first value and then add a space.

Note: Enclose the value in quotation marks if it is a text string.

2. Type the word **Or** and then add a space.
3. Type the next value and then add a space.
4. Repeat steps **2** and **3** to include as many items for the list as needed.

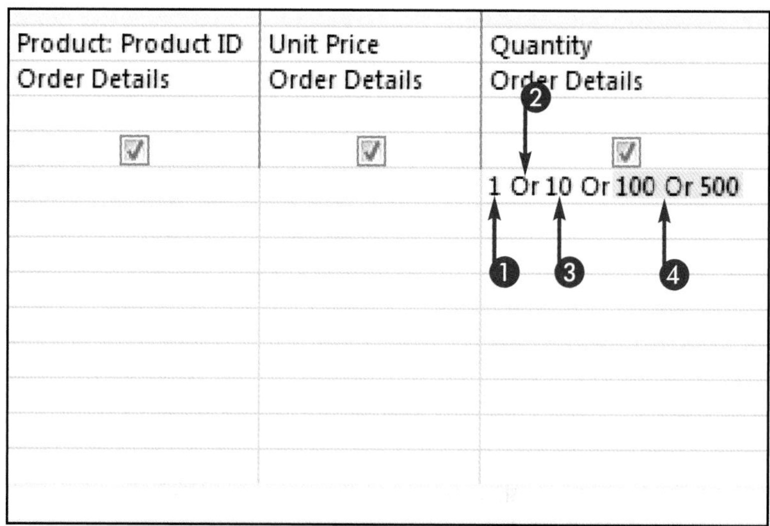

Create a List by Using *In*

1. In the Criteria row, type **In (**.
2. Type the list of values, separated by commas.

Note: If the values are text strings, enclose each one in separate quotation marks. Make sure that the commas are outside the quotation marks. You can use spaces to make the criteria easier to read, but Access ignores them unless they are within quotation marks.

3. Type **)**.

Product: Product ID
Order Details
Unit Price
Order Details
Quantity
Order Details
In (1, 10, 100, 500)

Hide a Field in the Query Results

You can hide a field without removing it from the query grid. This is useful when you need to include a field in a query in order to use it as a criterion but you do not want that field to show up in the results.

For example, suppose you are creating a query called Orders in Washington. You would need the State field to be included so you can show only Washington orders, but it would be redundant to have "WA" appear in a column for every record.

Hide a Field in the Query Results

1. In the Show row, deselect the check box for the field you want to hide.

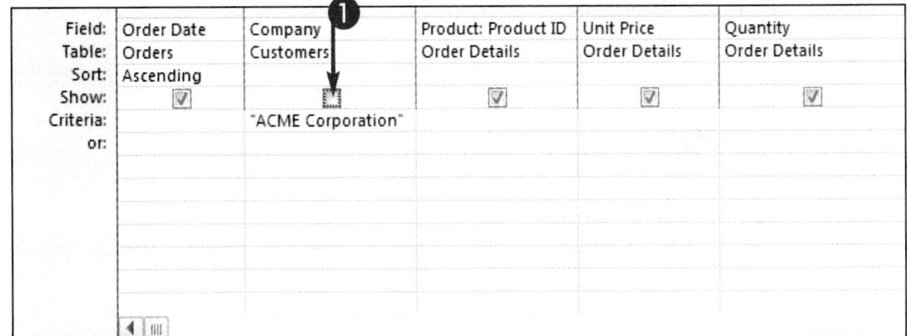

Field:	Order Date	Company	Product: Product ID	Unit Price	Quantity
Table:	Orders	Customers	Order Details	Order Details	Order Details
Sort:	Ascending				
Show:	☑	☐	☑	☑	☑
Criteria:		"ACME Corporation"			
or:					

2. Click **View** to check your work.

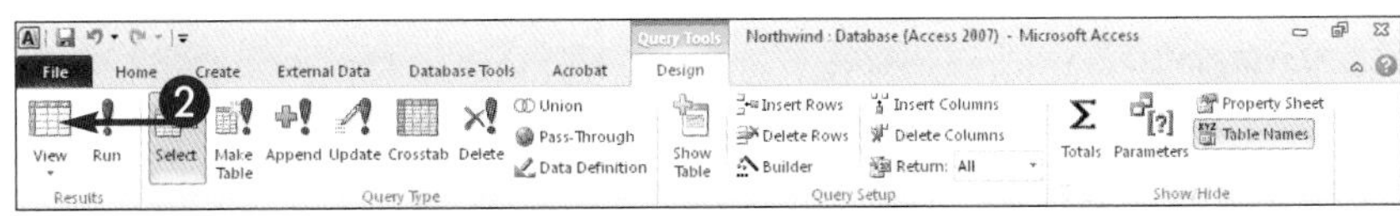

The datasheet opens, showing the query results. Only the records that match the criteria appear.

- The field providing the criteria does not appear.

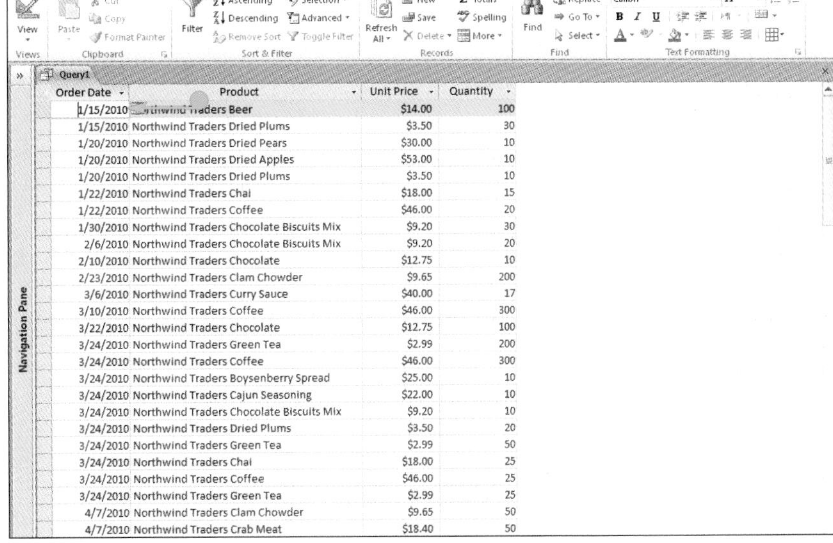

Order Date	Product	Unit Price	Quantity
1/15/2010	[illegible] Traders Beer	$14.00	100
1/15/2010	Northwind Traders Dried Plums	$3.50	30
1/20/2010	Northwind Traders Dried Pears	$30.00	10
1/20/2010	Northwind Traders Dried Apples	$53.00	10
1/20/2010	Northwind Traders Dried Plums	$3.50	10
1/22/2010	Northwind Traders Chai	$18.00	15
1/22/2010	Northwind Traders Coffee	$46.00	20
1/30/2010	Northwind Traders Chocolate Biscuits Mix	$9.20	30
2/6/2010	Northwind Traders Chocolate Biscuits Mix	$9.20	20
2/10/2010	Northwind Traders Chocolate	$12.75	10
2/23/2010	Northwind Traders Clam Chowder	$9.65	200
3/6/2010	Northwind Traders Curry Sauce	$40.00	17
3/10/2010	Northwind Traders Coffee	$46.00	300
3/22/2010	Northwind Traders Chocolate	$12.75	100
3/24/2010	Northwind Traders Green Tea	$2.99	200
3/24/2010	Northwind Traders Coffee	$46.00	300
3/24/2010	Northwind Traders Boysenberry Spread	$25.00	10
3/24/2010	Northwind Traders Cajun Seasoning	$22.00	10
3/24/2010	Northwind Traders Chocolate Biscuits Mix	$9.20	10
3/24/2010	Northwind Traders Dried Plums	$3.50	20
3/24/2010	Northwind Traders Green Tea	$2.99	50
3/24/2010	Northwind Traders Chai	$18.00	25
3/24/2010	Northwind Traders Coffee	$46.00	25
3/24/2010	Northwind Traders Green Tea	$2.99	25
4/7/2010	Northwind Traders Clam Chowder	$9.65	50
4/7/2010	Northwind Traders Crab Meat	$18.40	50

Combine Criteria

You can use multiple criteria to define your filtering conditions. Criteria combinations can be exclusive (And) or nonexclusive (Or).

You can have combinations of And and Or in your query specification. For example, you could filter for orders placed on either of two dates *and* placed by a certain customer.

Combine Criteria

Combine Exclusive Criteria (Using And)

1. Create a criterion for a field.

Note: *See the preceding sections for help if needed.*

2. On the same Criteria row, create a criterion for another field.

Field:	Order Date	Company	Product: Product ID
Table:	Orders	Customers	Order Details
Sort:	Ascending		
Show:	☑	☐	☑
Criteria:	#12/15/2010#	"ACME Corporation"	
or:			

Combine Nonexclusive Criteria (Using Or)

1. Create a criterion for a field.
2. On the first empty Or row, create a criterion for another field.

Note: *You can also create a criterion for the same field in step **2**, but if working with the same field, it would be easier to use the word Or in the Criteria line, as you learned earlier in this chapter.*

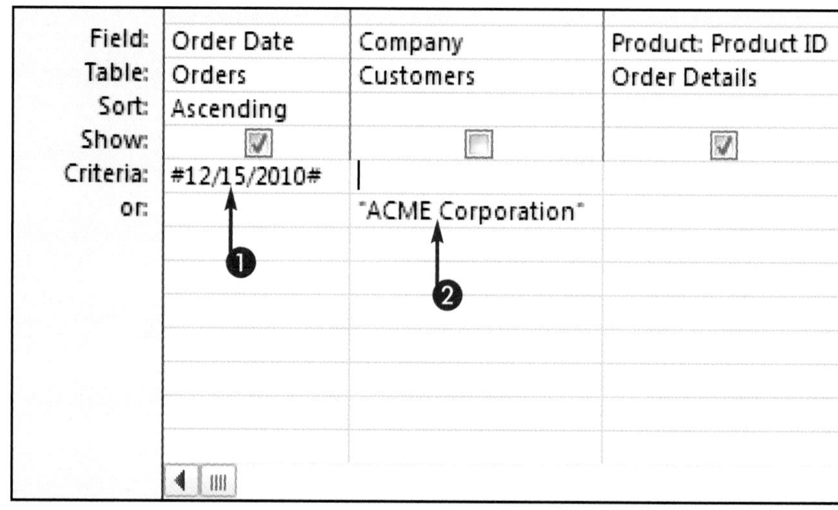

Limit the Records Returned

In addition to the various criteria that you can create, you can also limit the number of records that a query returns. You can limit it either by a number or by a percentage. For example, you could show only the top 5 records or you could show the top 5%.

Limit the Records Returned

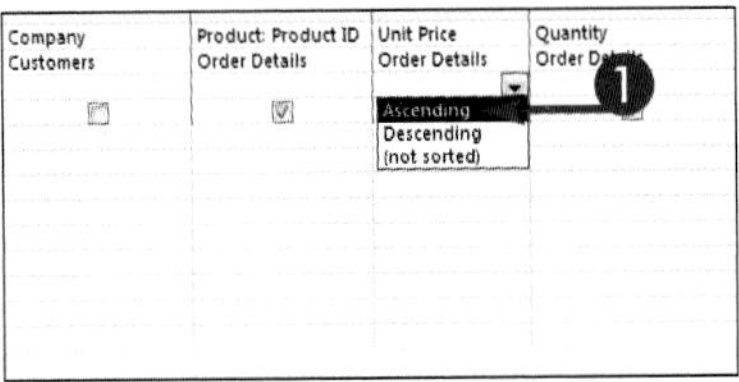

1. In Query Design view in the field by which you want to impose the limit, click here (▾) to choose **Ascending** or **Descending**.

Note: *The limit refers to the first field by which the query is sorted, if any. If there is no sorting specified, it refers to the leftmost field.*

2. Click here (▾) to choose the limit that you want.
3. Click **View** to view the filtered list.

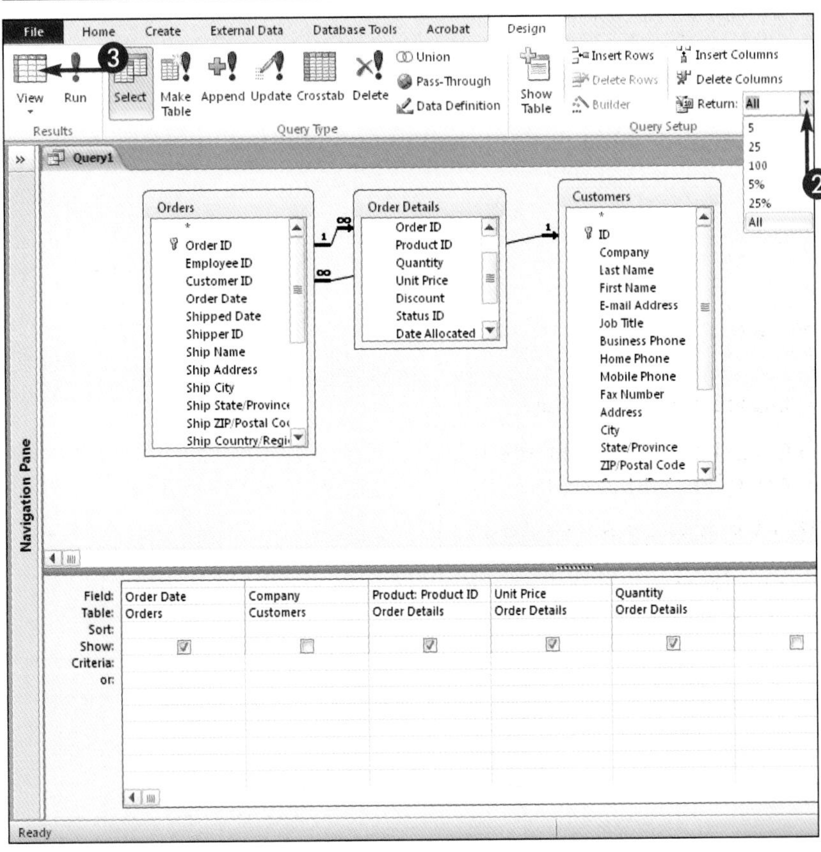

CHAPTER

Creating More Complex Queries

Queries can do much more than just sort and filter data from a table. They can summarize and calculate data, append data from one table to another, identify duplicate data, prompt the user for parameters at runtime, and much more. In this chapter, you learn how to take advantage of the powerful tools for special-purpose queries in Access 2010.

Understanding Summary Queries

A summary query distills a large quantity of data down into useful information. You can use summary queries whenever you do not care about the individual records but want to understand the big picture.

No individual records
Individual records do not appear in the results of a summary query. Each row in the query datasheet represents a summary of a group of records. It is possible but not typical for a group to consist of a single record.

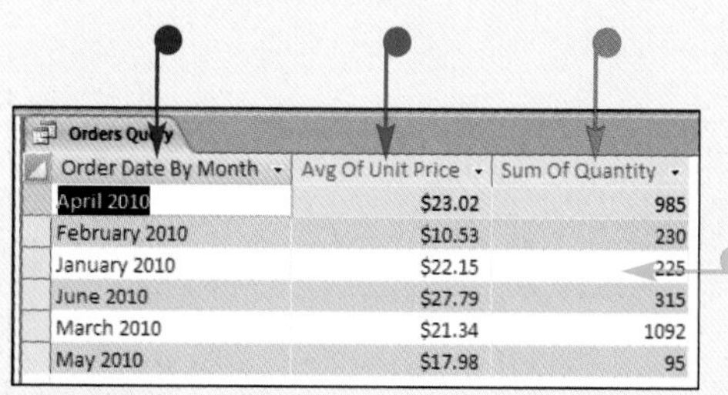

Orders Query

Order Date By Month	Avg Of Unit Price	Sum Of Quantity
April 2010	$23.02	985
February 2010	$10.53	230
January 2010	$22.15	225
June 2010	$27.79	315
March 2010	$21.34	1092
May 2010	$17.98	95

Group By
A summary query typically contains only a few fields. It needs only the field(s) by which you want to group the data and the field(s) by which you want to calculate. There is typically one field by which the data is grouped. In this example, each row represents a different month.

Average
The UnitPrice field has been set up to use the Average function to average the unit price values for the month as a whole. Access automatically generated the column title Avg Of Unit Price.

Sum
The Quantity field has been set up to use the Sum function to sum the Quantity values for the month as a whole. Access automatically generated the column title Sum Of Quantity.

Aggregate Functions

Summary queries summarize data using *aggregate functions* built into Access. These are math operations that calculate statistics about the data. Some of the aggregate functions require the data to be numeric, such as Sum; others, such as Count, work on any data type.

The following are the available aggregate functions:

Function	***Purpose***
Sum	Totals numeric values
Avg	Totals numeric values and divides by the number of records in the group
Min	Finds the lowest value (smallest number, first text alphabetically, earliest date)
Max	Finds the highest value (largest number, last text alphabetically, latest date)
Count	Finds the number of records in the group
StDev	Calculates the standard deviation. This is used to see how close the values are to the average.
Var	Calculates the variance. This is another way of measuring how close the values are to the average.
First	Finds the first record's entry in the group
Last	Finds the last record's entry in the group
Expression	Allows a custom formula to be entered
Where	Refers the query to the Criteria row. This enables you to include fields in the query purely for criteria purposes without grouping or calculating by that field.

Simple Query Wizard Summaries

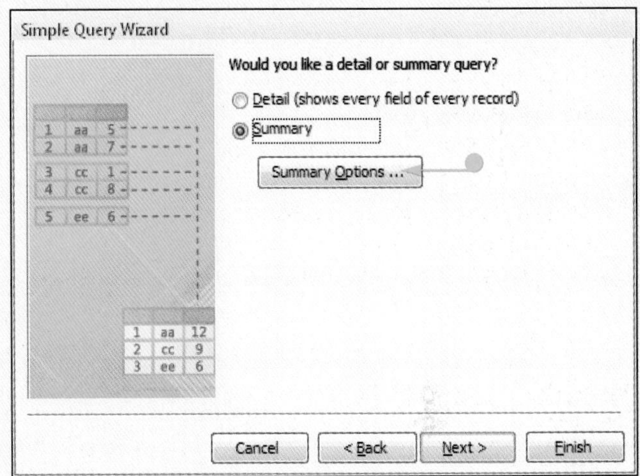

- **Summary Options**
  When you choose a summary query with the Simple Query Wizard, a Summary Options button becomes available in the wizard.

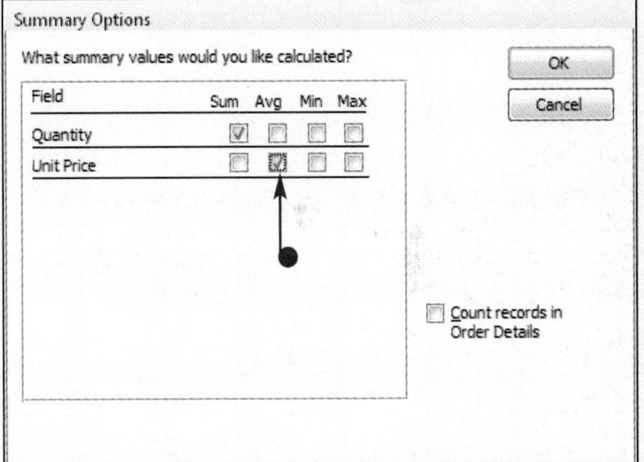

- **Select the Calculations**
  You can click check boxes for each calculation that you want (☐ changes to ☑). Each check box that you click translates into a column in the query results, so choose carefully to avoid information overload.

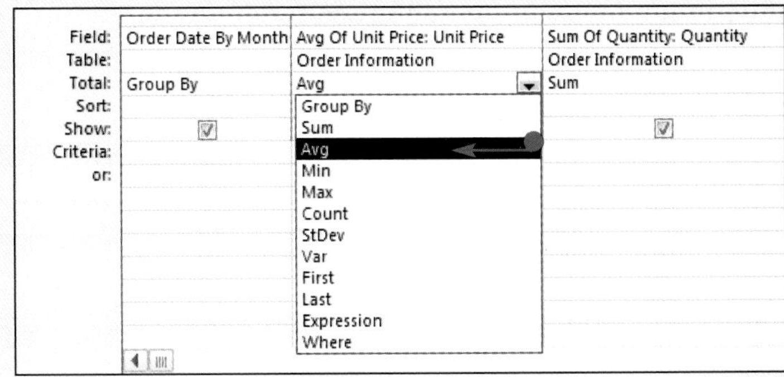

- **Query Design View Summaries**
  In Query Design view, you can display a Total row in the grid. For each field included, the Total row must be set either to Group By or to one of the functions shown in the previous table.

Create a Summary Query with the Simple Query Wizard

The easiest way to create a summary query is to use the Simple Query Wizard, as you learned in Chapter 7. As part of the wizard, you can specify a summary query and then set up the calculations that you want to use.

Create a Summary Query with the Simple Query Wizard

1. On the Create tab, click **Query Wizard**.

   The New Query dialog box opens.

2. Click **Simple Query Wizard**.
3. Click **OK**.

   The Simple Query Wizard opens.

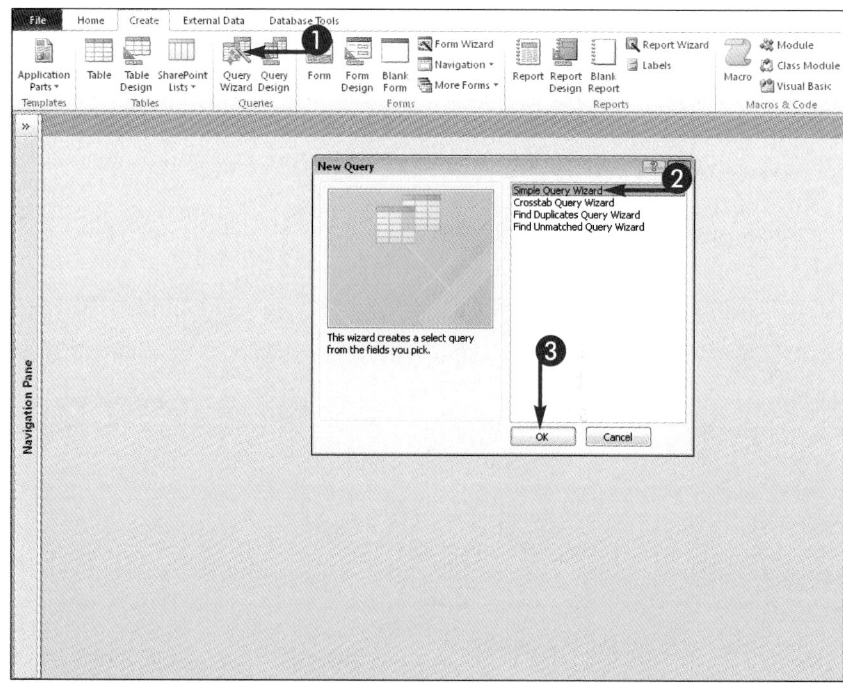

4. Click here to choose the table (or other query) from which you want to select fields.
5. Click a field.
6. Click here (>) to move the field to the Selected Fields list.

- You can also click here (>>) to move all the fields at once.

7. Repeat steps **5** and **6** to pull more fields from the same table.
8. If needed, repeat steps **4** to **7** to pull fields from another table.
9. Click **Next**.

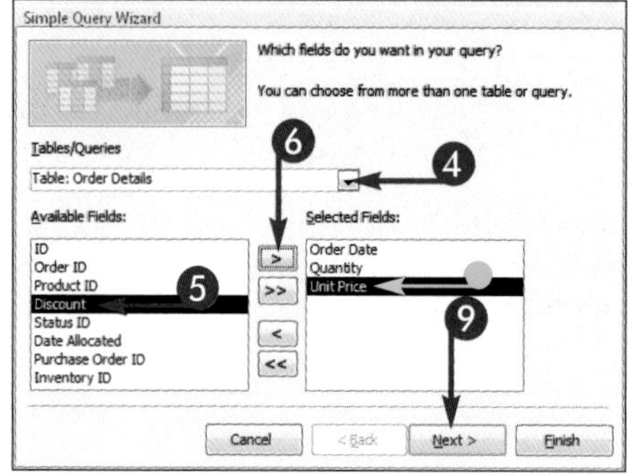

⑩ Click the **Summary** radio button (◎ changes to ◉).

⑪ Click **Summary Options**.

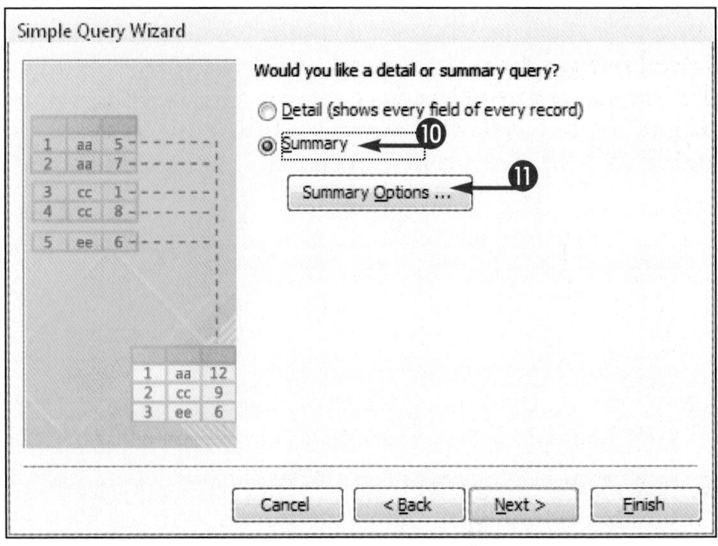

The Summary Options dialog box opens.

⑫ Click the check box for each calculation that you want to perform (☐ changes to ☑).

⑬ If you want a record count, click the **Count records in *table name*** check box (☐ changes to ☑).

Table name will be replaced by the name of the table or query from which that field is being taken. It is Order Details in this example.

⑭ Click **OK** to return to the Simple Query Wizard.

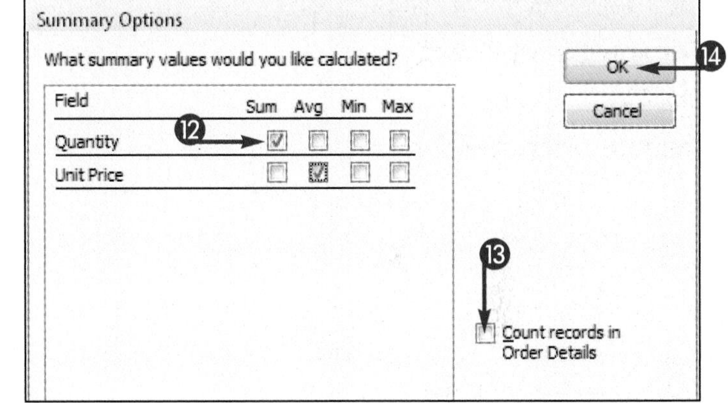

Which fields should I use?

A summary query is clearest and most concise when it uses very few fields. Include one field by which to group and then only the fields by which you want calculations to appear for those groups. If you use more fields than that, the datasheet becomes so complex that it defeats the purpose of a summary query — to summarize a large collection of data in a concise format.

Can I choose fields from different tables?

Yes. The same rules apply as with a detail query. Fields can come from different tables as long as those tables are related. Consult the Relationships window (File⇨Relationships) if you are not sure about the relationships.

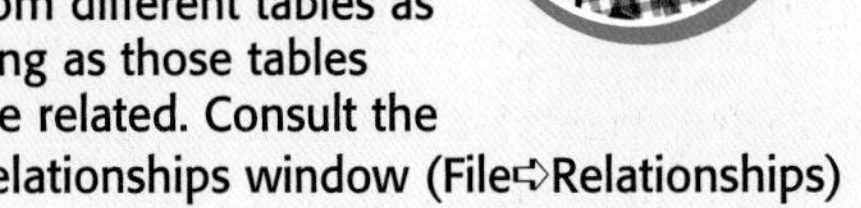

continued

Create a Summary Query with the Simple Query Wizard *(continued)*

When creating a summary query in which the field by which you are grouping has a Date data type, the wizard enables you to select a grouping interval for the dates. You can group by day, month, year, and so on.

This option alone makes the wizard very valuable. It is easy to set up such intervals in the wizard, but it is very complicated and difficult to set them up manually in Query Design view.

Create a Summary Query with the Simple Query Wizard *(continued)*

15. Click **Next**.

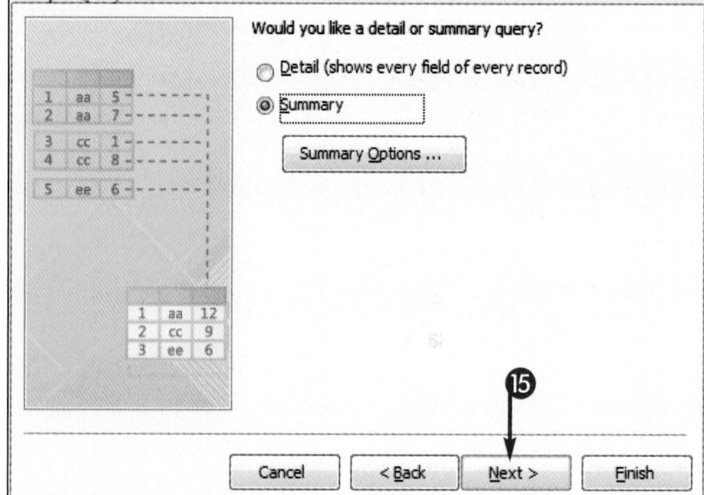

If the Group By field is a Date data type, you are prompted for an interval.

16. Click the grouping interval that you want (◎ changes to ◉).
17. Click **Next**.

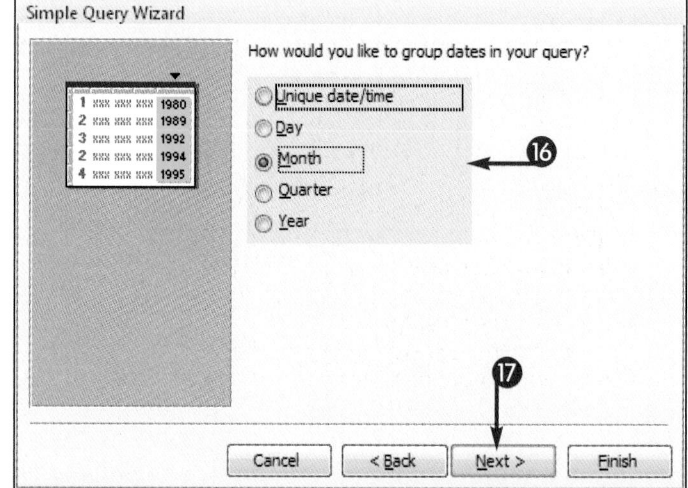

18 Type a name for the query here, replacing the default name.

19 Click **Finish**.

The query results appear in a datasheet.

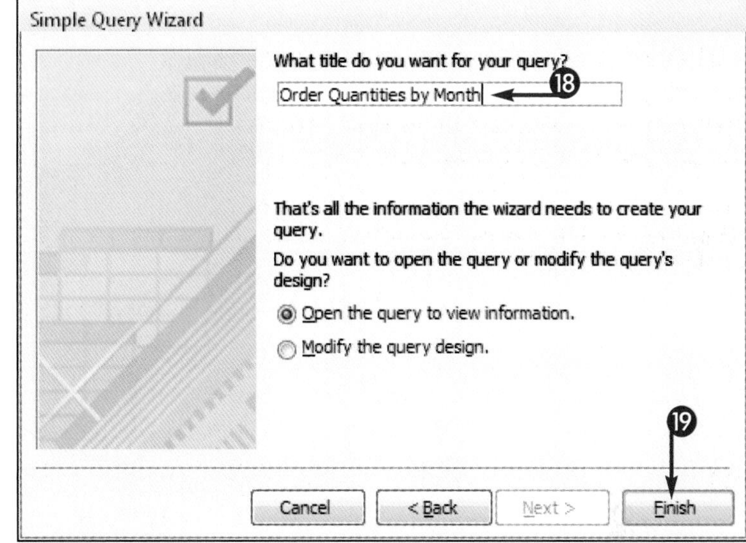

20 Widen the columns if needed to display the column headings.

***Note:** To automatically size a column to its content, double-click between the column headings. To manually size it, drag the right border of a column heading.*

21 Click the **Save** button (save icon).

The query definition is saved.

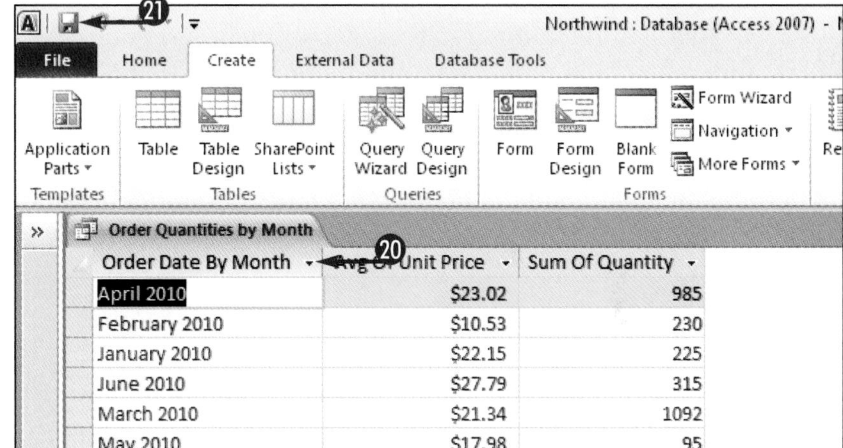

Order Date By Month	Avg Of Unit Price	Sum Of Quantity
April 2010	$23.02	985
February 2010	$10.53	230
January 2010	$22.15	225
June 2010	$27.79	315
March 2010	$21.34	1092
May 2010	$17.98	95

Can I make changes to a summary query after creating it with the wizard?

Yes. You can edit it in Query Design view. In most respects, a summary query is just like any other query. However, it has a Total row in the grid that detail queries do not have. You will learn more about summary queries in Query Design view in the next section.

When I view the query in Query Design view, why is there a weird extra field that starts with "Year"?

```
Year([Order Information].[Order Date])*12+DatePart('m',[Order Information].[Order Date])-1
```

When you specify grouping by a date range, the Simple Query Wizard adds a formula that represents the interval. Its syntax can be quite complex; that is why it is best to create such fields with the wizard. Widen its column in the grid to see the entire formula at once.

Create a Summary Query in Query Design View

You can also create a summary query in Query Design view by specifying the fields manually. If you know exactly what you want and if the syntax you need is not complicated, it can be faster to use this method than the wizard.

Create a Summary Query in Query Design View

1. On the Create tab, click **Query Design**.

   A new query design window opens, and the Show Table dialog box opens.

2. Double-click a table that you want to include in the query. Repeat as needed.

- You can also click a table and then click **Add**.
- You can also click the Queries tab and add an existing query, just like you would a table.

3. Click **Close**.

   The selected tables (or queries) appear as field lists in the top part of the window.

4. Drag the fields that you want on to the grid.

5. Click **Totals**.

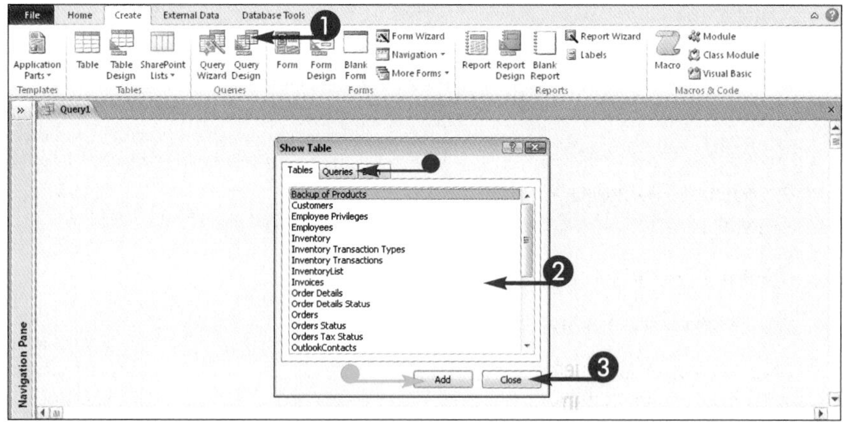

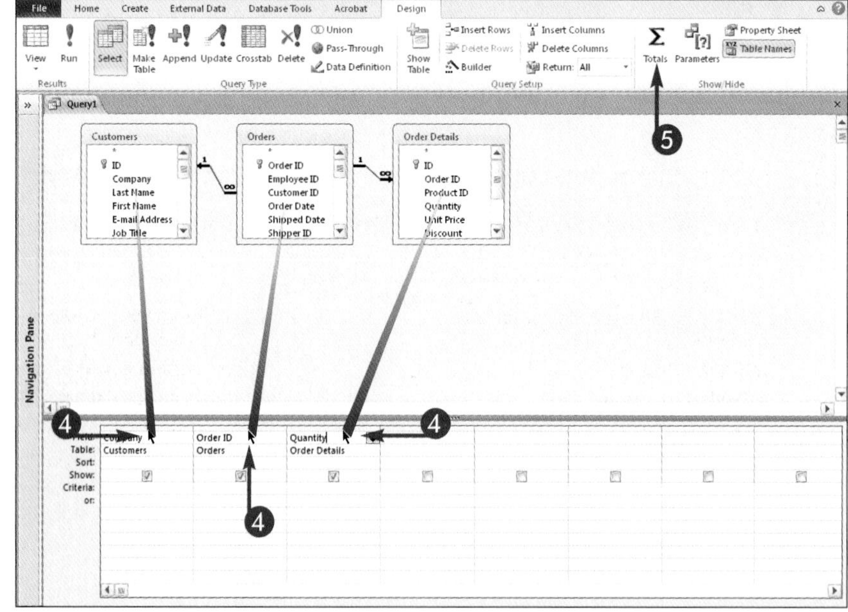

The Total row appears on the grid.

6 For each field, click here (▾) to choose the calculation to perform.

- Leave one field set to Group By; these groups will form the rows of the results.

7 Click **View**.

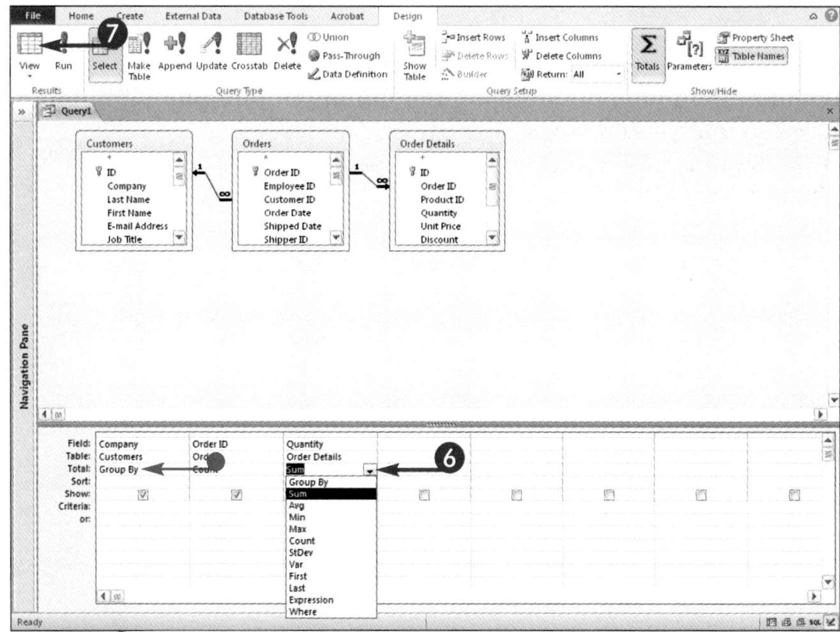

The query results appear in a datasheet.

8 Click the **Save** button (💾).

The Save As dialog box opens.

9 Type a name for the query, replacing the default name.

10 Click **OK**.

The query is saved.

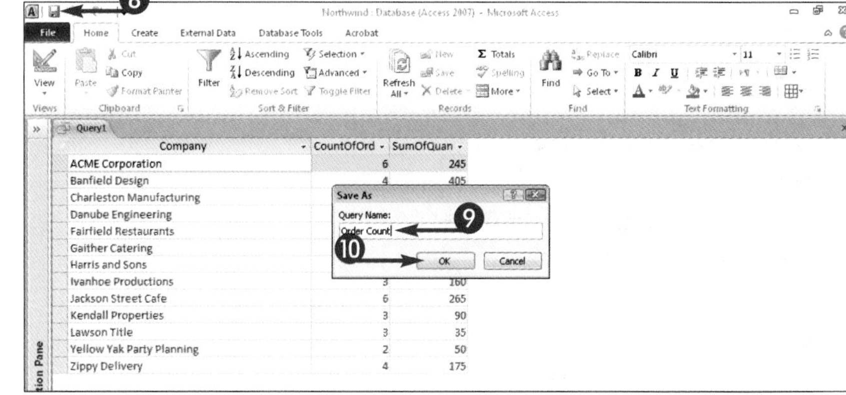

How can I rename the column headings?

Use an alias, as you learned to do in Chapter 7. In Query Design view, type an alias and a colon in front of the field name in the Field row.

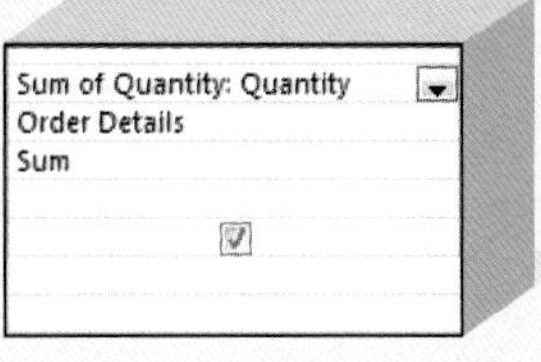

Can I sort and use filter criteria in a summary query?

Yes. A summary query is just like a detail query in most respects. You can even include a field in the query that does not appear in the query results just for filtering.

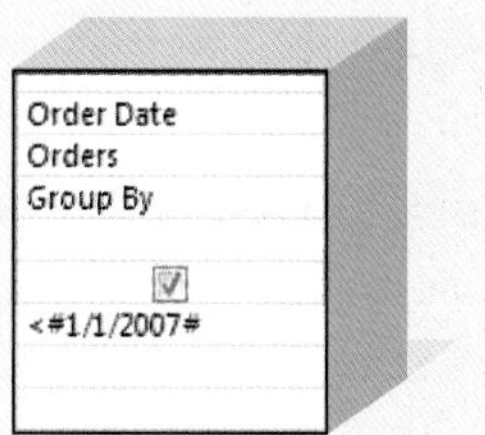

Understanding Calculated Fields

You can use queries to generate new columns on the fly that calculate values based on the contents of other fields. For example, you could create a Cost column in the query that multiplies Quantity by Unit Price.

Assign a Column Name

Use the same technique for naming the new column that you did with aliasing in Chapter 7, but do it in a blank column. Type the new name at the beginning of the Field box and then follow it with a colon.

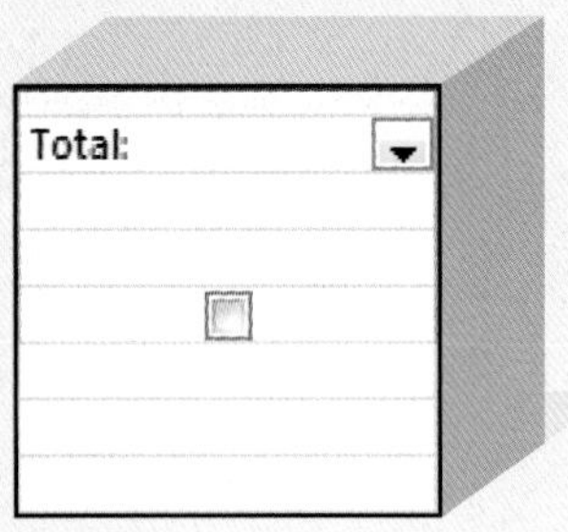

Write the Expression

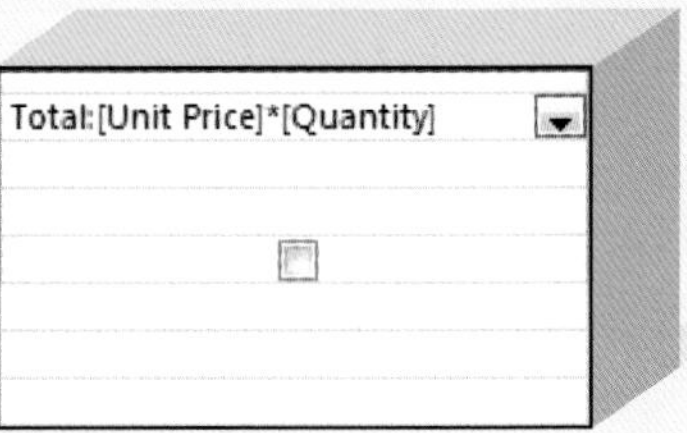

After the colon, write the expression — that is, the math formula — by using standard math operators, with field names enclosed in square brackets. For example, to multiply the Unit Price by the Quantity, type the following:

[Unit Price]*[Quantity]

Here are the math operators that Access recognizes:

Addition	+
Subtraction	–
Multiplication	*
Division	/
Exponentiation	^

Create a Calculated Field

You can use calculated fields to generate information about each record. For example, you can test the effect of increasing prices by 20% by creating a new column that multiplies the existing list price by 1.2.

Create a Calculated Field

Create a Calculated Field

1. In Query Design view in the Field row for a blank column, type a title for the new column, followed by a colon (:).
2. Type the formula to calculate.

***Note:** Remember to enclose field names in square brackets.*

Set a Number Format for the Calculated Field

1. Right-click on the calculated field.
2. Click **Properties**.

The Property Sheet opens.

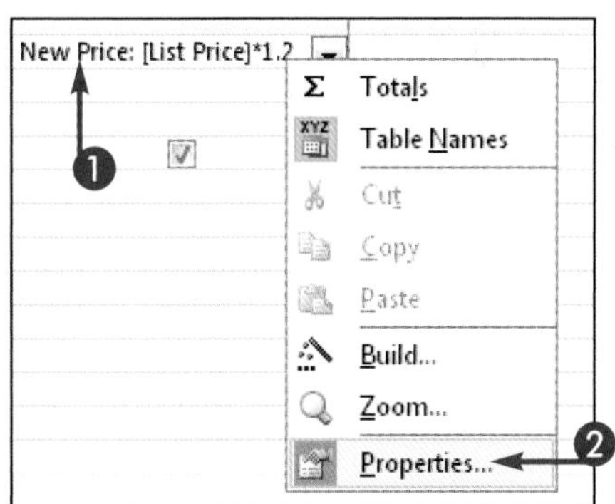

3. Click here (▾) to choose the number format for the calculated field.
4. Click here (☒) to close the Property Sheet.

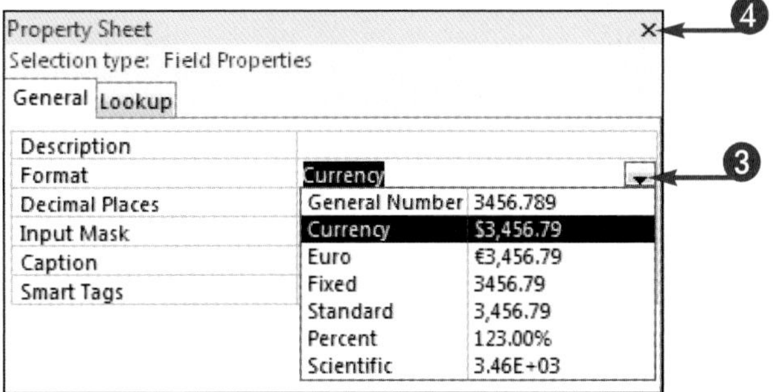

Understanding Action Queries

Action queries modify records based on criteria that you specify. Unlike a select query (the type of query you have worked with so far), an action query makes permanent changes to the table.

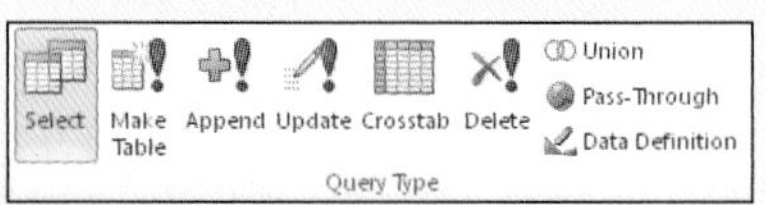

Types of Action Queries

In Query Design view, the Query Type group has buttons for the various types of queries. Here are the action queries that are available:

Make Table: This creates a new table; it is a way of copying records from an existing table to a new one.

Append: This adds records to the end of an existing table. This is a way of copying records from an existing table to another existing table.

Update: This changes values across the entire table based on criteria that you specify. For example, you can increase prices by a certain percentage.

Delete: This deletes records from the table based on criteria that you specify.

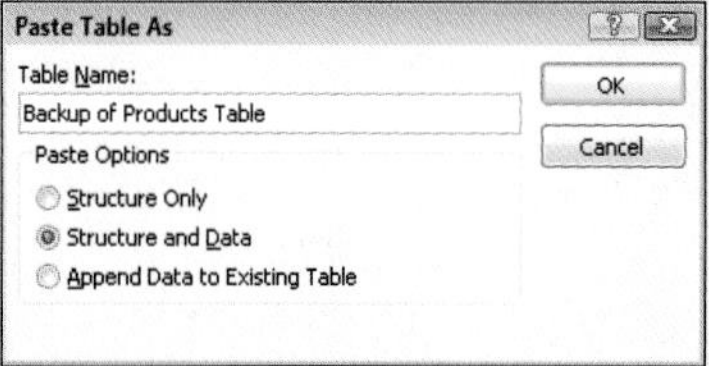

Be Careful!

Because action queries make permanent changes to tables, you should back up a table before running an action query on it. One way is to copy the table by selecting the table in the Objects list, pressing Ctrl + C, and then paste it by pressing Ctrl + V. In the Paste Table As dialog box, specify a name for the copy, and make sure that Structure and Data is selected as the Paste option.

To avoid accidentally re-running an action query later, either delete it from the Objects list when you are finished with it or hide it there by right-clicking on it and then choosing **Hide in This Group**.

To unhide hidden objects, right-click on the bar at the top of the navigation pane and choose Navigation Options. In the Navigation Options dialog box, click **Show Hidden Objects** and then click **OK**.

Run a Make Table Query

A Make Table query creates a new table. You can use this query to archive old records, for example, or to split a table into two separate tables based on the status of a certain field. After making the new table, you could then run a Delete query to remove the records from the original location.

Run a Make Table Query

1. Create the query as you would any other query in Query Design view.

Note: Make sure you include all the fields that the new table should contain. Also, make sure your criteria capture the needed records.

- To include all the fields for a table, drag * from the field list to the grid.
- To act only upon certain records, enter criteria.

2. To check your work before running the query, click **View**.

   Click **View** again to return to Query Design view.

3. On the Design tab, click **Make Table**.

   The Make Table dialog box opens.

4. Type a name for the new table.

Note: You can optionally choose to save the new table in another database.

5. Click **OK**.
6. Click **Run**.

   Access creates the new table.

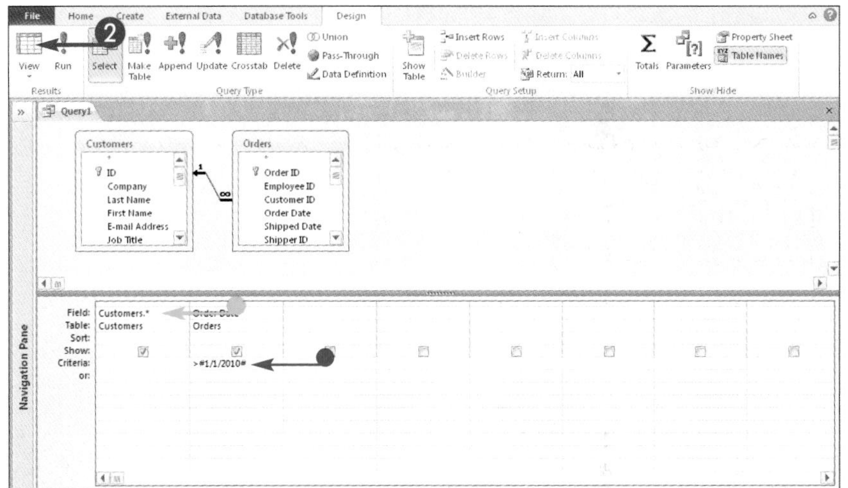

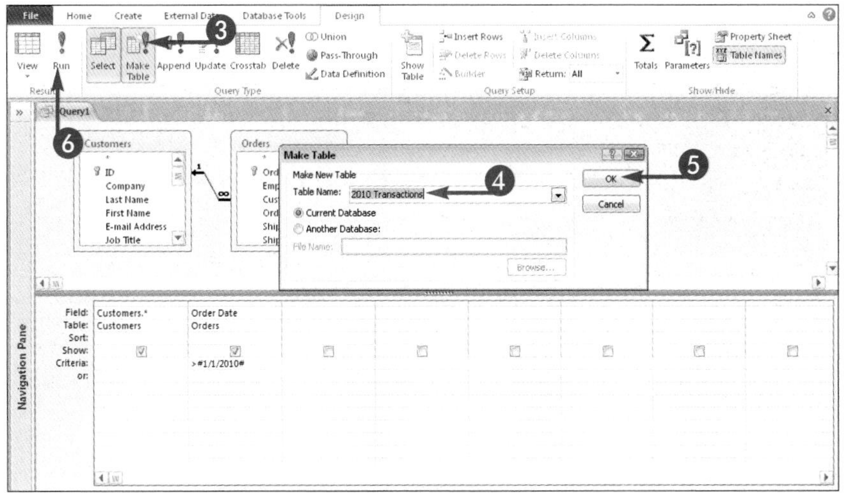

Run a Delete Query

A Delete query removes records that match the criteria you specify.

Delete queries are useful whenever you need to purge a table of a certain type of record. For example, you can use a Delete query to remove products from a supplier that has gone out of business.

Run a Delete Query

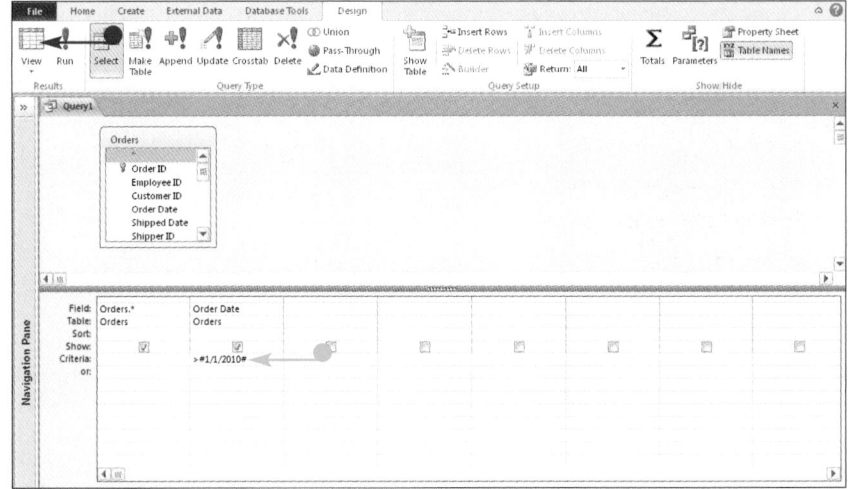

1. Create the query as you would any other query in Query Design view.

- Include criteria that identify the records to be deleted.

Note: *This query will act on entire records, regardless of the fields you include. Therefore, you need to include only fields by which you want to set up criteria.*

- To check your work before running the query, click **View**. Click **View** again to return to Query Design view.

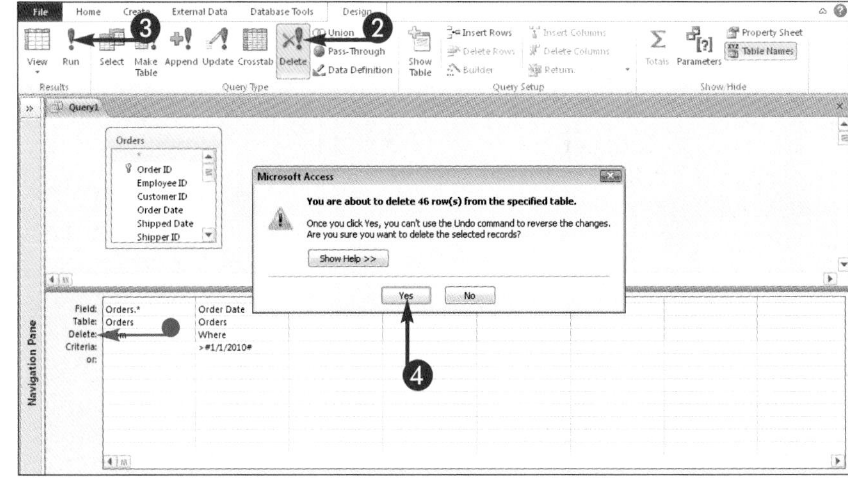

2. On the Design tab, click **Delete**.

- The rows in the grid change. The Sort and Show rows disappear, and a Delete row appears.

3. Click **Run**.

   A warning dialog box opens.

4. Click **Yes**.

   The records are deleted.

Run an Append Query

You can use an Append query to copy records from one table to another table. Appending records does not remove them from the original source.

The receiving table must have the same fields as the original table. You can use the Make Table query to create a new table with the same structure or you can copy the table and include only the structure in the copy, as shown in Chapter 3.

Run an Append Query

1. Create the query as you would any other query.

- Include criteria that identify the records to be appended to another table. All fields for the records will be appended.
- You need to specify only the field(s) containing the criteria. Including all fields makes it easier to check your work.

2. To check your work before running the query, click **View**. Click **View** again to return to Query Design view.
3. On the Design tab, click **Append**.

   The Append dialog box opens.

4. Click here to type the table name to which you want to append.

- Click here (▾) to choose from a list of tables in the current database.

5. Click **OK**.

   The dialog box closes.

6. Click **Run**.

   A warning dialog box opens.

7. Click **Yes**.

   The records are appended.

***Note:** The records are not appended where it would violate data integrity rules, such as duplicate records not being allowed for a certain field.*

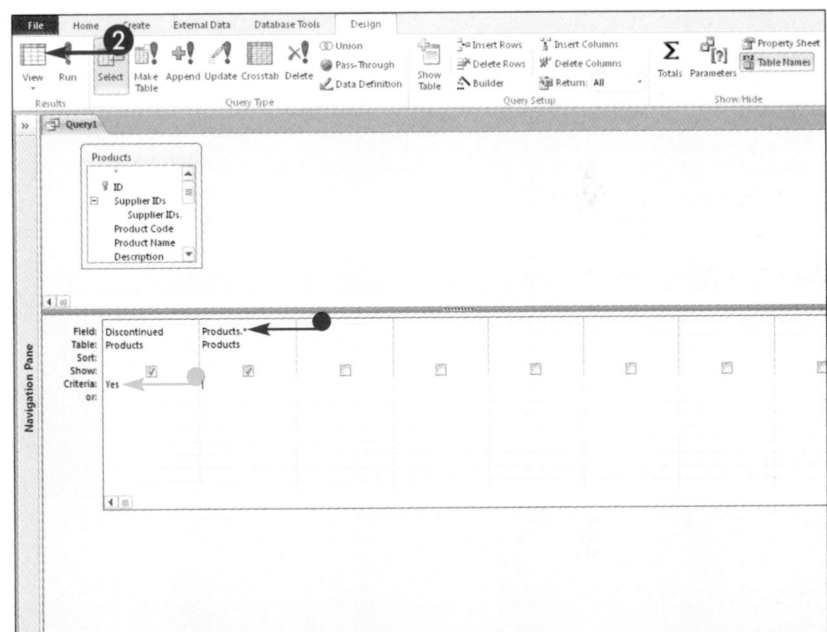

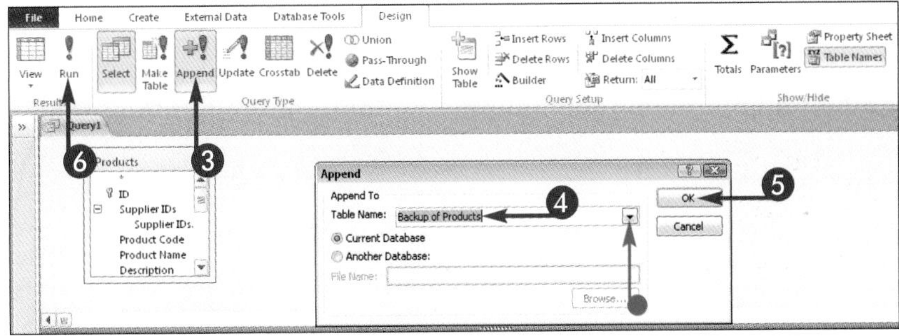

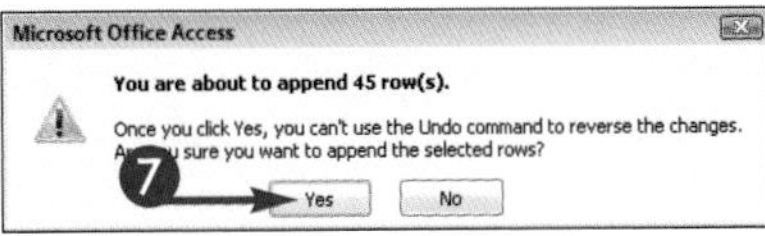

Run an Update Query

An Update query does not add or remove records from the table. Instead, it changes the value in a particular field for all records across the board. For example, you can use an update query to increase or decrease the prices of products by a fixed amount by using addition or by a percentage by using multiplication.

Run an Update Query

1 In Query Design view, click **Update**.

- An Update To row appears in the grid.

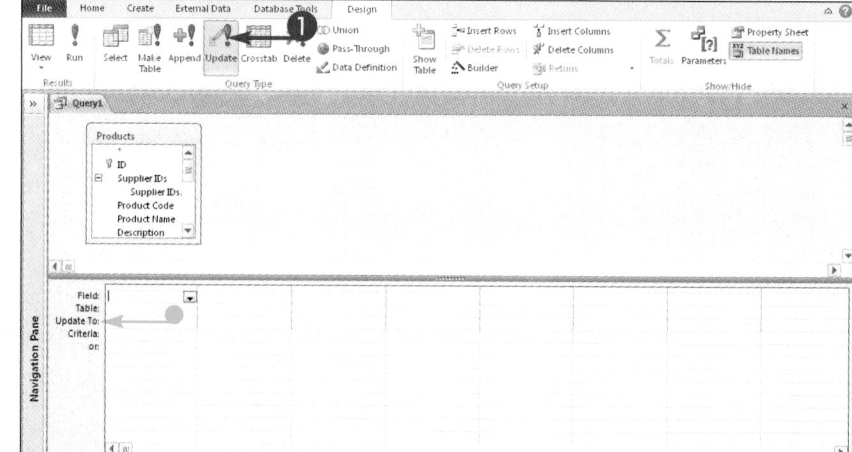

2 Double-click the field you want to update.

- The field is placed into the grid.

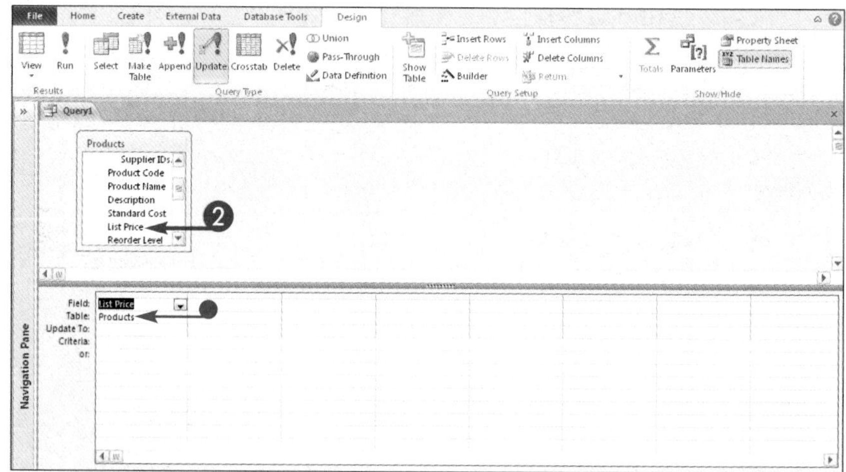

3 In the Update To row, type the formula to use for the update.

A 10% increase in the list price is shown here.

4 Click **Run**.

A warning dialog box opens.

5 Click **Yes**.

The query runs and updates the values.

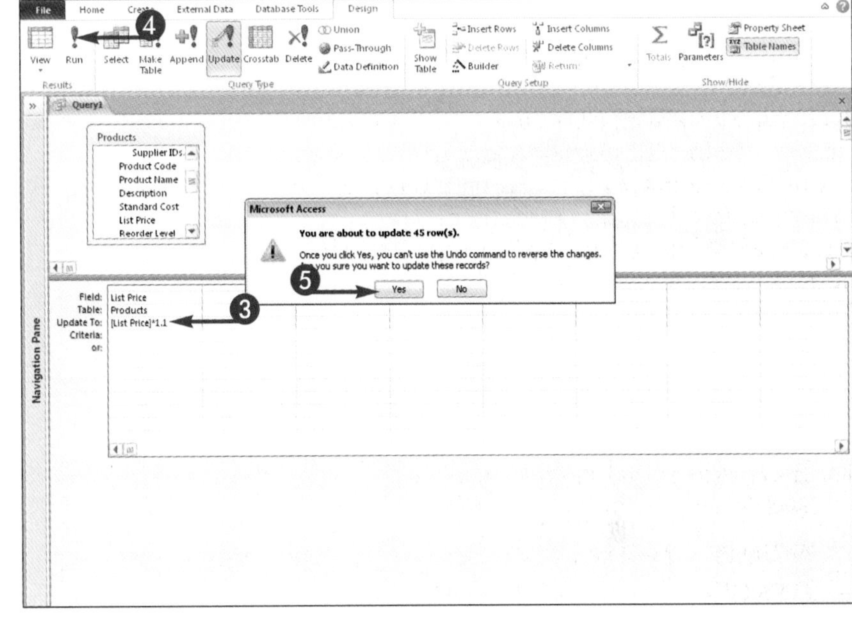

What is the correct syntax for an Update To formula?

Enclose field names in square brackets and use standard math operators:

- **+** (addition)
- **–** (subtraction)
- ***** (multiplication)
- **/** (division)
- **^** (exponentiation)

Do not use any currency symbols, and express numbers as plain digits.

What are some examples of formulas?

Some examples include the following:

- To increase Price by $2: **[Price]+2**
- To decrease Price by 5%: **[Price]*0.95**
- To decrease Price by one-third: **[Price]*0.67**
- To multiply Price by itself: **[Price]*[Price]** or **[Price]^2**

Prompt the User for a Parameter

Instead of creating many similar queries, you can create one query that prompts the user for a value to use as a variable. For example, if you use the same query to look up addresses in different states, you can create a parameter that asks for the state each time the query is run.

Prompt the User for a Parameter

Create the Prompt

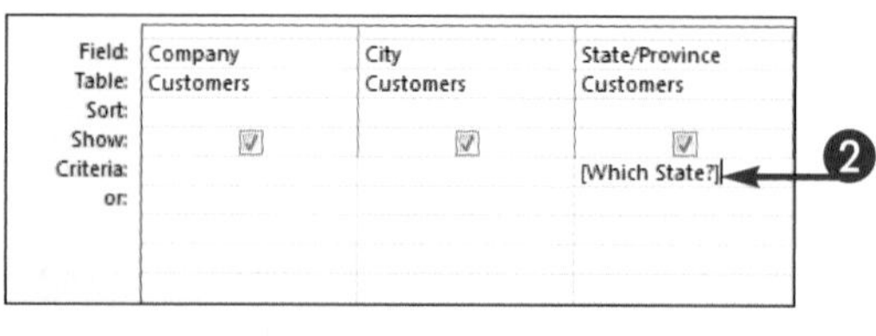

1. Create the query as you normally would in Query Design view.
2. In the Criteria row, type the prompt message in square brackets.

***Note:** You can be brief, as shown here, or you can provide much more direction than that. For example, you could clarify the instruction by adding **[Please type the two-character state abbreviation:]**.*

Test the Parameter

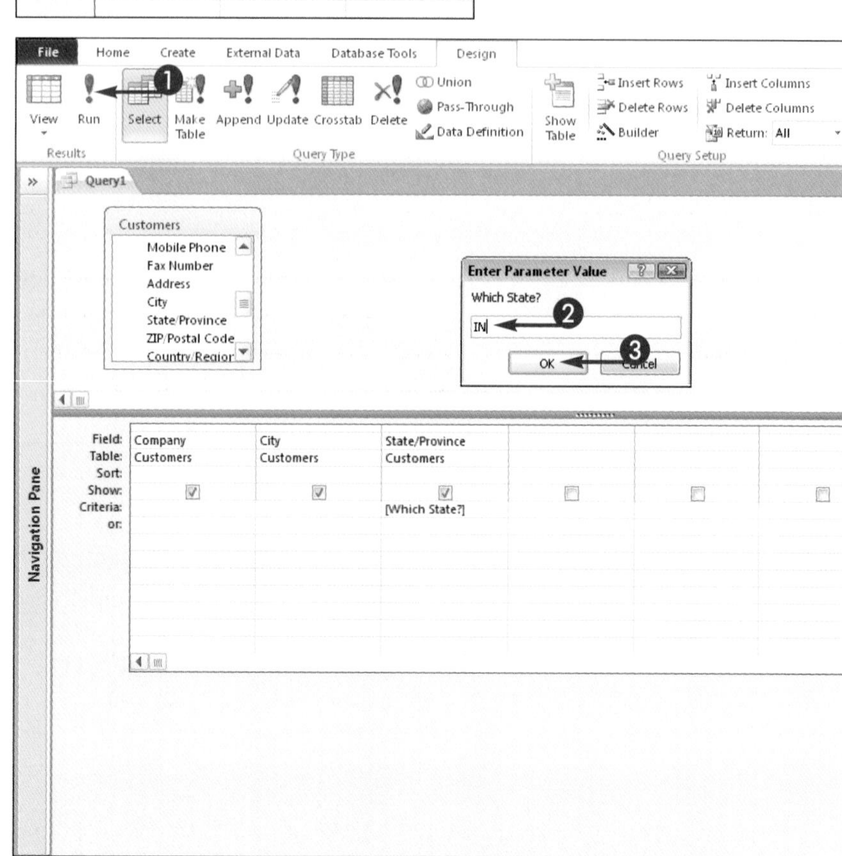

1. Click **Run**.

__Note:__ Because this is a select query, there is no difference between Run and View. You can use either one.

The prompt for the parameter appears.

2. Type the variable in the text box.
3. Click **OK**.

The datasheet opens with just the records that match the variable.

***Note:** If you want to re-run the prompt from Datasheet view without returning to Design view, press Shift + F9.*

Understanding Parameter Syntax

One of the difficulties in creating a parameter prompt is making it easy for users to enter the values that they want without generating an error or unwanted results. To help with this, you can modify the basic prompt and combine it with other criteria to permit a variety of responses.

Here are some examples that use the state prompt from the preceding section as their basis:

Entry in Criteria	*Permissible Responses*
[Which State?]	Entire state abbreviation
Like [Which State?]	Entire state abbreviation
	OR
	Any portion of field contents with a wildcard. For example, use **C*** to see CA, CO, and CT or ***A** to see CA, IA, PA, and WA.
Like [Which State?] or Is Null	Entire state abbreviation
	OR
	Any portion of field contents with a wildcard
	OR
	Press Enter or click **OK** without entering anything to display all records.
Like [Which State?] & "*"	Entire state abbreviation
	OR
	Any portion of field contents with a wildcard, where the wildcard applies to the value in any position. For example, ***A** displays all values with A anywhere in their name.
	OR
	Press Enter or click **OK** without entering anything to display all records.

Creating Forms

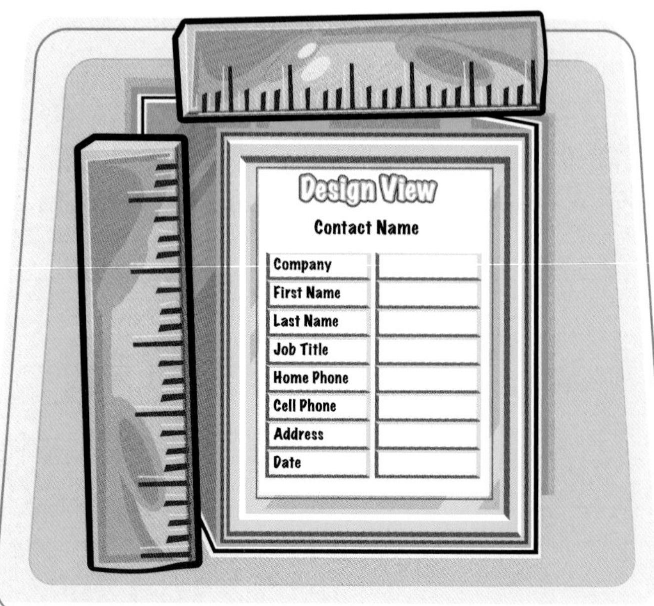

Forms provide an easy-to-use interface for data entry and editing. Forms are especially helpful for databases that will have less-experienced users assisting you because on-screen forms can mimic familiar paper forms. In this chapter, you learn how to create forms, group and arrange fields on them, and define their tab order.

Understanding Forms

A form is a view of one or more tables that is designed to be used for data entry and editing. By creating forms, you can make your database more user-friendly for inexperienced users who need to enter and edit records in it.

One Record at a Time
The default form shows the fields as fill-in boxes for one record at a time. This makes it easier for users to enter a new record without becoming confused by the multiple rows and columns of a datasheet.

Object Display
In Datasheet view, imported objects such as graphics appear as text names, but on a form, depending on the data type, Access might be able to display them as they actually appear. For example, pictures of employees can be displayed with each employee record.

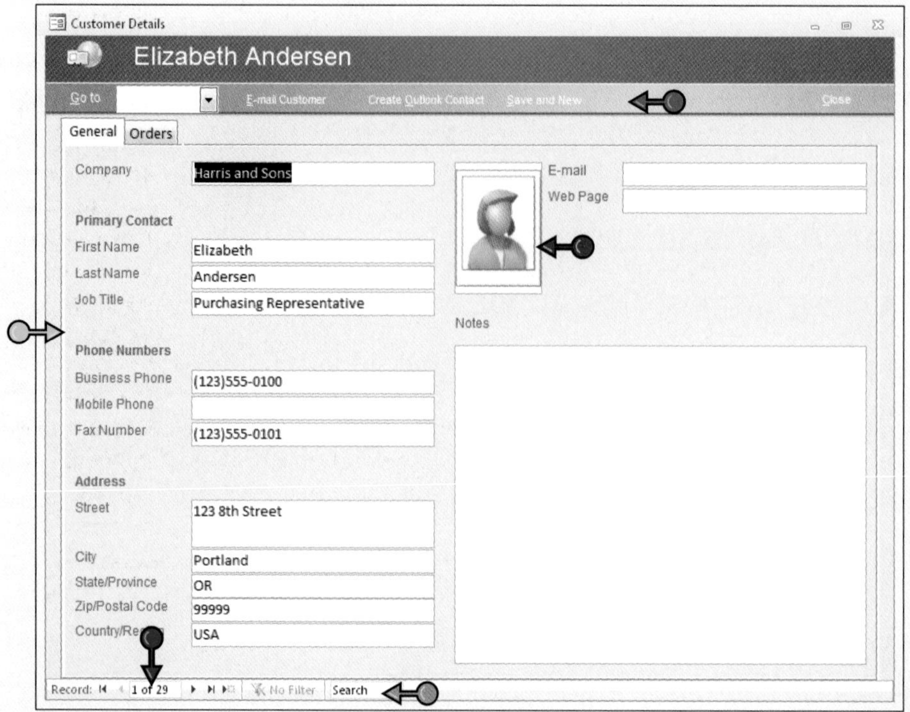

Form Header
A form can have a running header that appears the same no matter which record is displayed. You can put anything you want in this header. In this example, hyperlinks to other forms appear, making it easy for the user to navigate between forms.

Search
To search for a particular record, a user can type a word or phrase in the Search box and then press Enter. The records are filtered so that only records that contain the word or phrase appear when the user scrolls through them with the record navigation controls. Click **No Filter** to remove the filter.

Record Navigation
To move between records, users can use the Record Navigation buttons. These are the same as in a datasheet, but they are more useful here because you cannot see other records without them.

Tabbed or Pop-Up Forms
A form can appear on a tab, as shown here, or as a pop-up window, as shown on the preceding page. This is controlled by the pop-up setting in the form's properties.

Multitabbed Forms
A form can consist of multiple tabbed pages, with different form controls on each tab.

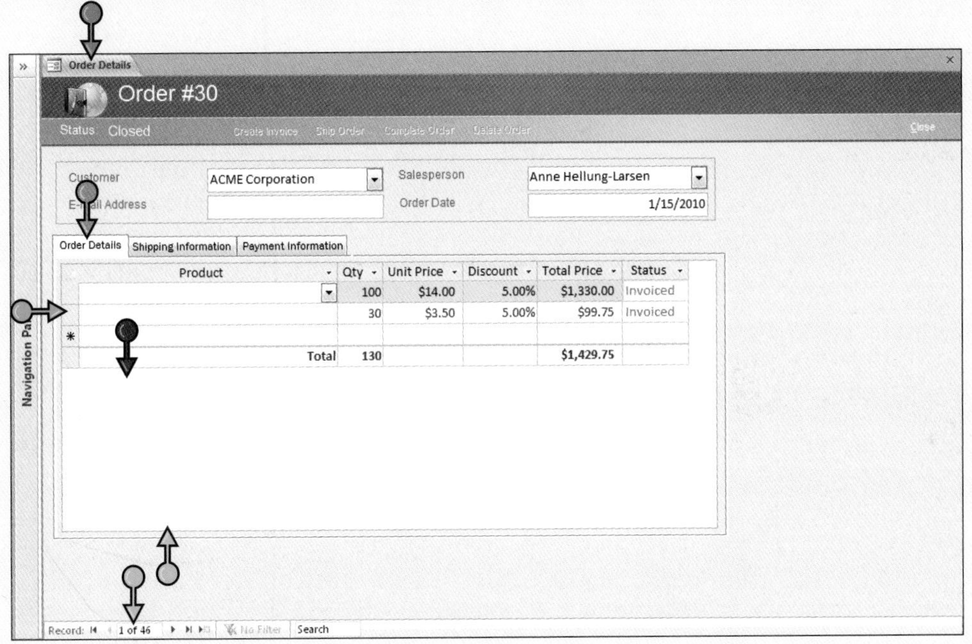

Datasheet-Style Forms
There are several design styles for forms besides the standard one shown on the preceding page. For example, a form can resemble a datasheet and can show multiple records at once.

Subforms
A subform shows the records from a different table or query that are related to the main record shown. For example, the orders for a particular customer are being pulled from the Orders table depending on which customer is chosen in the main form.

Navigation Buttons
This subform does not have navigation buttons at the bottom. That's because having two sets of buttons (one for the main form and one for the subform) would be confusing. Navigation buttons are turned off with the Navigation Buttons property for the subform.

Create and Save a Form

Access 2010 makes it very easy to create several simple types of forms based on a table or query. Just one click will do it.

You can create three types of forms this way: a plain form; a split form, showing both the datasheet and the form at once; and a multiple-item form, showing multiple records.

Create and Save a Form

Create a Basic Form

1. In the Objects list, click the table or query you want to use.
2. On the Create tab, click **Form**.

   The form appears.

- A subform appears, showing a related table, if any useable relationships exist.

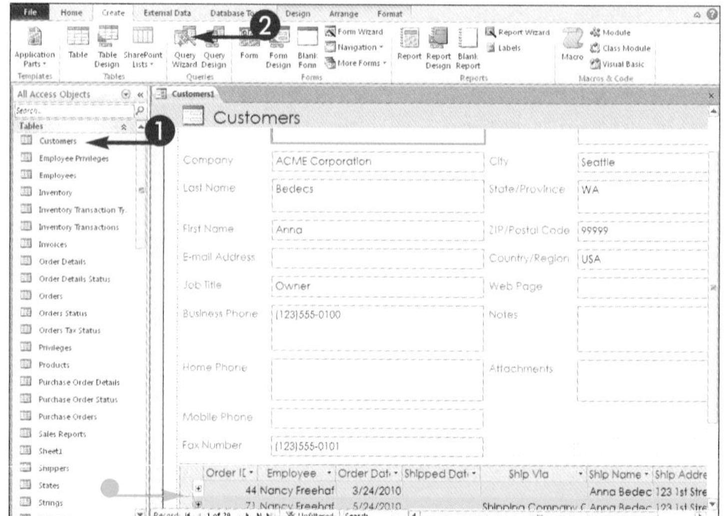

Create a Split Form

1. In the Objects pane, click the table or query you want to use.
2. On the Create tab, click **More Forms**.
3. Click **Split Form**.

- The form appears in the upper part of the screen.
- The datasheet for the table or query appears in the lower part of the screen.

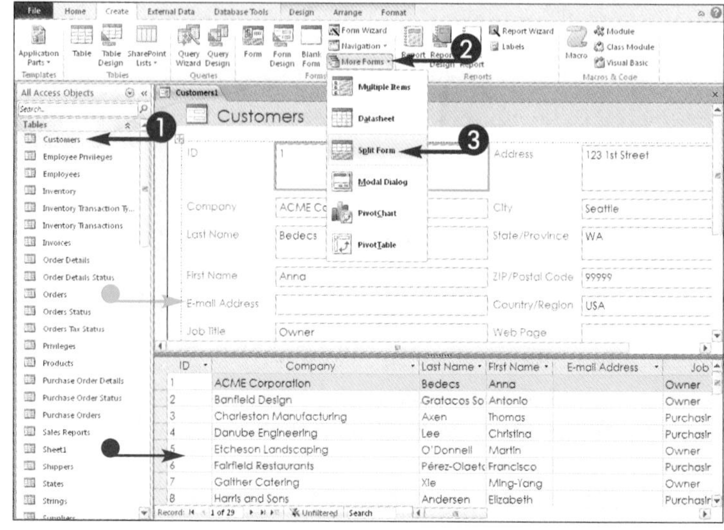

Create a Multiple-Item Form

1. In the Objects pane, click the table or query you want to use.
2. On the Create tab, click **More Forms**.
3. Click **Multiple Items**.

   A form appears with multiple records visible at the same time.

Save a Form

1. Click the **Save** button (💾).

   The Save As dialog box opens.

2. Type a name for the form.
3. Click **OK**.

   You can right-click on the form tab and then choose **Close** from the shortcut menu to close the form.

What other form types can I create?

From the More Forms button, you can create the following:

- **Datasheet:** This looks just like a regular datasheet, but it is actually a form. This is useful when you want to show a datasheet on a subform, for example.
- **Modal Dialog:** This looks just like a dialog box, but it is actually a form. This is useful for creating navigational menu systems.
- **PivotChart:** This is a graphical type of PivotTable, in which you can experiment with different charts that summarize the data. PivotCharts are covered in Chapter 14.
- **PivotTable:** This is a configurable PivotTable view of the data. You learn more about PivotTables in Chapter 12.

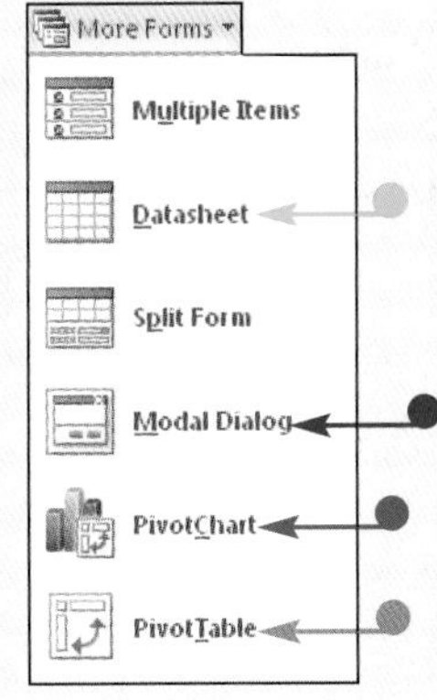

What if I do not want a subform on a form created with the Form button?

You can easily delete it. Select the subform so a thick border appears around it and then press Delete.

Create a Form with the Form Wizard

The Form Wizard enables you to create a form based on more than one table or query, not necessarily using all the available fields from them. With the Form Wizard, you gain some flexibility without having to do all the form design work yourself.

Create a Form with the Form Wizard

1. On the Create tab, click **Form Wizard**.

   The Form Wizard starts.

2. Click here (▾) to open a menu of tables and queries.
3. Click the table or query from which you want to pull fields.

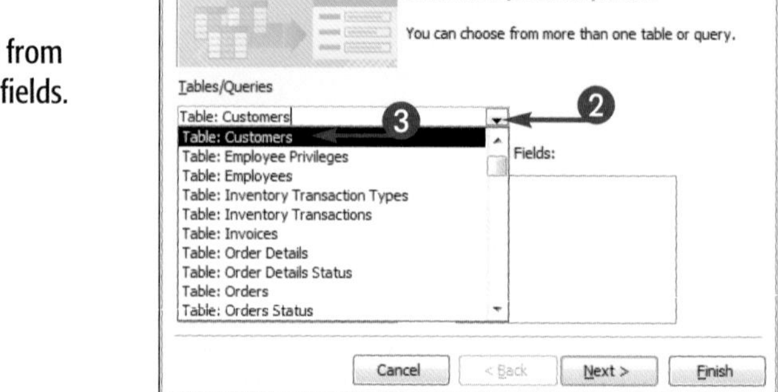

4. Click a field.
5. Click here (>) to move the field to the Selected Fields list.

***Note:** Add fields in the order in which you want them to appear on the form.*

- If you make a mistake, you can remove a field by clicking here (<).

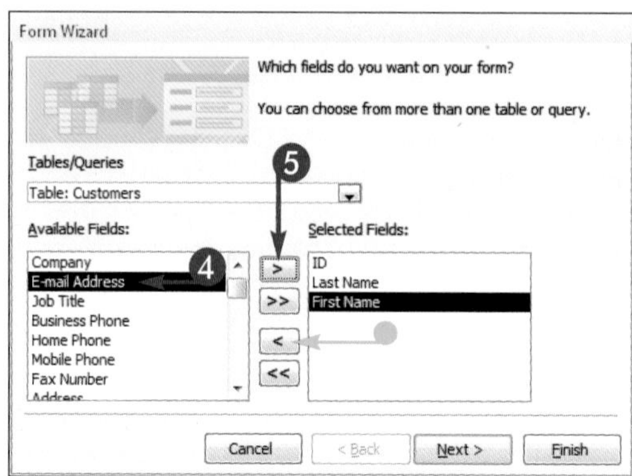

6. Repeat steps **4** and **5** to add more fields from the chosen table or query.

7. Repeat steps **2** to **6** for other tables or queries if needed.

Note: *If you choose fields from more than one table or query, they must be related.*

8. Click **Next**.

   If you chose fields from two different tables or queries, you are asked which one should be the subform.

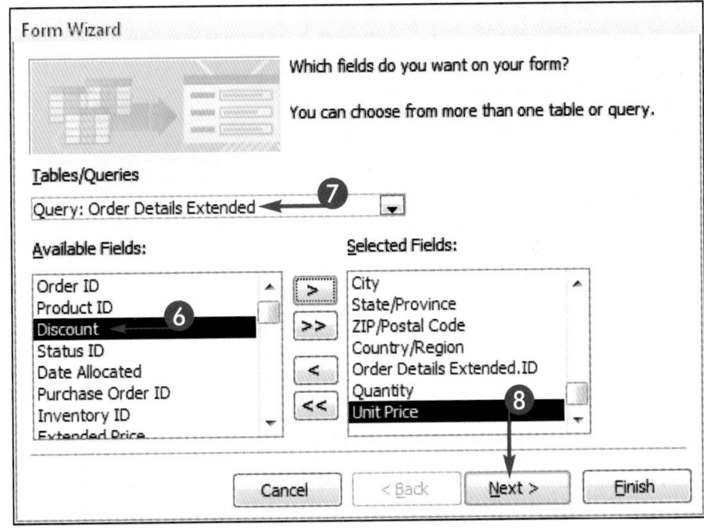

9. Click the option that best represents the layout that you want.

10. If you would rather have a linked form than a subform, click the **Linked forms** radio button (◎ changes to ◉).

11. Click **Next**.

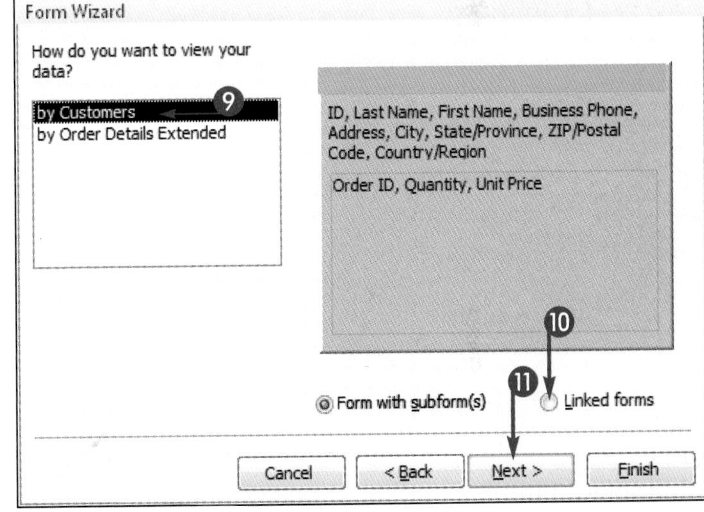

TIPS

Can I use fields from more than two tables or queries?

Yes. But you are not prompted for subform information. Instead, all the fields appear on a single form. It is possible to create subforms within subforms using Form Design view but not using the wizard.

Is it okay to not use all the fields from the table or tables?

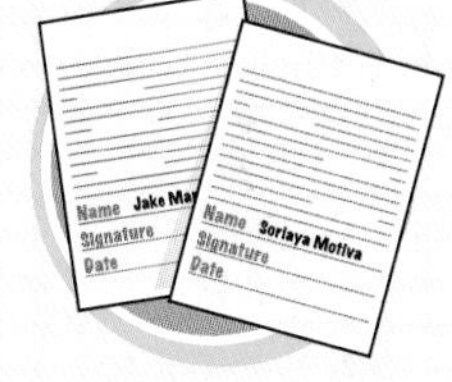

Yes. But keep in mind that users filling out that form will have no way of entering values into the fields that do not appear on the form. With an AutoNumber field, that is not a problem because the user cannot enter data into that field anyway, but any other field will be blank if it is not included on the form.

continued

Create a Form with the Form Wizard *(continued)*

The Form Wizard is useful not only for selecting the exact fields to include but also for choosing a format and appearance for the form. You can also change the fields and format later in Form Design view, but it is often easier to specify upfront what you want via the wizard.

Create a Form with the Form Wizard *(continued)*

⑫ Click a radio button for the layout you want for the form (◎ changes to ◉).

Note: *If you are creating a form with a subform, this screen asks you to choose the layout for the subform rather than for the main form. For a form/subform layout, the main form is always Columnar when constructed by the wizard.*

⑬ Click **Next**.

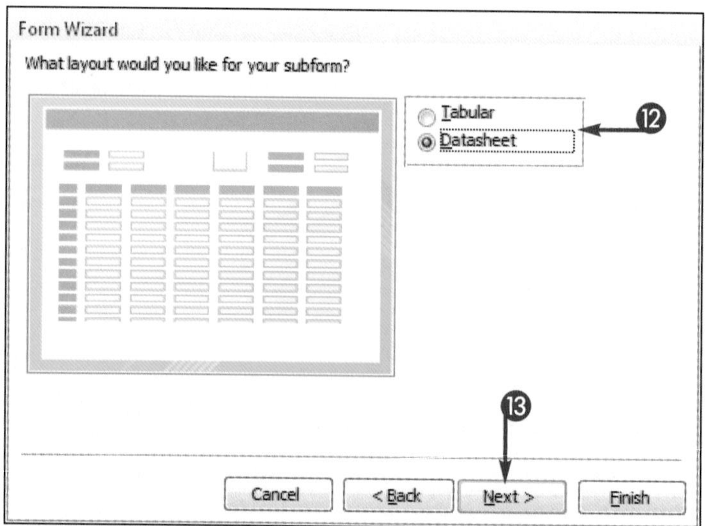

⑭ Type a name for the form, replacing the default name.

⑮ If you created a subform, type a name for the subform, replacing the default name.

⑯ Click **Finish**.

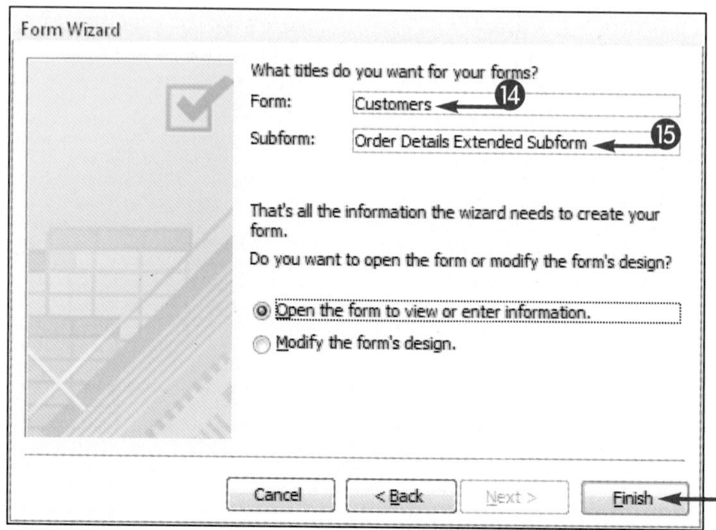

The form appears in Form view.

- Some of the labels may appear truncated; you can fix this problem in Form Design view.

Note: *See the section "Arrange Fields on a Form" for more on fixing truncated fields.*

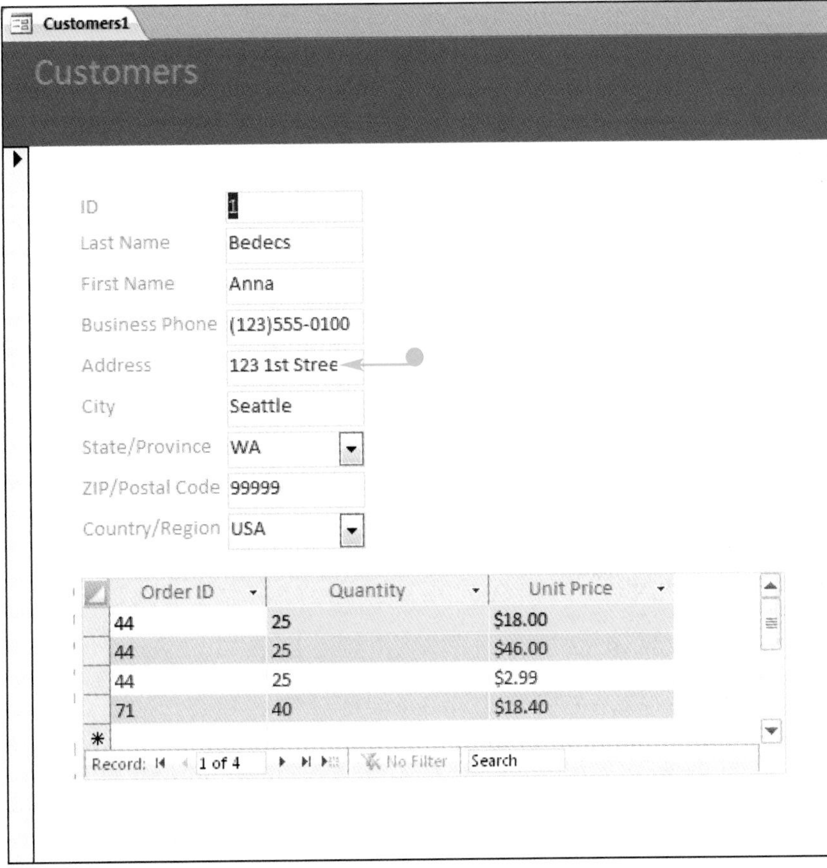

TIPS

Do I need to save the form before I close it?

No. When you specify a name in step **14** and optionally in step **15**, you are supplying the file names to be used. Access automatically saves the form and subform, if applicable, with those names.

I made a mistake; how do I delete the form I just created?

Delete the form as you would any other object:

1. Locate the form in the Objects list.
2. Right-click on the form name.
3. Click **Delete**.
4. In the warning dialog box that appears, click **Yes**.

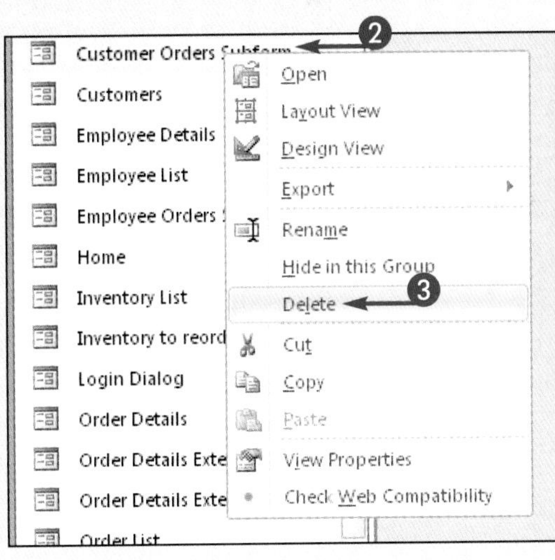

Create a Form in Layout View

Layout view lets you create a form by dragging and dropping fields onto a blank page. It is not as flexible as Form Design view, but it is much easier because you do not have to worry about fields and labels lining up correctly or using consistent spacing.

Create a Form in Layout View

Create the Form

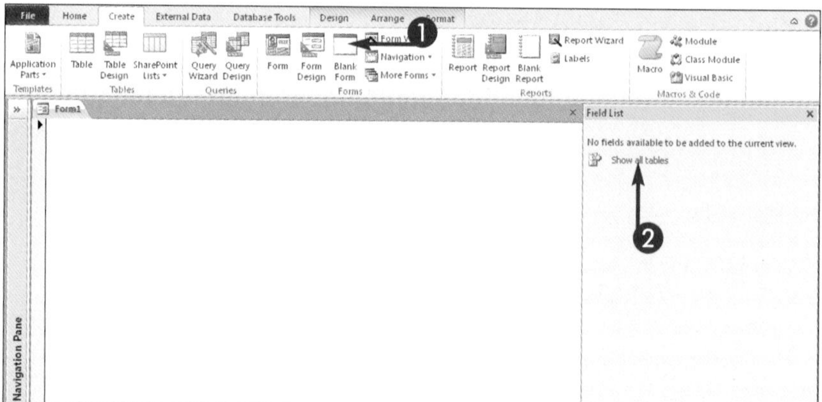

1. On the Create tab, click **Blank Form**.

   A blank form appears, along with a Field List pane.

2. Click **Show all tables**.

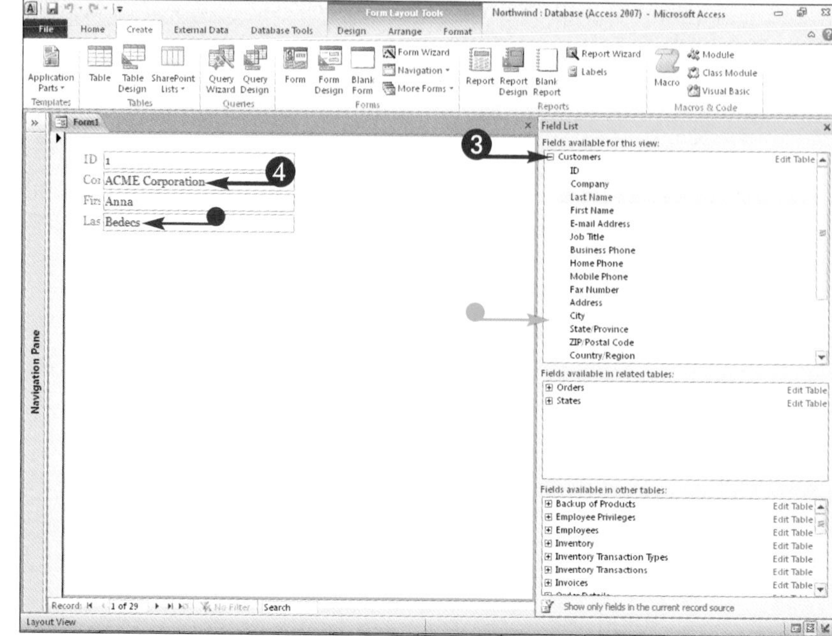

- A list of all the tables appears; each table's field list is collapsed.

3. Click ⊞ next to a table.

   A list of the fields in the table appears (⊞ changes to ⊟).

4. Drag a field from the Field List onto the form.

   You can also double-click a field to add it to the form.

5. Repeat step **3** to add more fields.

- Continue with the following steps if the labels are truncated, as shown here.

Adjust the Spacing between Labels and Fields

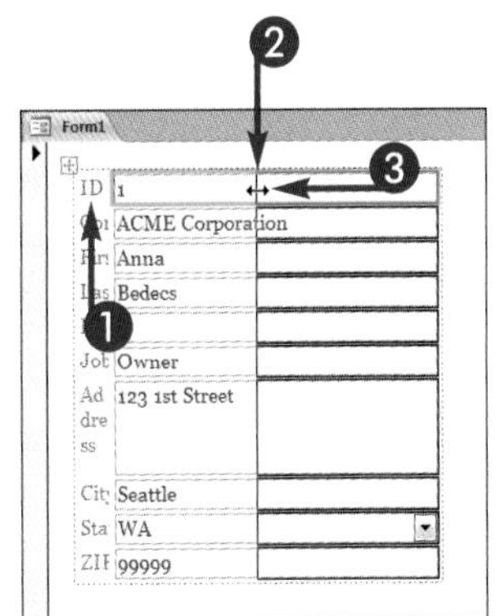

1. Click a label to select it.
2. Position the mouse pointer between the field and its label (↖ changes to ↔).
3. Drag to the left or right to change the spacing.

   The change affects all fields, not just the one that you dragged.

Adjust Label Alignment

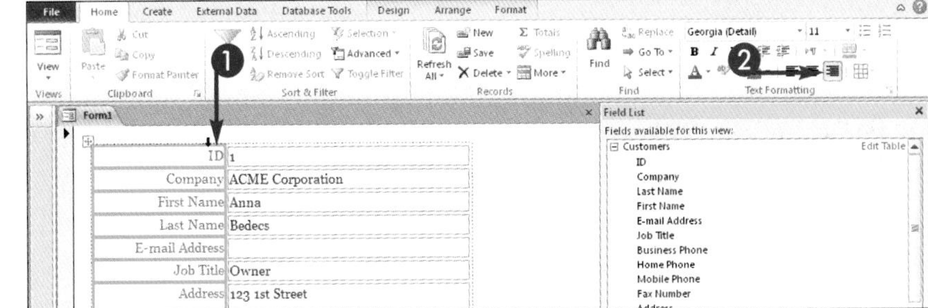

Note: *By default, labels are left-aligned. You can make them right-aligned with the fields if you prefer.*

1. Position the mouse pointer above the top label so that a black arrow appears (↖ changes to ⬇) and then click.

   The entire column is selected.

2. On the Home tab or the Format tab, click the **Align Text Right** button (≣).

   All the labels are right-aligned.

Can I rearrange fields after placing them on the layout?

Yes. Follow these steps:

1. Click the field's label to select it.
2. Press and hold down Shift and then click the field to also select it.
3. Position the mouse pointer over either the field or the label (↖ changes to ✥).
4. Click and drag up or down to move the field and its label.

- A horizontal line shows where the field is being moved.

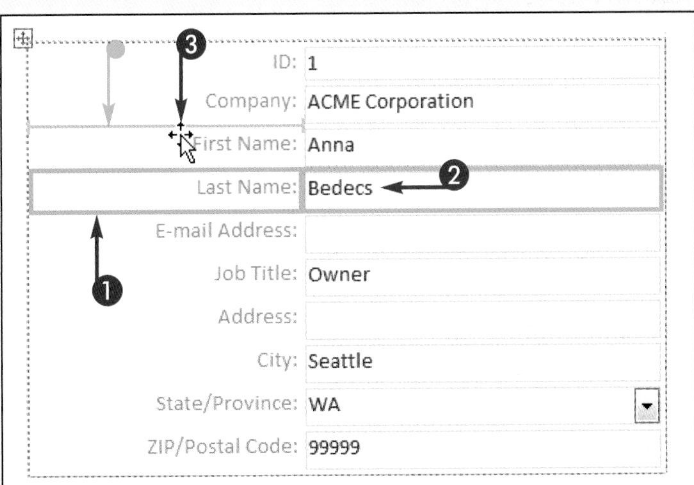

Create a Form in Design View

Design view provides the most flexibility for creating forms, although it can be tedious and time-consuming. You can create a form in Design view that arranges the fields and labels in exactly the way you want them. Fields and labels are not restricted in their placement, as they are in Layout view.

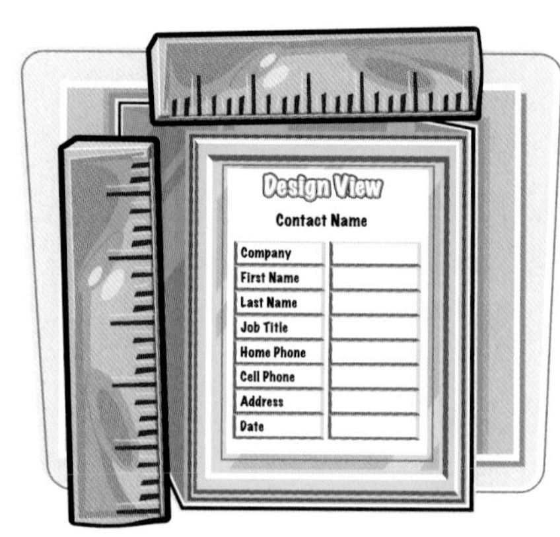

Create a Form in Design View

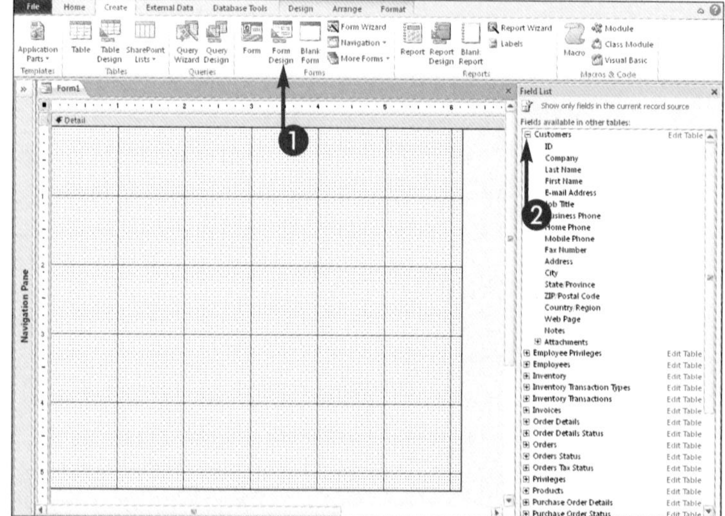

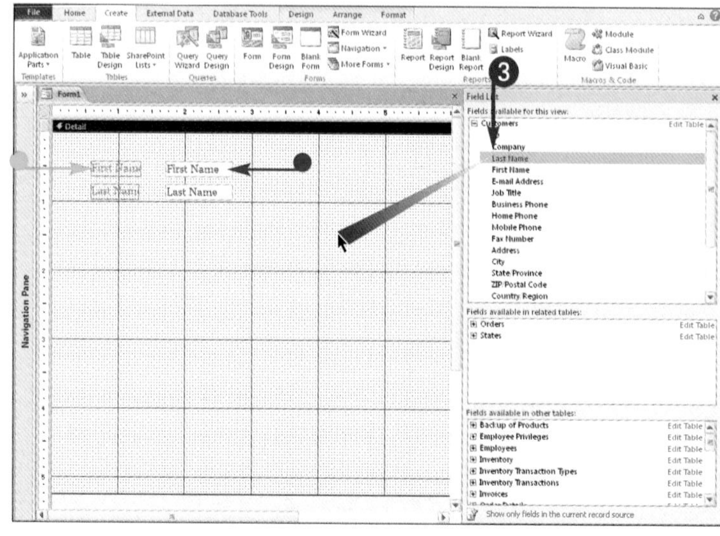

1. On the Create tab, click **Form Design**.

   A new form appears in Form Design view.

   The Field List appears.

Note: *If the Field List does not appear, click* ***Add Existing Fields*** *on the Design tab.*

   If you have previously expanded any table's field list, it still appears expanded.

2. If a table's field list is not expanded, on the Field List, click ⊞ next to the table from which you want to select fields.

   The ⊞ changes to ⊟, and the list of fields appears.

3. Click and drag a field onto the design grid.

   Both the field and an associated label appear.

- This is the field label.
- This is the field.

4. Drag and drop more fields onto the form.

Note: *You can drag more than one field at a time by selecting multiple fields on the Field List before dragging. Hold down* Ctrl *and then click the fields you want.*

Delete a Field from Design View

You can either remove an entire field, including its label, or remove only the label. When you remove the label, this enables the field to remain on the form but without a label. This can be useful, for example, when you want a single label, such as Name, followed by two different fields, such as FirstName and LastName. It can also be useful when fields on the form are obvious and do not need labels to name them, such as Notes or Memo.

Delete a Field from Design View

Delete a Field and Its Label

1. Click the field — not its label — to select it.

   A dark selection box appears around the field.

2. Press Delete.

   Both the field and its label are deleted.

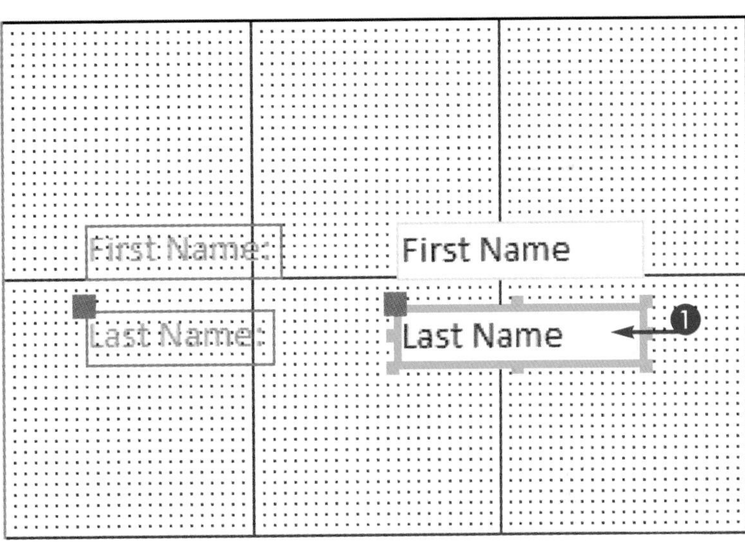

Delete a Field Label

1. Click the field label — not the actual field — to select it.

   A dark selection box appears around the label.

2. Press Delete.

   The label is deleted, but the field remains.

Note: *You cannot delete the field but leave its label. You can, however, place freestanding labels on a form. See Chapter 10 for more.*

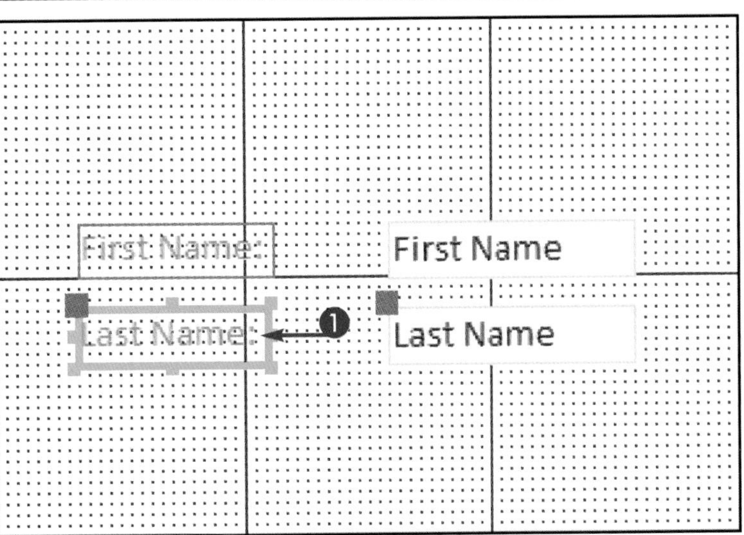

Arrange Fields on a Form

One advantage of working in Form Design view, as opposed to Layout view, is the flexibility it offers in arranging fields. You can freely drag a field around on the grid or make a field align or conform in size with other fields.

Resize a Field or Label Box

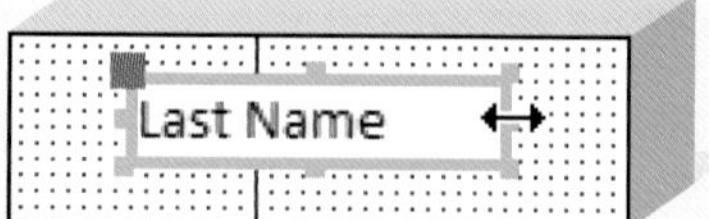

When you hover the mouse over a selection handle on a selected field or label, the mouse pointer (⇖) turns into a two-headed arrow (↔ or ↕). If you click and drag at this point, the field or label box is resized.

Move a Field

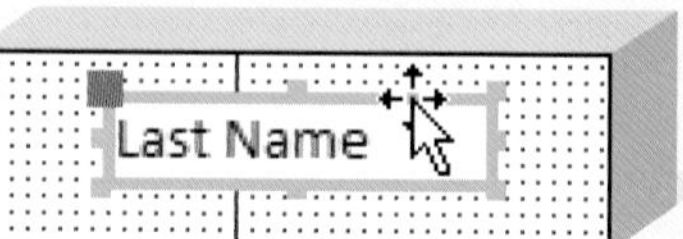

When you move a field, its label travels with it. To move a field, position the mouse pointer over the border of the selected field or label — but *not* over a selection handle — so the mouse pointer turns into a four-headed arrow (⇖ becomes ✥). Then, click and drag the field to its new location.

Move Only the Field or Only the Label

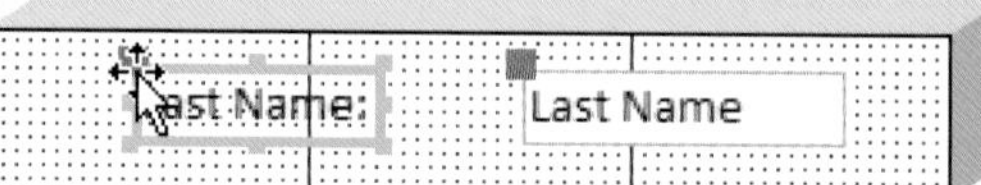

Each field and each field label has a larger selection handle in its upper-left corner. If you drag the box by that selection handle, it moves separately from its associated objects. So, for example, you can move a label independently of its field or vice versa. This can be useful if you want to place the label closer to the field or above the field.

Align Fields and Labels

It is often useful to right-align or left-align a series of fields or field labels. You can select several fields and then click one of these buttons to make the fields align neatly with one another. On the Arrange tab, click **Align** and then choose an alignment from the menu that appears.

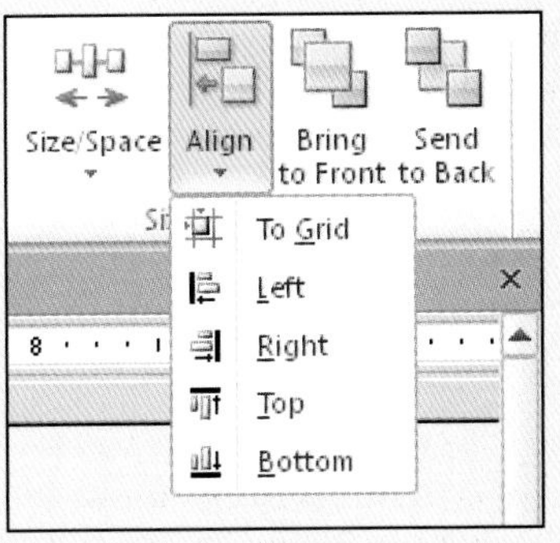

Make Field Sizes Consistent

Sometimes, a form looks best when all the fields are the same size. You can select multiple fields and then use the Size/Space button's menu from the Arrange tab to apply a standard size.

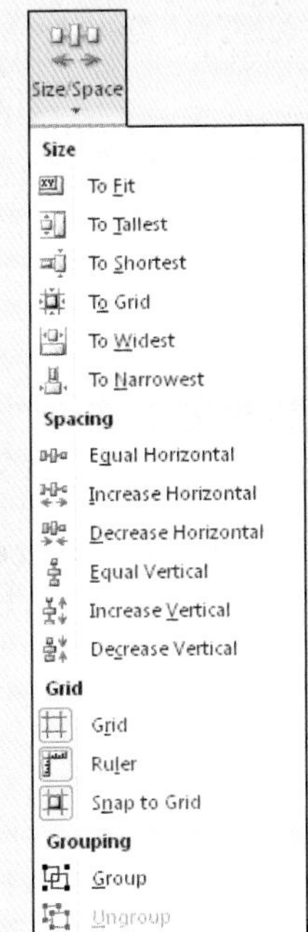

Align Fields in a Grid

You can quickly place fields in a Stacked or Tabular layout by selecting them and then clicking the **Stacked** or **Tabular** button on the Arrange tab. Doing so makes the field and label boxes consistent in size and position.

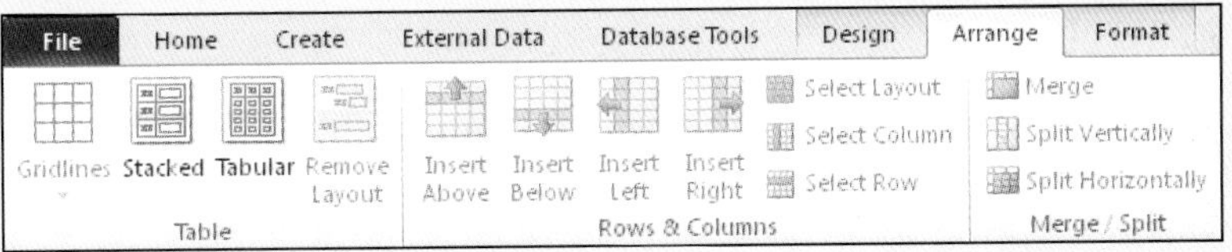

Group Fields Together

When moving fields around, it can be easier to work with a block of fields than to select and move each one individually. You can group several fields together so that any actions you perform on the group are applied to all individual fields within that group.

Group Fields Together

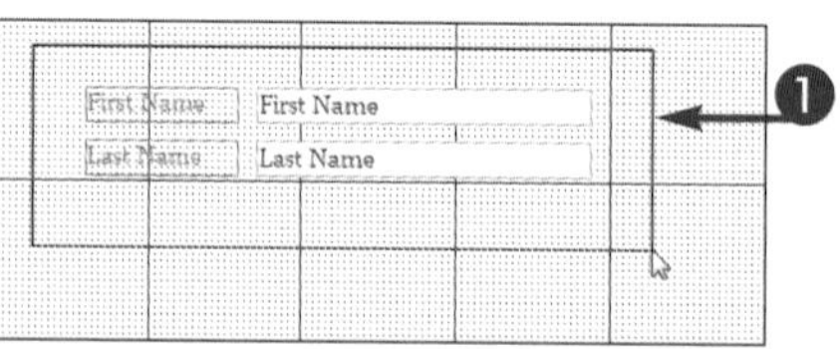

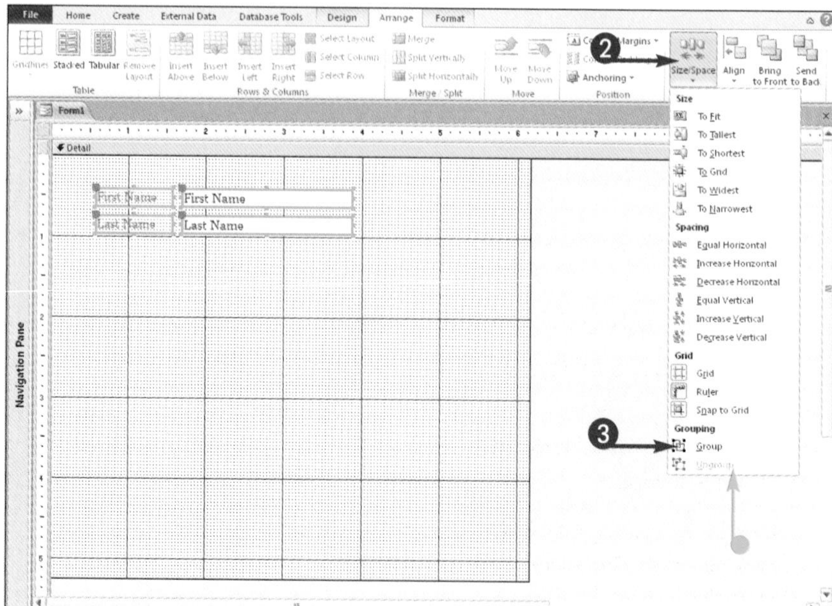

1. In Form Design view, drag a marquee around a group of fields to select them.

***Note:** To create a marquee, click and drag an imaginary box from a spot above and to the left of the fields to a spot below and to the right of the fields. You can also press and hold Shift and then click each field that you want to select.*

2. On the Arrange tab, click **Size/Space**.
3. Click **Group**.

- To ungroup the fields, you can follow steps **1** to **3** and then click **Ungroup**.

***Note:** Grouping works only with fields that are not part of a layout grid (stacked or tabular). If the Group command is unavailable, select the fields and then click **Remove Layout** on the Arrange tab to remove them from the grid.*

Define the Tab Order on a Form

The tab order is the order in which the insertion point moves from one field to another when the user presses Tab. The default tab order is the order in which the fields were added to the form. However, you can change this to any order that you prefer.

Define the Tab Order on a Form

1. On the Design tab, click **Tab Order**.

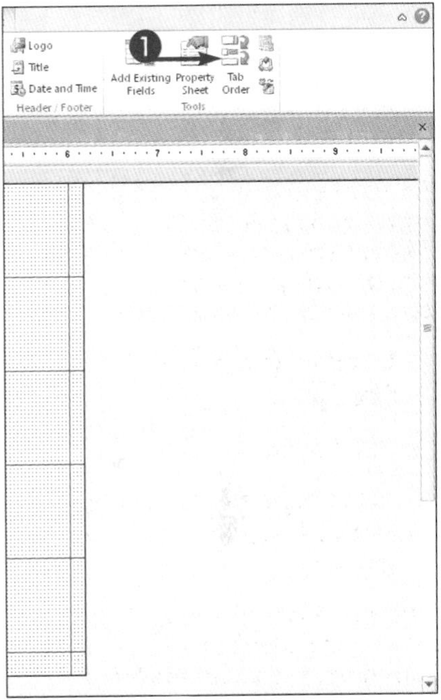

The Tab Order dialog box opens.

2. Click to the left of a field name to select it.
3. Drag the selected field name up or down in the list.

- Alternatively, you can click **Auto Order** to set the tab order based on the positions on the form.

***Note:** Auto Order orders fields from top to bottom. If two fields have the same vertical position, it orders them from left to right.*

4. Click **OK**.

The dialog box closes, and the new tab order goes into effect.

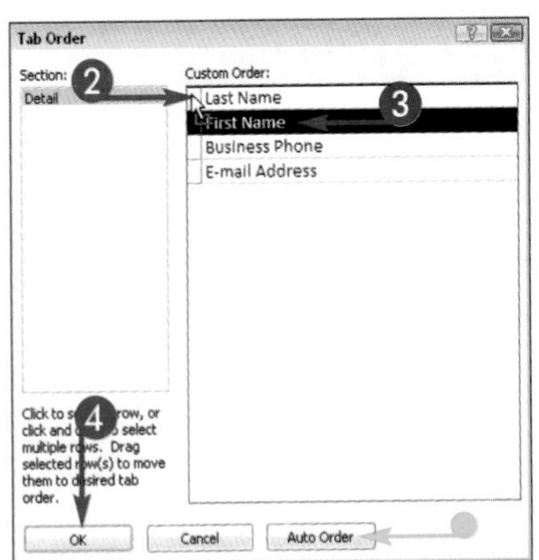

CHAPTER 10

Modifying and Formatting Forms

The basic forms you created in Chapter 9 can be improved by applying formatting and by using special sections, such as headers and footers. In this chapter, you will learn how to use formatting and design features to make forms easier to use and more attractive.

Display the Header and Footer

Each form can optionally have a header and a footer, where you can place information that should be the same, regardless of which record is displayed. This can include a title, buttons that open other forms or hyperlinks, and so on.

There are two header/footer sets: form and page. The form header/footer appears on every form on-screen; the page header/footer applies to each printed page when you print the form.

Display the Header and Footer

1. In Design view, right-click on one of the section bars (such as Detail).
2. Click the desired header/footer: **Form** or **Page**.

***Note:** The commands are toggles; click one again to turn the header/footer display off.*

- The header or headers appear at the top of the form, with their own title bars.
- The footer or footers appear at the bottom.

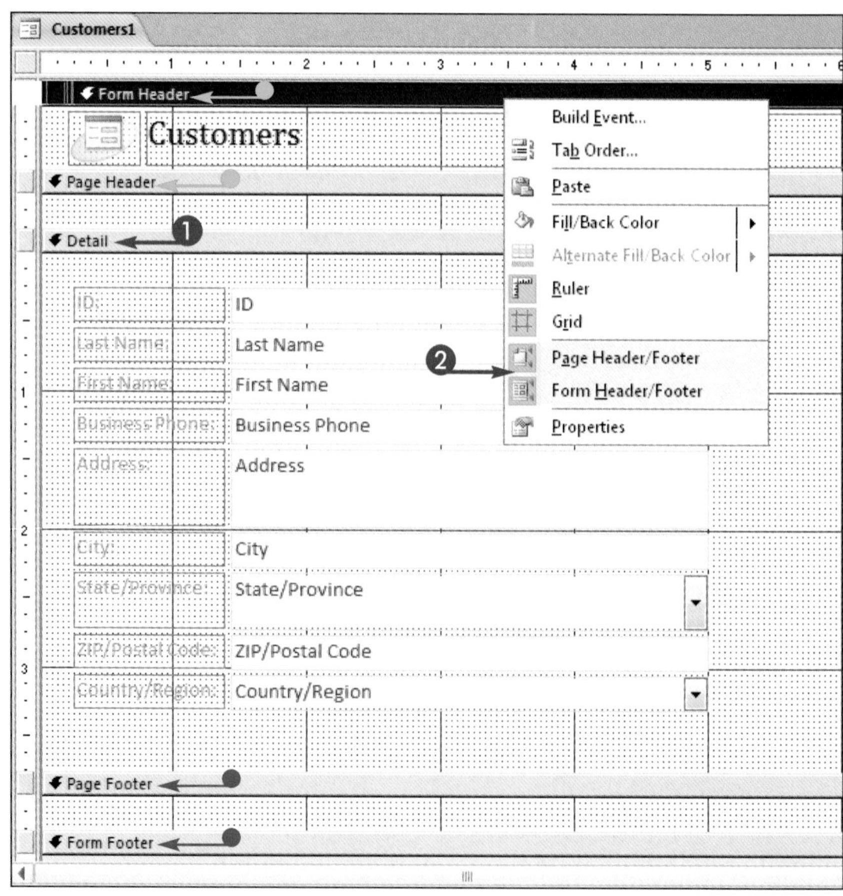

Resize Sections of a Form

Header and footer sections start out small vertically, but you can enlarge them as much as is needed to hold the content that you want to place there. You can also resize the main section of the form — the Detail section — to accommodate the fields there.

It is also sometimes helpful to temporarily enlarge a section so you have more room to work and then tighten the spacing up again when its content is finalized.

Resize Sections of a Form

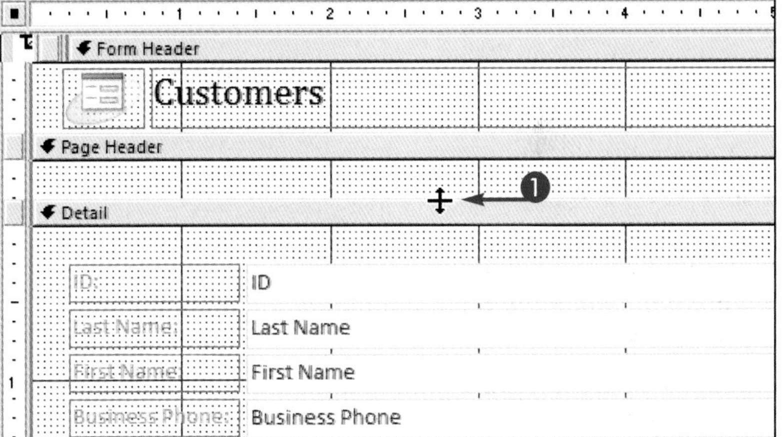

1. In Design view, position the mouse pointer at the bottom edge of a section of the form.

   For example, to enlarge the Page Header section, position the mouse pointer at the top of the section divider below it.

   The mouse pointer (↖) changes to a vertical, double-headed arrow (⇕).

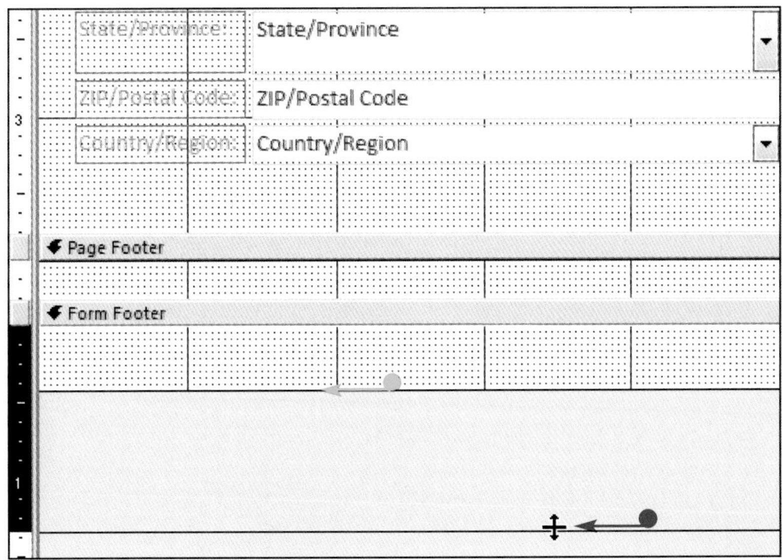

2. Drag up or down to change the height of that section of the form.

- The form footer does not have a divider below it.
- To enlarge the form footer, drag its bottom border down.

Note: *If you want only the header but not the footer, or vice versa, resize the unwanted section so that it takes up no space at all.*

Note: *If you do not want the header and footer at all, turn them off, as described in the section "Display the Header and Footer."*

Select Sections of a Form

After turning on headers and footers, you have a multisection form. Each section can be separately selected and acted on. For example, you can apply themes, which are covered later in this chapter, to individual sections.

To make sure that formatting applies to the correct sections, you must learn how to select a section and how to select an entire form.

Select Sections of a Form

Select an Individual Section

1. In Design view, click the title bar of the section that you want.

   The title bar turns black, indicating that the section beneath it is active.

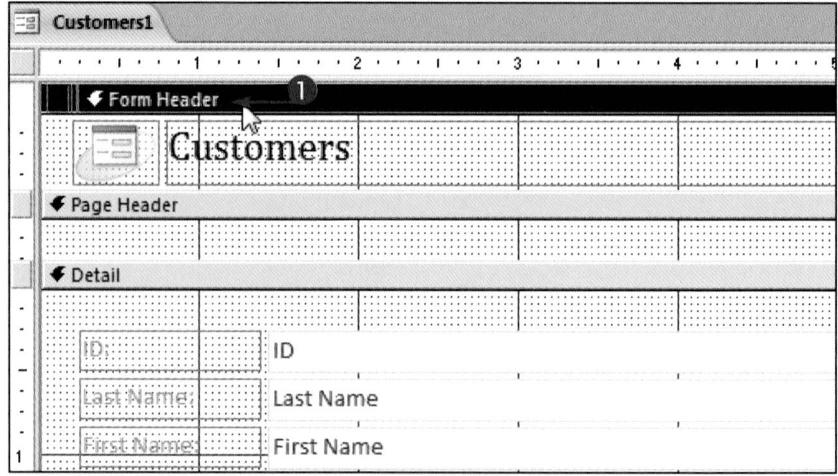

Select an Entire Form

1. In Design view, click the square in the upper-left corner of the form.

   A small black square appears within the square, indicating that the form is selected.

- Any individual section title bars that were previously selected become unselected.

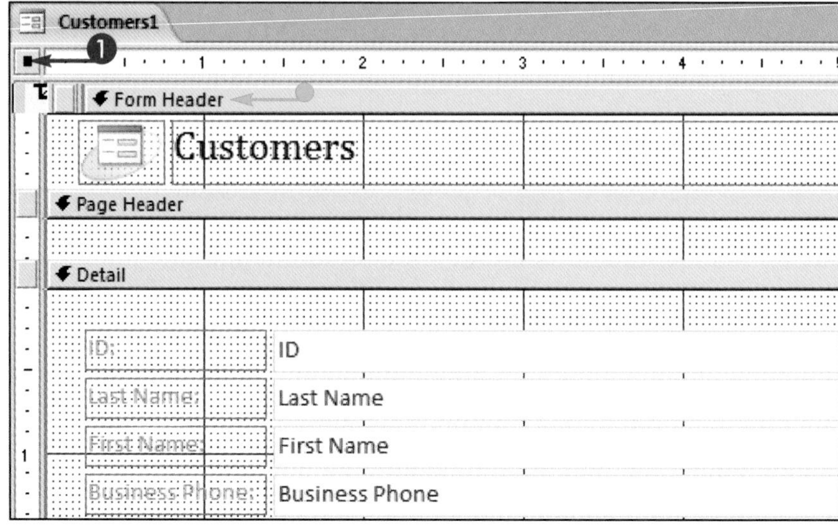

Add a Form Title

A form title appears in the form header and provides a name for the form. If the form header does not already appear when you insert a form title, Access turns on the form header.

You can manually create a form title by adding a label text box to the form header area, but Access makes it easy by providing a button on the Design tab specifically for this purpose.

Add a Form Title

1. In Design or Layout view, on the Design tab, click **Title**.
   - If the form header was not already visible, it now appears, containing a box with dummy text, such as Form1.

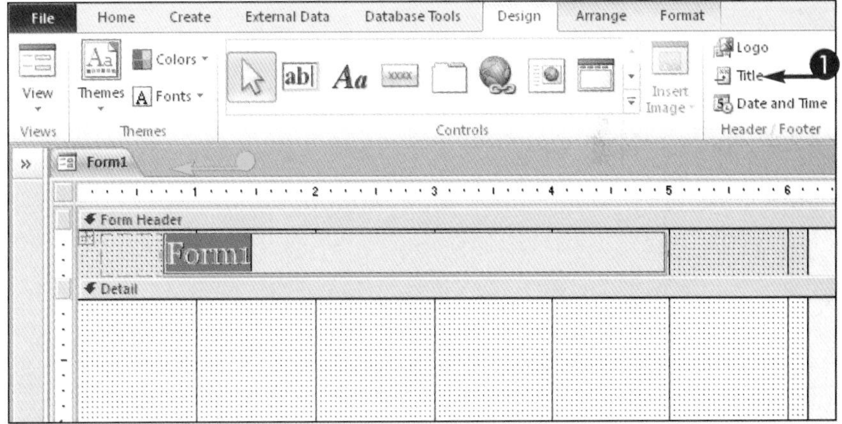

2. Type the text for the title.
3. Click outside the box when finished.

   Because the dummy text was already selected, typing new text replaces it.

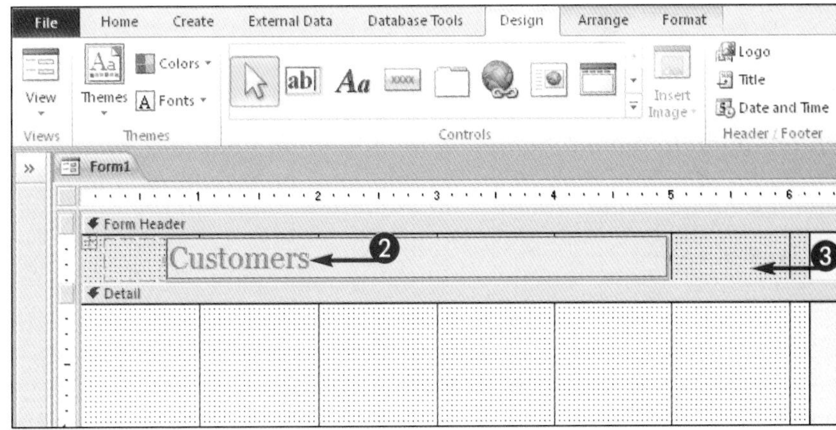

Apply a Theme

A *theme* is a preset collection of formatting that you can apply to your form. Themes are used consistently across all Office 2010 applications to apply formatting, allowing you to standardize color and font choices for everything you create, regardless of which application you create it in.

Generally speaking, themes define three formatting elements for the object to which they are applied: fonts, colors, and object effects. However, in Access, only colors and fonts are affected.

Apply a Theme

1. In Design or Layout view, on the Design tab, click **Themes**.

   A gallery of themes appears.

2. Click the theme that you want.

- You can point to a theme without clicking it to see a preview of it on the form.

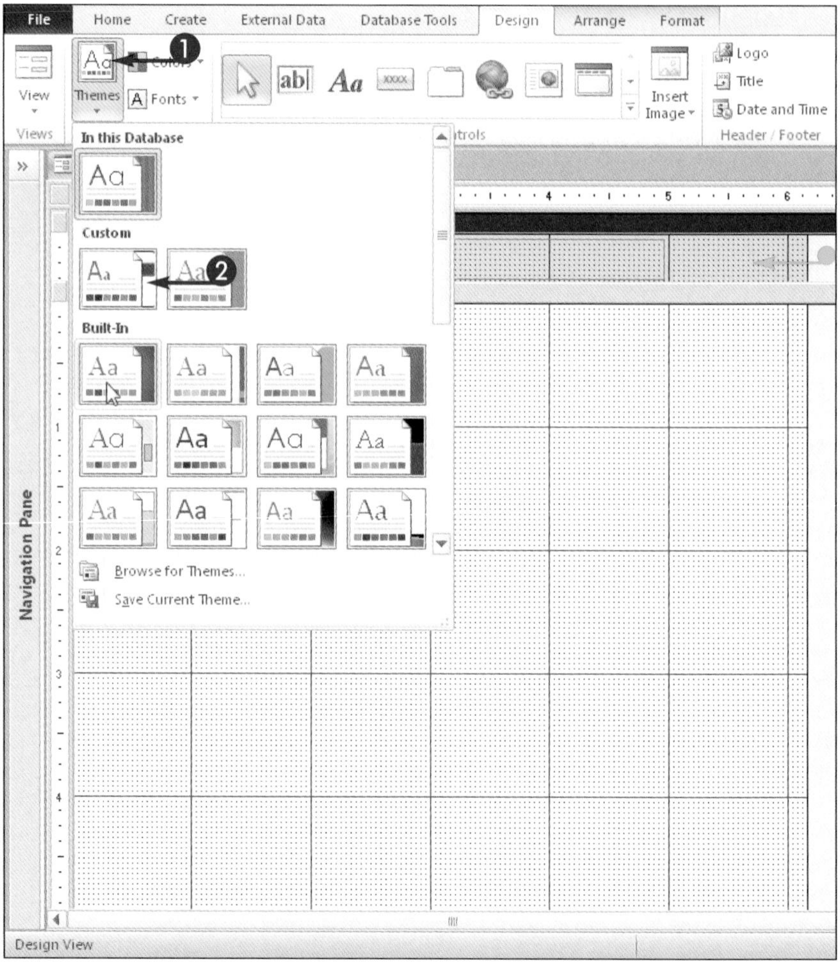

Apply a Font Theme or Color Theme

Applying a theme changes both the fonts and the colors used. If you want to change only the fonts or the colors, you should apply a font theme or a color theme instead. Each has its own separate gallery that you can access from the Design tab.

Like regular themes, font and color themes are consistent across all Office applications and can be shared among them to create consistency among all the business documents, spreadsheets, databases, and presentations you create.

Apply a Font Theme or Color Theme

Apply a Font Theme

1. In Design or Layout view, on the Design tab, click **Fonts**.

   A gallery of font themes appears.

2. Click the desired font theme.

   The new fonts are applied to the form.

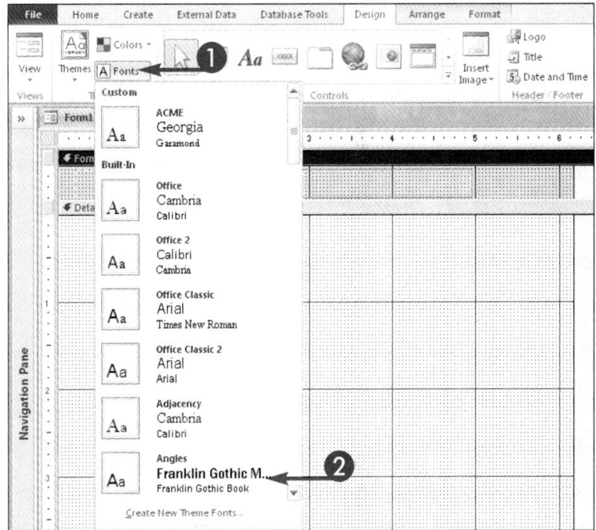

Apply a Color Theme

1. In Design or Layout view, on the Design tab, click **Colors**.

   A gallery of color themes appears.

2. Click the desired color theme.

   The new colors are applied to the form.

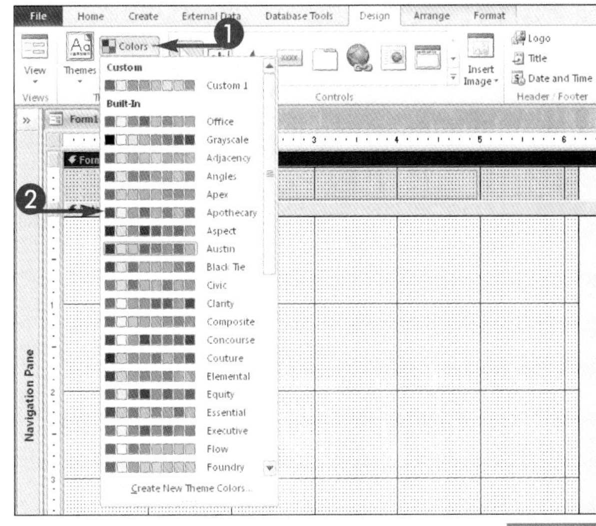

Create a Custom Font Theme

A font theme is a combination of two font choices: one for headings and one for body text. If you do not like any of the font themes that Office provides, you can create your own by defining any fonts you like for the heading and body placeholders.

Any custom font themes you create are also accessible by other Office applications, such as Word and PowerPoint.

Create a Custom Font Theme

1. In Design or Layout view, on the Design tab, click **Fonts**.

   A gallery of font themes appears.

2. Click **Create New Theme Fonts**.

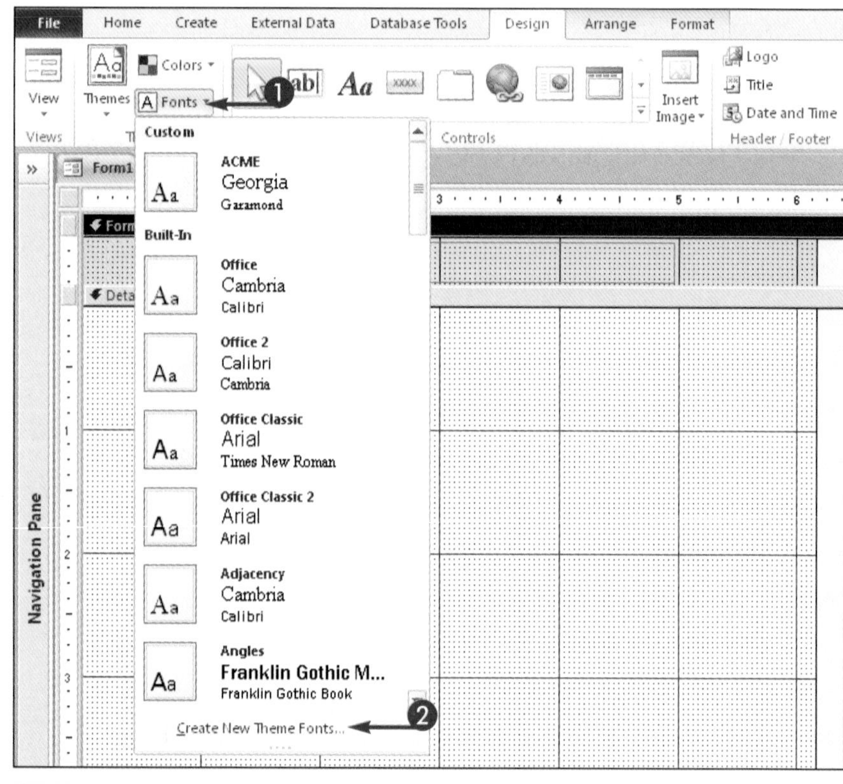

The Create New Theme Fonts dialog box opens.

3. Choose the desired fonts from the Heading font and Body font drop-down menus.

   The Sample preview box shows what the heading and body fonts look like.

4. Type a name for the new font theme in the Name box.

5. Click **Save**.

   The new font theme will be available in the font theme gallery the next time you use it.

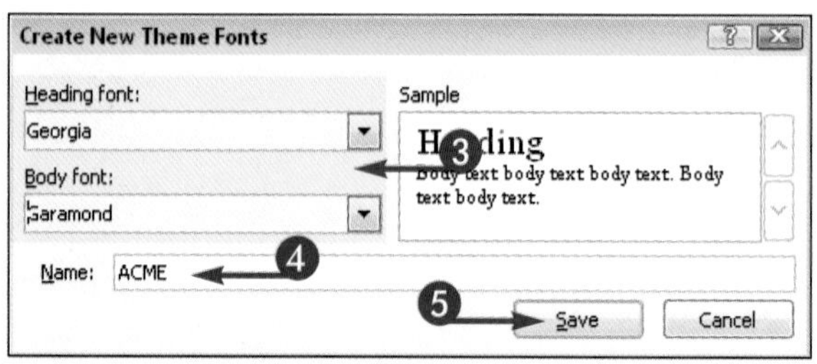

Create a Custom Color Theme

A color theme defines colors for 12 placeholders that Office applications use when formatting a document. Not all these colors are used in Access when formatting a form, but they are all used (or at least available) in one way or another. For example, the Hyperlink color placeholder defines the color of underlined hyperlinks in tables and forms. In addition, whenever you use a color picker — such as on the Font Color button's drop-down menu — the colors from the current theme are available for selection.

You can create your own custom color themes if none of the existing ones meet your needs. Just like with font themes, you can share color themes among all your Office applications.

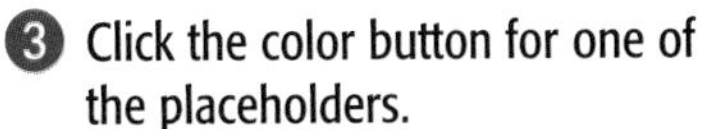

1. In Design or Layout view, on the Design tab, click **Colors**.

   A gallery of color themes appears.

2. Click **Create New Theme Colors**.

   The Create New Theme Colors dialog box opens.

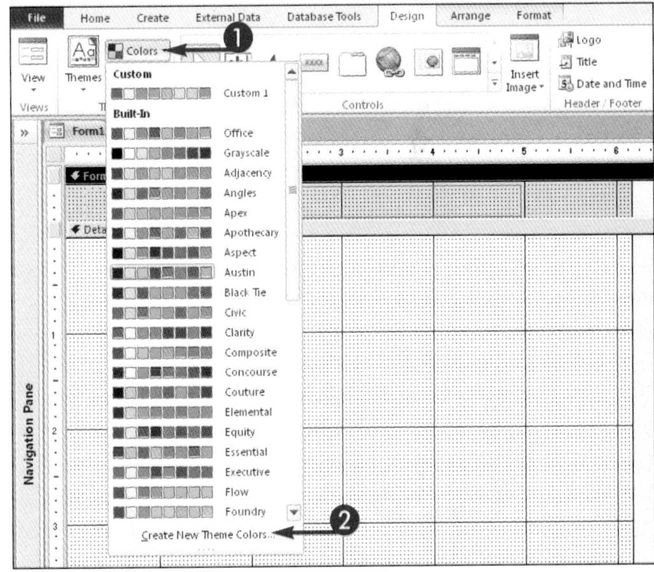

3. Click the color button for one of the placeholders.

   A palette of color choices opens.

4. Choose the desired color.

5. Repeat steps **3** and **4** for each placeholder you want to change.

6. Type a name for the new color theme in the Name box.

7. Click **Save**.

   The new color theme will be available in the color theme gallery the next time you use it.

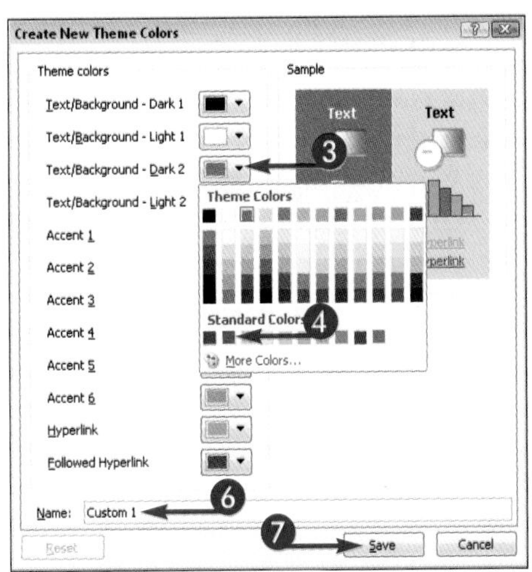

Create a Custom Theme

You can create a theme that combines your preferred fonts and colors so you do not have to go through the two-step process of applying a certain color theme and a certain font theme each time you want to format a form or other object.

First, you define the form's colors and fonts the way you want them. You can do this by applying any of the preset color and font themes or by creating your own custom color and font themes, as you learned earlier in this chapter. Then, you use the following steps to save them as a new theme.

Create a Custom Theme

1. In Design or Layout view, apply the colors and fonts that you want to be used in the theme.
2. On the Design tab, click **Themes**.

   A gallery of themes appears.
3. Click **Save Current Theme**.

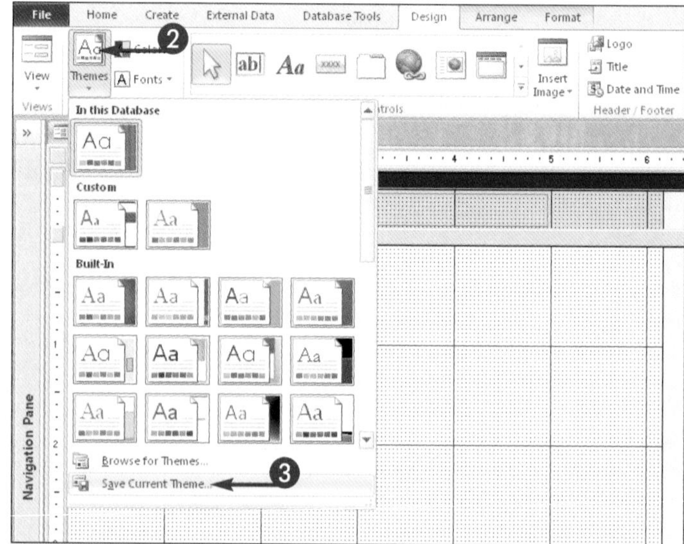

The Save Current Theme dialog box opens.

4. Type a name for the theme in the File Name box.
5. Click **Save**.

   The new theme will appear in the Themes list the next time you use it.

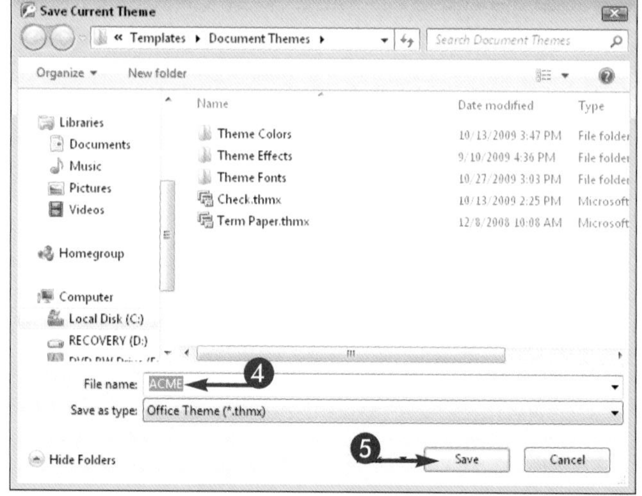

Browse for a Theme to Apply

The list of themes that appears when you click the Themes button is compiled from two specific locations on your hard disk. The built-in themes are taken from C:\Program Files\Microsoft Office\Document Themes 14, and any custom themes you have created are taken from C:\Users*username*\AppData\Roaming\Microsoft\Templates\Document Themes (where *username* is the name you are logged into in Windows).

If you want to apply a theme that is stored in some other location, such as on a network or on a CD that a coworker has given you, you must browse for it.

Browse for a Theme to Apply

1. In Design or Layout view, on the Design tab, click **Themes**.

   A gallery of themes appears.

2. Click **Browse for Themes**.

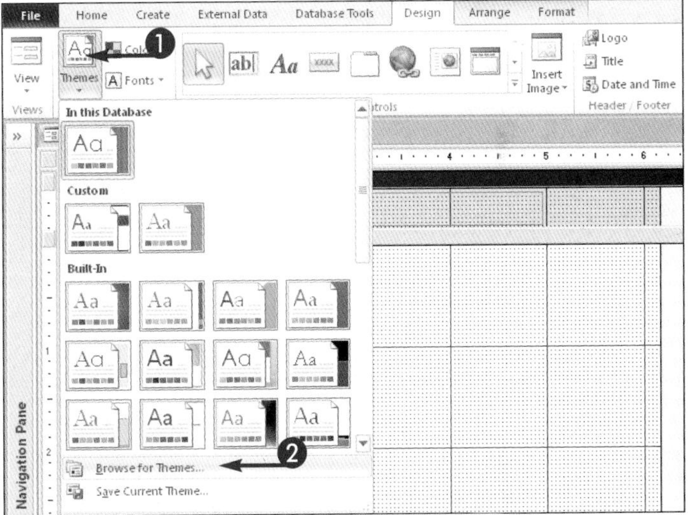

The Choose Theme or Themed Document dialog box opens.

3. Choose the theme or other file from which you want to apply font and color settings.

- You can choose a data file from another Office application to copy theme settings from instead of directly choosing a theme file.

4. Click **Open**.

   The theme is applied.

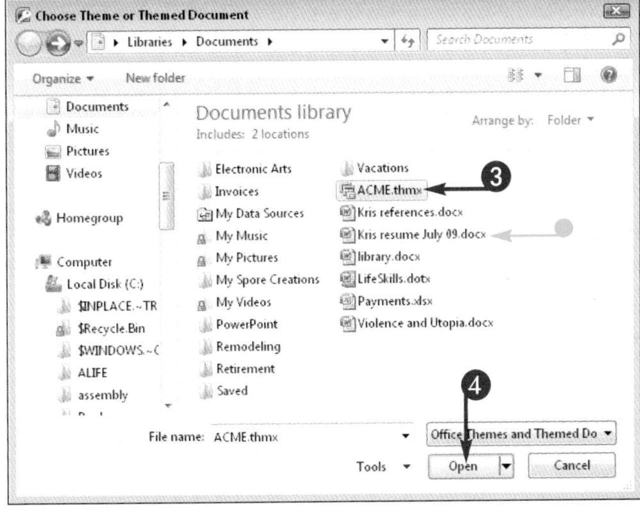

Adjust Internal Margins and Padding

The *margin* setting for a field is the amount of space inside its box between the edge and the text. You can adjust the margins for individual fields, but forms look better if all the fields have the same margins.

The padding setting is the amount of space outside the box. When you adjust the padding, you change the amount of space between fields and between a field and its label.

Adjust Internal Margins and Padding

Change the Margins

1. In Design view, select the field(s) you want to affect.

   Selecting the section bar does not select the fields; however, you can lasso the fields you want.

   To lasso fields, drag an imaginary box around them while holding down the left mouse button. When you release the mouse button, everything inside the area you dragged across will be selected.

2. On the Arrange tab, click **Control Margins**.
3. Click the margin setting you want.

   The margin setting is applied to the selected fields.

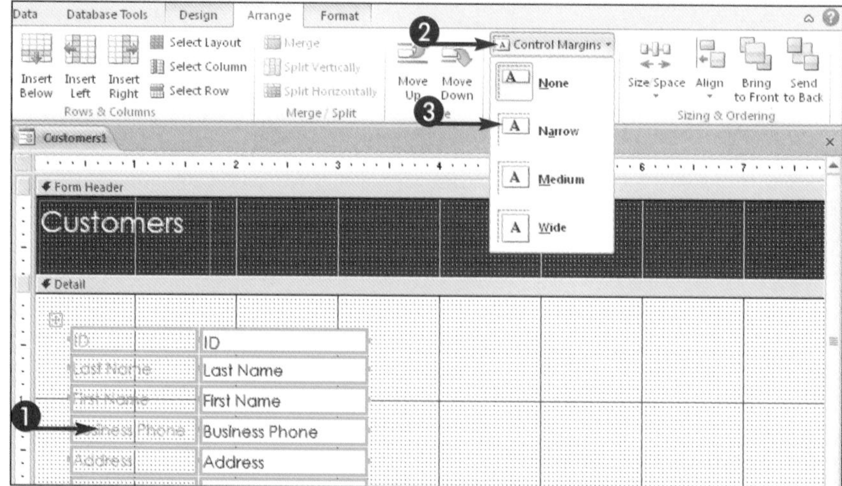

Change the Padding

1. In Design view, select the field(s) you want to affect.
2. On the Arrange tab, click **Control Padding**.
3. Click the padding setting you want.

   The new padding setting applies to the selected fields.

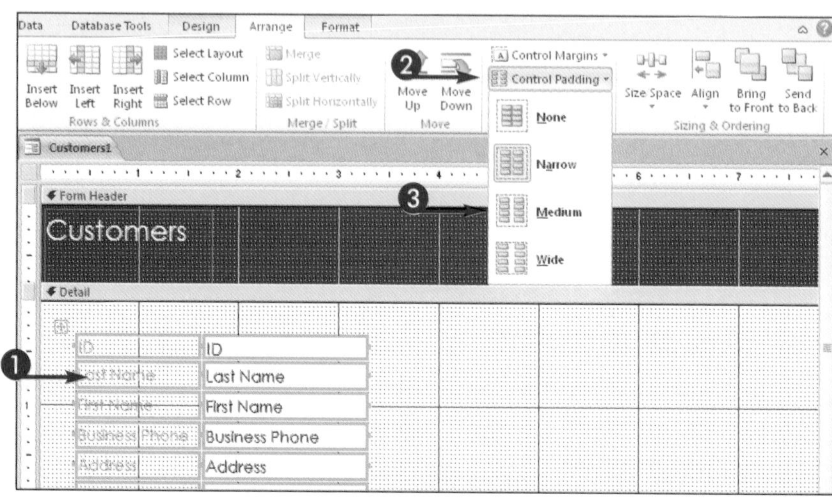

***Note:** You can also change margins and padding in Layout view.*

Add a Label

A *label* is a text area that is not connected to a field or function. It exists on a form purely for informational purposes. Earlier in this chapter, you learned how to create a form title, which is a type of label. You can also manually create other labels anywhere you like in the form.

Add a Label

1. In Design view on the Design tab, click the **Label** button (Aa).

   The mouse pointer changes from ↖ to +A.

2. Drag a box where you want the label to be and then release the mouse button.

   A label box appears, containing a flashing insertion point.

3. Type the label text.

4. Click outside the label when finished.

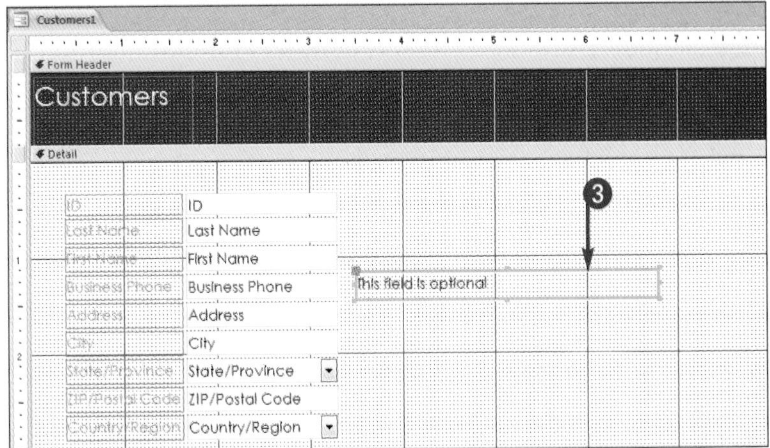

Format Label Text

You can apply some of the same types of formatting to a label as you would to text in a word-processing program, such as changing the font and size and applying bold, italic, and underline formatting.

The main difference is that in Access, text formatting is available only when the outer frame of the label is selected; you cannot select different formatting for certain characters within a single label box.

Format Label Text

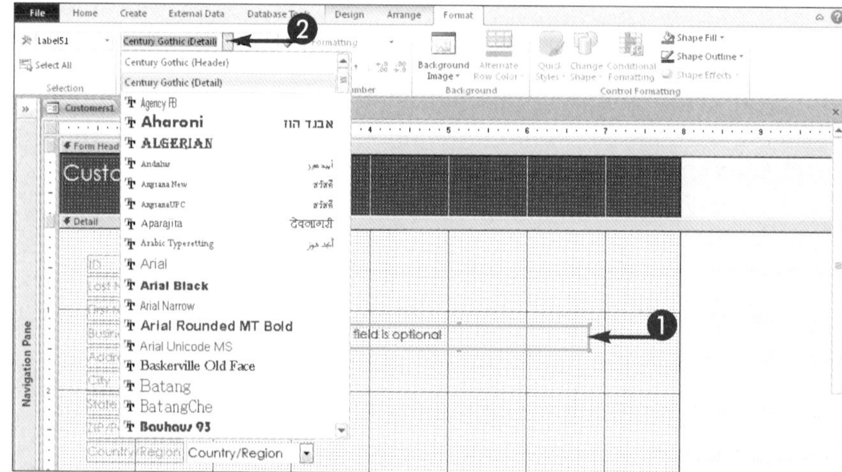

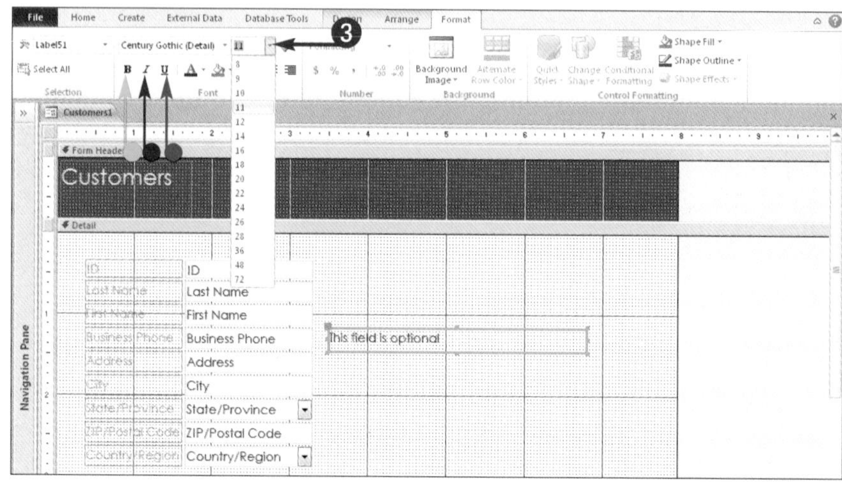

1. In Design view, click the frame of the label you want to be formatted.

   You can select multiple labels at once by holding down Shift as you click each one.

   You can format both labels you have created yourself and labels that are associated with fields.

2. On the Format tab, click here (▾) to open the Font list and then choose a font.

   You can also use the Font list on the Home tab.

3. Click ▾ to open the Size list and then choose a size.

4. Click one or more of these buttons to apply formatting:

- Bold
- Italic
- Underline

5 Click an alignment button:

- Left
- Center
- Right

6 Click ▾ to open the Font Color list and then choose a color.

7 To place a colored background in the label box, click ▾ and then choose a color.

- You can click **Transparent** to remove the colored background.

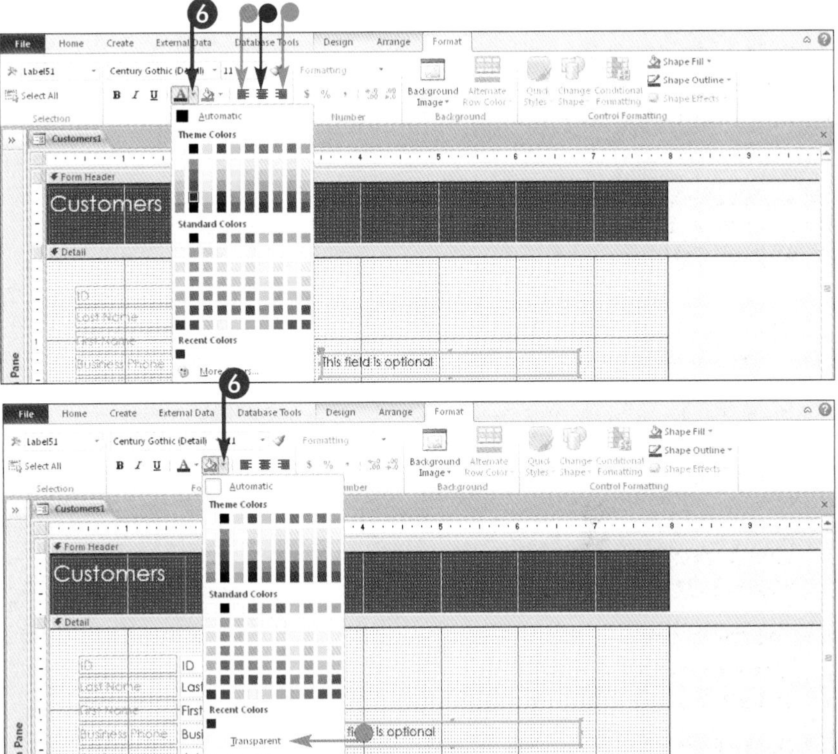

Can I format the text in a field?

Yes. Just select a field instead of a label and then apply the formatting as you learned in this section. It works exactly the same way.

What is the paintbrush button on the Format tab?

This is the Format Painter button. It copies formatting from one place to another. To use it:

1 Select a label or field that is already formatted correctly.

2 Click the **Format Painter** button ( ).

3 Click the label or field to which you want to apply the formatting.

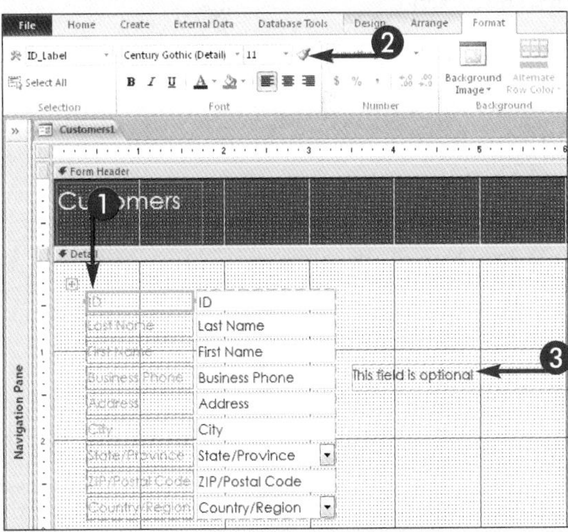

If you want to click more than one field or label in step **3**, double-click instead of single-clicking in step **2**. Click the button again to turn it off when finished.

Change the Background Color

You can set a background color for each section individually. For example, this would allow the form header to be in a contrasting color to the detail section. Alternatively, you can set all the sections in the same color for a uniform appearance.

Change the Background Color

1. In Design view, click the title bar of the section.

   The title bar becomes black.

2. On the Format tab, click ▾ to display the available colors.
3. Click **More Colors**.

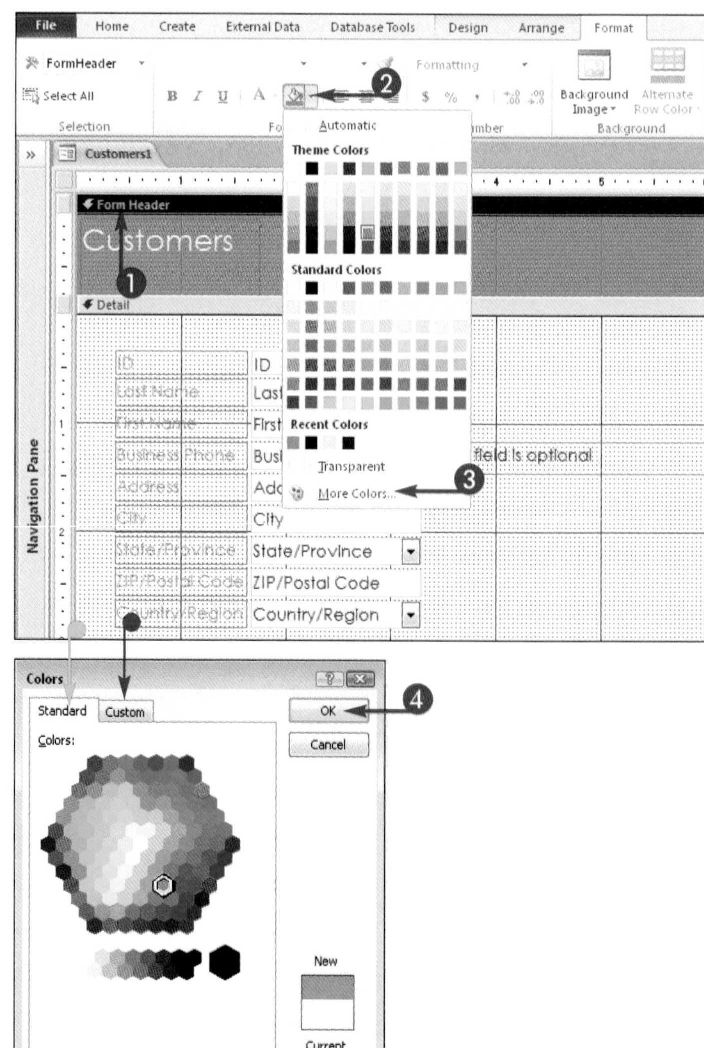

The Colors dialog box opens.

- Click the **Standard** tab to choose from basic colors.
- Click the **Custom** tab to define a color numerically.

4. Click **OK** when you have selected a color.

   The color is applied to the background.

Use a Background Image

A background image can add interest to a form. As the name implies, it sits behind the fields, providing a backdrop. For best results, choose an abstract image rather than a photo of a person or building.

By default, the fields have a solid filled background, so they will contrast nicely with the background and stand out for easy viewing. If you prefer the fields to blend into the background, set the fill for each field to Transparent, as you learned to do in the section "Format Label Text." Labels are already set to Transparent fill by default.

Use a Background Image

1. On the Format tab, click **Background Image**.
2. Click **Browse**.

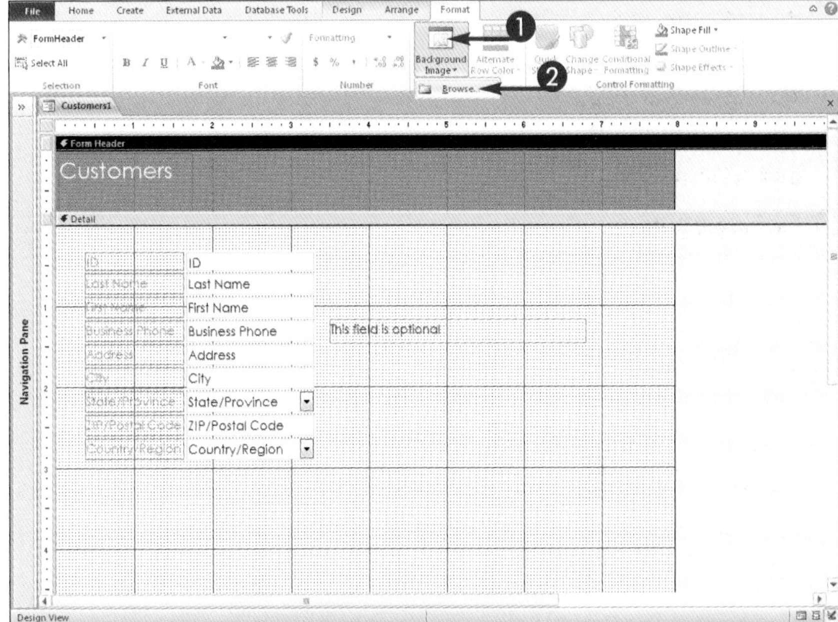

The Insert Picture dialog box opens.

3. Navigate to the folder containing the image you want to use.
4. Choose the image.
5. Click **OK**.

The image appears behind all sections of the form.

***Note:** To remove the background image from the form, on the Design tab, click **Property Sheet**. Choose **Form** from the drop-down menu on the property sheet. Click the **Format** tab and then delete the file name from the Picture property.*

Add a Hyperlink

Hyperlinks on a form are like labels, except that they are live links to the destinations they represent.

The hyperlinks you learn to create in this section exist only on the form; they are not stored in database fields. If you want to store hyperlinks in a table, you can use a Hyperlink field type. See "Change a Field's Data Type" in Chapter 3 to learn how to change a field type to Hyperlink.

Add a Hyperlink

1. In Design view, click the bar of the section in which you want to place the hyperlink.
2. On the Design tab, click here (▾) to open the gallery in the Controls group.

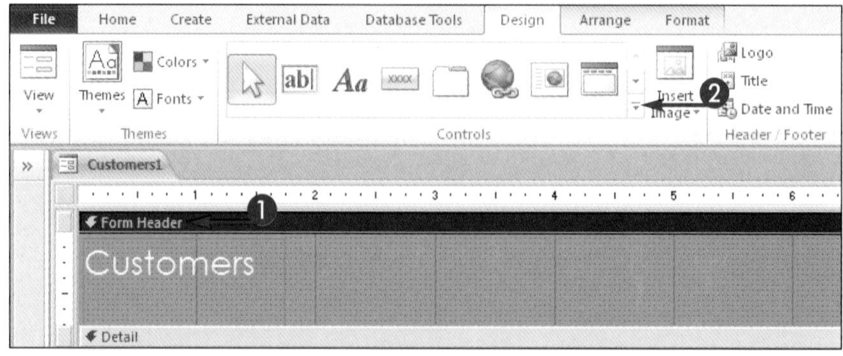

3. Click the **Hyperlink** button (🌐).

   The Insert Hyperlink dialog box opens.

Note: The Controls group's gallery contains many different content types that you can insert in a form. You may want to explore some of the others on your own.

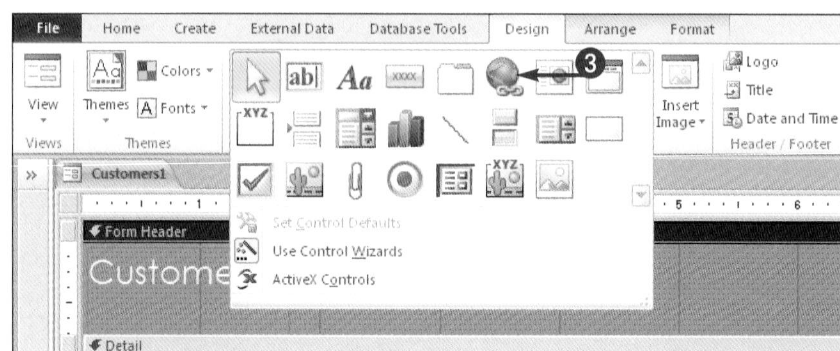

4. Type the URL in the Address box.

- You can also click **Browsed Pages** to choose a recently used URL.

5. Type the text that should appear on the form.

6. Click **ScreenTip**.

   The Set Hyperlink ScreenTip dialog box opens.

Note: *A screen tip is text that pops up when the user points at the hyperlink with the mouse pointer.*

7. Type the screen tip text you want to use.

8. Click **OK**.

   You are returned to the Insert Hyperlink dialog box.

9. Click **OK**.

   The hyperlink is added to the form in the upper-left corner of the section you chose in step **1**.

10. Click the hyperlink's frame and then drag it to the desired location.

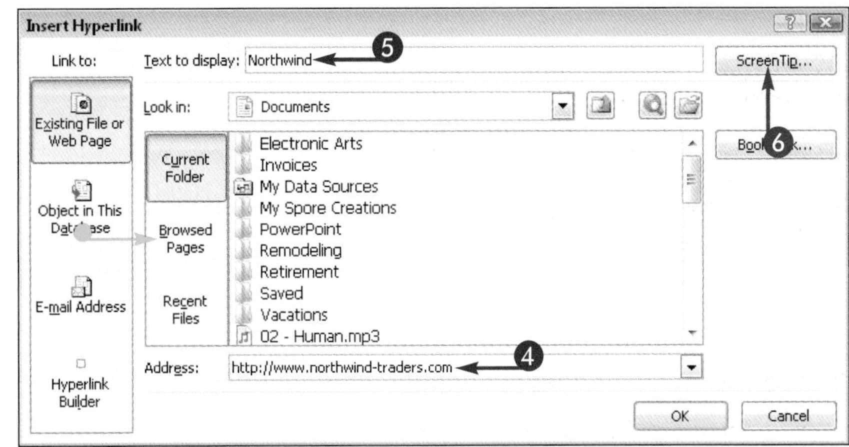

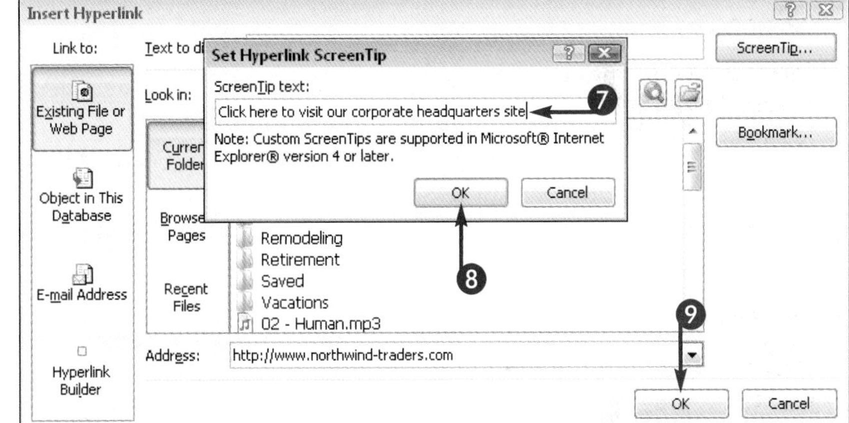

Can I hyperlink to other locations besides the Internet?

Yes. A hyperlink can link to any file in any location, including your own hard disk or network; it does not have to be on the Internet.

- By default, in the Insert Hyperlink dialog box, the current folder contents are displayed. You can browse your hard disk or network locations using this interface to choose any accessible file.

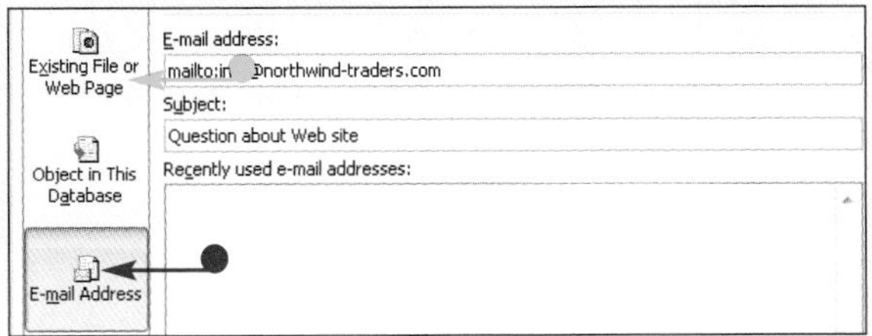

What does the E-mail Address type of hyperlink do?

- It inserts a hyperlink that, when clicked, opens a new message window in your default e-mail program. To set up an e-mail address hyperlink, click the **E-Mail Address** button in the Insert Hyperlink dialog box and then fill in the fields provided.

Add a Tabbed Section

When there are too many fields or labels to fit on a form at a useable size, you can use a tab control to create multiple tabs, or pages, on the form. Like the tabs on the Ribbon in Access, the tabs on the form can be clicked to switch to their associated set of fields and other controls.

Add a Tabbed Section

Add a Tab

1. On the Design tab, click the **Tab Control** button (□).
2. Drag to create a rectangle representing the tab area and then release the mouse button.

   A tab control appears on the form with two tabs.

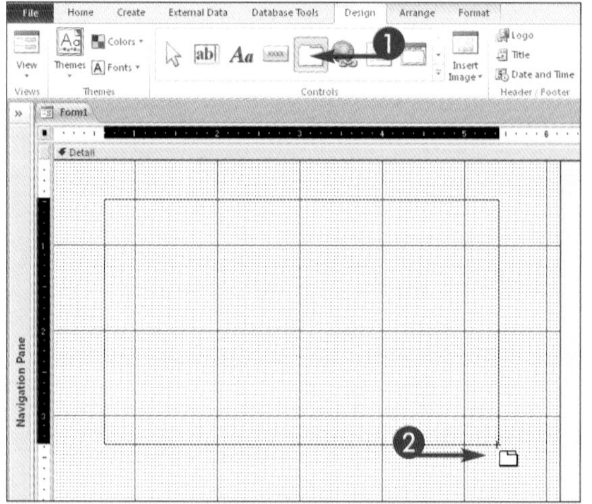

3. Click a tab.

   A frame appears, representing that tab's page.
4. Click **Add Existing Fields**.

   The Field List pane appears.
5. Click the plus sign (⊞ changes to ⊟) next to a table name.

   The list expands to show that table's fields.

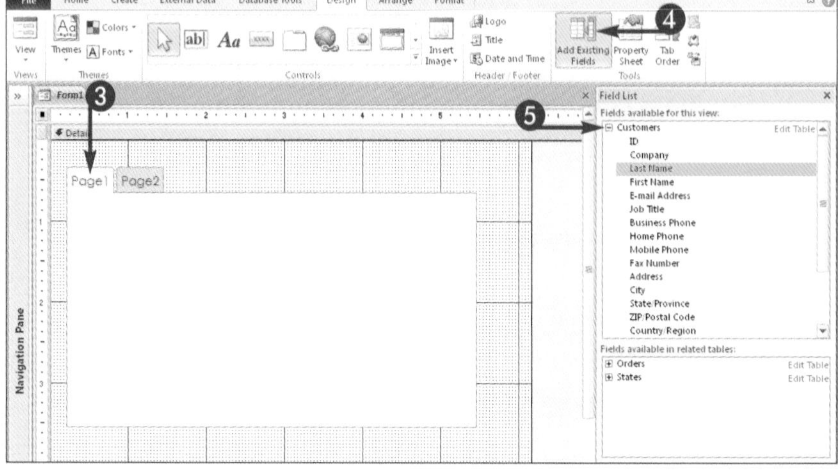

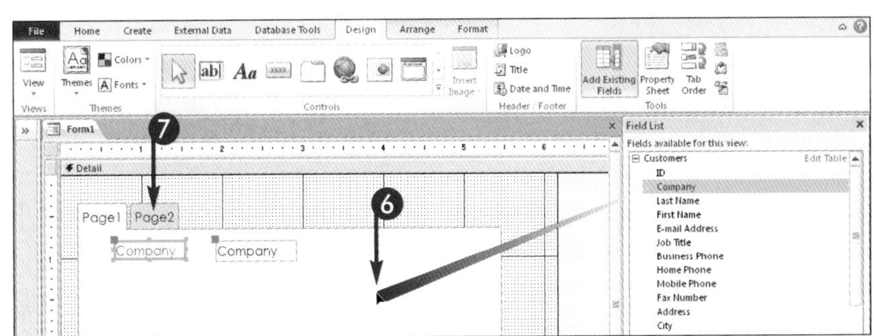

6 Drag and drop fields from the Field List onto the frame.

Note: *You can also add nonfield items, such as labels and hyperlinks.*

7 Click the other tab to add fields to it.

Add Another Tab

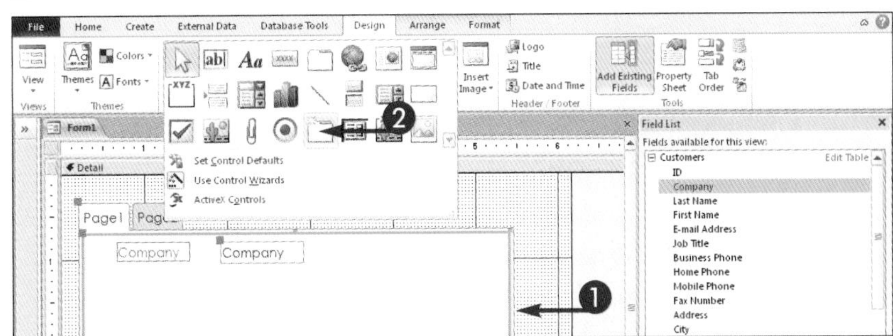

1 Click the outer frame of the tab control.

2 On the Design tab, open the Controls gallery and then click the **Insert Page** button ().

Another tab appears in the tab control.

Rename a Tab

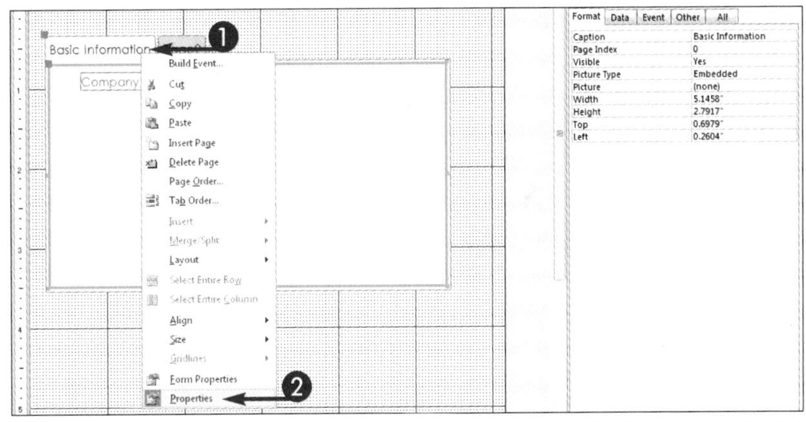

1 Right-click on the tab you want to rename.

2 Click **Properties**.

3 In the Caption box, type the text that should appear on the tab.

How do I delete a tab?

Right-click on the tab and then choose **Delete Page** from the shortcut menu.

How can I hide a tab without deleting it?

To hide a tab, set its Visible property to No:

1 On the Design tab, click **Property Sheet**.

2 Click ▾ to choose the tab page.

3 Click ▾ to choose No.

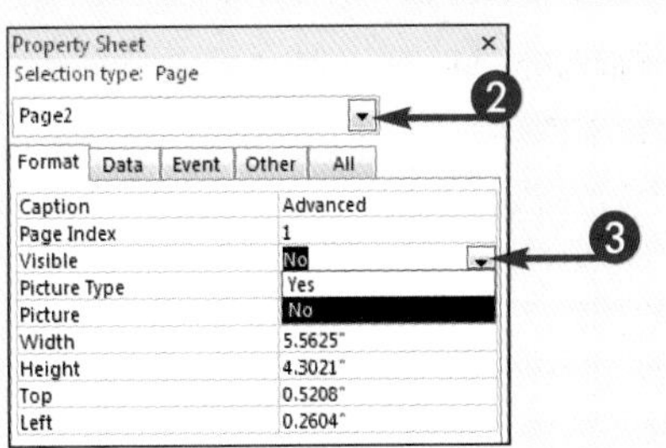

Insert a Logo or Image

Just as the Title feature inserts a label in the form header, the Logo feature inserts a graphic in the form header.

If you want to insert a graphic anywhere else, you can use the Image feature. Images are like logos, except that you can choose where to put them and you can define the size of the frame.

Insert a Logo or Image

Insert a Logo

1. On the Design tab, click **Logo**.

   The Insert Picture dialog box opens.

2. Click the picture to be inserted.
3. Click **OK**.

   The picture is inserted in the Form Header section.

   Depending on the resolution of the image file, it may cause the Form Header section to expand. The form header may also change its background color.

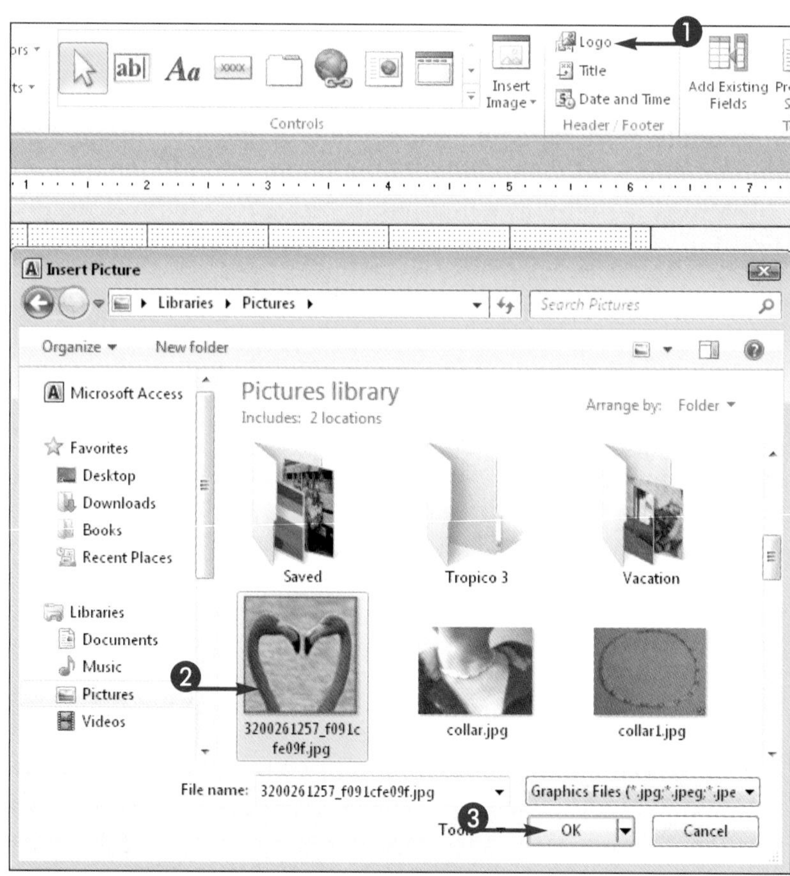

Resize a Logo

1. If needed, expand the Form Header section to make room for the image to be enlarged.
2. Click the logo.
3. Drag a corner selection handle to resize the frame (↖ changes to ↘).

Note: *If you do not maintain the proportions, extra blank space may appear on either the sides or the top and bottom, but the picture will not be distorted.*

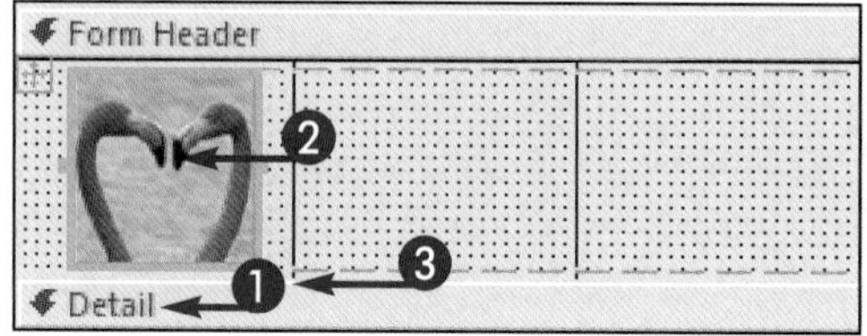

Insert an Image

1. On the Design tab, click **Insert Image**.

2. Click **Browse**.

   The Insert Picture dialog box opens.

3. Click the picture you want to insert.

- Navigate to a different location if needed.

4. Click **OK**.

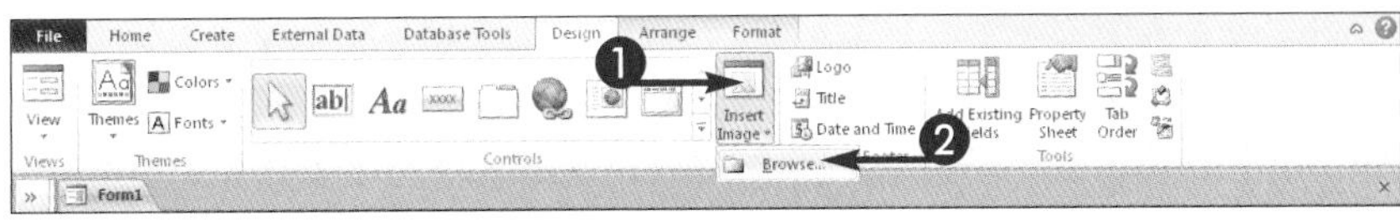

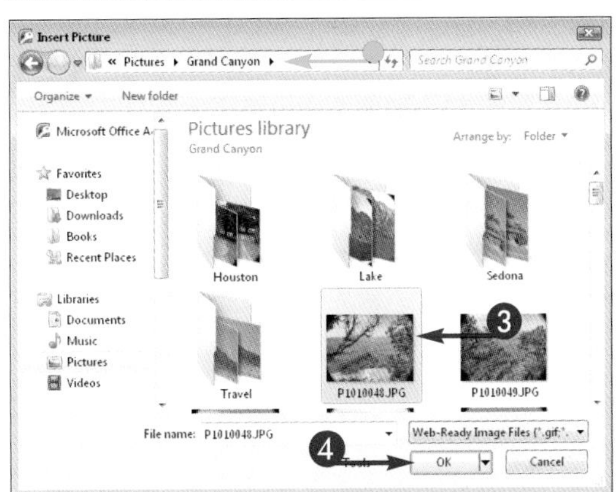

The mouse pointer changes from to .

5. Drag the mouse to create the desired picture frame size and then release the mouse button.

   The picture appears in the frame you just drew.

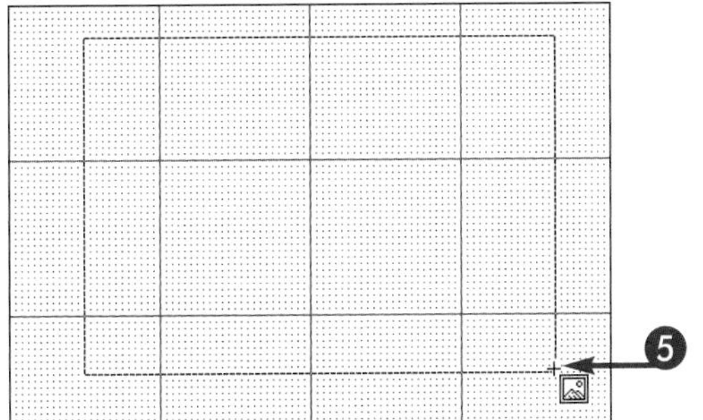

How can I make sure a picture has exact measurements?

Set the picture's Height and Width properties:

1. Click the picture.
2. On the Design tab, click **Property Sheet**.
3. On the Property Sheet, click the **Format** tab.
4. Click in the Width field and then type a value in inches.
5. Click in the Height field and then type a value in inches.

Set Conditional Formatting

Conditional formatting applies certain formatting if the data in a field meets a condition that you specify and other formatting if it does not. For example, you could set up a Balance field to display its value in red if the balance is negative or you could color the Order Total field gold for customers whose order amount exceeds a certain value.

Set Conditional Formatting

1. In Design view, click the field you want to format.

Note: *Make sure that you select the field, not its label.*

2. On the Format tab, click **Conditional Formatting**.

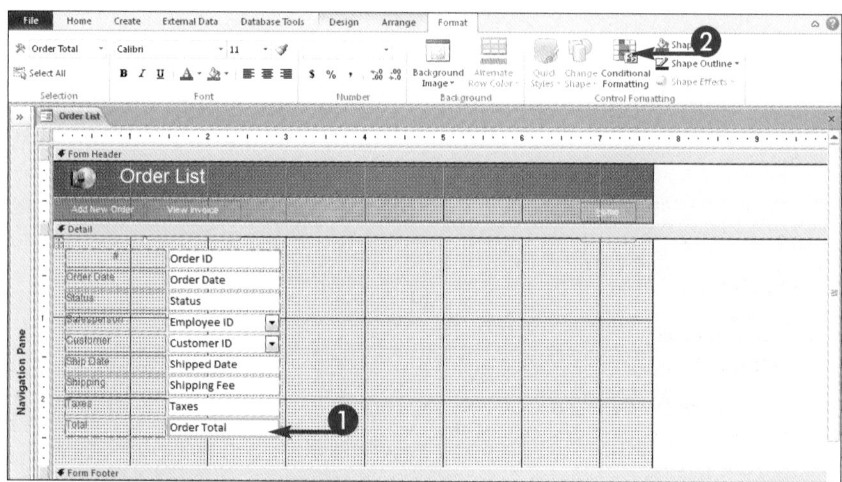

The Conditional Formatting Rules Manager dialog box opens.

3. Click **New Rule**.

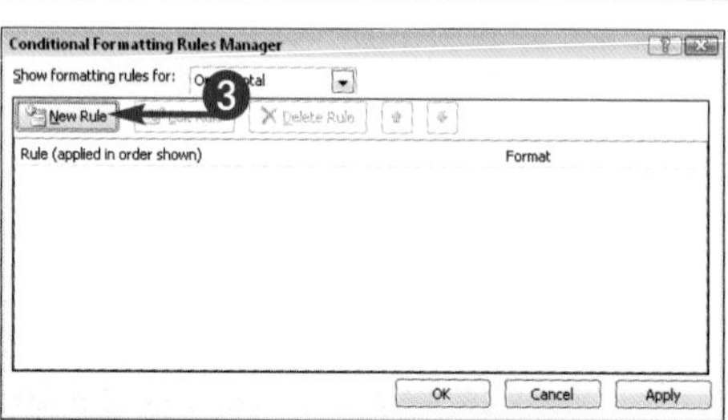

The New Formatting Rule dialog box opens.

4. Click a rule type.
5. Click ▾ to choose a condition.
6. Click ▾ to choose a comparison operator.
7. Click here to type the value or text string.

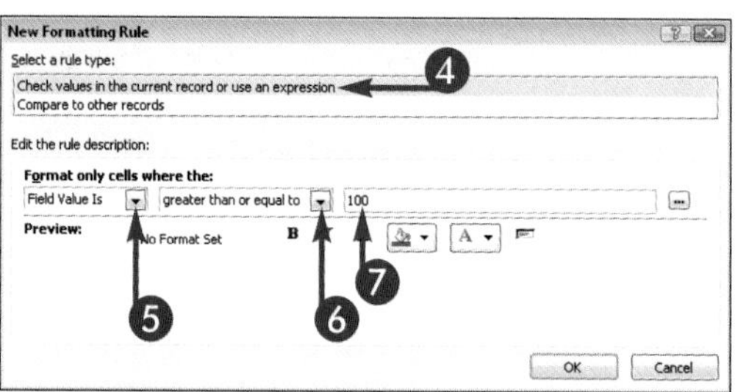

8. Choose formatting in the Preview area to define the formatting for records where the condition is met:

- Bold
- Italic
- Underline
- Background Color
- Font Color
- The Enable/Disable button toggles the display of the formatting.

9. Click **OK**.

   The new rule appears in the Conditional Formatting Rules Manager dialog box.

10. To add another rule, you can repeat steps **3** to **9**.

11. Click **OK**.

   The conditions are applied to the selected field.

Note: *You do not see the results immediately because you are in Design view.*

You can switch to Form view and then scroll through a few records to check the conditional formatting.

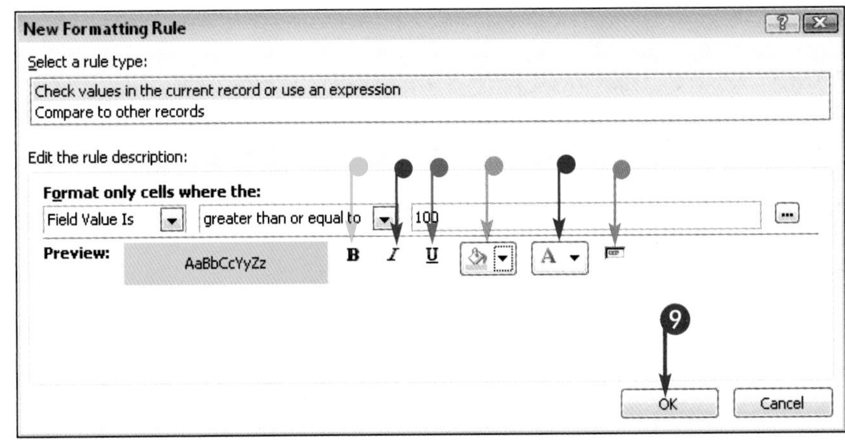

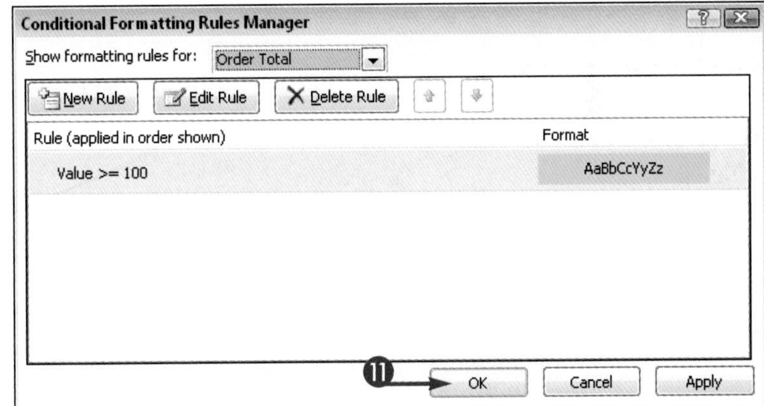

Why would I want to use the Enable/Disable button?

You can toggle off the conditional formatting with the Enable/Disable button for either Default Formatting or for any of your conditions in order to preserve your conditional settings without using them all the time. For example, perhaps you only want to use conditional formatting when a form is viewed on-screen, so you would turn it off before printing the form.

How do I delete one of the multiple conditions that I have set up?

- To remove a rule, open the Conditional Formatting Rules Manager dialog box, click the rule you want to delete and then click **Delete Rule**.

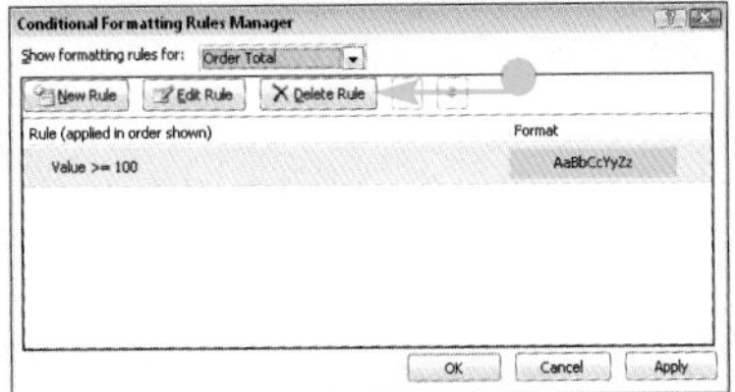

CHAPTER 11

Creating and Formatting Reports

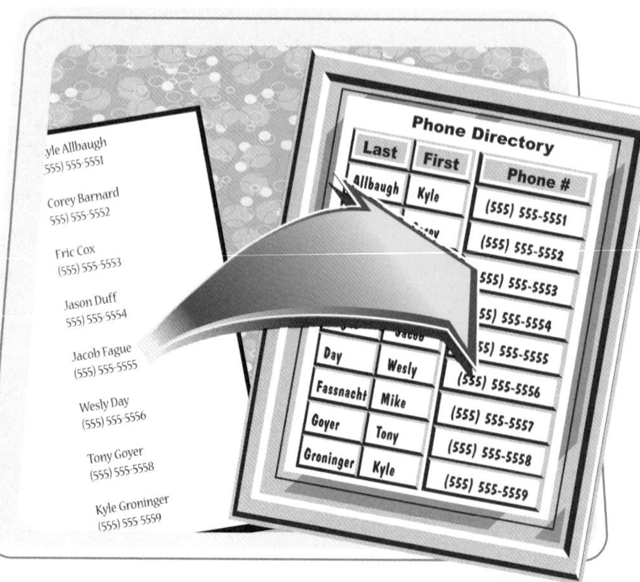

Reports are views of your data, as are forms, queries, and table datasheets, but reports have a special purpose: They are designed to be printed. A report can have more elaborate formatting and layouts than other objects you can print. You can create basic reports with default settings or you can create custom layouts by using the exact settings that work best for your situation.

Understanding Report Views

You have several choices of views for working with reports. Each has a specific function for which it is best suited.

Print Preview

Print Preview shows the report exactly as it will be printed. It shows page margins by simulating the edges of the paper on-screen. If the report is too wide to fit on the paper, it is truncated where the page break would truncate it. You cannot edit the report in Print Preview.

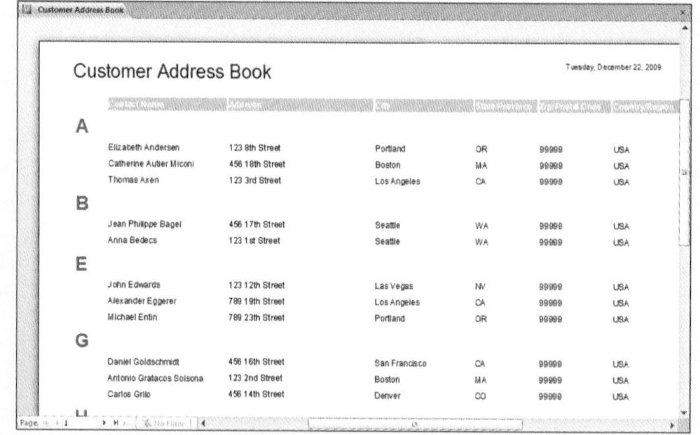

Report View

Report view shows the report approximately as it will be printed, but it does not simulate the edges of the paper on-screen, so you cannot see the actual margins that will be used. Even if the report is too wide to fit on the paper, it still appears on-screen as one whole page. You cannot edit the report in Report view.

Layout View

Layout view enables you to configure the overall formatting and layout of the report but not to change individual elements, such as text boxes. You can add grouping and sorting levels, totals, and other information as well as apply themes.

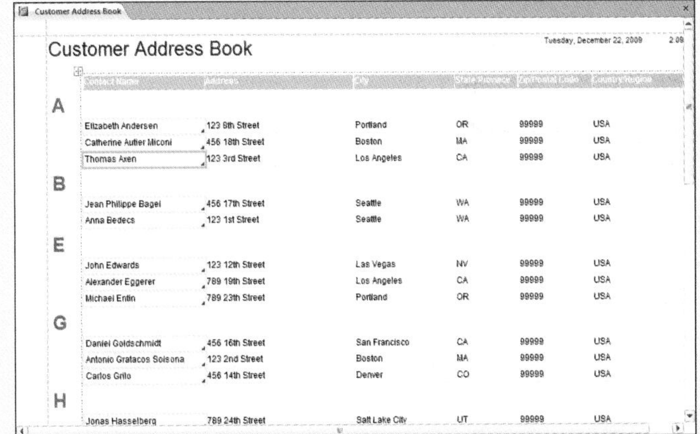

Design View

Design view is where you can fine-tune the fields and labels to be included on the report. Only in this view can you add and remove fields and add nonfield controls, such as labels. The report in Design view often bears little resemblance to the finished layout. For example, compare the Design and Layout views shown here; Layout view shows approximately how the fields will appear in the actual printout. However, Design view shows items according to section and does not always place everything where it will actually be. As you are learning to use Design view, it is often best to begin the report by using the Report Wizard or another automated method to help you set up the fields.

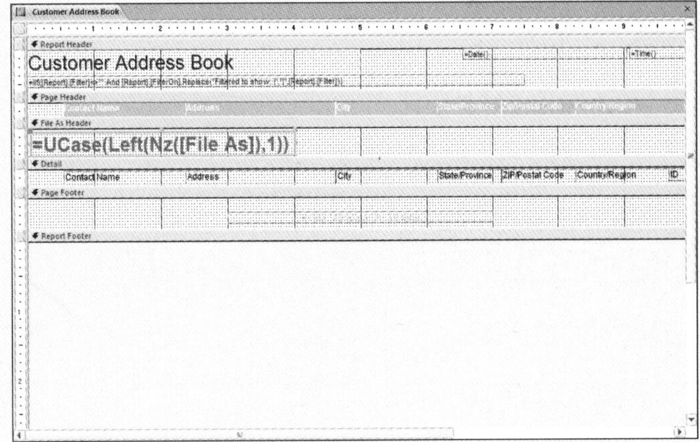

Create a Simple Report

Rather than print a form or datasheet, you may prefer to generate a report. By using the default settings, you can create a report very quickly. You can then save the report for later reuse or simply re-create it the next time you need it.

Create a Simple Report

1. Click the table or query in the Objects list.
2. On the Create tab, click **Report**.

   The report appears in Layout view.

3. To save the report, click the **Save** button (💾).

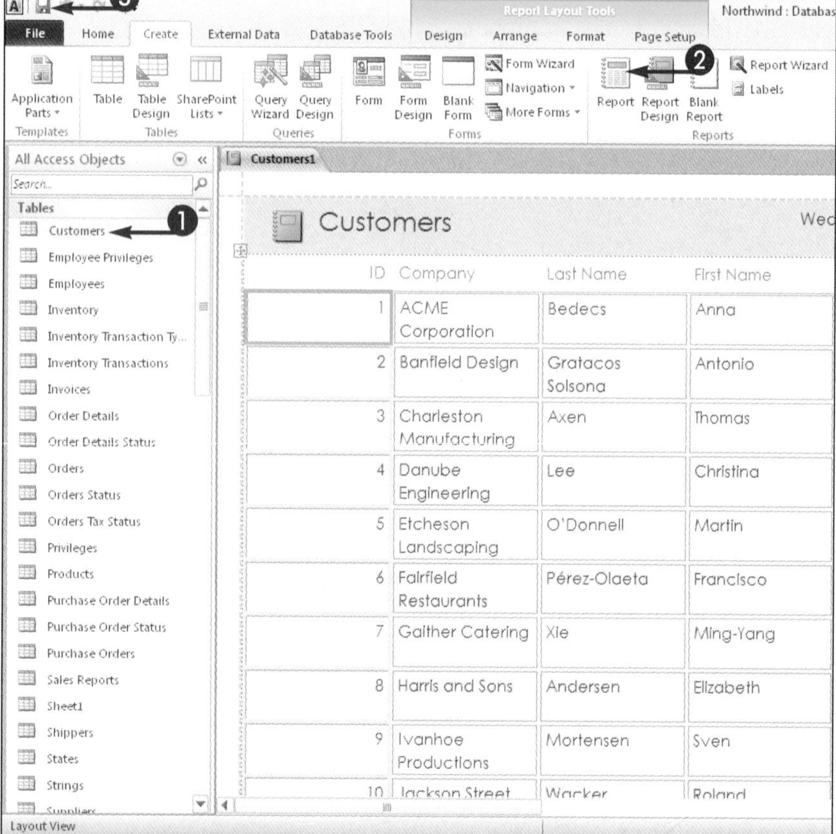

The Save As dialog box opens.

4. Type a name for the report.
5. Click **OK**.

   The report is saved.

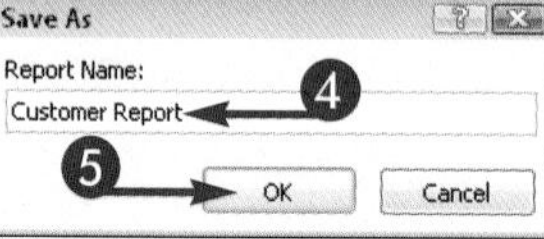

Apply a Theme to a Report

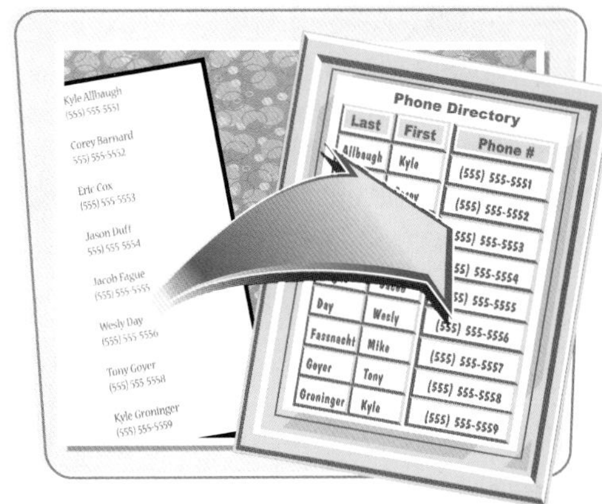

A theme applies certain fonts and colors to a report. You can use a theme to quickly apply consistent formatting to a report so it matches other reports or company specifications.

Themes work the same way for reports as for forms; for more, see Chapter 10.

Apply a Theme to a Report

1. In Layout view on the Design tab, click **Themes**.

   A gallery of themes appears.

   You can point to a theme to see a preview of it on the report.

2. Click the theme that you want.

Note: *Review Chapter 10 for more on creating your own custom themes. Chapter 10 also explains how you can apply color themes or font themes separately.*

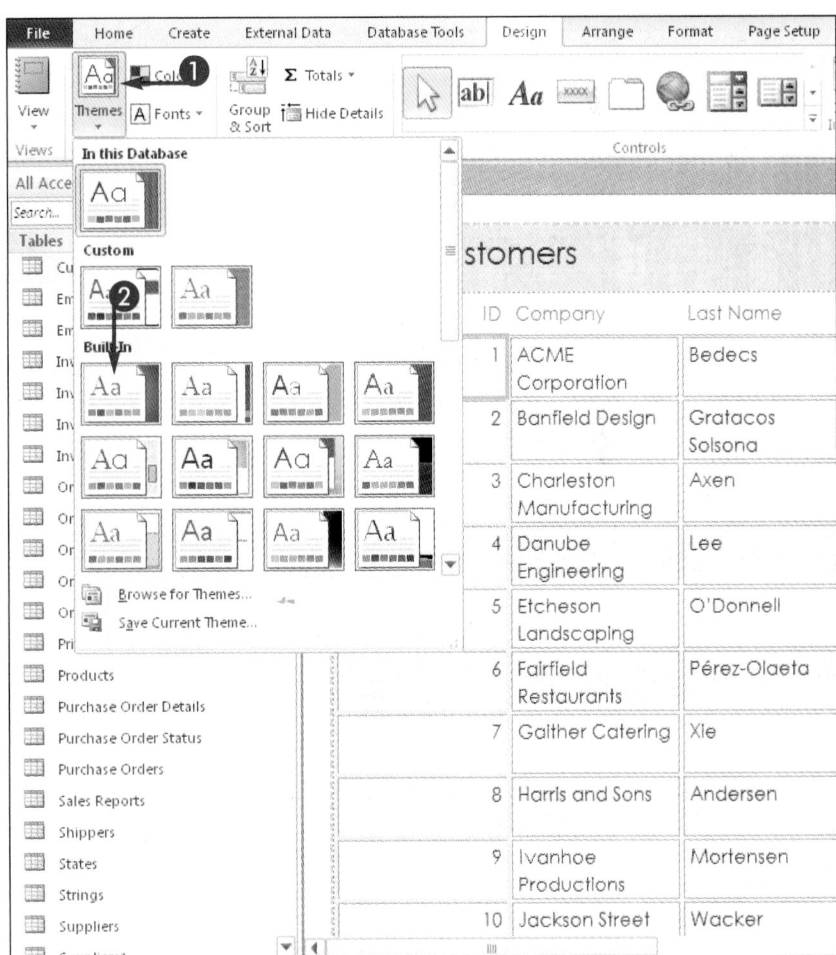

Preview and Print a Report

After creating a report, you will probably want to print it. You can check the report first in Print Preview to make sure that it is the way you want it or you can print it directly from any other view.

Preview and Print a Report

Open a Report in Print Preview

1. In the Objects list, right-click on the report you want to open.
2. Choose **Print Preview** from the shortcut menu.

   The report appears in Print Preview.

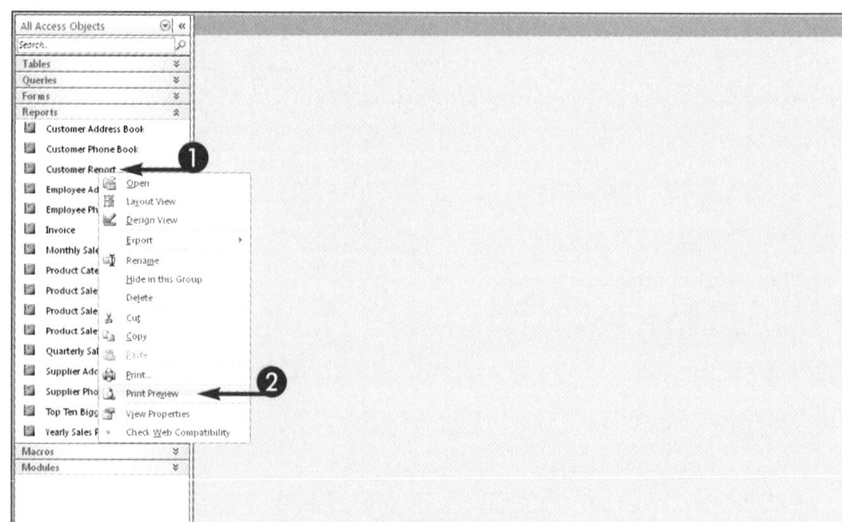

Switch an Open Report to Print Preview

1. Right-click on the report's tab.
2. Choose **Print Preview** from the shortcut menu.

   The report appears in Print Preview.

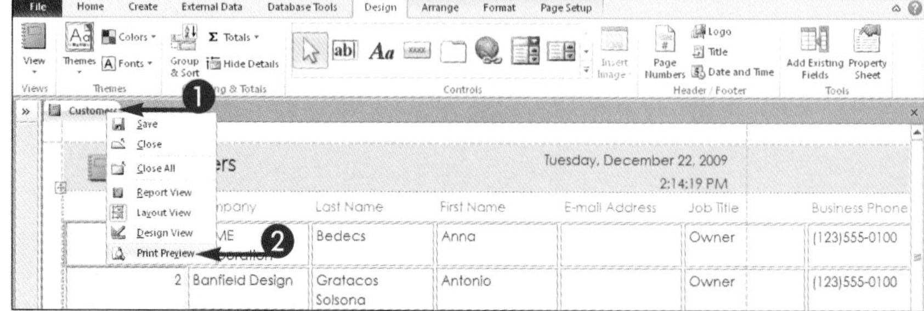

Print a Report from Print Preview

1. On the Print Preview tab, click **Print**.

   The Print dialog box opens.

2. Change any print settings, if necessary:

   - Click here to choose a different printer.
   - Click here to set a page range (◎ changes to ◉).
   - Click here to specify a number of copies to print.

3. Click **OK**.

   The report prints.

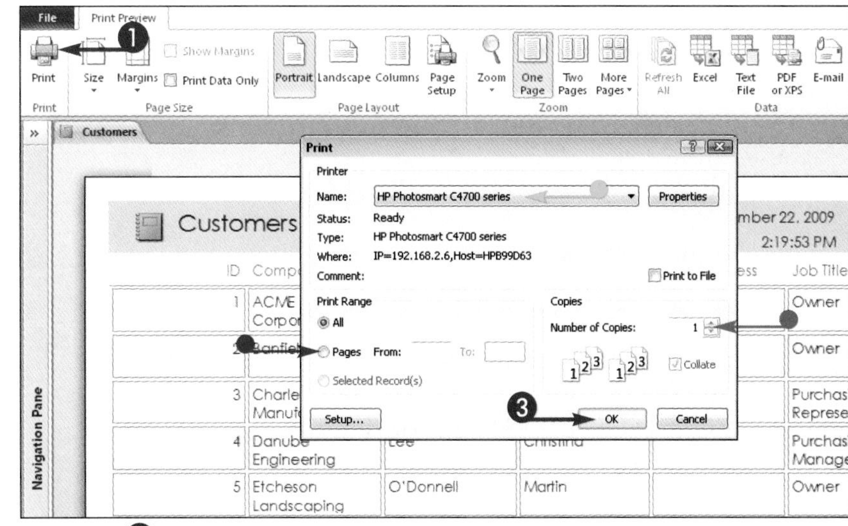

Print a Report from Other Views

1. Click **File**.

   The File menu opens.

2. Click the **Print** category.
3. Click **Print**.

   The Print dialog box opens.

4. Perform steps **2** and **3** in the section "Print a Report from Print Preview."

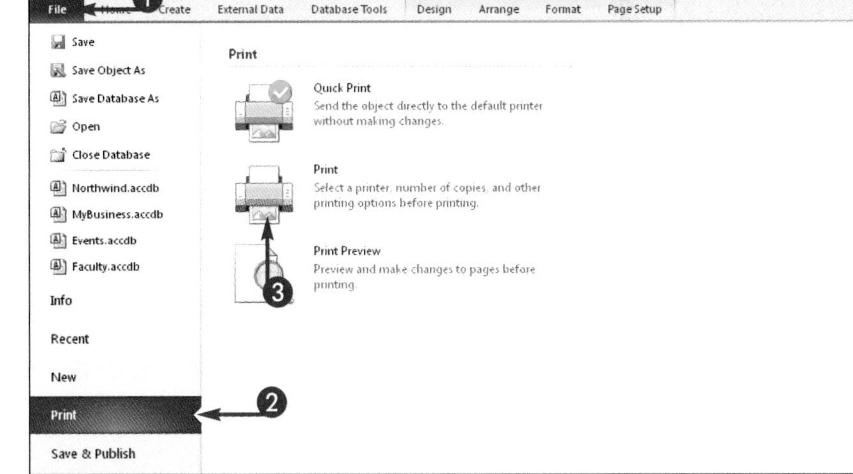

How can I see more of the report at once?

The Zoom group on the Print Preview tab contains buttons for One Page, Two Pages, and More Pages. If you click **More Pages**, you can choose a four-, eight-, or twelve-page display.

How can I export the report?

The Data group on the Print Preview tab contains buttons for exporting to Microsoft Word (in rich text format), to a text file, to an Excel file, and to several other formats.

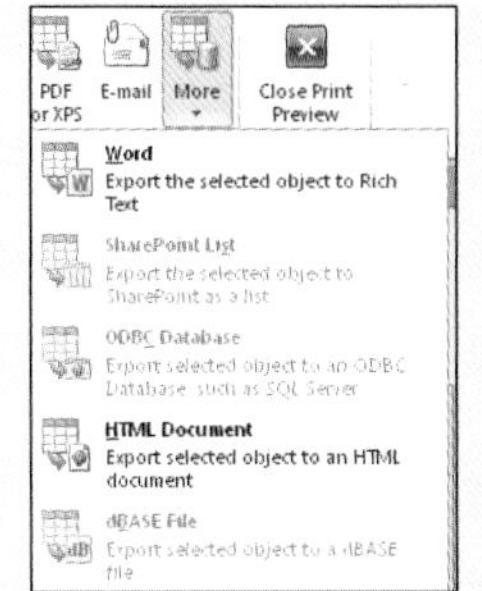

Create a Report with the Report Wizard

You can use the Report Wizard to create a report without having to manually design it while still having some control over its layout and formatting.

After creating a report this way, you can then edit it in Design view to fine-tune its appearance.

Create a Report with the Report Wizard

1. On the Create tab, click **Report Wizard**.

   The Report Wizard dialog box opens.

2. Click here (▾) to choose a table or query on which to base the report.

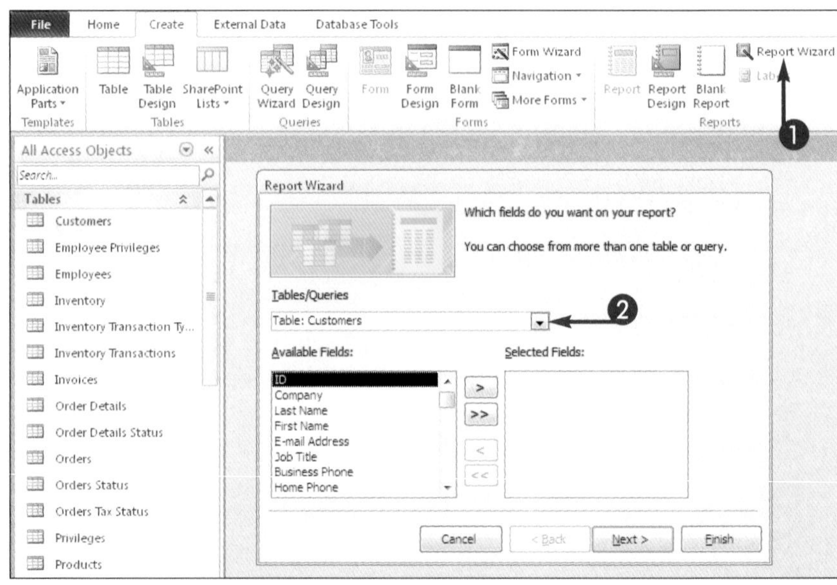

3. Click a field.
4. Click here (>) to move the field to the Selected Fields list.
5. Repeat steps **3** and **4** for all the fields you want to include.

- Click here (>>) to add all the fields at once.
- Click here (<) to remove a field.
- Click here (<<) to clear the Selected Fields list.

6. Click **Next**.

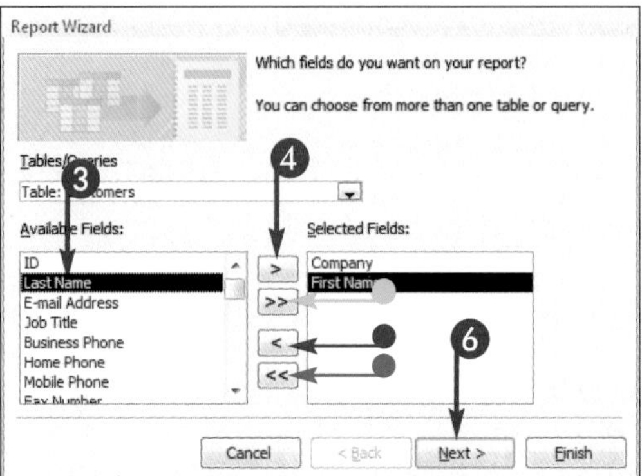

7. Click a field by which you want to group.
8. Click here (>) to group by the chosen field if you chose one in step **7**.

- The sample changes to show grouping by that field.

9. Click **Next**.

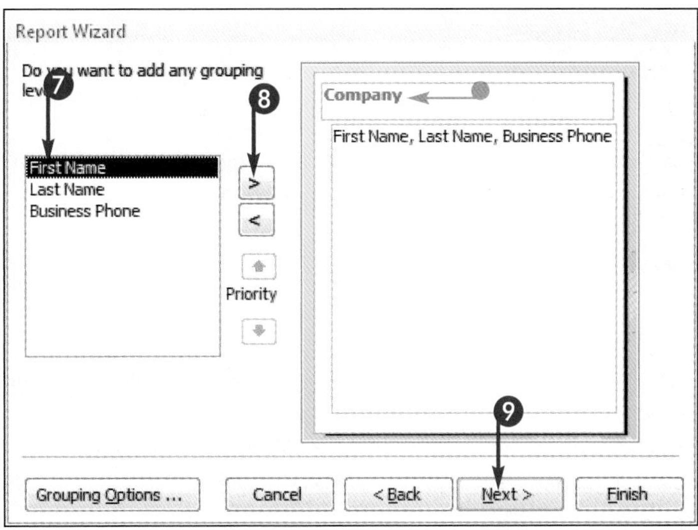

10. Click here (▾) to choose a field by which you want to sort.
11. Click here to switch between an Ascending and a Descending sort.

- You can define additional sort levels, if needed.

12. Click **Next**.

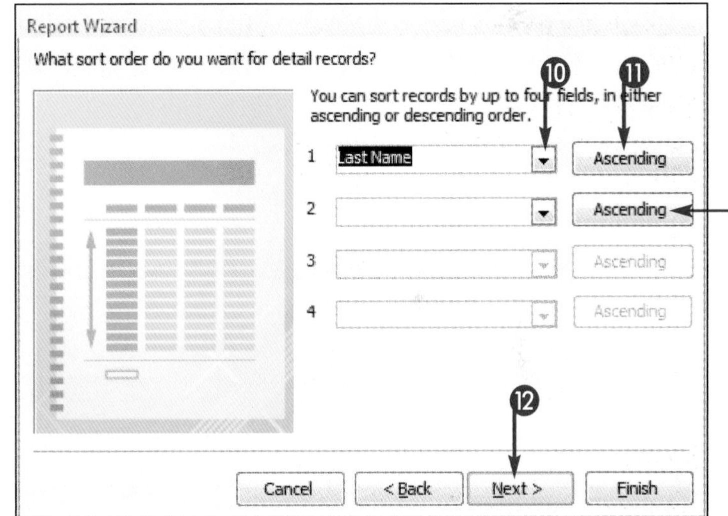

How can I group by something other than unique values?

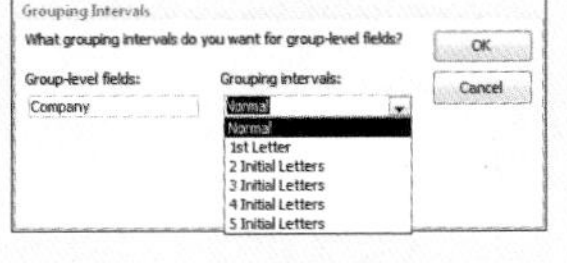

Click **Grouping Options** after step **8** to access a Grouping Intervals dialog box. From there, you can define a grouping interval. For text, you can group by the first letters of the entry. For numeric values, you can group by numbers (such as 10s or 100s).

Can I have fields from more than one table or query in the same report?

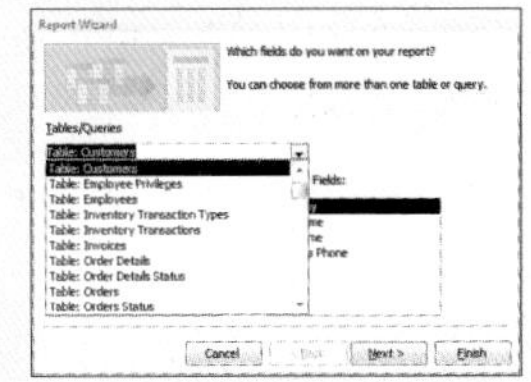

Yes. Repeat steps **2** through **5** to select another table or query before clicking **Next** in step **6**. As long as the tables or queries are related in some way, Access will pull data from them, just as it does when you create a query.

Create a Report with the Report Wizard *(continued)*

The Report Wizard not only lets you specify what fields and grouping you want but also allows you to choose the report layout, orientation, and formatting. You can fine-tune this formatting in Design view if needed.

Create a Report with the Report Wizard *(continued)*

13. Click the layout you want to use (◎ changes to ◉).
14. Click the page orientation you want (◎ changes to ◉).
15. Click **Next**.

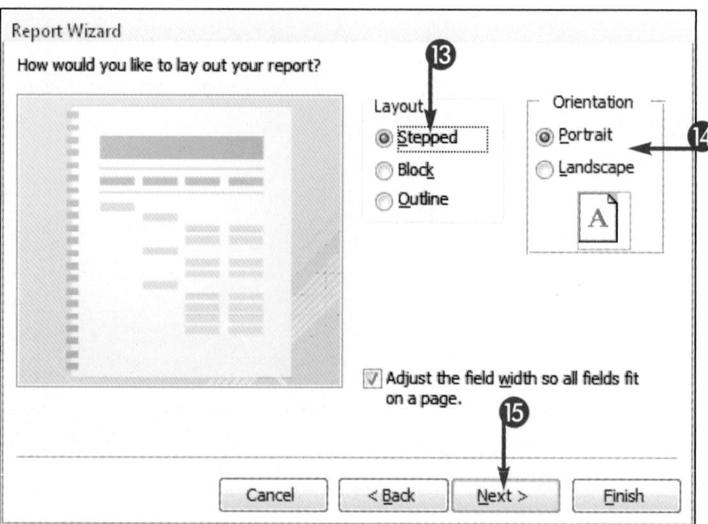

16. Click here to type a name for the report, replacing the generic name that appears.
17. Click a radio button (◎ changes to ◉) to choose how the report should be viewed after it is created.
18. Click Finish.

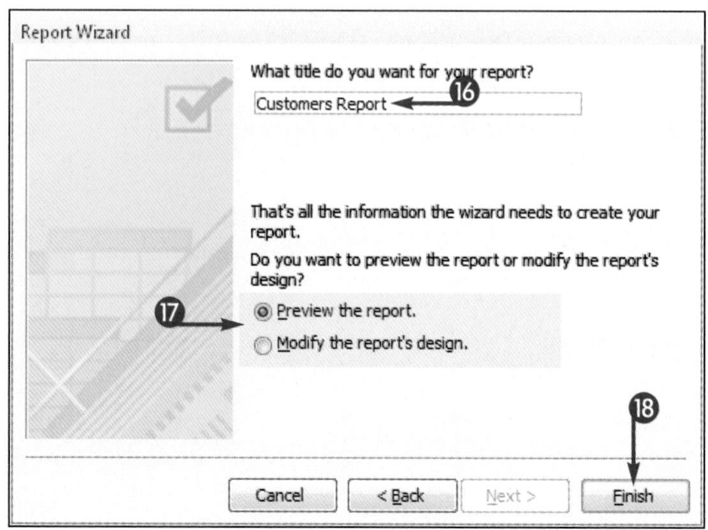

If you clicked the Preview the report radio button in step **17**, the report appears in Print Preview.

If you clicked the Modify the report's design radio button in step **17**, the report appears in Design view.

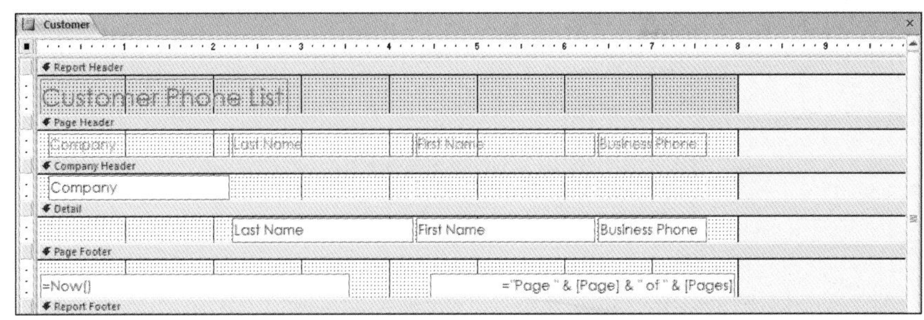

How can I change the name of a report after creating it with the Report Wizard?

First, close the report. Then, from the Objects list, right-click on the report and choose **Rename** from the shortcut menu. Type a new name and then press Enter.

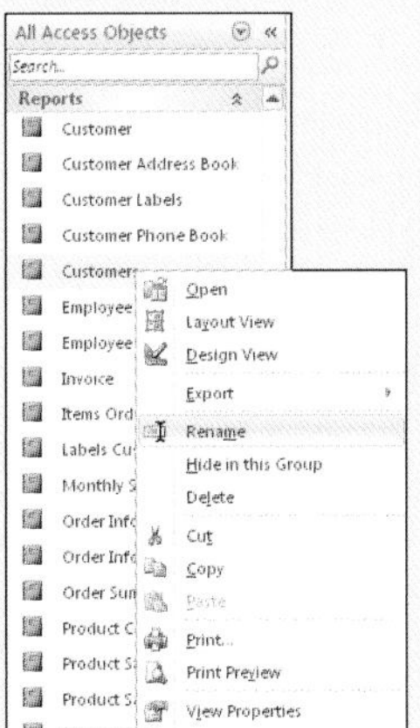

How can I make the report extend to multiple pages horizontally if the fields do not fit on a single page width?

Before step **15**, deselect the Adjust the field width so all fields fit on a page check box (☑ changes to ☐). The report will then expand horizontally to fill as many pages as needed so all the fields are at their original sizes.

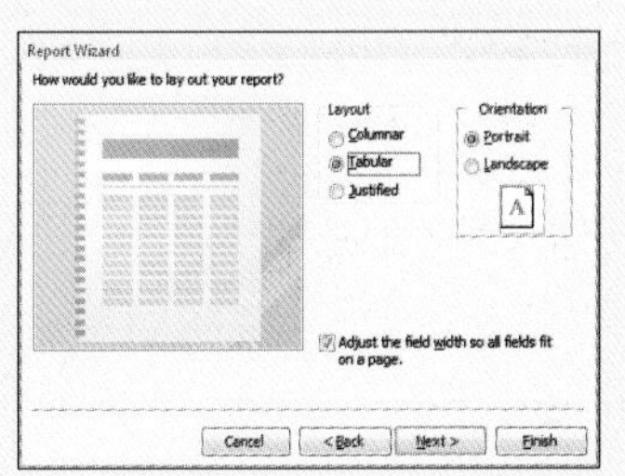

Create a Report in Layout View

You can design your own reports from scratch by using either Layout view or Design view. However, Layout view is much easier to work in because it more closely resembles how the report will actually appear.

Because you can easily switch between views, you can do the initial layout in Layout view and then fine-tune it in Design view.

Create a Report in Layout View

1. On the Create tab, click **Blank Report**.

   A blank report window appears in Layout view.

2. In the Field List, if a list of tables does not already appear, click **Show all tables**.

3. Click the plus sign (⊞ changes to ⊟) next to a table's name to expand its field list.

4. Drag a field onto the report.

- The field name appears at the top, and records from the table appear beneath it.

5. Repeat step **4** to add other fields to the report as needed.

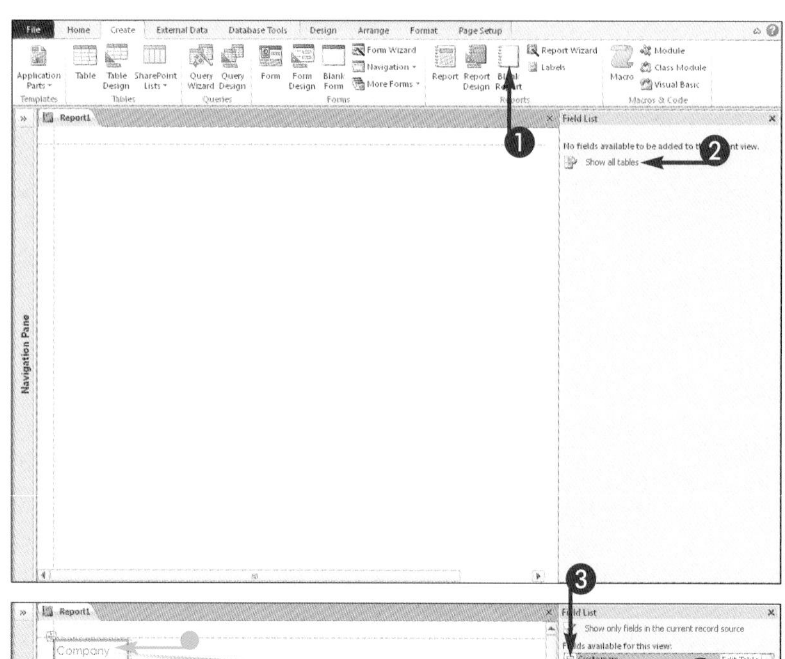

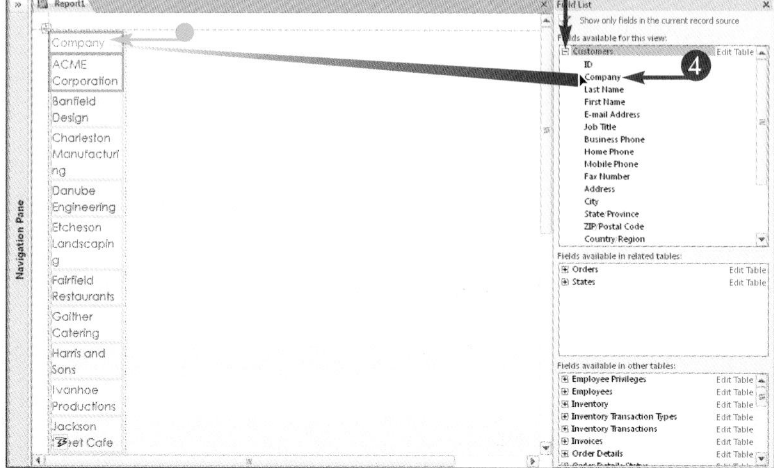

Set the Page Size and Orientation

The default page size for a report is the Letter size, which is 8.5 inches × 11 inches. You can set the page to any size you like as well as switch between portrait and landscape.

Set the Page Size and Orientation

Set the Page Size

1. In Design or Layout view, on the Page Setup tab, click **Size**.
2. Click a paper size.

   The page is resized.

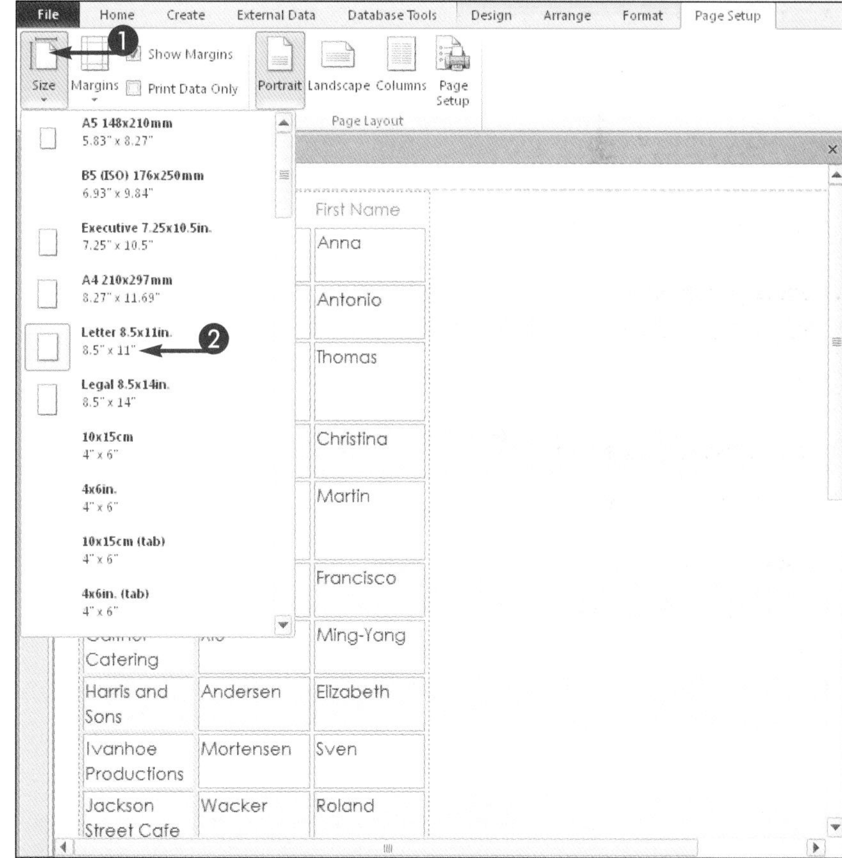

Set the Page Orientation

1. In Design or Layout view, on the Page Setup tab, click **Portrait** or **Landscape**.

   The page orientation changes to the setting that you chose.

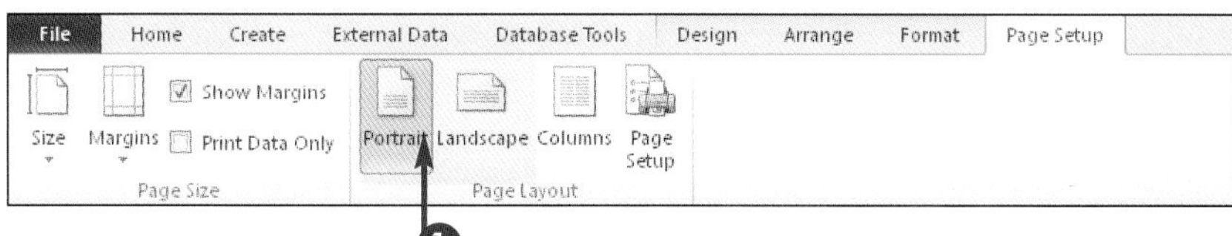

Change the Report Layout Type

You can choose to make a report either tabular or stacked. A tabular report resembles a table (datasheet), with records in rows and fields in columns. A stacked report shows each record in a separate, self-contained section.

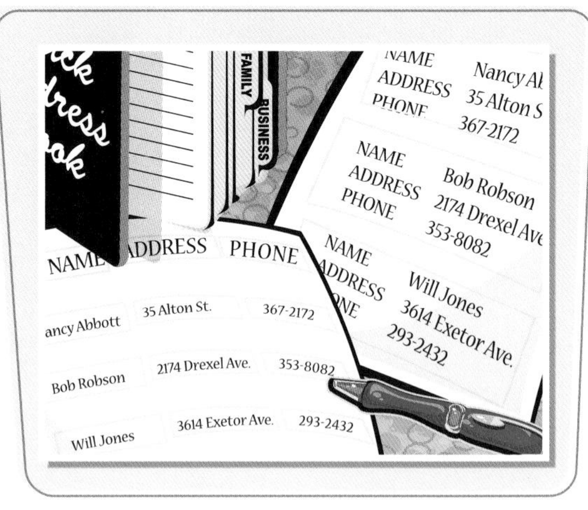

- The default type of report created in Layout view is Tabular.

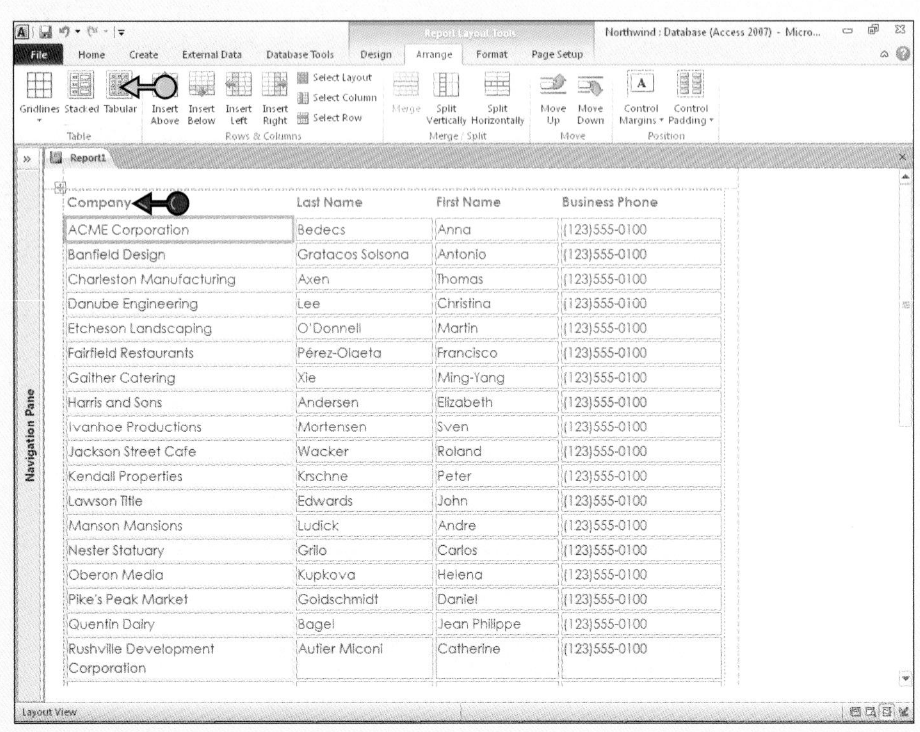

- Tabular layout places each field name across the top row, with the individual records beneath.

- You can click here to change to a Stacked layout.
- A Stacked layout places each record in its own area, one on top of the other, with all its fields in one place.

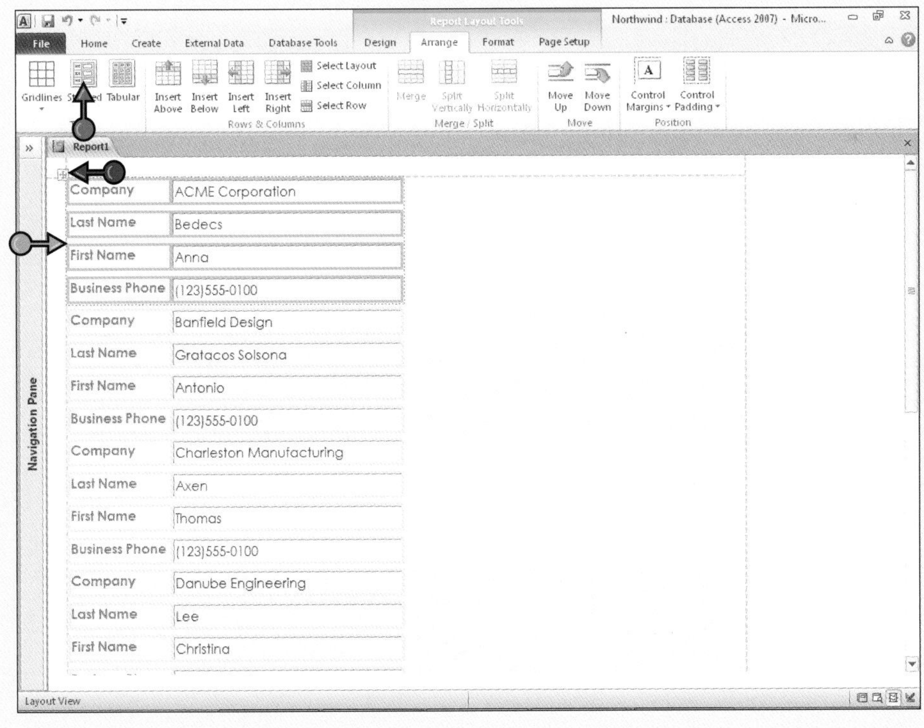

- When switching between Stacked and Tabular layouts, make sure you click here (⊞) to select the entire data grid before making the change. If you select only certain fields, only those fields will be changed. That enables you to create layouts in which some fields are arranged in a tabular layout and others are stacked.

Set Page Margins

You can set page margins for your report; these refer to the overall white space around the outside of the report on the printed page.

Set Page Margins

Use a Page Margin Default

1. In Design or Layout view, on the Page Setup tab, click **Margins**.
2. Click a margin setting.

   The margin setting is applied.

- By default, margins appear on-screen in Print Preview. If you do not want this to happen, deselect the Show Margins check box (☑ changes to ☐).

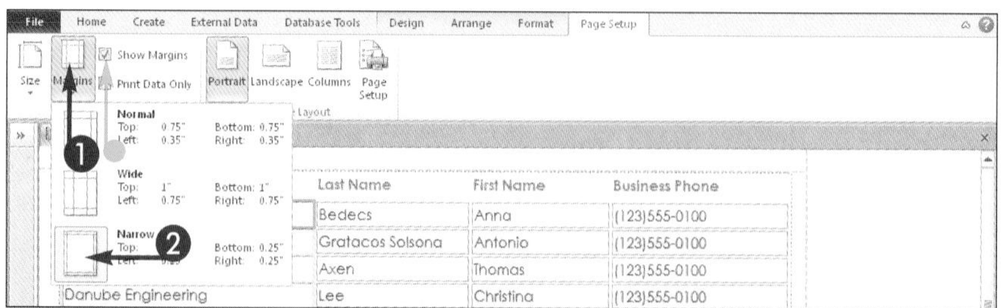

Set Custom Page Margins

1. On the Page Setup tab, click **Page Setup**.

   The Page Setup dialog box opens.
2. Click in a text field and then type a margin setting for that side of the page.
3. Click **OK**.

   The margin setting is applied.

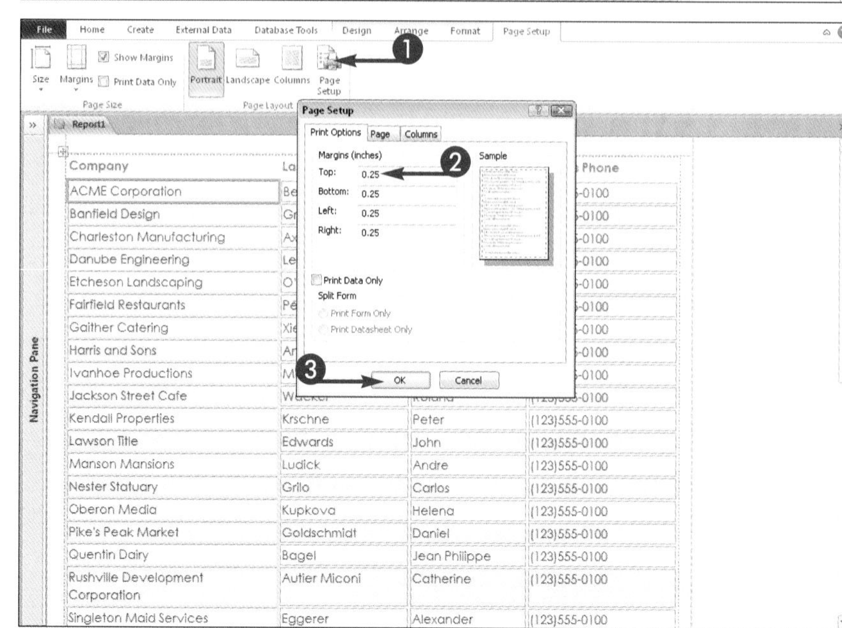

Set Control Margins and Padding

You can set margins for the individual controls on a form. The margin controls for individual items are for the text within the text boxes or label frames.

You can also set an amount of padding for one or more controls. Padding is like margins, but it refers to the space between fields – that is, the extra white space on the outside of a text box or another control.

Set Control Margins and Padding

Set Control Margins

1. In Design or Layout view, choose the controls you want to affect.

Note: *Hold down* Shift *and then click multiple controls; you can also drag a lasso around them.*

2. On the Arrange tab, click **Control Margins**.

3. Click the setting that you want.

   The control margin setting is applied.

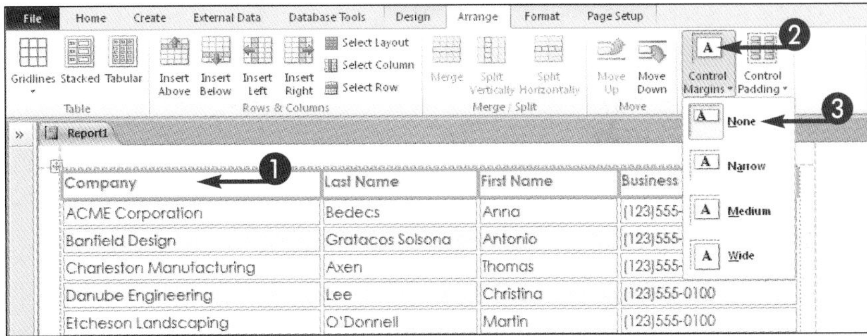

Set the Control Padding

1. In Design or Layout view, choose the controls you want to affect.

Note: *Hold down* Ctrl *and then click multiple controls; you can also drag a lasso around them.*

2. On the Arrange tab, click **Control Padding**.

3. Click the setting that you want.

   The control padding setting is applied.

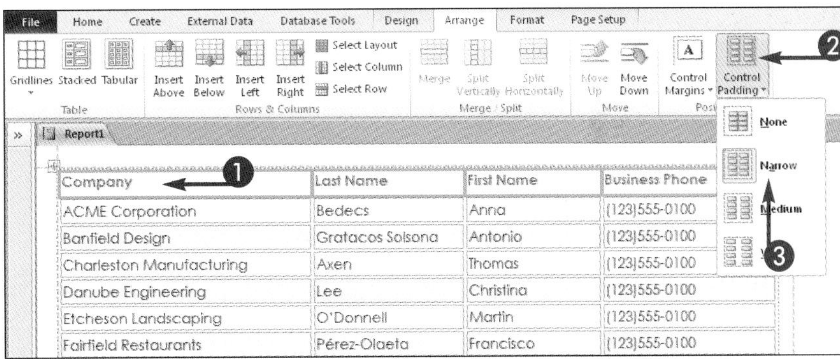

Format Report Text

When you apply a theme to a report, the font formatting is applied automatically. You can modify this formatting, selecting specific fonts, sizes, colors, and text attributes as needed.

As with forms, font formatting on reports applies to entire boxes only, not to individual characters. Therefore, if you want characters formatted differently from others, they must be in separate controls or labels.

Format Report Text

Set the Font

1. In Design or Layout view, click the label or field you want to format.

   To select more than one label or field, hold down Ctrl as you click them.

2. On the Format tab, click here (▾) to choose the font you want.

   The font is applied.

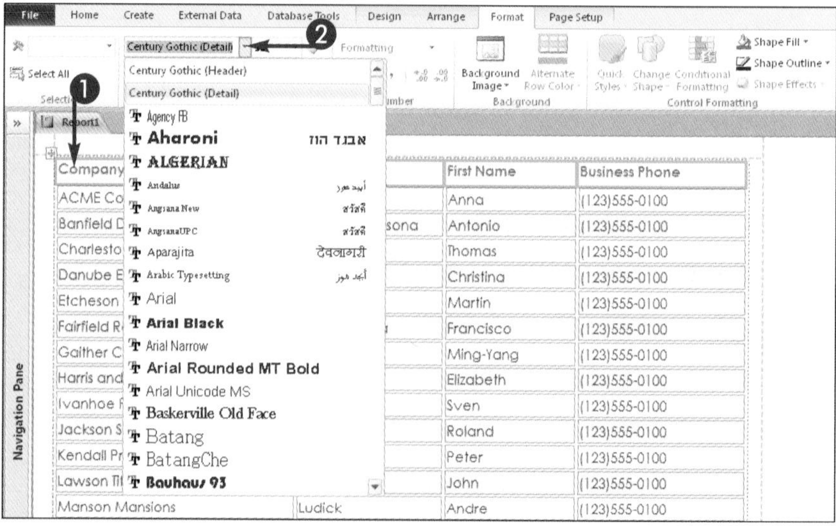

Set the Font Size

1. Click the label or field you want to format.

   To select more than one label or field, hold down Ctrl as you click them.

2. On the Format tab, click here (▾) to choose the font size.

Note: *If you choose a larger size, the text may appear truncated. Enlarge a field's box if needed, moving other boxes to make room.*

Note: *To automatically resize a field name box to accommodate its entry, double-click a selection handle in the direction you want to expand. For example, to expand to the right, double-click the right selection handle.*

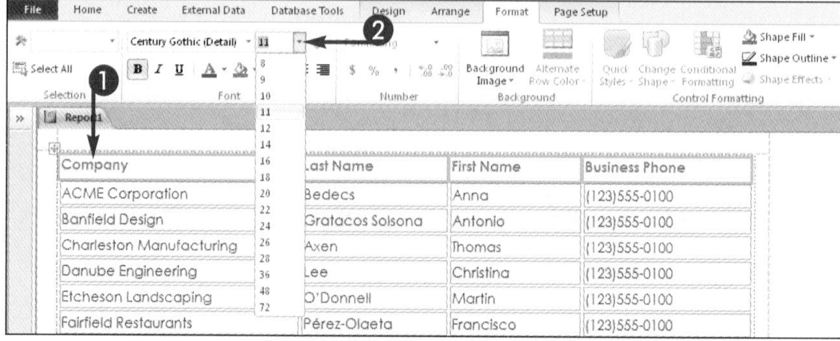

Set the Font Attributes

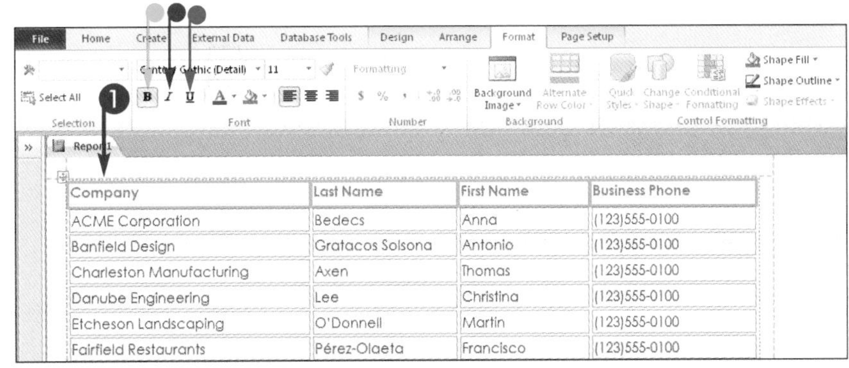

1. Click the label or field you want to format.

   To select more than one label or field, hold down Ctrl as you click them.

2. On the Format tab, click the button for the attributes that you want:

- Bold
- Italic
- Underline

The font attributes are applied.

Set the Font Color

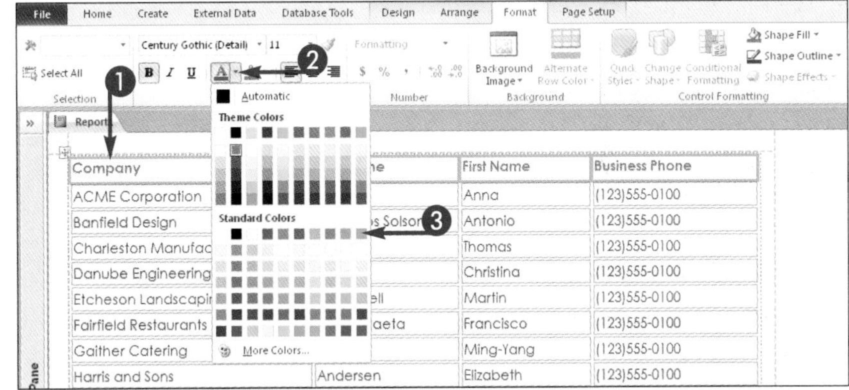

1. Click the label or field you want to format.
2. On the Format tab, click here (▾) to open the Font Color palette.
3. Click the color you want.

The color is applied.

What are the different color sections in the Font Color palette?

- **Theme Colors** refer to the color themes you can apply throughout Office applications in Office 2010. These colors shift when you apply a different theme.
- **Standard Colors** are fixed colors that do not change with the color theme.
- **Recent Colors** are colors that you have already applied in this database. Using one of these colors ensures consistency across objects.

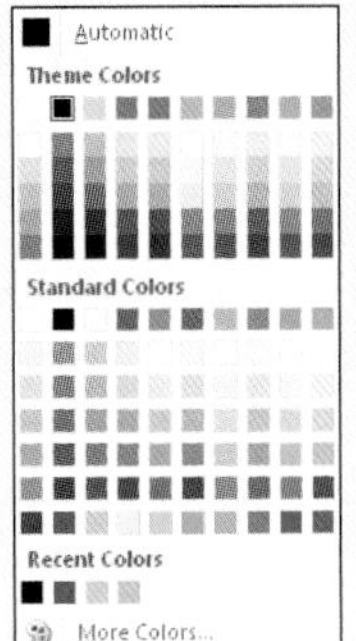

What does the Fill Color button do?

The Fill Color button (🖌) applies a background fill to controls. For example, you may want to use a colored background for certain labels. Keep in mind that if you use a dark fill color, you should set the text color to white (or a light color).

Size and Align Report Fields

As you design your report, you may need to adjust the sizing and alignment of the fields and their labels. When you change the width of a field, its label also changes automatically, and the fields to its right shift to make room or to reduce the space.

When you create a form in Layout view, the fields are usually properly aligned with one another, but if you created or modified the form in Design view, some of the fields may not be quite aligned with one another. You can easily align multiple fields by selecting them and then choosing an alignment type.

Size and Align Report Fields

Size a Field

1. In Design or Layout view, click the label or field you want to size.
2. Position the mouse pointer over the right edge of the control (⇖ changes to ↔) and then drag to the right or left.

   The field is resized, and any fields to its right are moved.

Company	Last Name	First Name	Business Phone
ACME Corporation	Bedecs	Anna	(123)555-0100
Banfield Design	Gratacos Solsona	Antonio	(123)555-0100
Charleston Manufacturing	Axen	Thomas	(123)555-0100
Danube Engineering	Lee	Christina	(123)555-0100
Etcheson Landscaping	O'Donnell	Martin	(123)555-0100
Fairfield Restaurants	Pérez-Olaeta	Francisco	(123)555-0100
Gaither Catering	Xie	Ming-Yang	(123)555-0100
Harris and Sons	Andersen	Elizabeth	(123)555-0100
Ivanhoe Productions	Mortensen	Sven	(123)555-0100
Jackson Street Cafe	Wacker	Roland	(123)555-0100
Kendall Properties	Krschne	Peter	(123)555-0100
Lawson Title	Edwards	John	(123)555-0100
Manson Mansions	Ludick	Andre	(123)555-0100
Nester Statuary	Grilo	Carlos	(123)555-0100
Oberon Media	Kupkova	Helena	(123)555-0100
Pike's Peak Market	Goldschmidt	Daniel	(123)555-0100
Quentin Dairy	Bagel	Jean Philippe	(123)555-0100
Rushville Development Corporation	Autier Miconi	Catherine	(123)555-0100
Singleton Maid Services	Eggerer	Alexander	(123)555-0100
Trambull and Sons	Li	George	(123)555-0100
Uline Packaging Concepts	Tham	Bernard	(123)555-0100

Align Fields with One Another

1. In Design view, select the controls you want to align.

   Note: *Hold down* Shift *as you click each control.*

2. On the Arrange tab, click **Align**.
3. Click the alignment that you want.

   The selected labels align with one another.

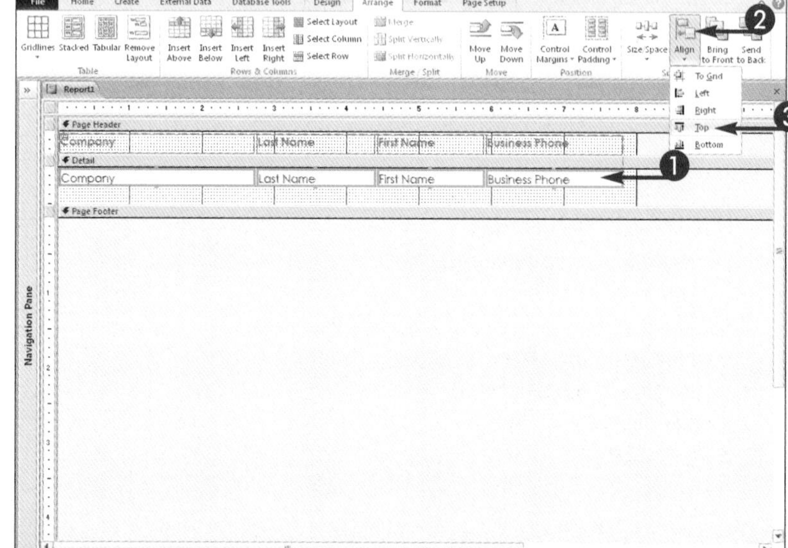

Insert a Page-Numbering Code

Because reports are designed to be printed, they should include page-numbering codes. Reports generated with the Report Wizard or other quick methods contain a page-numbering function in the Page Footer section. In reports that you generate from blanks, you must insert your own page-numbering codes.

Insert a Page-Numbering Code

***Note:** These steps are for reports that do not already contain page numbering.*

1. In Design view on the Design tab, click **Page Numbers**.

   The Page Numbers dialog box opens.

2. Click the desired page number format (◯ changes to ◉).

***Note:** Page N will display the word "Page" along with the number, like this: Page 2. Page N of M will display the word "Page" along with the current page number, the word "of," and the total page count, like this: Page 2 of 4.*

3. Choose a position for the page numbers (◯ changes to ◉).

   Page numbering can be placed in either the report header or footer.

4. Click here (▾) to choose an alignment for the page numbers.

- You can deselect the Show Number on First Page check box (☑ changes to ☐) to omit the page number from the first page.

5. Click **OK**.

- The page numbering code is inserted in either the header or the footer depending on your selection in step **3**.

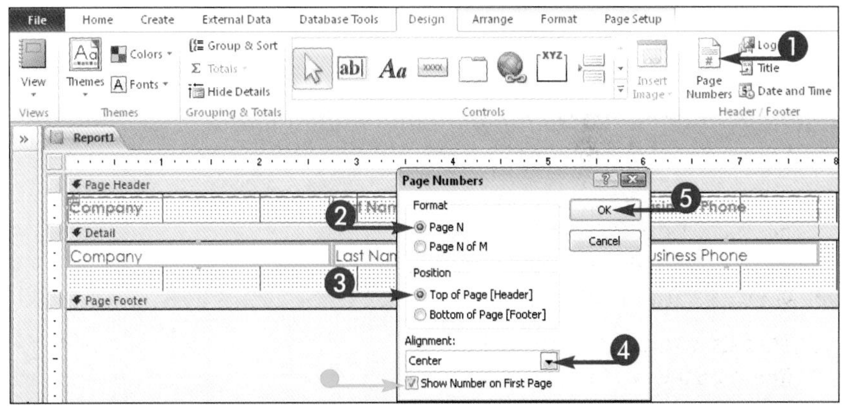

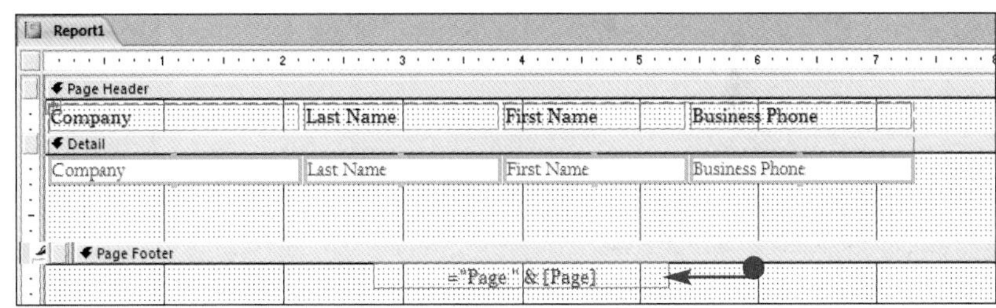

CHAPTER

12

Grouping and Summarizing Data

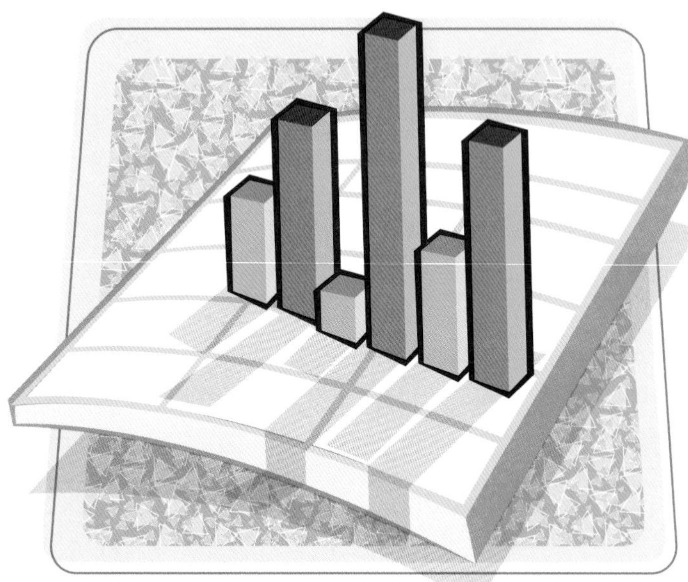

The reports you learned about in Chapter 11 provide a complete listing of the records in the data set. In this chapter, you will learn how to create reports that group and summarize data, distilling down a large amount of information into a manageable, meaningful report.

Understanding Grouping and Summarizing

When you have a lot of data, it can be difficult to discern its overall meaning. Access provides several ways of grouping and summarizing data to make it easier to understand.

- **Grouping**
  You can group a report by a field, such as by company. In this example, each company has its own section of the report.

- **Aggregate Functions**
  You can summarize each group with one or more aggregate functions, such as Sum (shown here), Average, or Count.

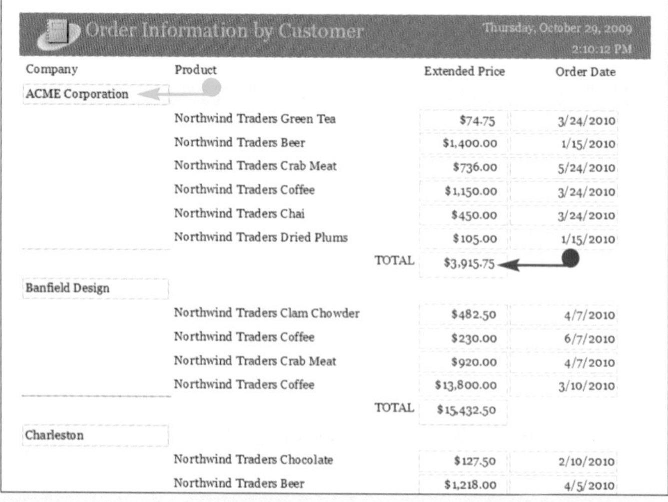

Order Information by Customer — Thursday, October 29, 2009 2:10:12 PM

Company	Product		Extended Price	Order Date
ACME Corporation				
	Northwind Traders Green Tea		$74.75	3/24/2010
	Northwind Traders Beer		$1,400.00	1/15/2010
	Northwind Traders Crab Meat		$736.00	5/24/2010
	Northwind Traders Coffee		$1,150.00	3/24/2010
	Northwind Traders Chai		$450.00	3/24/2010
	Northwind Traders Dried Plums		$105.00	1/15/2010
		TOTAL	$3,915.75	
Banfield Design				
	Northwind Traders Clam Chowder		$482.50	4/7/2010
	Northwind Traders Coffee		$230.00	6/7/2010
	Northwind Traders Crab Meat		$920.00	4/7/2010
	Northwind Traders Coffee		$13,800.00	3/10/2010
		TOTAL	$15,432.50	
Charleston				
	Northwind Traders Chocolate		$127.50	2/10/2010
	Northwind Traders Beer		$1,218.00	4/5/2010

- **Reports Based on Summary Queries**
  As you learned in Chapter 8, you can create summary queries that distill table data into aggregate functions. You can then create reports based on one of those queries.

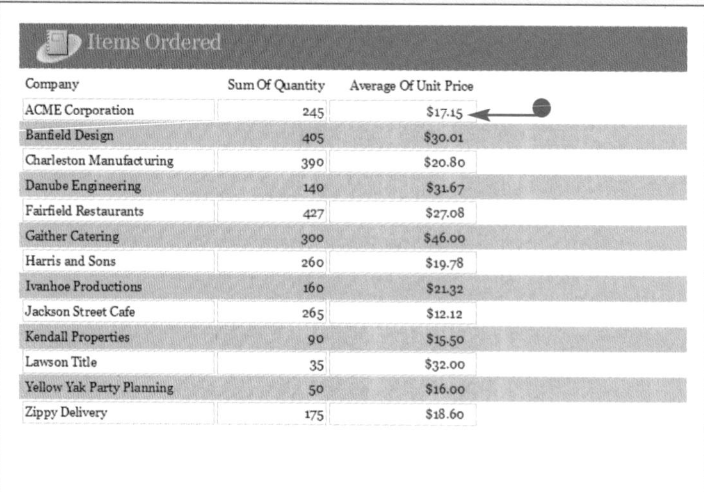

Items Ordered

Company	Sum Of Quantity	Average Of Unit Price
ACME Corporation	245	$17.15
Banfield Design	405	$30.01
Charleston Manufacturing	390	$20.80
Danube Engineering	140	$31.67
Fairfield Restaurants	427	$27.08
Gaither Catering	300	$46.00
Harris and Sons	260	$19.78
Ivanhoe Productions	160	$21.32
Jackson Street Cafe	265	$12.12
Kendall Properties	90	$15.50
Lawson Title	35	$32.00
Yellow Yak Party Planning	50	$16.00
Zippy Delivery	175	$18.60

- **PivotTables**
  When you want to summarize data without creating a report or query, a PivotTable works well. A PivotTable is a dynamic view of a table or query.
- **Grid with Placeholders for Fields**
  A PivotTable starts out as a blank grid with placeholders like this one.
- **Draggable Fields**
  You drag fields onto the grid to create the PivotTable.
- **Collapsible Group for Summary**
  You can click [+] or [−] to expand or collapse a group to show a summary.

- **PivotChart**
  A PivotChart is like a PivotTable, except that it displays the data graphically.
- **Filter**
  You can filter any of the fields to show only certain values. You can also do this with a PivotTable.

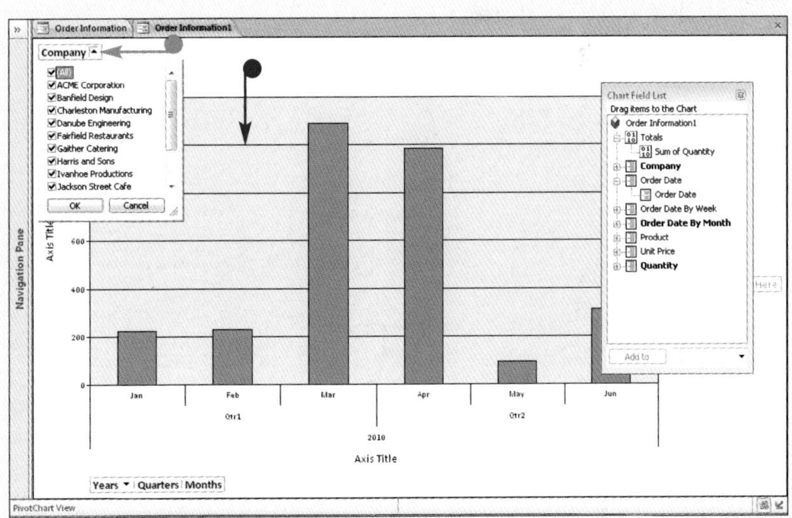

Group Report Results

If you use the Report Wizard to create a report, as detailed in Chapter 11, you have the opportunity to specify grouping in the wizard.

You can also set up grouping in Layout or Design view afterward or change the grouping. If you arrange the grouping in Layout view, the grouping field is moved automatically into the newly created group header. If you arrange it in Design view, you must manually cut and paste the field.

Group Report Results

Group from Layout View

1. In Layout view, click **Group & Sort**.

   The Group, Sort, and Total pane appears.

2. Click **Add a group**.

   A shortcut menu appears, showing the available fields by which you can group your data.

3. Click the field by which you want to group.

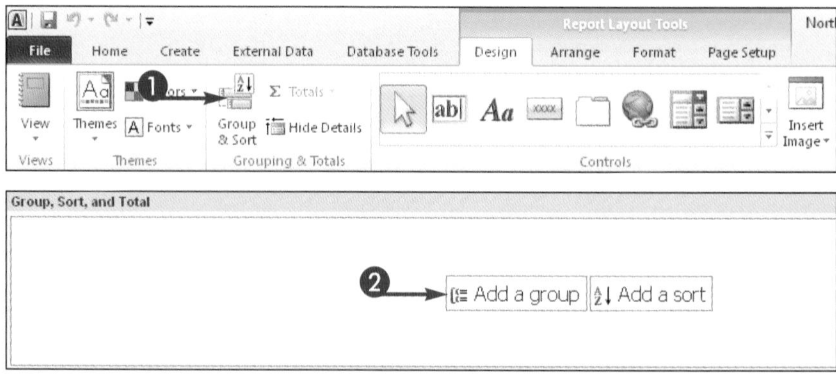

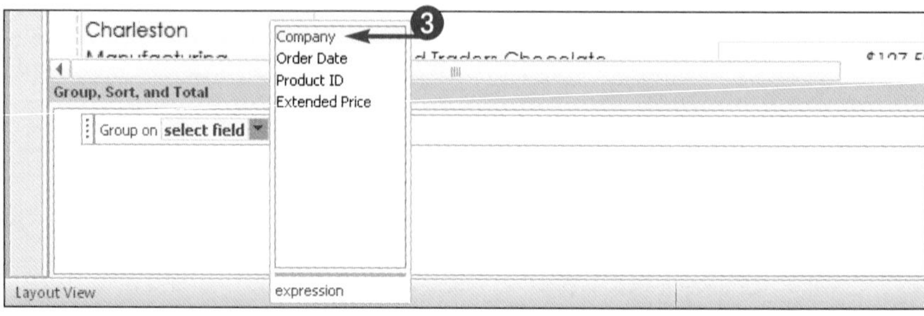

- A Group On line appears.
- An additional set of buttons appears for creating another level of grouping, if desired.

Group from Design View

1. In Design view, perform the steps in the section "Group from Layout View" to create a grouping.
2. On the design grid, click the field on which you have grouped and then press Ctrl + X to cut it to the Clipboard.
3. Click the header for the field on which you have grouped.
4. Press Ctrl + V to paste the field into that header section.
5. Click **View** to check the results in Report view.

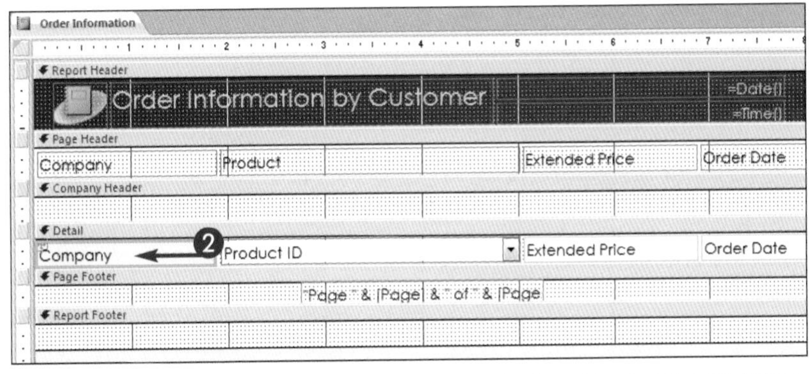

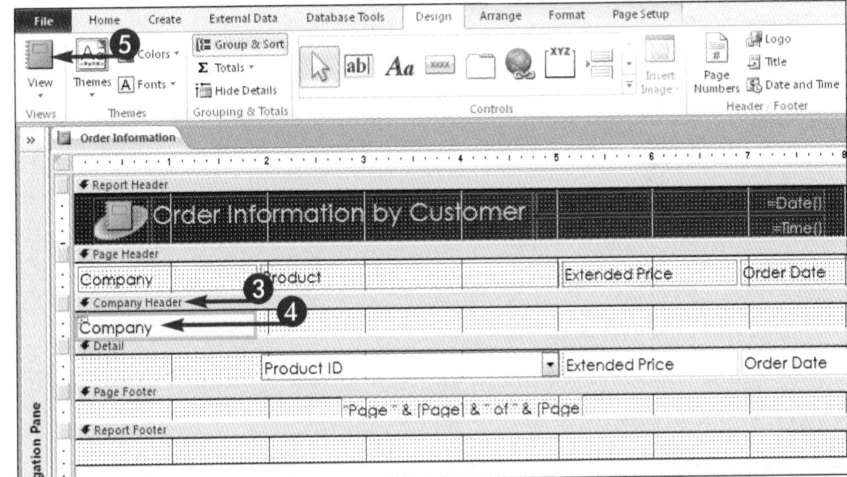

Can I have multiple levels of groupings?

Yes. After you create a grouping, a fresh set of Add a group and Add a sort buttons appears below it. Click **Add a group** to create a group subordinate to your original one.

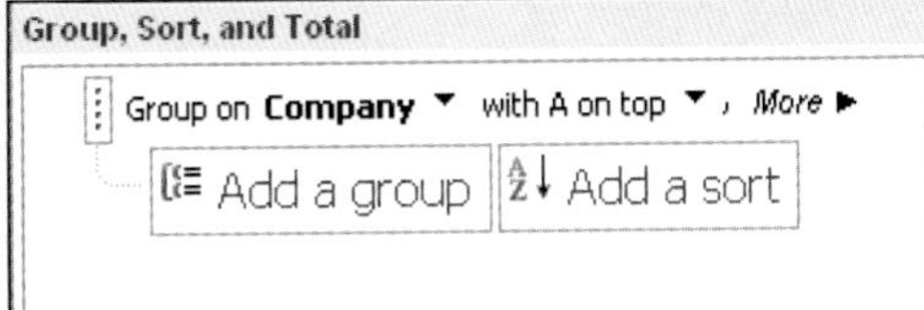

How can I set grouping options?

Click **More** on the group's bar. Additional drop-down lists appear for setting options. For example, you can choose grouping intervals, choose to have only a group header or footer, or choose whether or not to keep a group together on one page.

Sort Report Results

You can sort the results in a report, with or without grouping. If you group, you define the sorting in the context of that group by setting group options. If you do not group, you define the sorting separately.

Sort Report Results

Sort the Groups

Note: *Begin these steps in Design view, with a group already defined.*

1. Click here (▾) to choose a sort order.

   For a text field, you can sort with A on top or Z on top. For a numeric field, you can choose smallest to largest or largest to smallest.

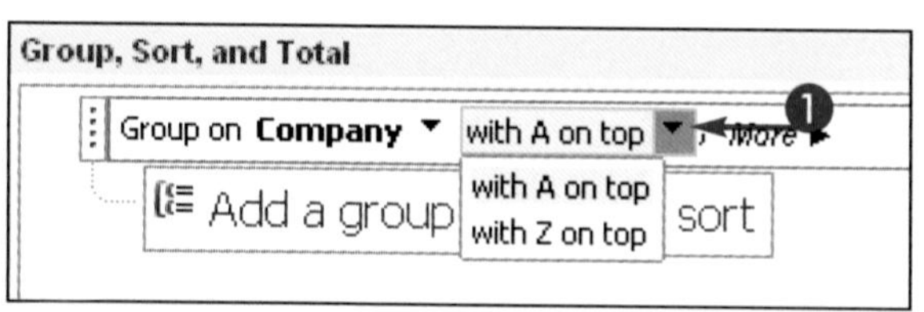

Sort Entries within a Group or with No Grouping

1. Click **Add a sort**.

   A list of available fields appears on which you can sort your data.

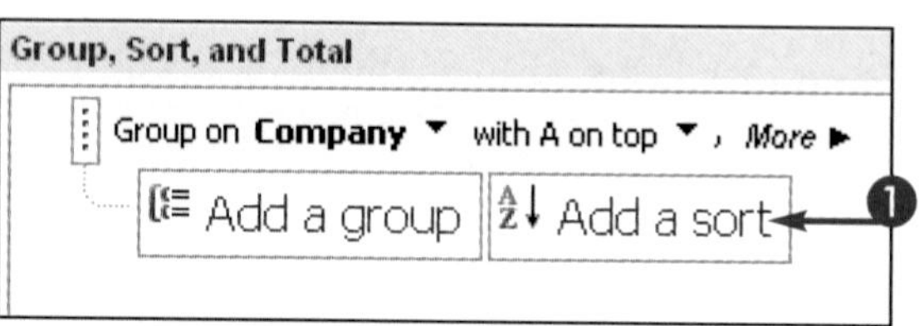

2. Click the field on which you want to sort.

   A sort bar appears.

   For a date field, you can sort oldest to newest or newest to oldest.

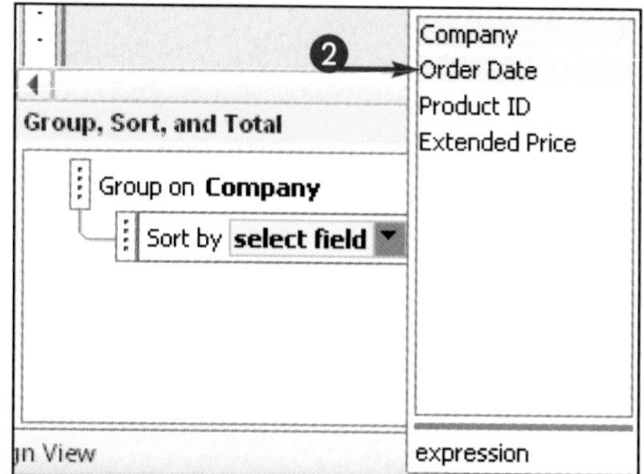

- To reverse the sort order, click here (▾) to choose the opposite setting.

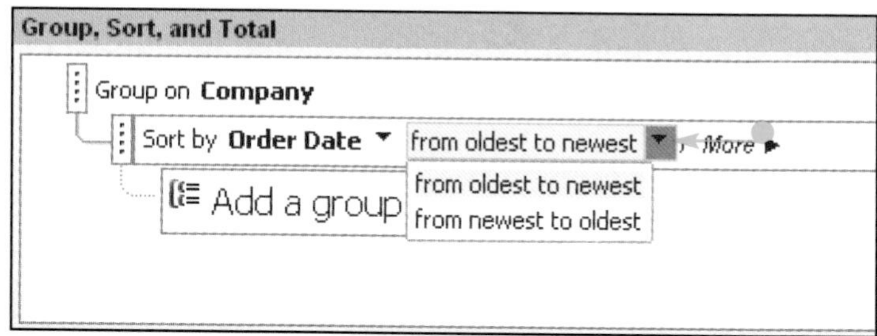

Count Records

You can use a Count function in a report to list the number of records, either within each group individually or within the entire report.

Count can be set either from a sorting or a grouping specification.

Count Records

***Note:** Begin these steps in Design view, with a group or sort specification already defined.*

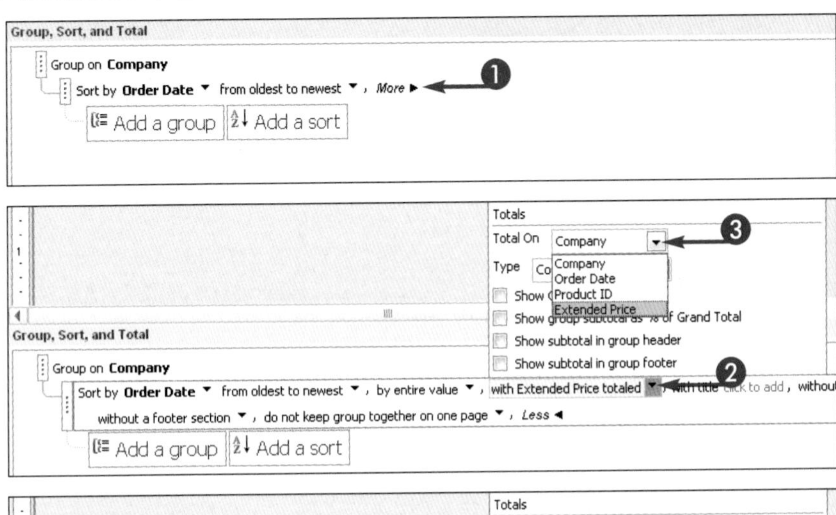

1. Click **More**.

   The available options expand. The options may be different than shown here depending on the field type.

2. Click here (▾) to open a menu of options.

3. Click here (▾) to choose the field on which you want to total.

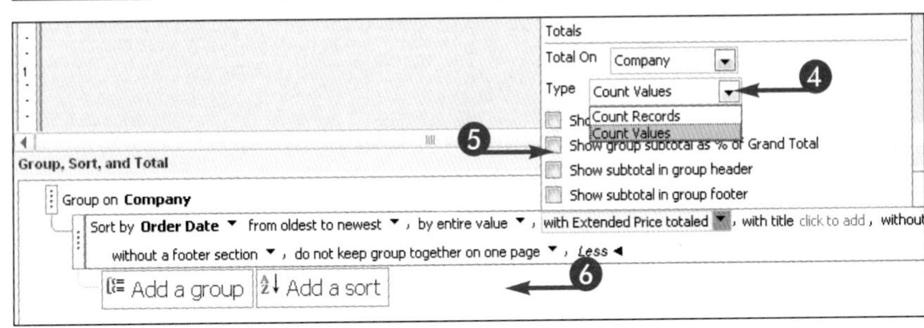

4. Click here (▾) to choose **Count Values** if it does not already appear.

5. Click the check boxes to indicate where and how the count should appear (☐ changes to ☑).

6. Click away from the menu to close it.

Add an Aggregate Function

Counting is only one of many math operations you can perform on records in a report. You can also add other functions, including sum, average, minimum, maximum, and standard deviation. These are all referred to as *aggregate functions* because they summarize (aggregate) data.

Add an Aggregate Function

***Note:** Begin these steps in Design view, with a group or sort specification already defined.*

1. Click **More** if the extended options do not already appear.

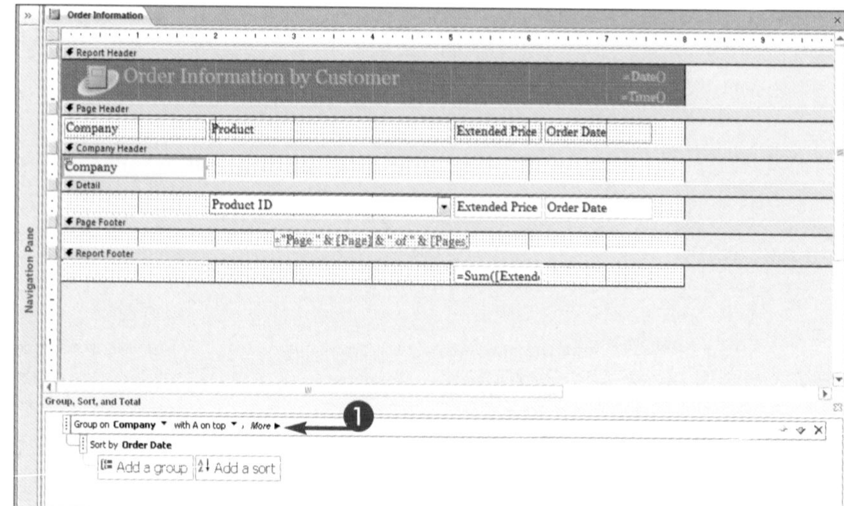

2. Click here (▾) to open a menu of total options.

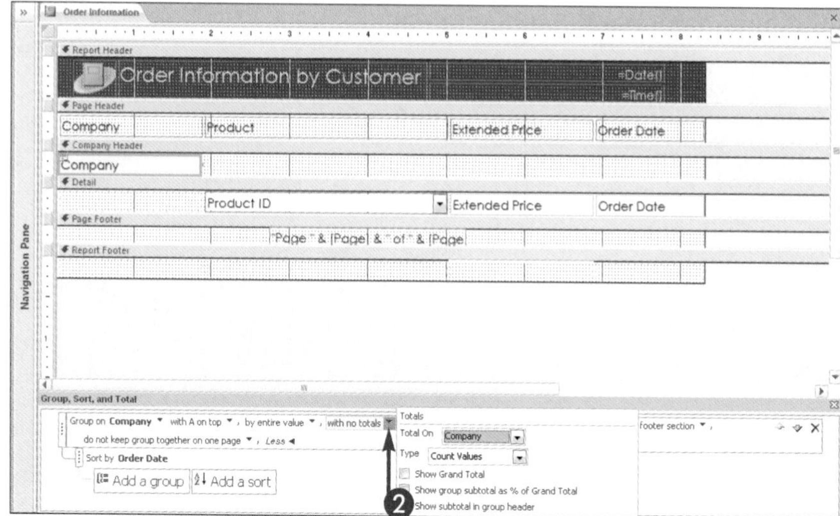

3 Click here (▾) to open a list of fields and then choose the field on which you want to total.

4 Click here (▾) to open a list of functions, and choose the function you want.

5 Click the check boxes to indicate where and how the function should appear (☐ changes to ☑).

6 Click away from the menu to close it.

- The function appears in the report design.

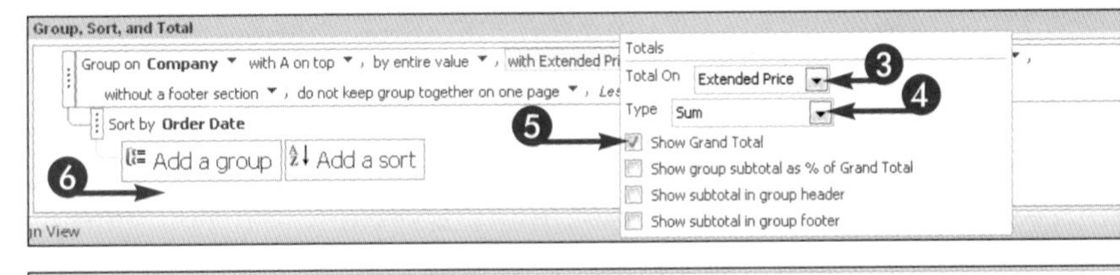

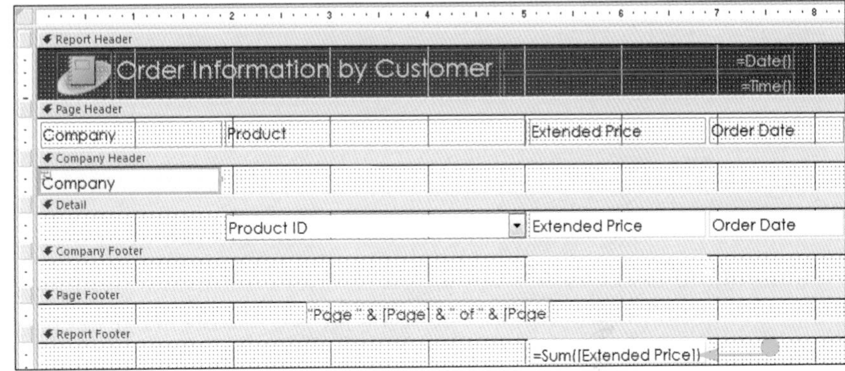

How can I move a function between sections?

A function is in an unbound text box. You can move unbound text boxes between sections with a cut-and-paste operation but not with a drag-and-drop operation. Select the text box containing the function and then press Ctrl + X. Click the bar for the section into which you want to insert the function and then press Ctrl + V.

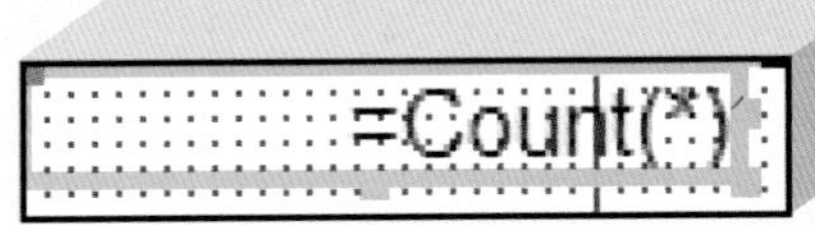

Can I use other functions besides the ones on the list?

Yes. Add an unbound text box to the report and then manually type the function into it. Use the Help system to get the proper syntax.

1 On the Design tab, click the **Text Box** button (ab|) in the Controls gallery.

2 Drag to create the text box.

3 Select the text box label and then press Delete to remove it.

4 Click inside the text box and then type the function, starting with an equals sign (=).

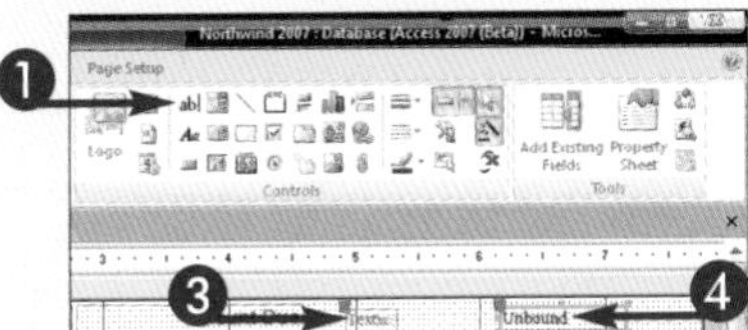

Summarize a Datasheet with a PivotTable

You can use a PivotTable to experiment dynamically with various summary views of your data. Rather than define a fixed report, you can create many different views of your data with the PivotTable before deciding which one is most useful.

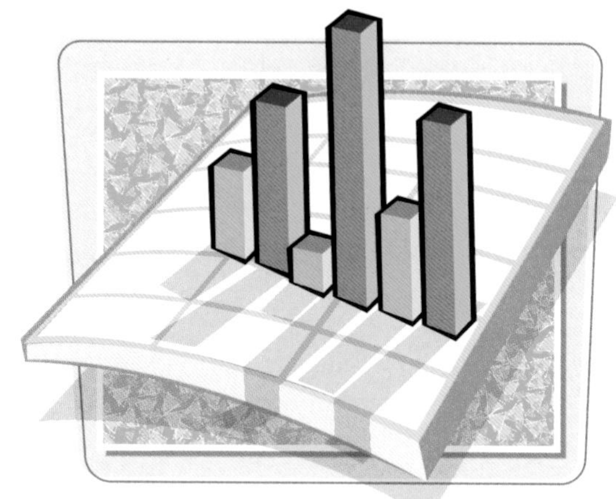

Summarize a Datasheet with a PivotTable

Create a PivotTable

1. From a table or query in Datasheet view, right-click on the tab for the datasheet.
2. Choose **PivotTable View** from the shortcut menu.

   A blank PivotTable grid appears with placeholders.

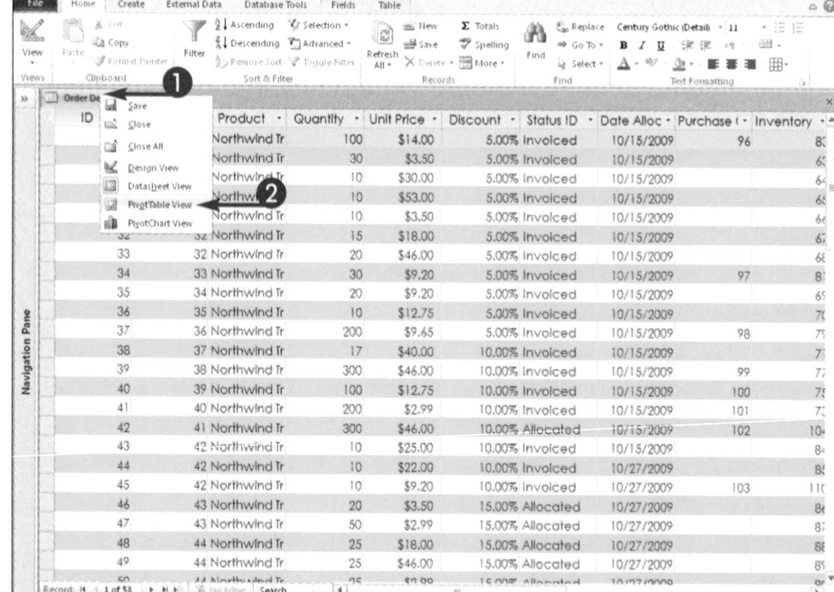

- If the Field List does not appear, click **Field List** to display it.

3. Drag a field onto the Drop Row Fields Here placeholder.

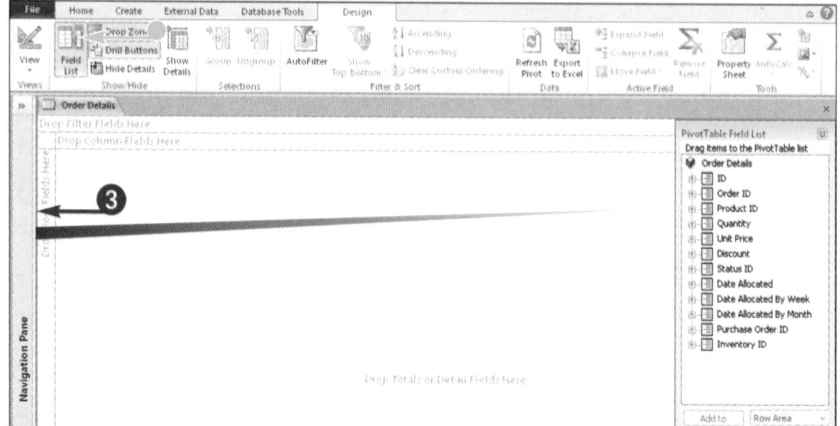

- Data from that field appears in a column at the left.

4 Drag a field onto the Drop Column Fields Here placeholder.

5 Drag a field onto the Drop Totals or Detail Fields Here placeholder.

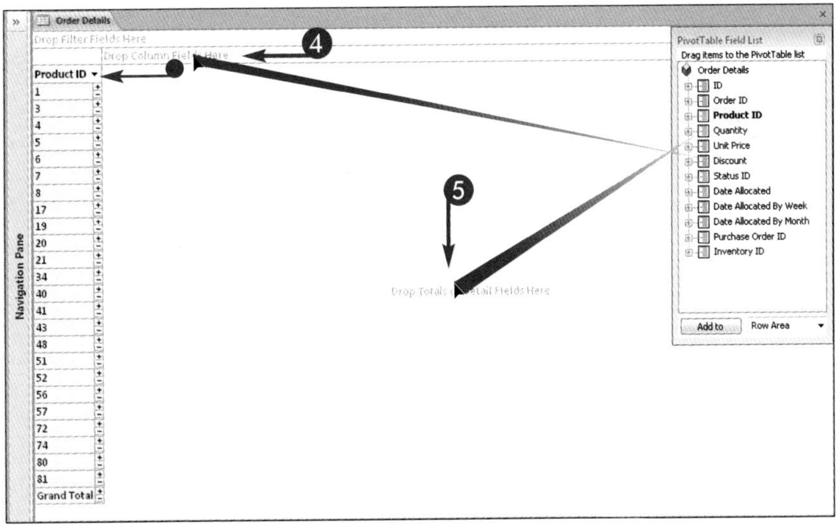

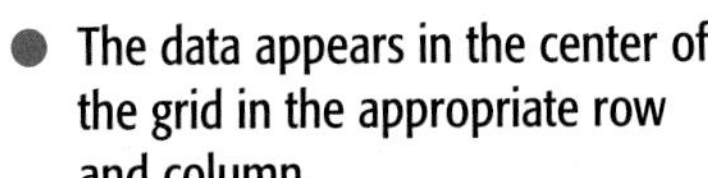

- The data appears in the center of the grid in the appropriate row and column.

TIPS

Can I have more than one field in each placeholder?

Yes. Just drag multiple fields into the same placeholder area. If there is already a field there, drag the other one on top of it. In this example, there are two fields as columns, and the second one is grouped by the first one.

Discount							
5.00%		10.00%		15.00%		Grand Total	
Quantity	Unit Price	Quantity	Unit Price	Quantity	Unit Price	Quantity	Unit Price
15	$18.00			25	$18.00	15	$18.00
						25	$18.00
30	$22.00	10	$22.00			10	$22.00
						30	$22.00
25	$21.35					25	$21.35
90	$25.00	10	$25.00			10	$25.00
						90	$25.00
10	$30.00					10	$30.00
30	$30.00					30	$30.00

What do the ⊟ and ⊞ buttons do?

They collapse (⊟) and expand (⊞) the summary. You can collapse any item to summarize it, or expand it to see all the details for it. This flexibility is one of the main benefits of a PivotTable.

continued

Summarize a Datasheet with a PivotTable *(continued)*

After you have the basic PivotTable in place, you can enhance it by filtering by certain fields. You can add fields to it specifically for the purpose of filtering or you can exclude certain values from individual rows or columns.

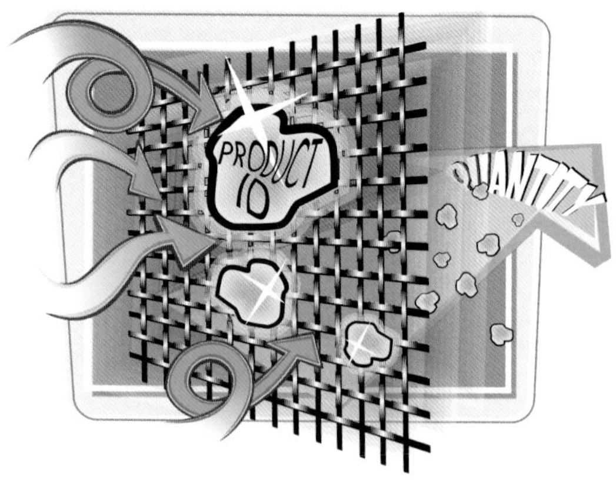

Summarize a Datasheet with a PivotTable *(continued)*

Filter for Certain Values in Individual Fields

1. Click ▾ next to a field name.
2. Deselect the check box for each value that you do not want to include (☑ changes to ☐).
3. Click **OK**.

The results change to exclude the values that you cleared.

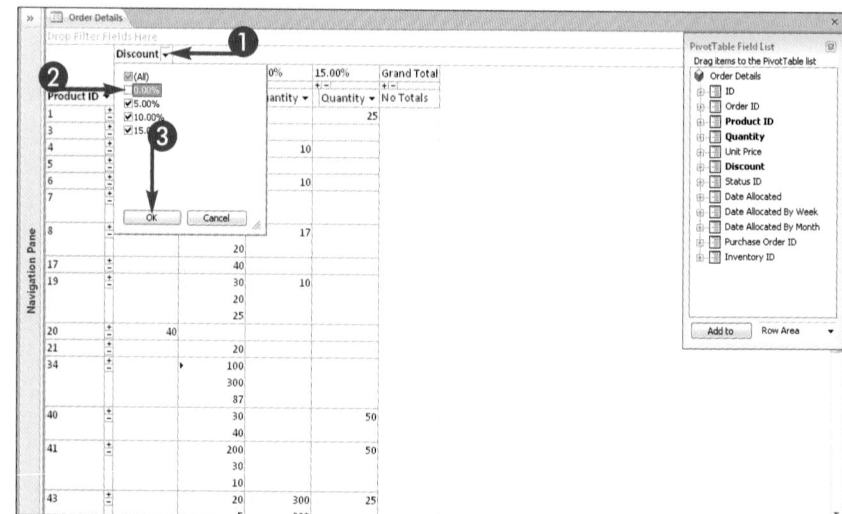

Filter a PivotTable

1. Drag the field by which you want to filter to the Drop Filter Fields Here area.

- Depending on the field types, the Field List may contain not only the individual fields but also some special entries that enable you to group records. For example, for the Date Allocated field, you might have Date Allocated by Week and Date Allocated by Month.

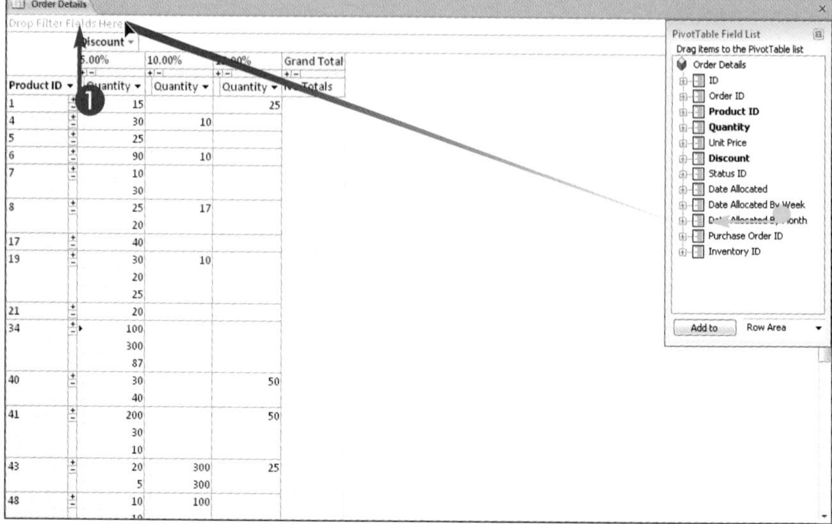

2. Click ▾ to the right of the filter field to open its menu.

- If needed, click ⊞ to expand a category (⊞ changes to ⊟).

3. Deselect the check boxes for any values you do not want (☑ changes to ☐).

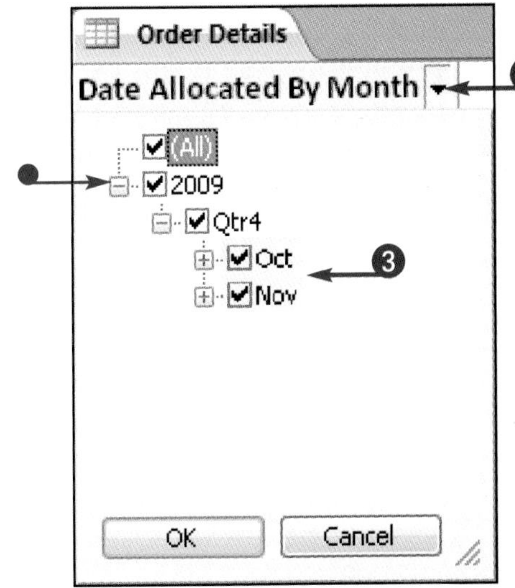

- When a category is partly selected, its check box appears gray (☐ changes to ☑).

4. Click **OK**.

The filter is applied, and a note appears under the filter field saying what has been excluded.

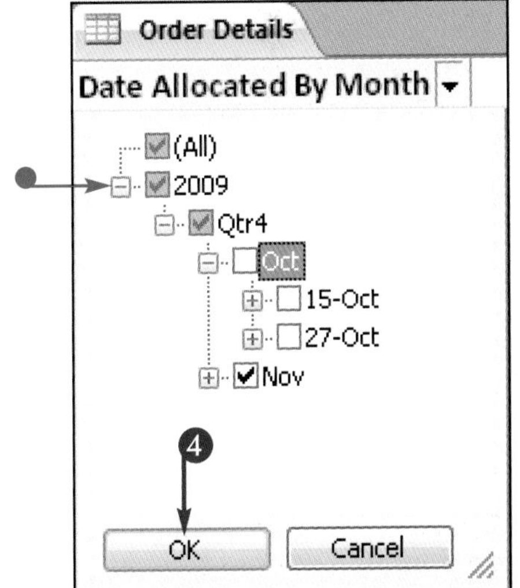

TIPS

Nothing appears in the Grand Total category; it just says No Totals. How can I display this information?

1. Click ⊞ under Grand Total to see the totals.

- The ⊞ and ⊟ buttons are called Drill Buttons, and you can turn them on or off with the Drill Buttons button on the Design tab.

How can I show or hide all details?

2. Click **Show Details** to show all details.

3. Click **Hide Details** to hide all details.

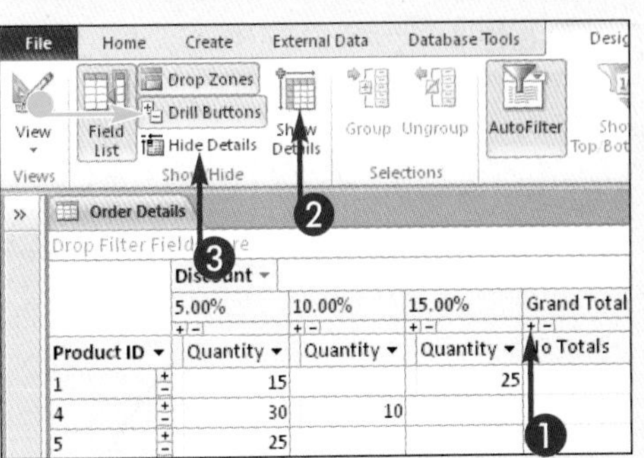

Add and Delete Aggregate Functions in a PivotTable

You can use AutoCalc to easily add aggregate functions to a PivotTable view. For example, you can add sums, averages, and so on.

Add and Delete Aggregate Functions in a PivotTable

Add an Aggregate Function

1. In PivotTable view, click the field in the PivotTable on which you want to aggregate.
2. Click **AutoCalc**.
3. Click the aggregate function that you want to use.

   The function appears as a new row (or column) for each grouping.

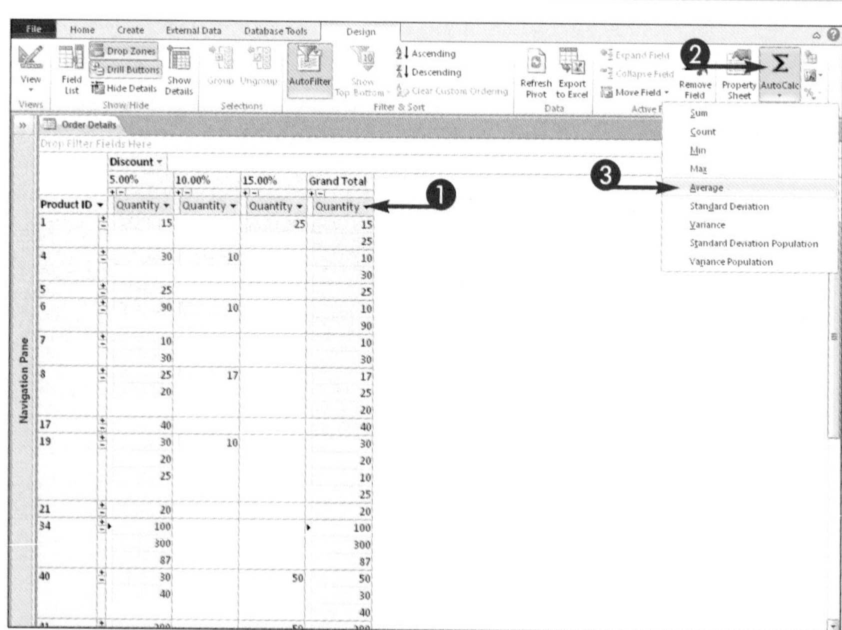

Delete an Aggregate Function

1. To delete an aggregate function, find it under Totals in the Field List.
2. Right-click on the aggregate function and then choose **Delete** from the shortcut menu.

   The function is removed from the field list.

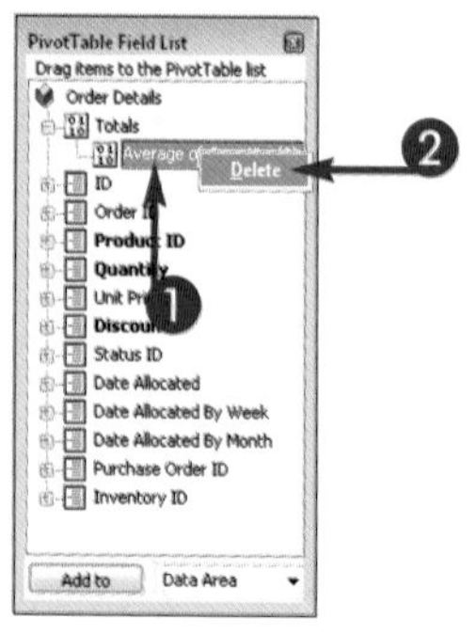

Group and Ungroup PivotTable Content

After creating a PivotTable view, you may decide that it contains too many individual entries to be meaningful. You can group these individual entries into summary items to make the data more useful.

Group and Ungroup PivotTable Content

Group Entries

1. In PivotTable view, select the individual entries that you want to group.
2. Click **Group**.

   The entries are grouped into a generically named Group1.

- You can change the group's name by right-clicking on it and then choosing **Properties** from the shortcut menu.
- Then, change the group name on the Captions tab.

You can click ⊞ to expand the group or ⊟ to collapse it.

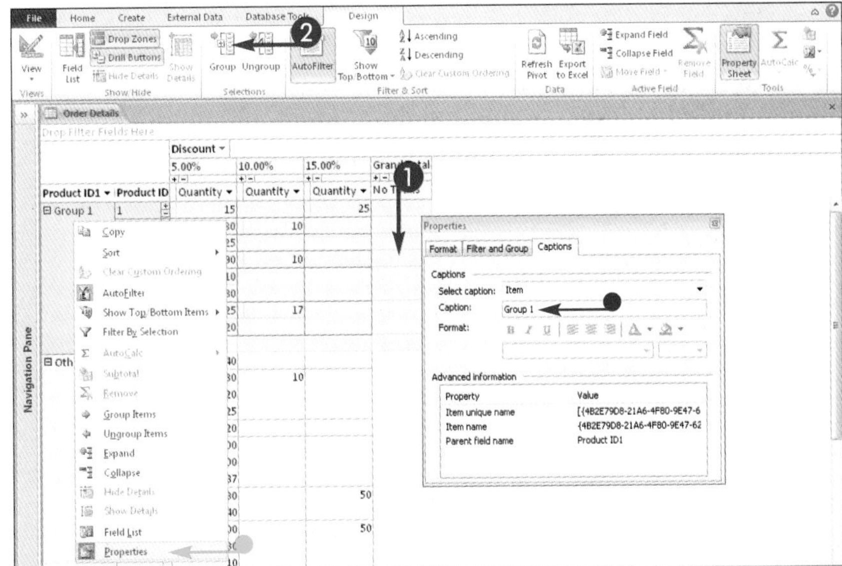

Ungroup a Grouped Entry

1. Select the group that you want to ungroup.
2. Click **Ungroup**.

   The single entry separates back into individual entries.

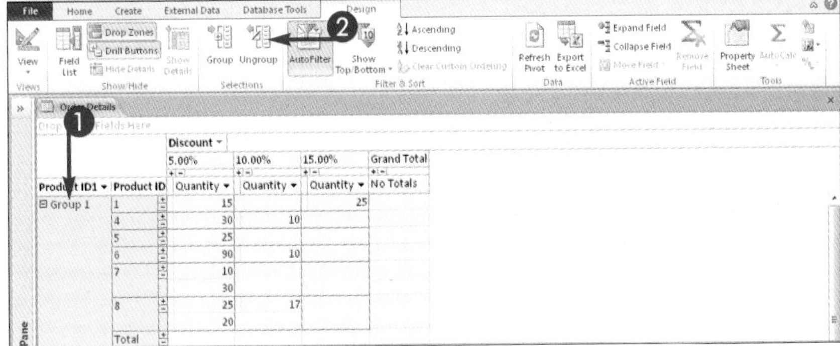

Clear a PivotTable Grid

A PivotTable stays populated with the fields you put into it until you clear them. The fields you put into a PivotTable also carry over to a PivotChart.

You do not have to clear the PivotTable grid before switching back to Datasheet view.

Clear a PivotTable Grid

❶ In PivotTable view, right-click on the field you want to remove.

❷ Click **Remove**.

The field is removed from the grid.

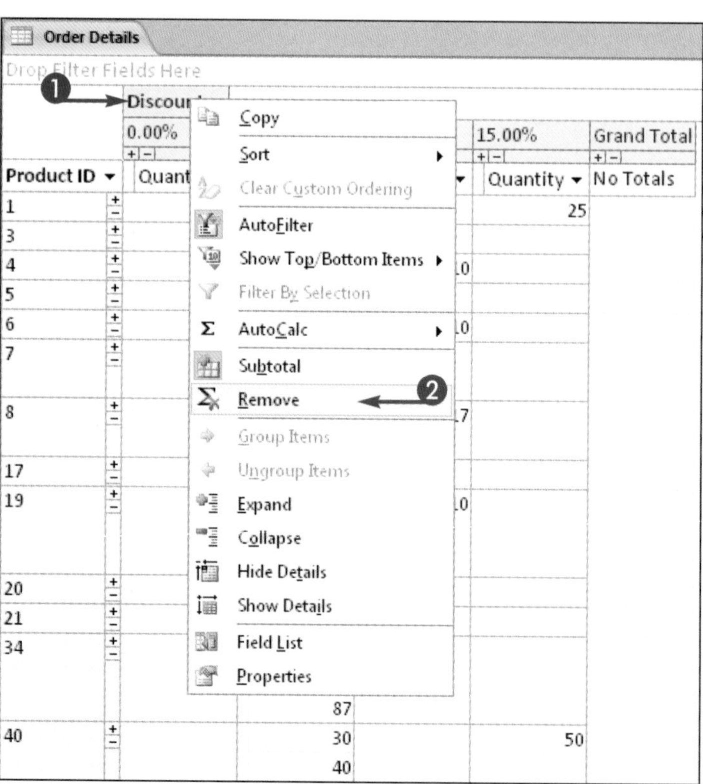

- If there are no fields remaining in that placeholder, the placeholder box appears empty.

❸ Repeat steps **1** and **2** for other fields you want to remove from the grid.

Order Details

Drop Filter Fields Here

Drop Column Fields Here

Product ID	Quantity
1	15
	25
3	50
4	10
	30

Note: *Another way to clear the grid for a PivotTable or PivotChart is to close the table or query without saving your changes to it.*

Switch a PivotTable to a PivotChart

PivotTables and PivotCharts are two different views of the same data, so you can switch easily between them.

If you switch to PivotChart view while there are fields in PivotTable view, the fields carry over unless they are cleared first.

Switch a PivotTable to a PivotChart

1. Right-click on the tab for the PivotTable.
2. Click **PivotChart View**.

A PivotChart grid appears. If there were fields in the PivotTable view, those same fields carry over into the PivotChart view.

You can switch back to PivotTable view by repeating these steps and then choosing PivotTable View in step **2**.

Note: *You will learn more about PivotCharts in Chapter 14.*

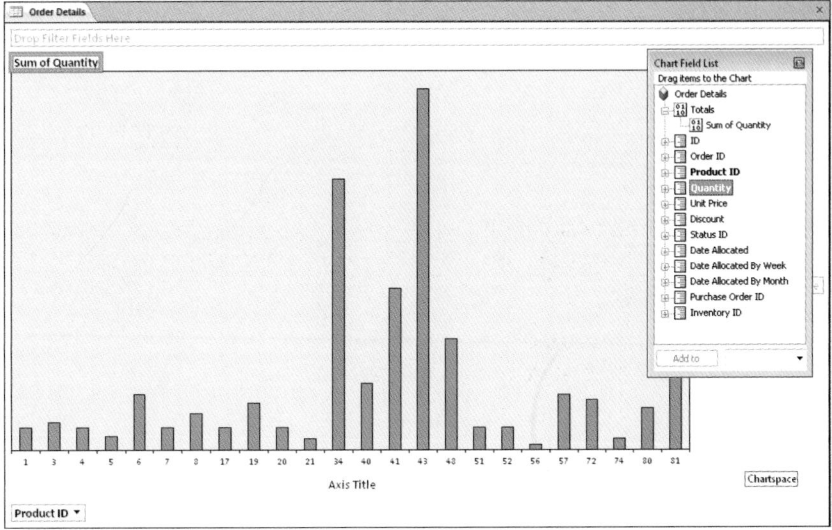

CHAPTER 13

Creating Mailing Labels

In addition to standard reports, Access can also create mailing labels. This enables you to print labels without first exporting the data into a word-processing program as well as set up reusable label definitions for recurring mailings.

Labels are a special type of report. They print multiple records per page in a layout designed to correspond to self-stick labels that feed into your printer.

Create Labels

1. In the Objects list, click the table or query containing the fields that you want.
2. On the Create tab, click **Labels**.

   The Label Wizard dialog box opens.
3. Click here (▾) to choose the label manufacturer.

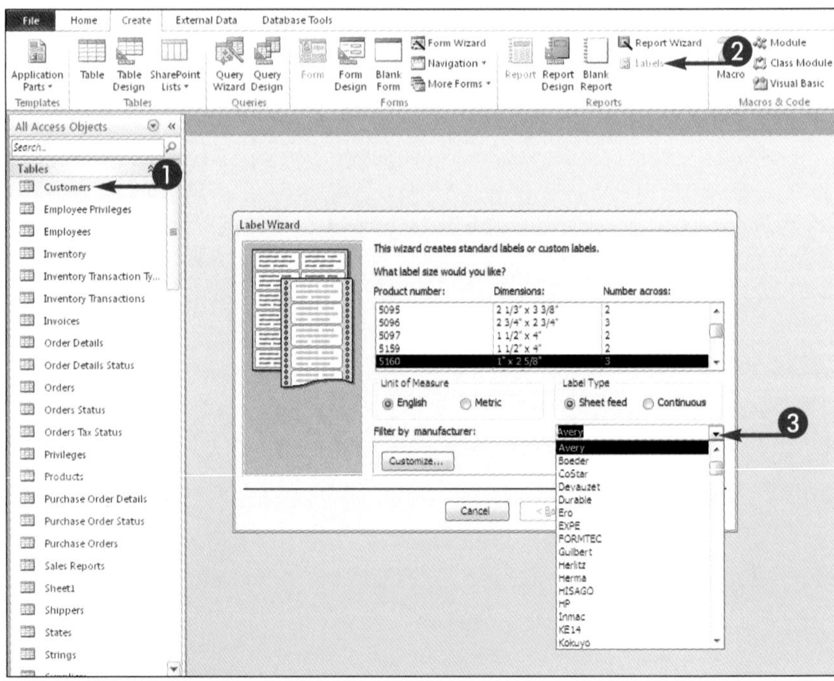

4. Click the unit of measure you want to use (◎ changes to ◉).
5. Click the label type (◎ changes to ◉).

Note: *Continuous-feed labels are typically used only by dot matrix printers.*

6. Click the label product number.

Note: *If you do not know the product number, choose one that matches the dimensions and number of labels across that you have.*

7. Click **Next**.

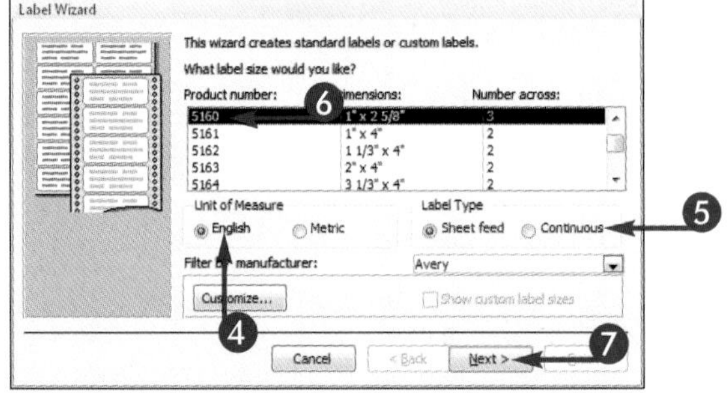

8 Click here (▾) to choose a font for the labels.

9 Click here (▾) to choose a font size.

10 Click here (▾) to choose a font weight.

11 If needed, click the **Italic** check box (☐ changes to ☑).

12 If needed, click the **Underline** check box (☐ changes to ☑).

13 Click here (...) to open the Color dialog box.

14 Click a color for the text.

- For more choices, you can click **Define Custom Colors**.

15 Click **OK**.

16 Click **Next**.

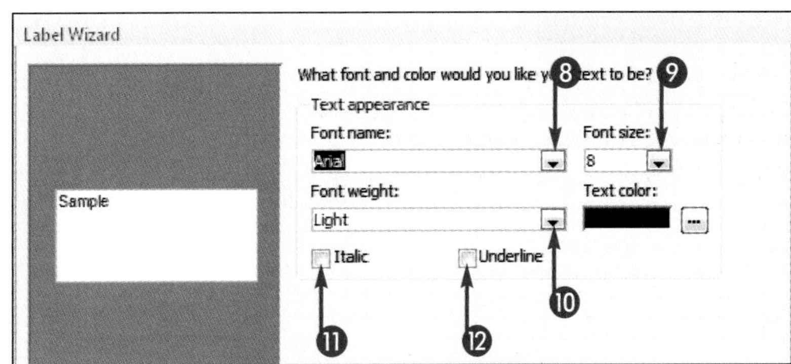

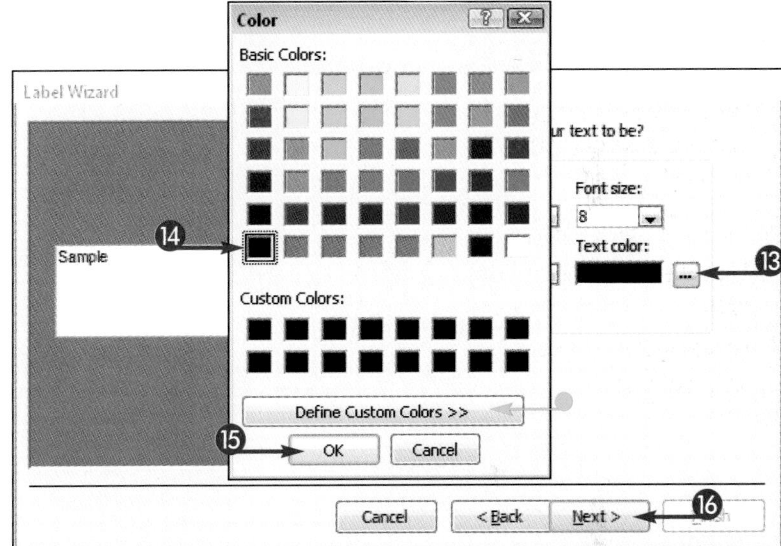

TIP

How can I create a custom label definition?

1 In the first screen of the Label Wizard, click **Customize** to open the New Label Size dialog box.

2 Click **New** to open the New Label dialog box.

3 Define the new label according to its size, type, and orientation.

4 Type a name for the new label definition.

5 Click **OK**.

6 Click **Close** in the New Label Size dialog box.

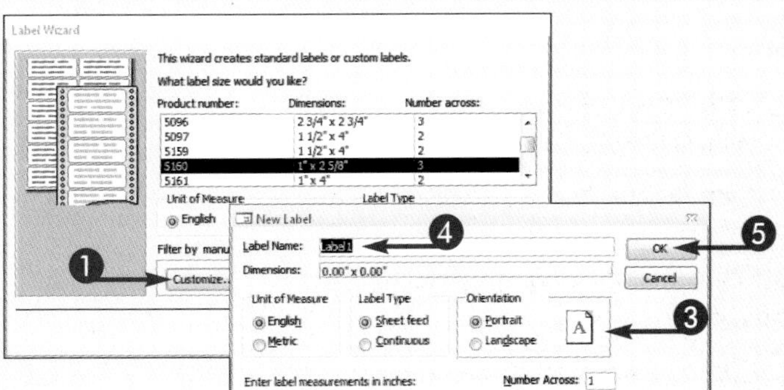

Create Labels *(continued)*

After choosing the size and formatting for the label, you set up the fields that should appear on it. These come from the table or query that you selected before you started the wizard.

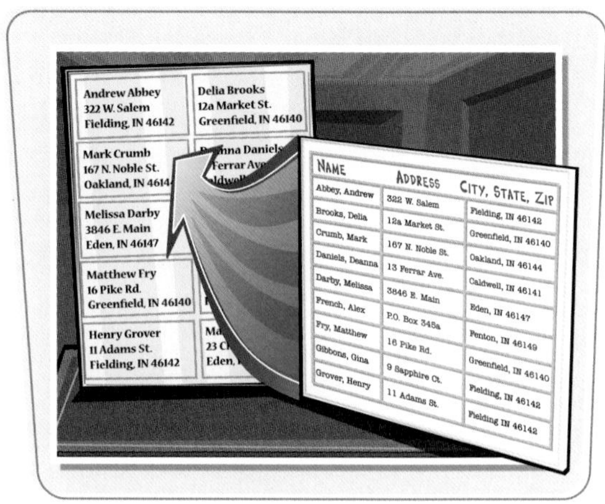

Create Labels *(continued)*

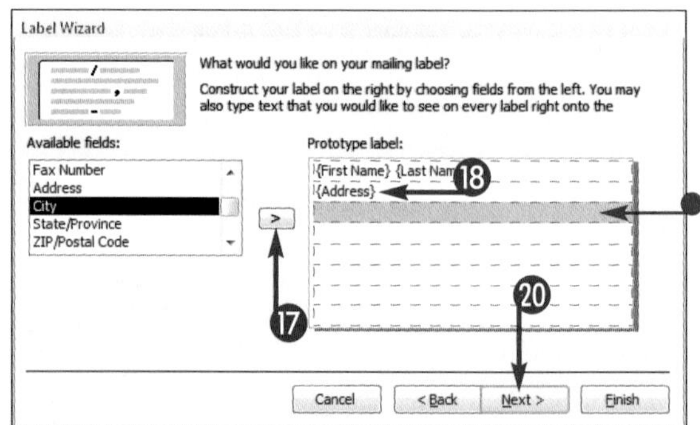

⑰ Click a field and then click here (>) to move it to the prototype label.

● Click a line to move the insertion point into it.

⑱ Type any spaces or other punctuation that should separate the fields within a line.

⑲ Repeat steps **17** and **18** as needed to create the complete label.

⑳ Click **Next**.

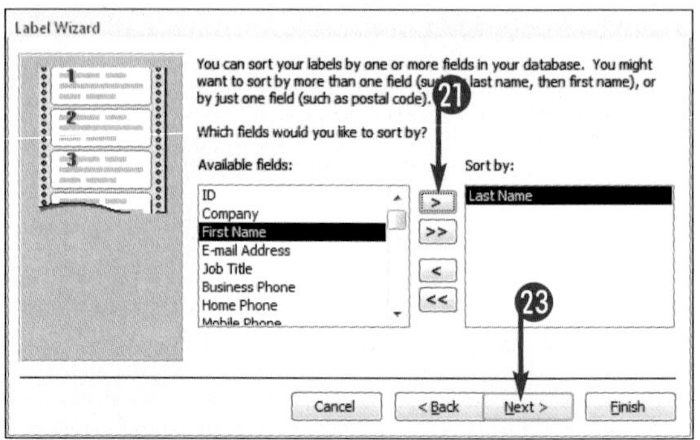

㉑ Click a field by which you want to sort and then click > to move it to the Sort by list.

㉒ Repeat step **21** to specify additional sorting if needed.

㉓ Click **Next**.

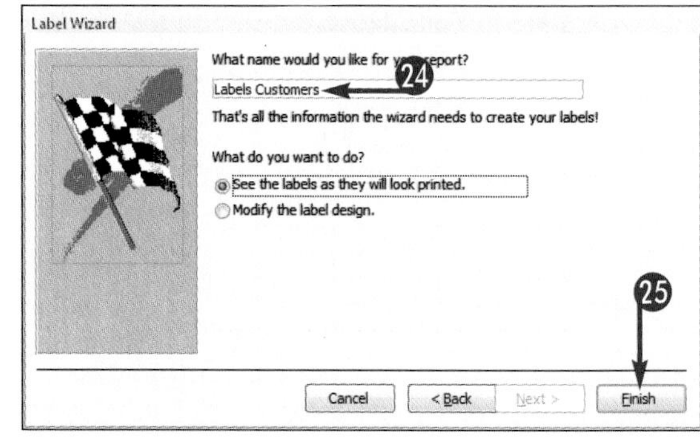

㉔ Type a name for the label report.

㉕ Click **Finish**.

26 If a warning appears about spacing, click **OK**.

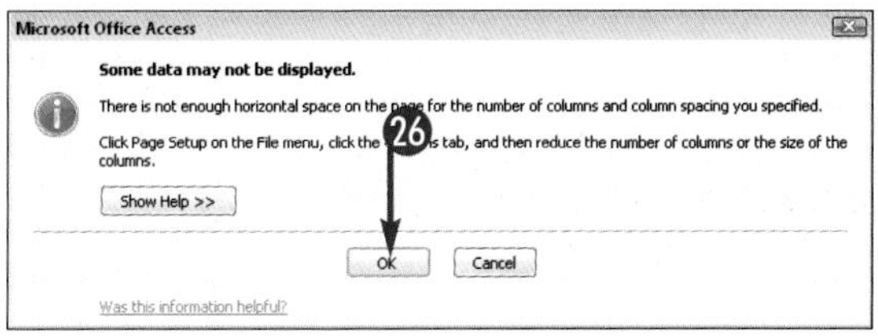

The report appears in Print Preview, ready to print on label paper.

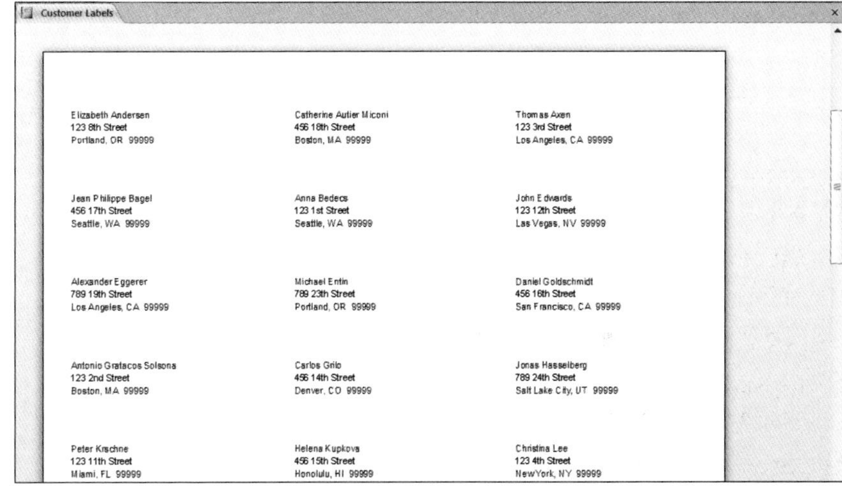

TIPS

How can I change the font after the report has been generated?

1. Right-click on the report's tab and then choose **Layout View** from the shortcut menu.
2. Click the **Format** tab.
3. Select the text you want to format.
4. Use the controls in the Font group to format the text.

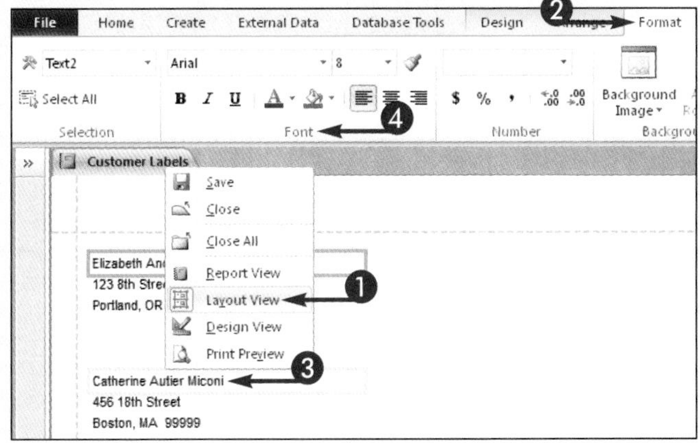

When I look at the labels in Design view, the fields are enclosed in a =TRIM() function. Why?

The =TRIM() function removes extraneous spaces around entries. For example, if the First Name field's entry has several spaces after it and you do not use =TRIM(), those spaces will appear between the first and last names on the label.

Detail
=Trim([First Name] & " " & [Last Name])
Address
=Trim([City] & ", " & [State/Province] & " " & [ZIP

Add a Field to an Existing Line

Labels generated with the Label Wizard concatenate multiple fields in a single text box within a =TRIM() function. If you want to add or remove a field within a line of the label, you must understand the syntax used to construct the function.

Syntax of the =TRIM() function

Syntax	*Explanation*
=Trim([City] & ", " & [State/Province])	This is an example of a complete =TRIM() function.
=Trim( )	The =TRIM() function trims off any excess blank spaces in the fields.
[City]	Field names appear in square brackets.
&	Fields are concatenated with an ampersand.
", "	Literal text or space is enclosed in quotation marks.

Additions to a =TRIM() function

To add another field within an existing =TRIM() function, you must make sure that the new field is enclosed in square brackets, separated from other fields by an ampersand sign (&), and separated from other fields with any literal text or punctuation marks in quotation marks.

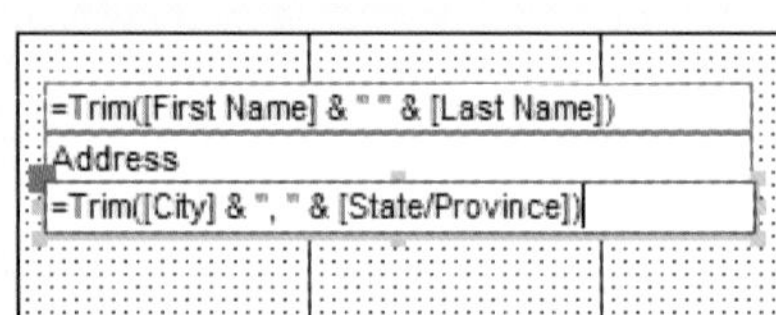

So, to add the ZIP/Postal Code field to the example shown here, you would change the function's code to **=Trim([City]&", "&[State/Province]&" "&[ZIP/Postal Code])**.

Add a Field to a Label as a Separate Line

In addition to adding a field to an existing =TRIM() function on a label, you can also add fields as separate text boxes on their own lines. For example, if you forgot to add an Address line, you could insert one in Design view.

If the field will be by itself in its own text box, you do not have to use the =TRIM() function; you can simply add the field as you would on a form or ordinary report.

Add a Field to a Label as a Separate Line

1. In Design view, drag the existing fields to make room for the new line, if necessary.

Note: To move a field, click the mouse pointer on its border and then drag.

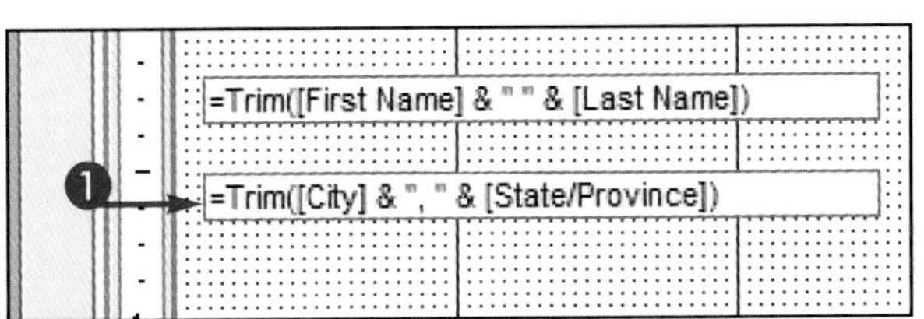

2. Click the Text Box button (ab|).
3. Click and drag to create a new text box where you want to place the field.

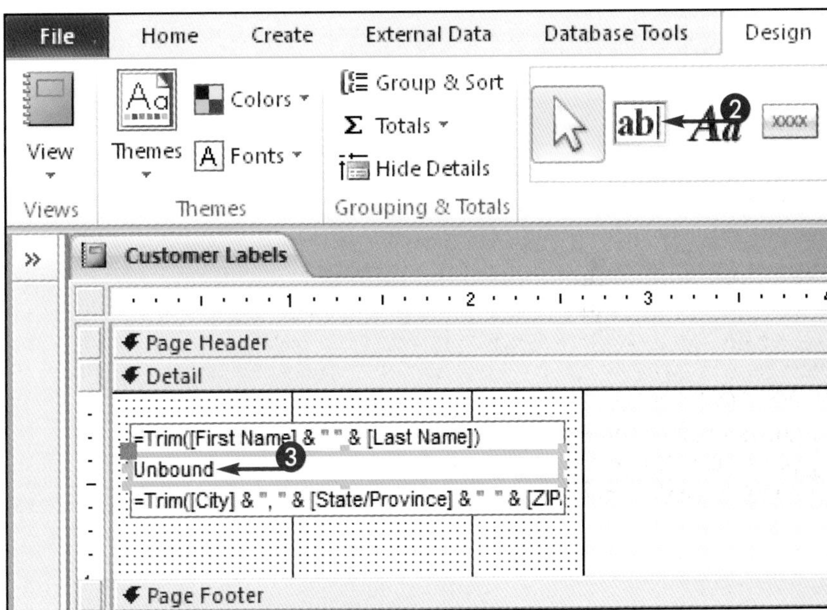

4. Type the field name in the new text box (if a single field).

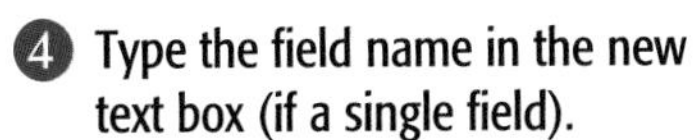

Note: You can also type a =Trim() function to include multiple fields on the same line; see the section "Add a Field to an Existing Line" for more.

The field name appears in the box.

Note: To delete a field, select it and then press Delete.

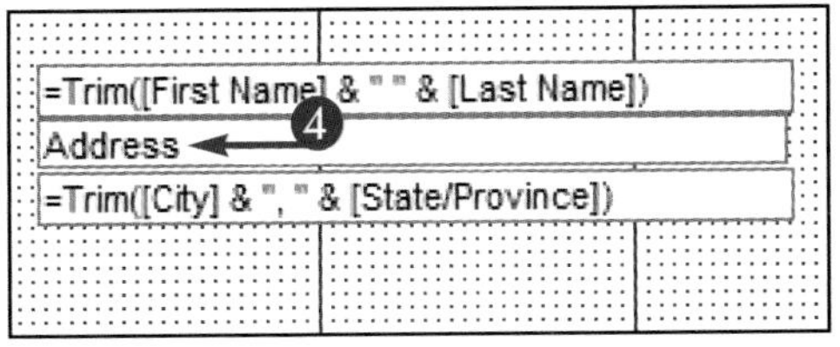

Color the Label Background

There are two ways to color a label background: You can color the overall background of the label or you can color the individual text boxes in which the text appears.

Color the Label Background

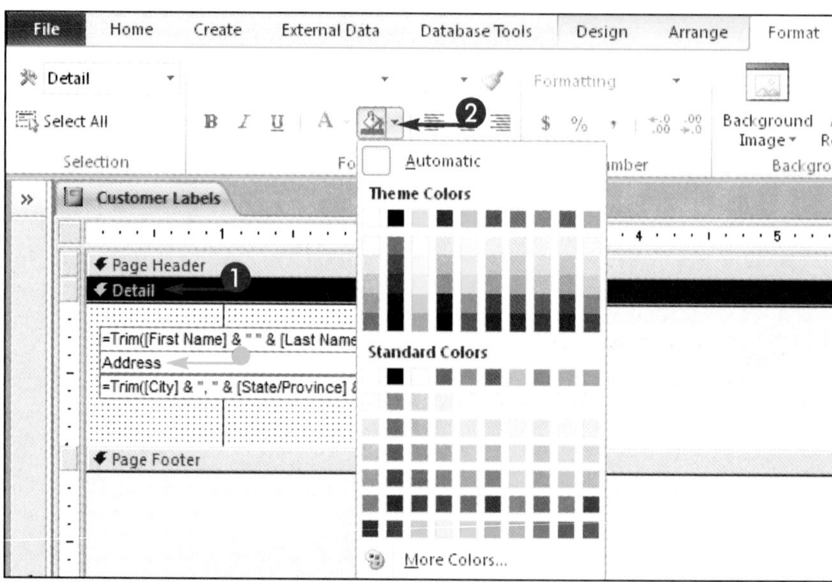

1. In Design view, click **Detail** to select the entire Detail section.

- You can also click an individual text box to select it.

2. On the Format tab, click here (▾) to choose a background color.

***Note:** You can click **Automatic** to remove an existing color from the label background or **Transparent** to remove an existing color from an individual text box.*

***Note:** You can click **More Colors** to open the Colors dialog box, from which you can choose more colors.*

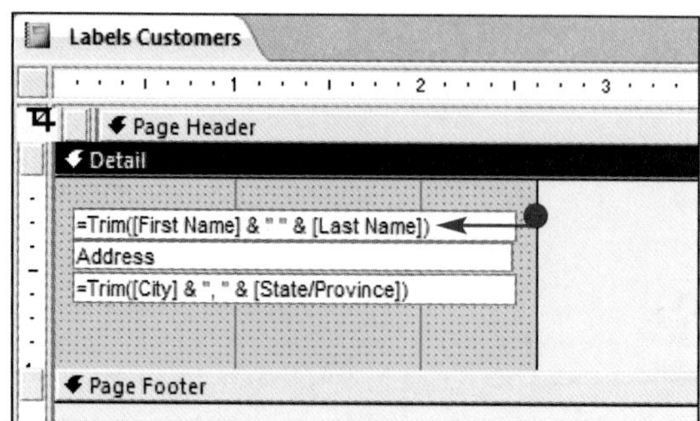

The chosen background color is applied to either the entire label or the individual text box.

- Fields on the label remain white by default; you can set their colors to Transparent if you prefer.

Color the Label Text

You can change the color of a label's text. This is especially useful after changing the label background color so the text continues to contrast with the background for good visibility. For more, see the section "Color the Label Background."

Color the Label Text

1. In Design view, click the text box containing the text you want to color.

***Note:** You cannot select only part of the text in a text box for a different color; you must select the entire text box.*

***Note:** You can select multiple text boxes by holding down Shift as you click each one. You can also drag a lasso around them.*

2. Click the **Font Color** drop-down arrow (▾) to choose a text color.

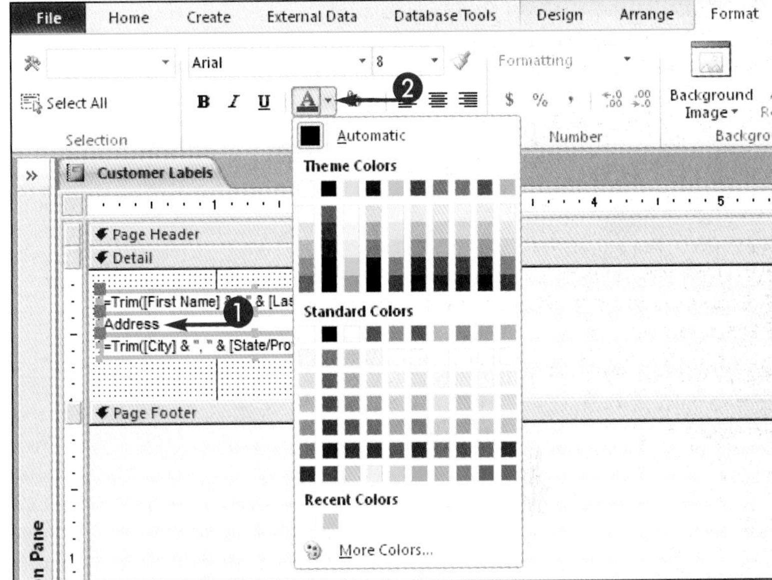

The chosen color is applied to the text in the text box you selected.

- You can click **Automatic** to make the text either black or white.
- You can click **More Colors** to open the Colors dialog box, from which you can choose more colors.

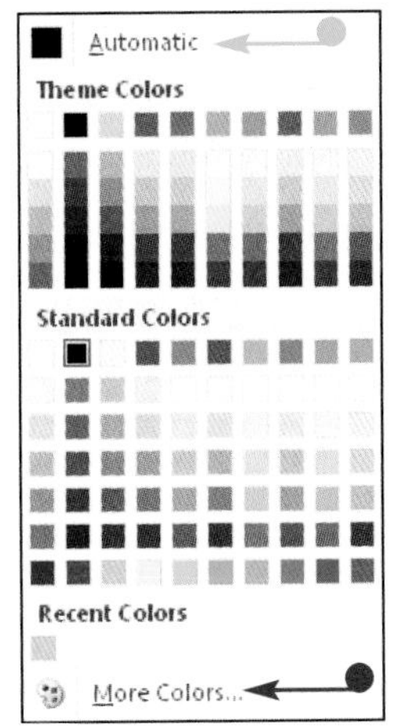

Apply Font Formatting to Label Text

You can change the font formatting for the label text in the same way in Design view that you can using the Label Wizard: font, size, bold, italic, and underline. You can also set the horizontal alignment and copy formatting between text boxes with the Format Painter tool.

Apply Font Formatting to Label Text

Change the Font

1. In Design view, click the text box you want to format.
2. Click here (▾) to choose a different font.

   The font is applied.

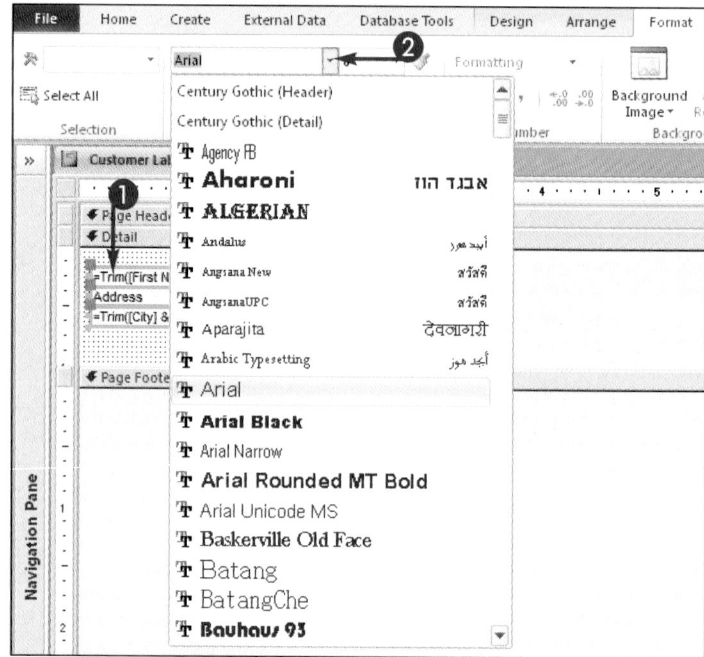

Change the Font Size and Attributes

1. Click the text box you want to format.
2. Click here (▾) to choose a different size.

   The font is resized.
3. You can click one or more of these buttons to apply more attributes:

- Bold
- Italic
- Underline

The font attributes are applied.

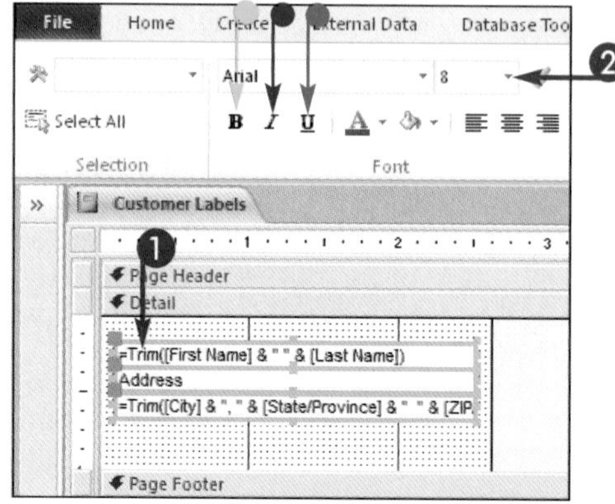

Change the Text Alignment

1. Click the text box you want to format.
2. Click one of the alignment buttons:

- Left
- Center
- Right

The alignment is applied to the text.

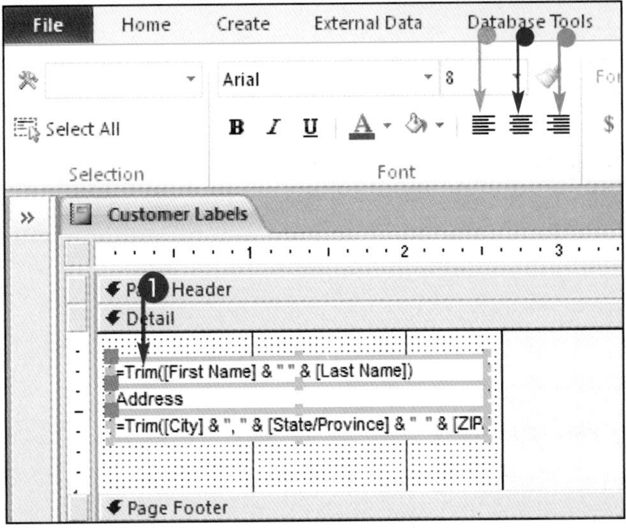

Copy Formatting to Another Text Box

1. Select a text box that is already formatted the way you want.
2. Click the **Format Painter** button ( ).
3. Click the text box you want to format.

The formatting is copied to the second text box.

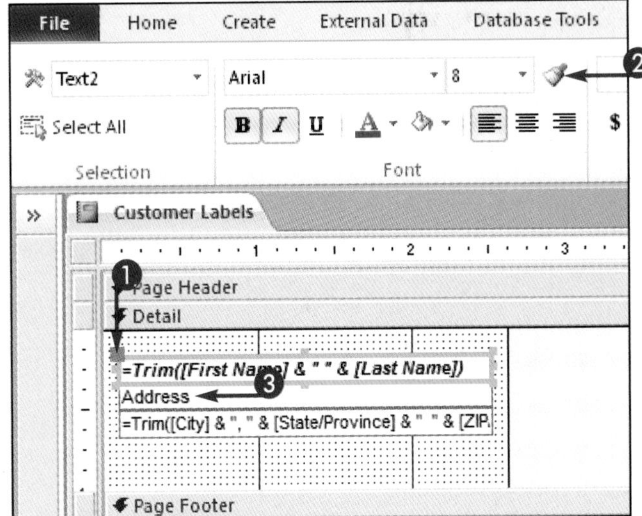

How can I format one field in a text box differently from the others?

You cannot. Font formatting is applied to the entire text box, not to individual characters. If you want a certain field to be formatted differently, place it in its own text box.

After enlarging the font, the text appears truncated. How can I fix this?

You may need to resize the text box to adjust for the larger font size. You can do this in one of the following ways: dragging a selection handle; double-clicking a selection handle; or right-clicking on the text box, choosing **Size**, and then choosing **To Fit**. Keep in mind, however, that in Design view, the text in the text boxes is the code to produce the label text, not the label text itself. Switch to Layout view for a more realistic picture of whether or not the text on the labels will be truncated.

Export Labels to Word

You may prefer to print labels in Microsoft Word rather than Access because of the increased options that are available in Word for formatting. You can use the Export Wizard to export the labels — or any other report — to a new Word document.

Export Labels to Word

1. On the External Data tab, in the Export group, click **More**.
2. On the menu that appears, click **Word**.

   The Export – RTF File Wizard opens.

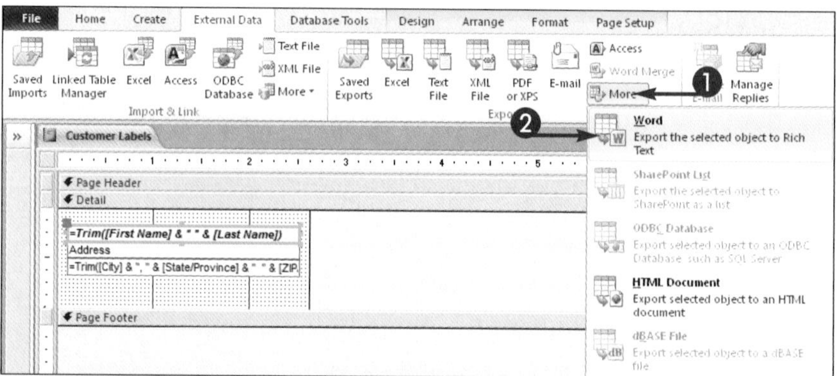

3. Change the path and file name if needed.

   - You can click **Browse** to choose a location.

4. Click here to open the file in Word after the export (☐ changes to ☑).
5. Click **OK**.

   If you see a message about some data not being displayed, click OK to continue.

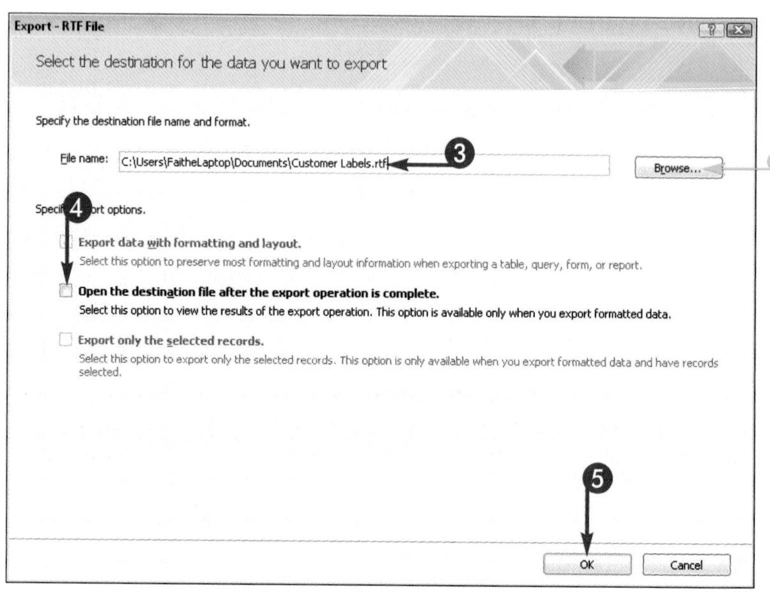

The final screen of the Export Wizard appears with a confirmation.

- You can click here to save the export steps and then recall them later from Saved Exports on the External Data tab (☐ changes to ☑).

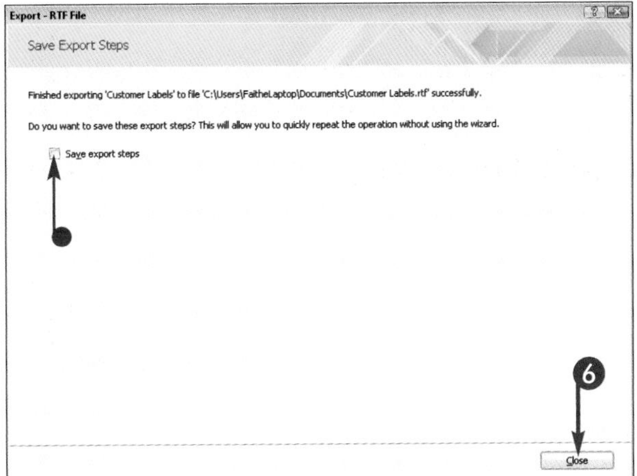

6 Click **Close**.

The labels open in Word.

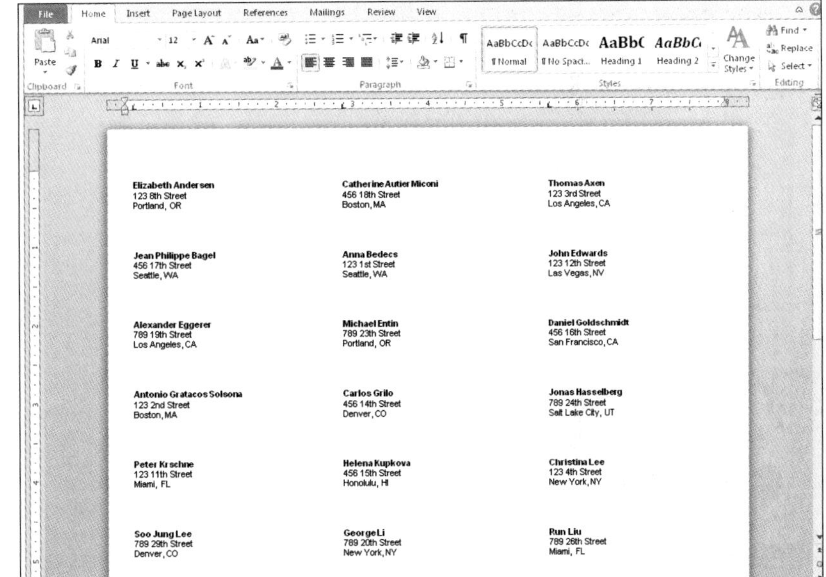

TIP

Should I be worried about a message that warns that some data may not be displayed?
Not necessarily. In most cases, the results are fine when exported into Word. If needed, you can adjust margins, columns, and other formatting settings in Word after the export.

CHAPTER

14

Creating Charts

Charts can help you summarize and display data from your tables. Often, a chart can explain the meaning of the data better than text. For example, a pie chart shows how the parts contribute to the whole, while a bar chart shows how values stack up against one another. There are two ways of using charts in Microsoft Access 2010: You can either create a PivotChart or you can embed a Microsoft Graph chart object on a form or report. You will learn both of those methods in this chapter.

Understanding Charts in Access

The main chart functionality in Access is contained in its powerful and flexible PivotCharts. Using a PivotChart, you can explore different data scenarios and compare the contents of various fields to one another in any way you like.

PivotChart
A PivotChart graphically displays and summarizes data from a table or query. In this example, the sum total of all entries in the Quantity field for each Customer appears as a bar on the graph.

Data Field(s)
The fields from which the numeric data are pulled appear here.

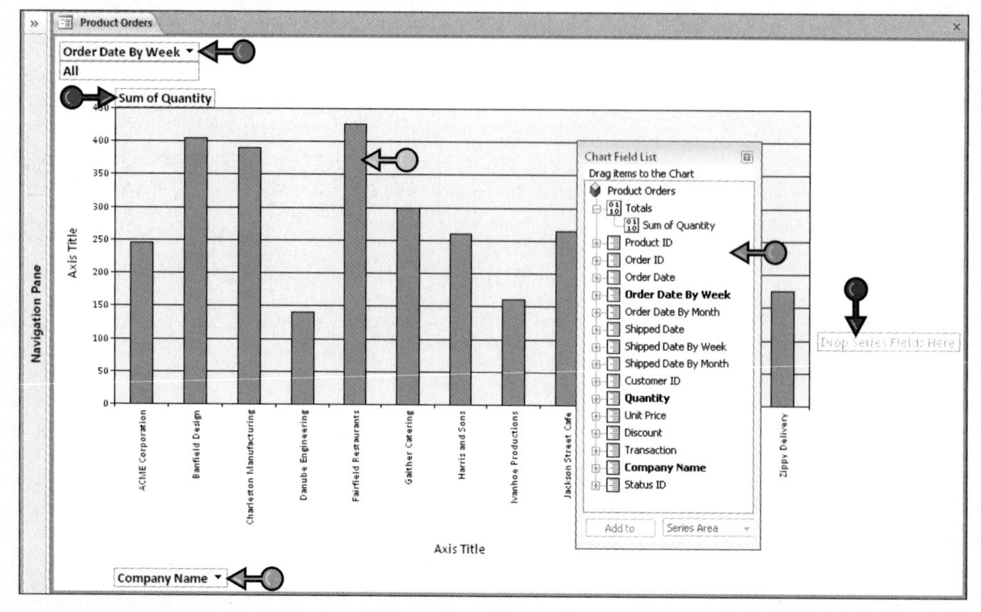

Filtering Field(s)
You can optionally filter to show only certain values in one or more fields. If used, the filter fields appear here.

Category Field(s)
The fields you place here appear as categories on the horizontal axis. In this case, the horizontal axis contains company names.

Series Field(s)
Some charts have multiple data series, each represented by a different bar color. The chart shown here does not have multiple data series, but if it did, the field name would appear here.

Field List
Drag and drop field names from the field list onto the placeholder areas to populate the placeholders on the PivotChart.

Microsoft Graph Objects

As an alternative to using a PivotChart, you can create a Microsoft Graph object on a form or report.

Summarizing for Individual Records

A Microsoft Graph object can show information from a linked table or query that is specific to each record as it is displayed. For example, this chart shows the quantity of each product that the customer ordered on the horizontal axis.

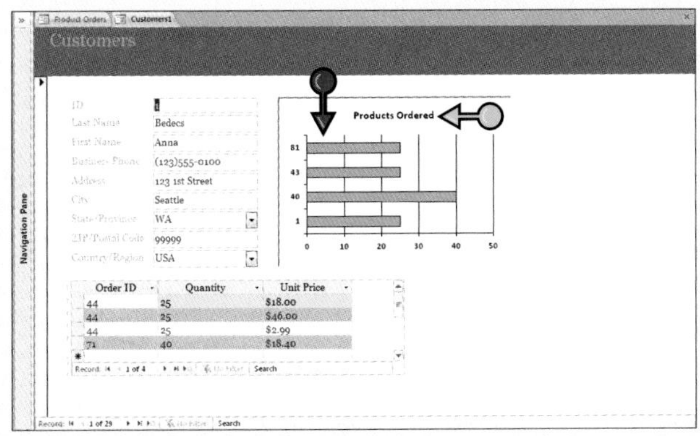

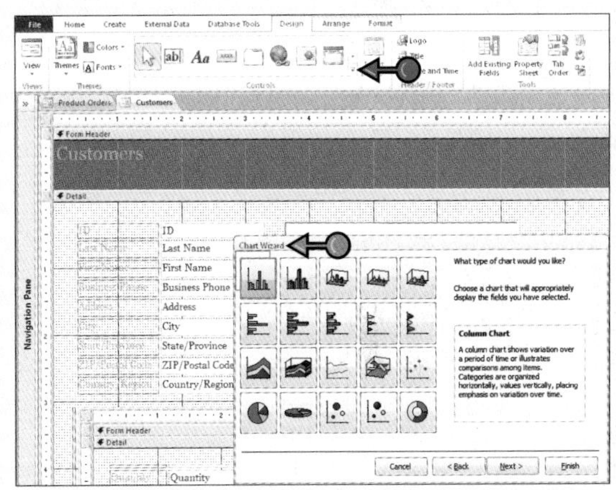

Placing a Chart on a Form or Report

To create a Microsoft Graph object, you can use the Chart Wizard. You can access it from Design view for a form or report by choosing the Chart object type from the Controls gallery.

Chart Wizard

The Chart Wizard walks you step by step through the process of choosing a table or query, selecting fields from it, choosing a chart type, and so on.

Open a PivotChart View

A PivotChart is like a PivotTable, except it expresses the data graphically rather than as text and numbers.

You can open a PivotChart view for any table or query and then experiment with different charting scenarios by dragging fields into its placeholders.

Open a PivotChart View

❶ In Datasheet view, right-click on the datasheet's tab.

❷ Click **PivotChart View**.

An empty PivotChart grid appears, unless you have previously set up a PivotTable or PivotChart for this table or query.

Note: *If there are already fields in use in the placeholder areas, delete them. See Chapter 12 for more.*

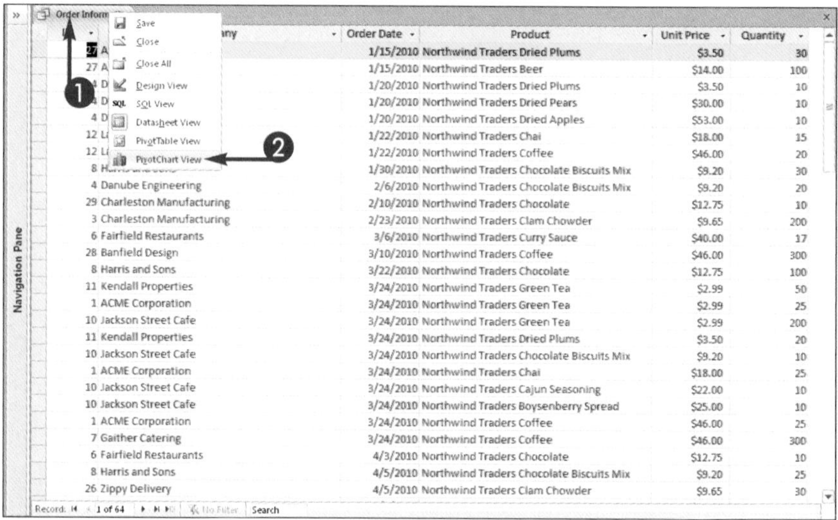

- You can drag the Chart Field List around on-screen by its title bar; by default, it covers up the Drop Series Fields Here placeholder.

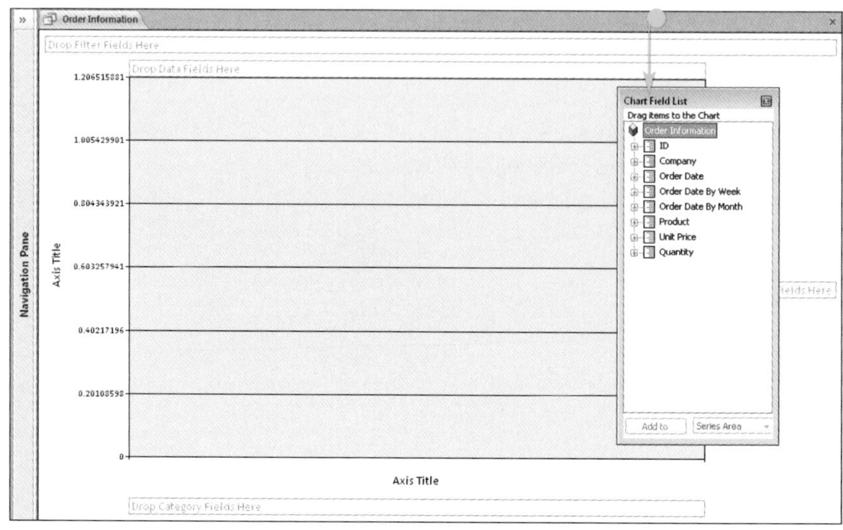

Start a PivotChart Form

If you think you will want to save and reuse a PivotChart, you should create it as a new form rather than simply viewing it from the table or query. By doing so, you create a form object that you can easily reopen whenever you want to see or print the chart. You can also embed the form on a report (which is explained later in this chapter).

Start a PivotChart Form

1. In the Navigation pane, select the table or query on which you want to base the PivotChart.
2. Click the **Create** tab.
3. Click **More Forms**.
4. Click **PivotChart**.

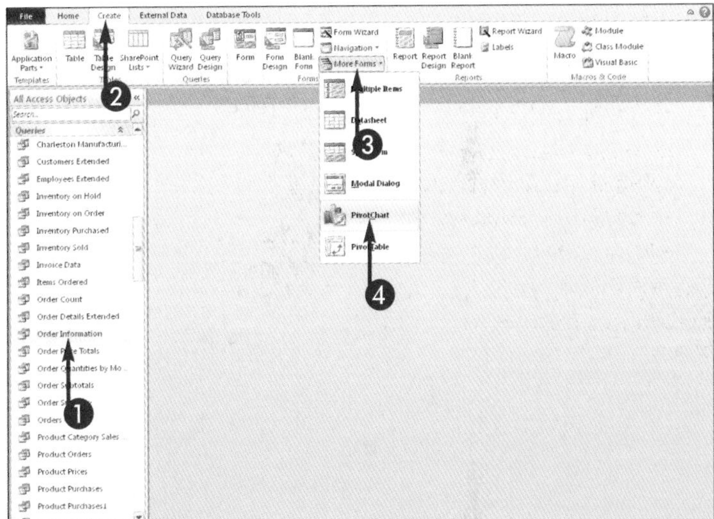

- A PivotChart grid appears, embedded in a form.
- If the field list is not visible, you can click the Field List button twice — once to toggle it off and then again to toggle it back on.

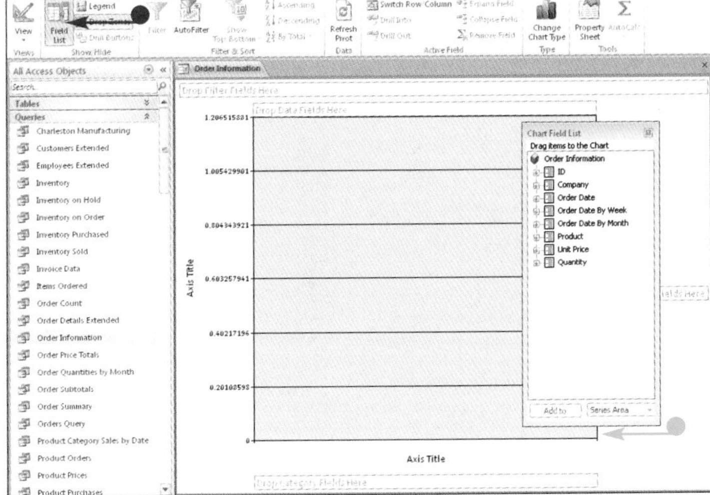

Construct a PivotChart

After opening a PivotChart view, you can create a variety of different PivotCharts by dragging fields onto the various placeholders in the grid.

This is just like creating a PivotTable, except that the result is graphical rather than text-based. For more on creating a PivotTable, see Chapter 12.

Construct a PivotChart

1. Display a PivotChart view.

Note: *See the section "Open a PivotChart View" for more.*

2. Drag a field onto the Drop Category Fields Here placeholder.

   That field appears as the categories (bars) along the horizontal axis.

3. Drag a field onto the Drop Data Fields Here placeholder.

   That field appears as the values (the heights of the bars) along the vertical axis.

- If the field contains numeric data, its values are summed. You can tell what math operation is in use by the text that appears here.
- If you want a different math operation, right-click on the placeholder, click **AutoCalc**, and then click a different math operation.
- You can also drag a field onto the Drop Series Fields Here placeholder if you want to separate the results into different series.

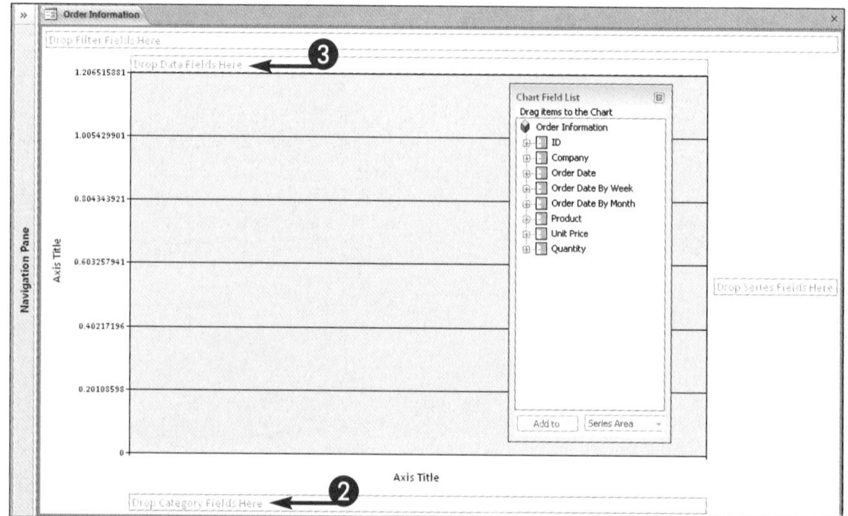

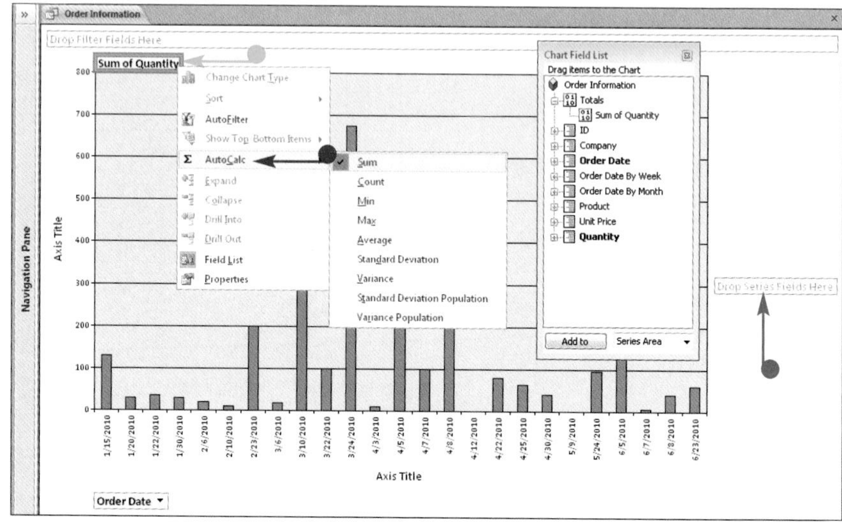

Group Data in a PivotChart

The chart you are using may have a lot of small bars because each individual date has its own bar. In this case, you may find it more useful to group the chart by date.

You can group by numeric intervals, dates, or other values depending on the type of data that the field contains.

Group Data in a PivotChart

1. In PivotChart view, click the field placeholder.
2. Click the **Design** tab.
3. Click **Property Sheet**.

   A Properties dialog box opens.
4. Click the **Filter and Group** tab.

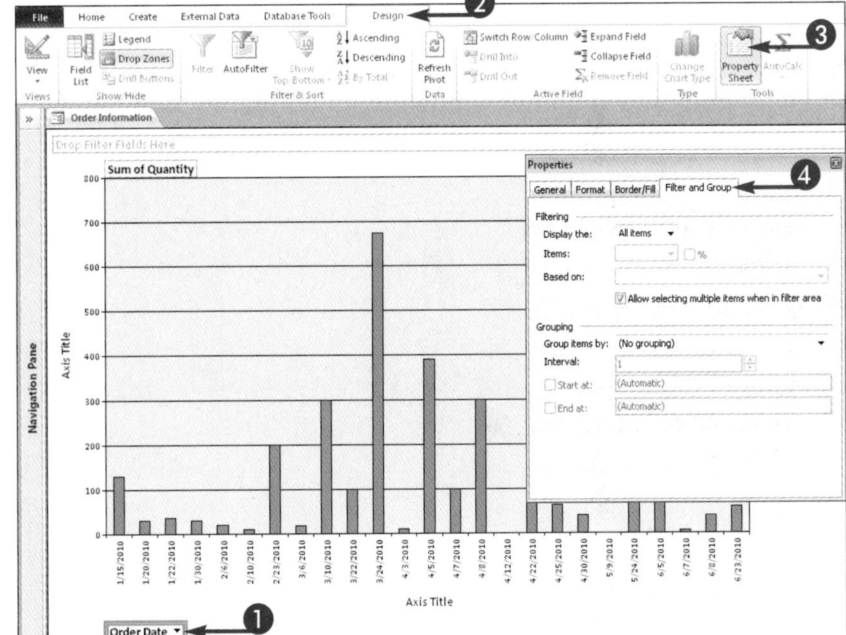

5. Click here (▾) to choose a grouping interval.
6. Click here (⊠) to close the dialog box.

   The data is grouped as you have specified.

Properties
General | Format | Border/Fill | Filter and Group
Filtering
Display the: All items
Items:
Based on:
Allow selecting multiple items when in filter area
Grouping
Group items by: Months
Interval:
Start at:
End at:
(No grouping)
Years
Quarters
Months
Weeks
Days
Hours
Minutes
Seconds

Change the PivotChart Type

You can set a PivotChart to use a different chart type on the Design tab. Access offers most of the chart types that are available in full-featured charting programs, including bars, pies, and lines.

In addition, for some chart types, you can switch between rows and columns. This switches the fields between the category axis (horizontal) and the value axis (vertical).

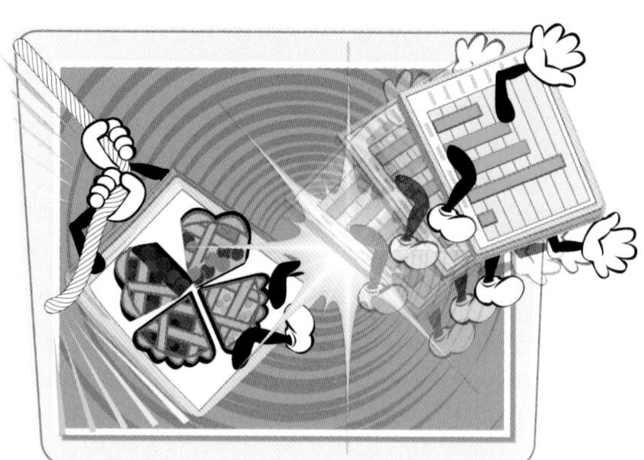

Change the PivotChart Type

1. Click the outer frame of the PivotChart.
2. On the Design tab, click **Change Chart Type**.

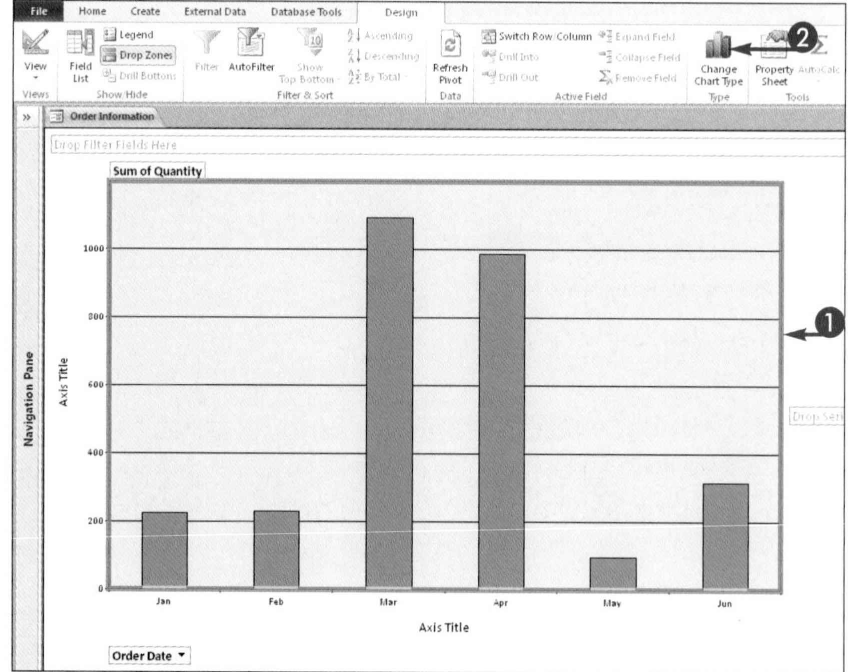

The Properties dialog box opens with the Type tab displayed.

3. Click a chart category.
4. Click a chart type.
5. Click here (▣) to close the dialog box.

The chart is changed to the new type.

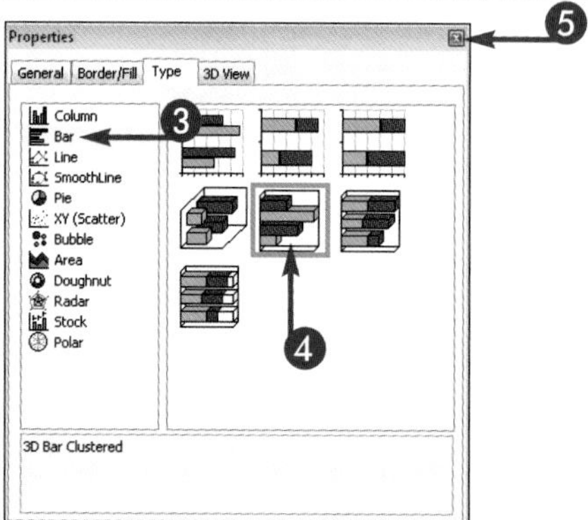

Change Chart Colors

You can change the colors of the bars — or lines, slices, or whatever shapes the data appears in — for a chosen chart type. You can change one data point or an entire data series.

When you click a bar for the first time, only that bar is selected; if you click it again, you select its entire series.

Change Chart Colors

1. In PivotChart view, click the data point (the bar, slice, or other shape) whose color you want to change.

   That single data point's shape becomes selected.

   You can select all data in a series by clicking the data point again.

2. On the Design tab, click **Property Sheet**.

   The Properties dialog box opens.

3. Click the **Border/Fill** tab.

4. Click here (▾) to choose a fill type.

   The default, Solid color, usually works. You can use a pattern if you plan to print in black and white.

5. Click here (▾) to choose a fill color.

- You can click **Default** to restore the default color.
- You can click **None** to remove the color.
- You can click **Custom** to display a Color dialog box.

6. Click here (☒) to close the dialog box.

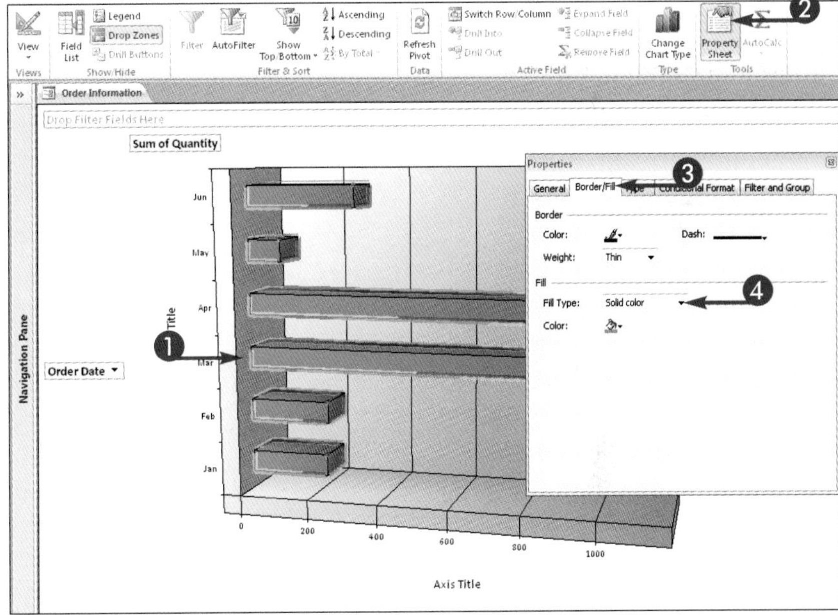

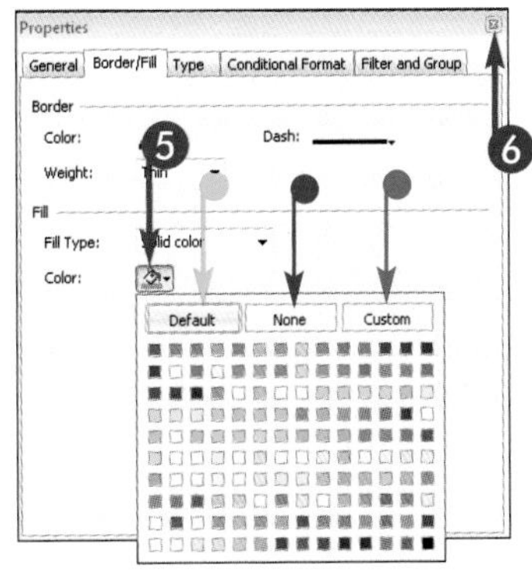

Create an Embedded Chart Object

You can also add embedded chart objects to forms and reports. These charts use a different charting technology — Microsoft Graph. You create a chart with the Chart Wizard.

You place Microsoft Graph objects on a form or report in Design view. You can make a chart take up an entire report or form body (in the Details section) or you can add a chart to an existing form or report. If you add a chart to a form or report that shows data, the chart reflects only the associated data for the displayed record.

Create an Embedded Chart Object

1. Open the form in Design view.
2. If needed, move and size the existing objects to clear a space for the chart.
3. Click here (▾) to open the Controls gallery.

   Depending on your display resolution, you might not need to perform step **3**; the Chart icon may appear already.

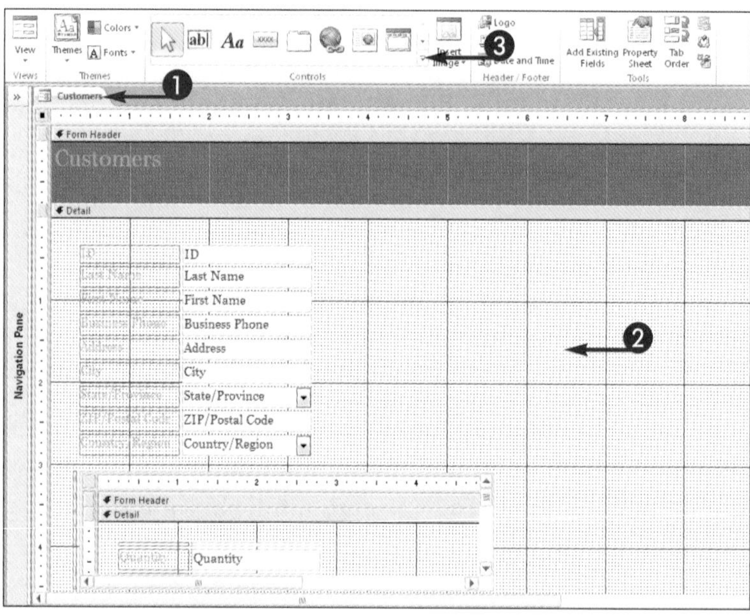

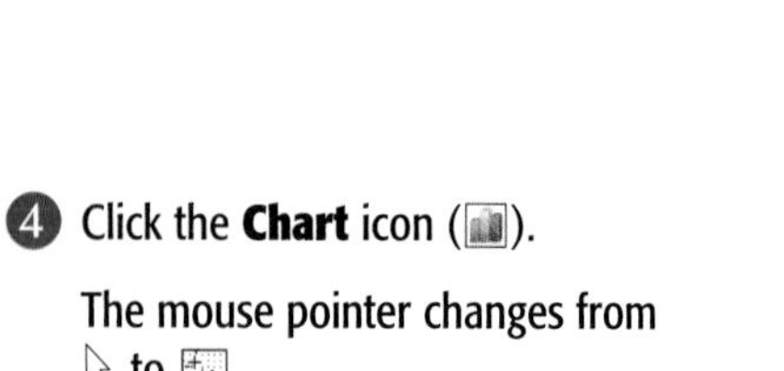

4. Click the **Chart** icon (📊).

   The mouse pointer changes from ↖ to a chart pointer.

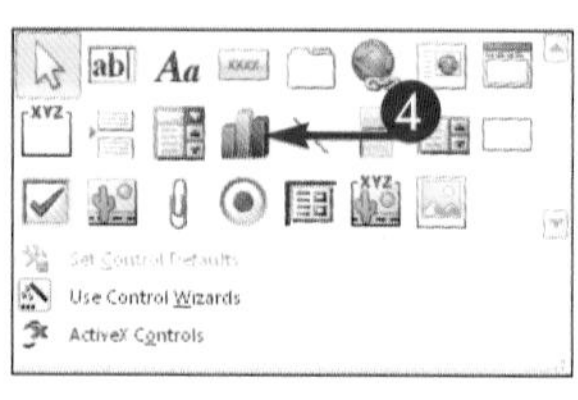

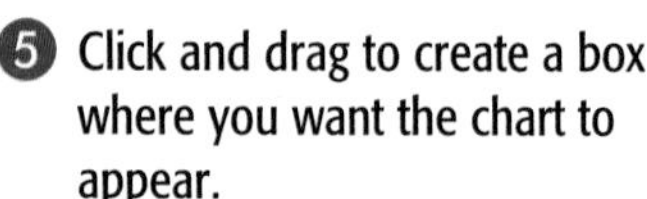

5. Click and drag to create a box where you want the chart to appear.

   When you release the mouse button, Access launches the Chart Wizard.

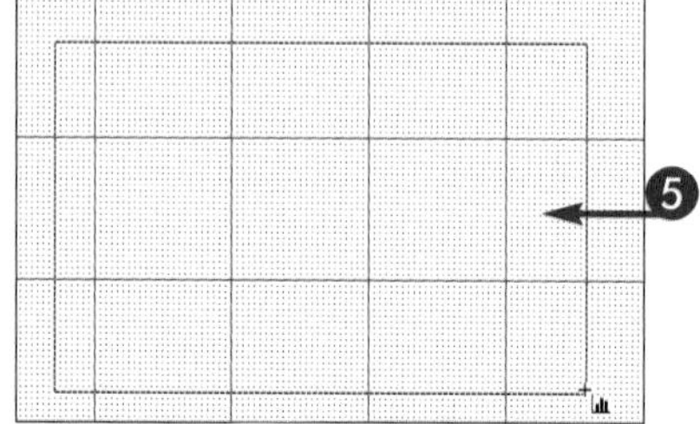

6. Click the table or query on which the chart should be based.

- You can filter the list to show only tables or only queries (◎ changes to ◉).

***Note:** If you want the chart to change depending on which record is active on the form, make sure you choose a table or query that has a relationship to the one on which the form is based.*

7. Click **Next**.

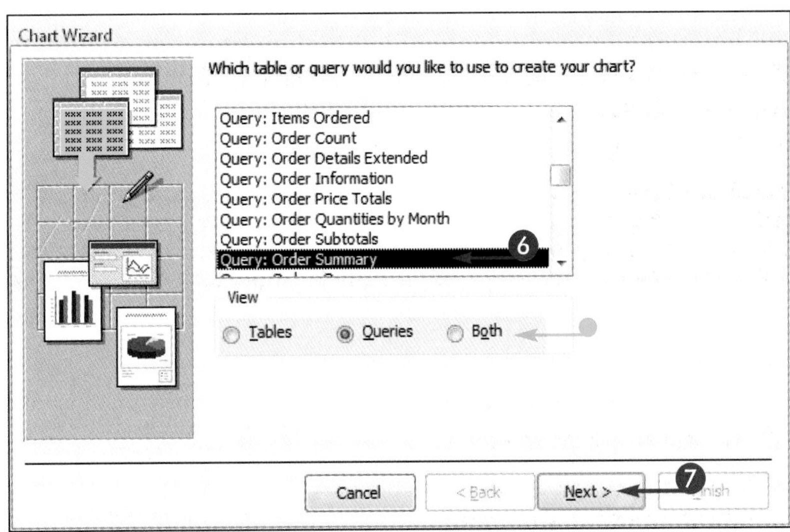

8. Click a field you want to include in the chart.

9. Click here (>) to move the field to the Fields for Chart list.

10. Repeat steps **8** and **9** for each field you want in the chart.

11. Click **Next**.

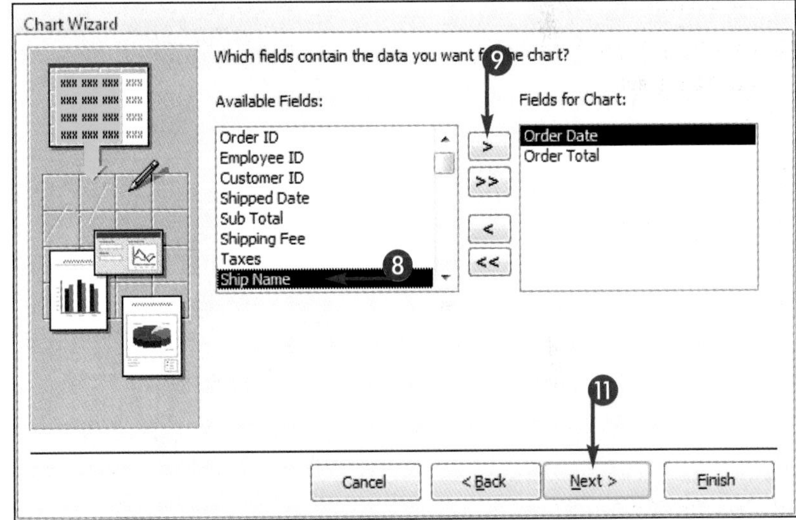

What if I can't find a table or query that contains the fields I want for the chart (step 6)?

You might need to create a query specifically for this purpose. Cancel the Chart Wizard and then create a new query. (See Chapter 7 for more.) To make it easier to find the query when you return to the Chart Wizard, name the query to reflect its purpose.

How do I find out what tables and queries are related to each other (step 6)?

Cancel the Chart Wizard and then use the Relationships window on the Database Tools tab, click **Relationships** to see which tables and fields are related. For a query, open the query in Design view and see which tables its fields come from.

Create an Embedded Chart Object *(continued)*

The Chart Wizard helps you build a chart that is appropriate for the location in which you are placing it. It assists you in selecting the fields you need, selecting a chart type, placing the fields in the chart areas, and more.

Create an Embedded Chart Object *(continued)*

12 Click the desired chart type.

13 Click **Next**.

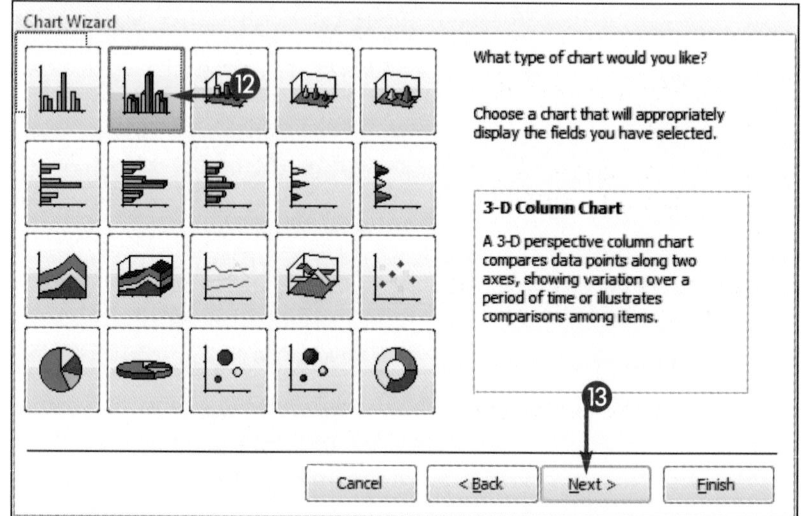

14 If the field placements are not what you want, drag the field names to different placeholder areas on the sample.

***Note:** The Series placeholder is used only if you want a multiseries chart. This example does not use the Series placeholder.*

15 Click **Next**.

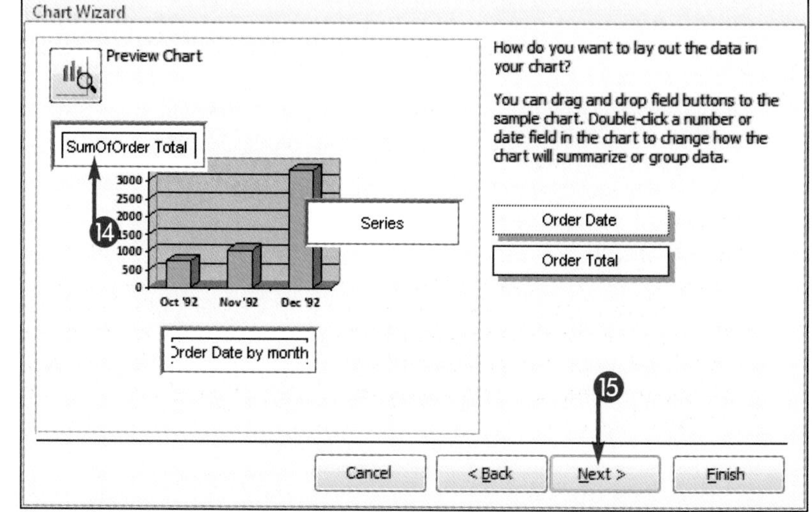

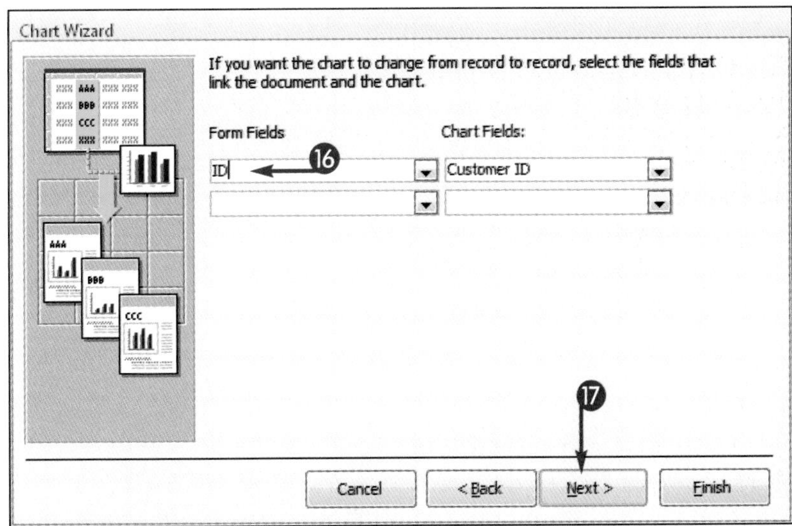

16 Confirm the choice of fields to connect between the form data and the chart. If needed, open one of the drop-down lists to choose a different field to match up.

17 Click **Next**.

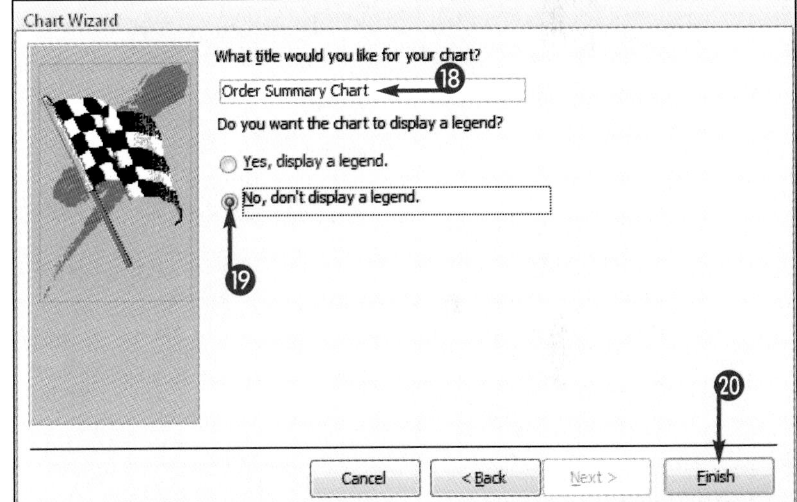

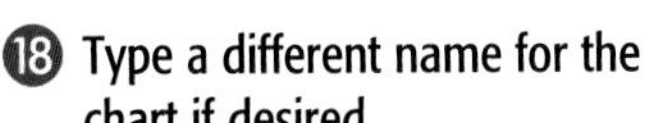

18 Type a different name for the chart if desired.

For example, you might want to include the word "chart" in the name.

19 If you do not want a legend, click here to omit it (◎ changes to ◉).

20 Click **Finish**.

The chart appears on the form.

TIPS

The chart shows some dummy data and not my data. How can I fix this?

Switch to Form view to update the chart data. It does not update automatically in Design view because the chart changes based on the individual records displayed, and in Design view, there are no individual records displayed.

I see a warning about having to add a field to my record source. Why does this warning appear?

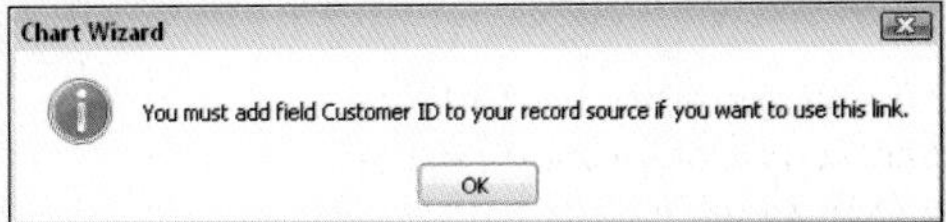

This message appears if Access cannot find a relationship between the fields on the form and the fields in the table or query you have selected to base the chart on. You need to choose a different query or table on which to base the chart. You might need to create a query for this purpose.

CHAPTER 15

Working with External Data

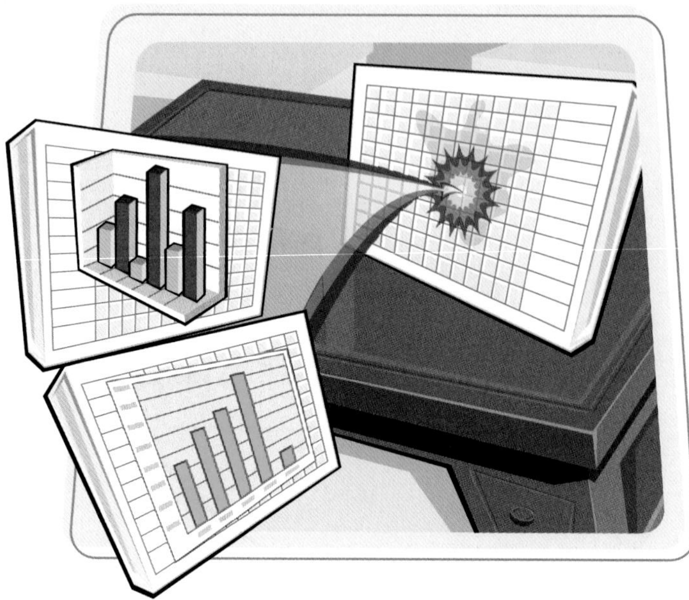

One of the strongest features of Access is its ability to work with outside data. You can import and export data from and to other Access databases, from Excel, and even from plain text files.

Import an Excel Worksheet

You can import data from an Excel worksheet into Access to create a new table. This new table becomes a part of the Access database; it does not retain any ties to Excel.

Excel data that is database-oriented, with field names as the top row, imports well into Access. Data that includes formulas and functions does not import well.

Import an Excel Worksheet

❶ On the External Data tab in the Import & Link group, click **Excel**.

The Get External Data – Excel Spreadsheet dialog box opens.

❷ In the File name field, type the path and file name for the Excel file.

- You can click **Browse** to browse for the file if you prefer.

❸ Click the **Import the source data into a new table in the current database** radio button (◎ changes to ◉).

❹ Click **OK**.

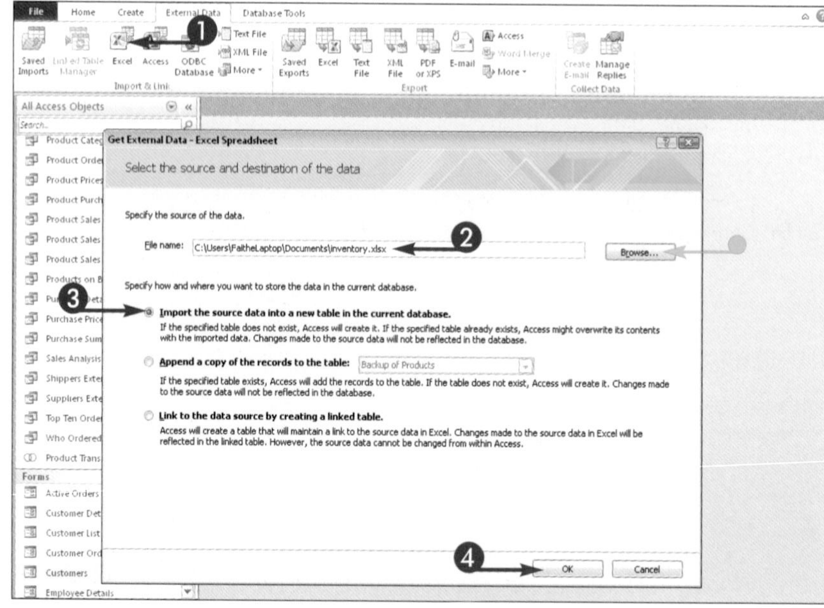

The Import Spreadsheet Wizard opens.

❺ Click the sheet you want to import.

- A preview of the data on that sheet appears.
- You can alternatively choose from named ranges (◎ changes to ◉).

❻ Click **Next**.

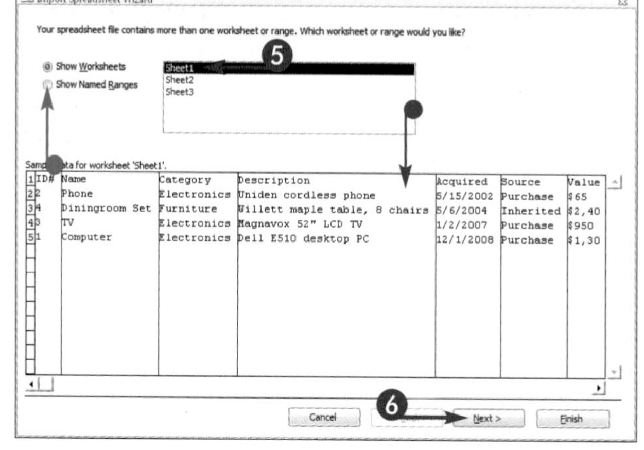

7 If the first row contains column headings, click the **First Row Contains Column Headings** check box if it is not already selected (☐ changes to ☑).

8 Click **Next**.

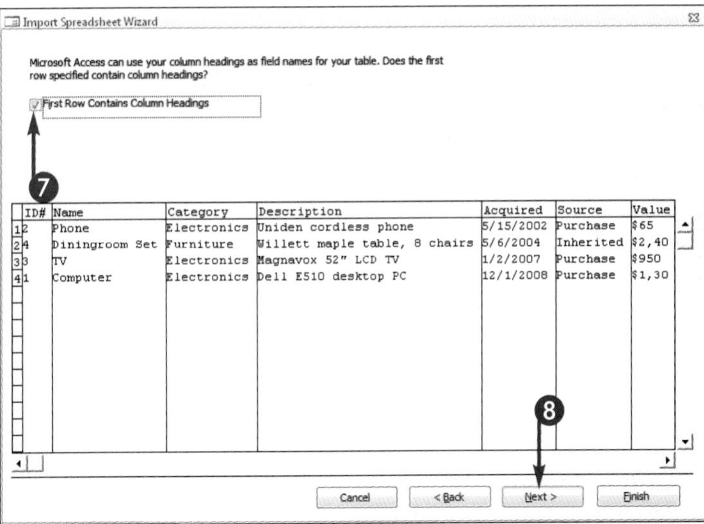

- You can change the field name for the first field in the Field Options area.

9 Click here (▾) to choose the data type you want.

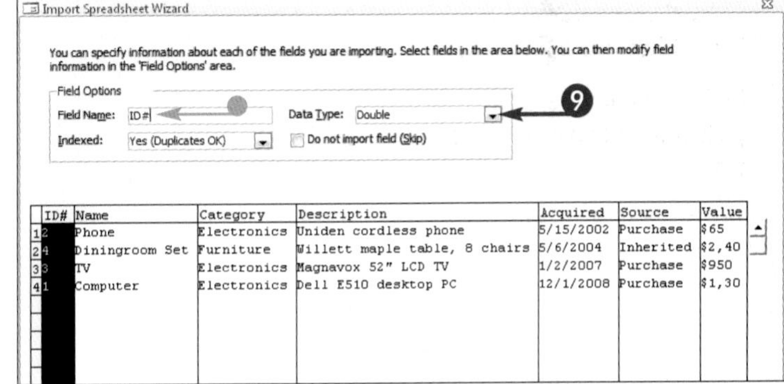

How should I prepare the Excel worksheet before importing it?

For Excel data to import correctly into Access, it must be set up to mimic a datasheet in Access. Follow these guidelines in Excel:

- Place the field names in row 1.
- Remove any blank rows or titles above the field names.
- Place each record in a separate row, starting immediately below the row containing the field names.
- Do not include any formulas or functions. Omit cells containing them from the range to import or convert them to values.

Can I import only part of a worksheet?

Yes. In step **5**, you can choose to import from a named range if you prefer. However, you must set up the range in Excel first. To create a named range in Excel, follow these steps:

1 Select the range.

2 Click here to type a name for the range.

3 Press Enter.

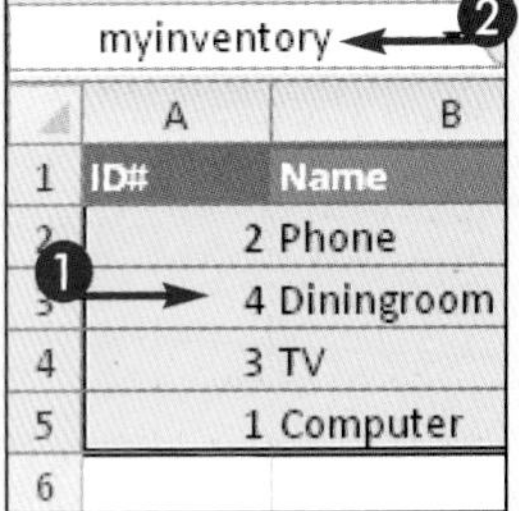

Import an Excel Worksheet *(continued)*

The Import Spreadsheet Wizard asks you about several setup options that you would ordinarily configure when creating a new table, such as whether fields should be indexed and whether duplicates are okay.

The Import Spreadsheet Wizard also gives you the opportunity to set a primary key and to name the table.

Import an Excel Worksheet *(continued)*

⑩ Click here (▾) to choose whether the field should be indexed and whether duplicates are okay.

- You can click the **Do not import field (Skip)** check box (☐ changes to ☑) to exclude a field from being imported.

⑪ Click the next column and then repeat steps **9** and **10**.

⑫ When you have set up all fields, click **Next**.

⑬ If the imported data already contains a field you want to use as the primary key, click the **Choose my own primary key** radio button (○ changes to ◉) and then click here (▾) to choose that field from the drop-down menu.

- You can click the **Let Access add primary key** radio button (○ changes to ◉) to allow the wizard to create a new field to be used as a primary key.

- You can click the **No primary key** radio button (○ changes to ◉) to decline to use a primary key in the table.

⑭ Click **Next**.

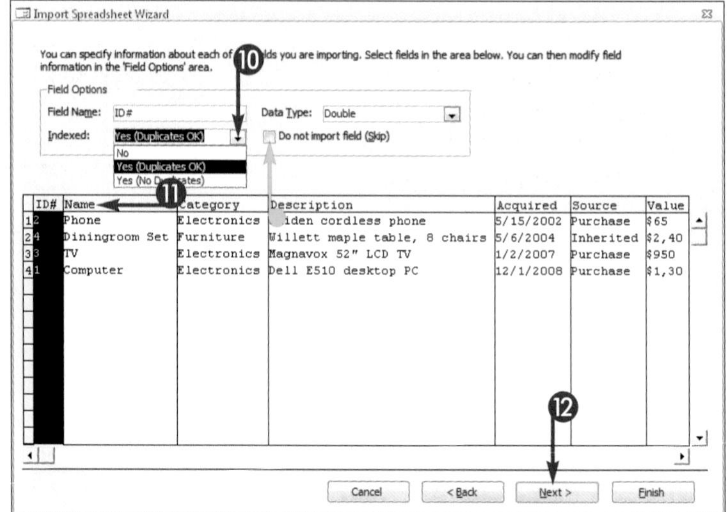

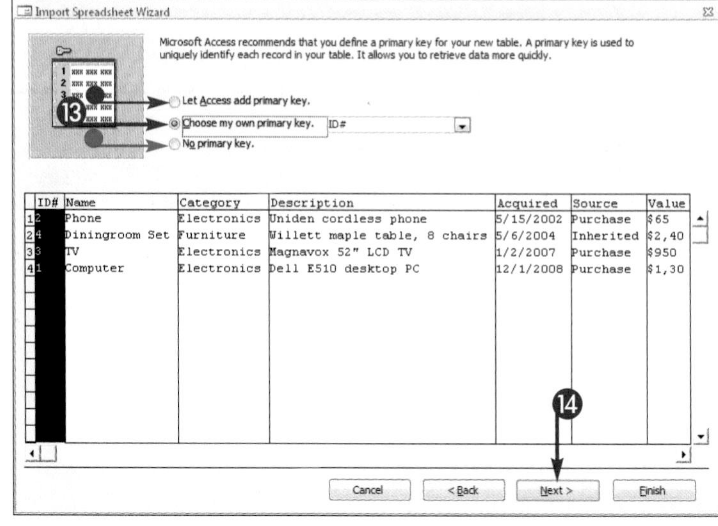

⓯ Type the name for the table.

Note: *The default name is the name of the tab from the worksheet.*

⓰ Click **Finish**.

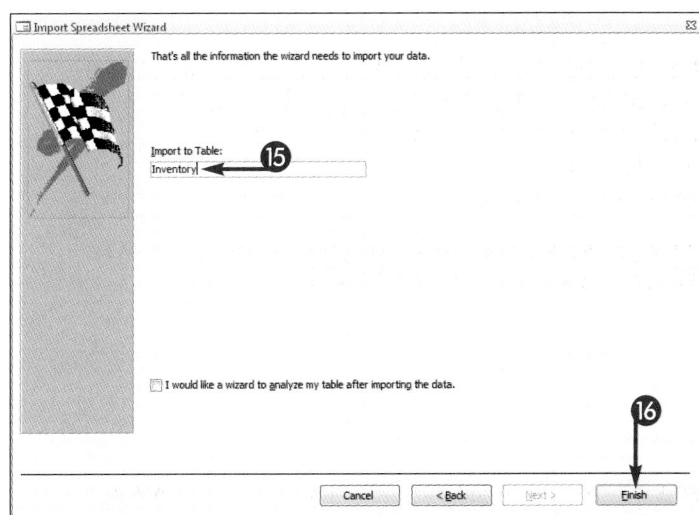

- You can save the import steps by clicking the **Save import steps** check box (☐ changes to ☑).

Note: *You will learn more about saving import steps later in this chapter.*

⓱ Click **Close**.

The Excel data is imported as a new table on the Objects list.

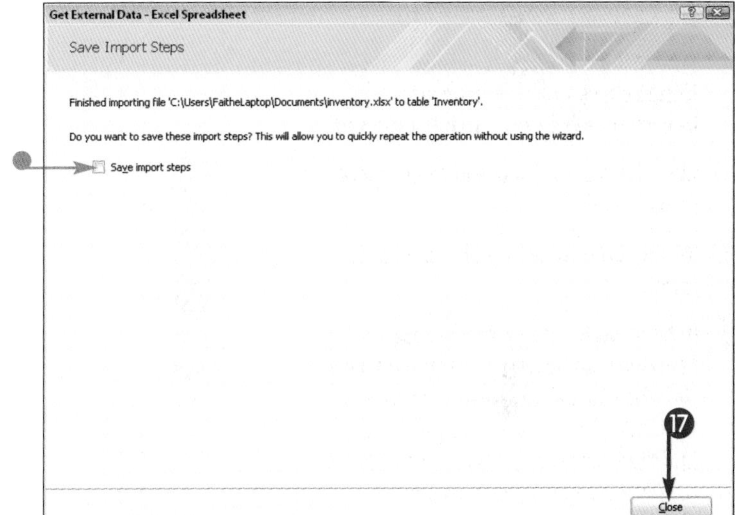

TIPS

Should I allow the wizard to create a primary key field?

It depends on whether you already have a field in the data that contains unique entries for each record and that will always contain unique entries. If you do, make that one the primary key. However, if you do not have any fields that fit that description, you should allow the wizard to create one for you.

Should I save the import specifications?

If you plan on doing this same import again later, then yes. For example, perhaps you have a table that a colleague maintains in Excel, and every month, you have to use it in Access. You could save the import settings to make it easier to import that file in the future. An even better approach, though, would be to link to the worksheet, as covered in the section "Link to an Excel Worksheet."

Link to an Excel Worksheet

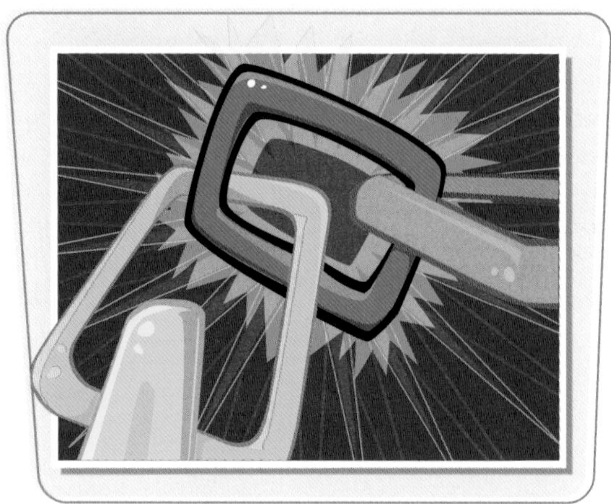

If you frequently need to reimport the same data from Excel, consider linking to that worksheet instead of repeatedly reimporting it.

With a link, the data is always up to date. Each time you open the linked worksheet in Access, Access refreshes the link to the data. That means, however, that the Excel file must always be in the expected location or else an error occurs.

Link to an Excel Worksheet

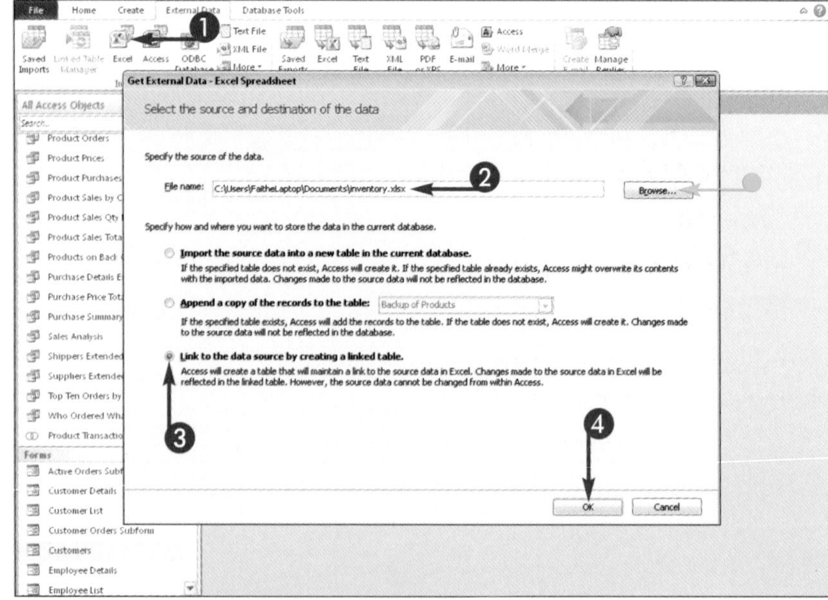

1. On the External Data tab in the Import & Link group, click **Excel**.

   The Get External Data – Excel Spreadsheet dialog box opens.

2. In the File name field, type the path and file name for the Excel file.

- You can click **Browse** to browse for the file if you prefer.

3. Click the **Link to the data source by creating a linked table** radio button (◎ changes to ◉).
4. Click **OK**.

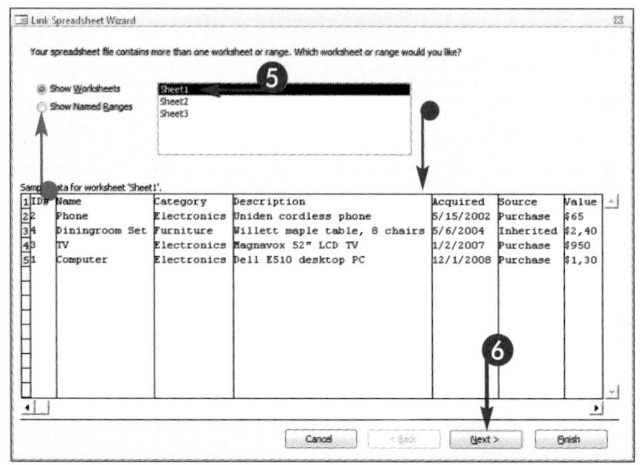

The Link Spreadsheet Wizard opens.

5. Click the sheet you want to import.

- A preview of the data on that sheet appears.
- You can alternatively choose from named ranges (◎ changes to ◉).

6. Click **Next**.

7. If the first row contains column headings, click the **First Row Contains Column Headings** check box (☐ changes to ☑).
8. Click **Next**.

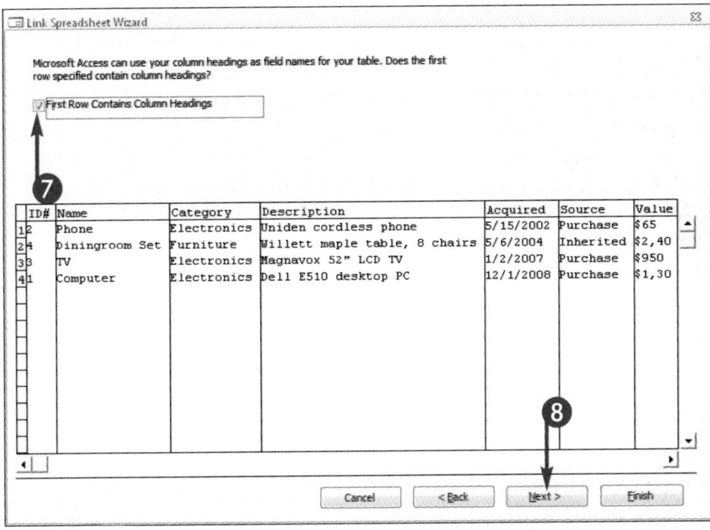

9. Type a name for the linked table.

   This will be the name that appears in the list of tables.
10. Click **Finish**.

    A confirmation window appears.
11. Click **OK**.

    The linked table appears in the Objects list in the Tables category.

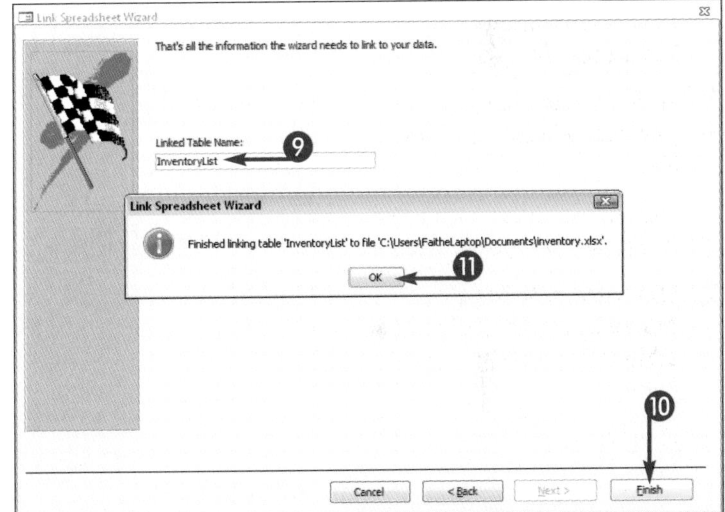

What happens if I need to move the Excel sheet later?

Use the Linked Table Manager, as described in the section "Manage Linked Tables." If the table has moved and Access can no longer find it, prompts can help you locate it again.

How can I tell what tables are actually linked Excel sheets?

- Linked Excel sheets have an Excel icon next to them in the All Access Objects list.

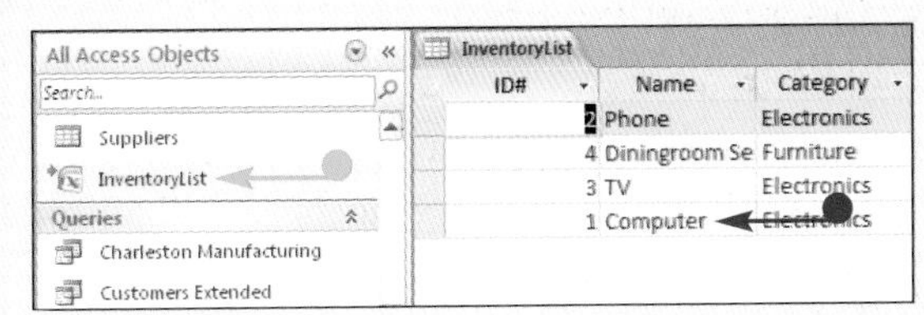

- When you open a linked object as a datasheet, it looks like a regular table.

Link to an Outlook Folder

If you use Microsoft Outlook as your main contact management program, there may be times when you want to use the Outlook Contacts list as a data source in Access. For example, if you store your customer information in Access, you may want to link certain orders or invoices to customers there.

Link to an Outlook Folder

1. On the External Data tab in the Import & Link group, click **More**.

   A menu opens.

2. Click **Outlook Folder**.

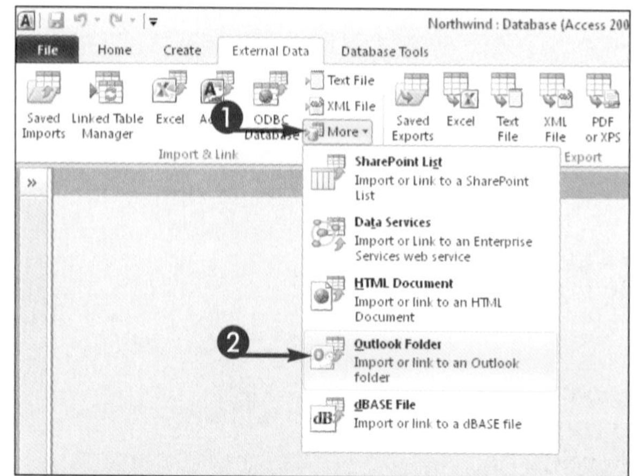

The Get External Data – Outlook Folder dialog box opens.

3. Click the **Link to the data source by creating a linked table** radio button (◎ changes to ◉).
4. Click **OK**.

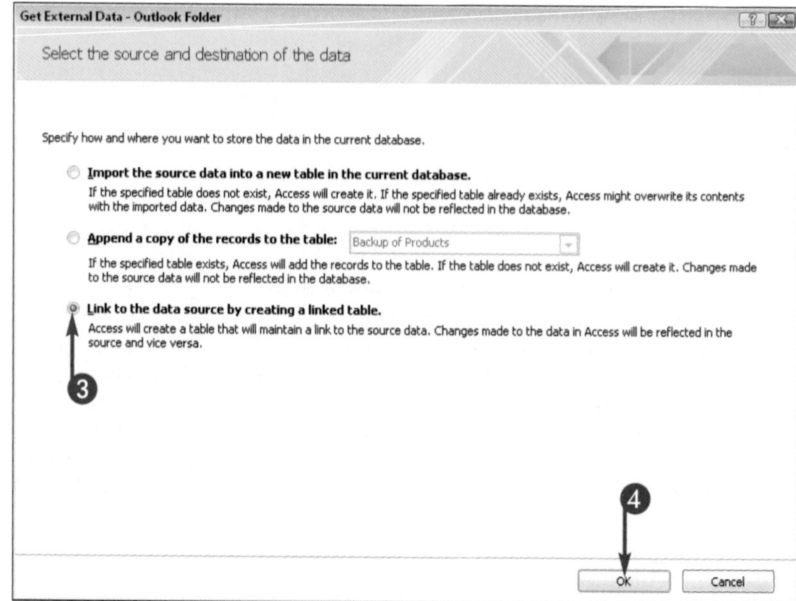

The Import Exchange/Outlook Wizard opens.

5 Click the plus signs (⊞) to expand the available categories and then select the desired Outlook folder.

6 Click **Next**.

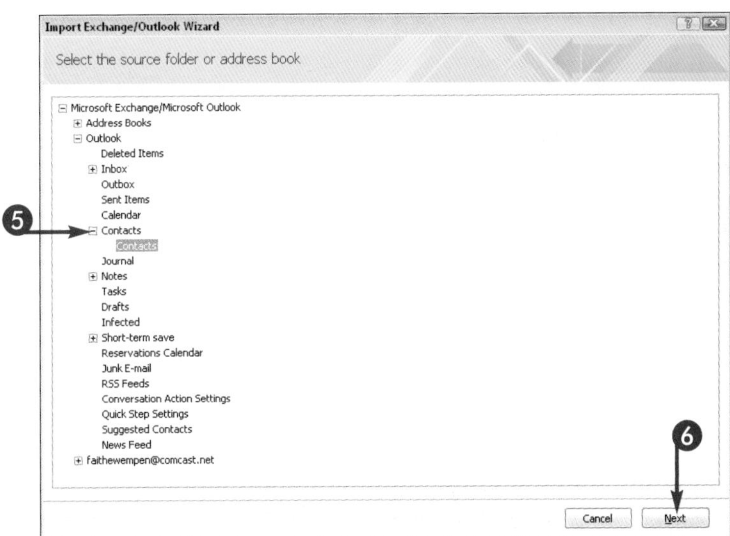

7 If desired, change the default name for the linked table.

8 Click **Finish**.

A dialog box opens, saying that it is finished linking the table.

9 Click **OK**.

The link is complete, and the new linked table appears in the Tables category of the Objects list.

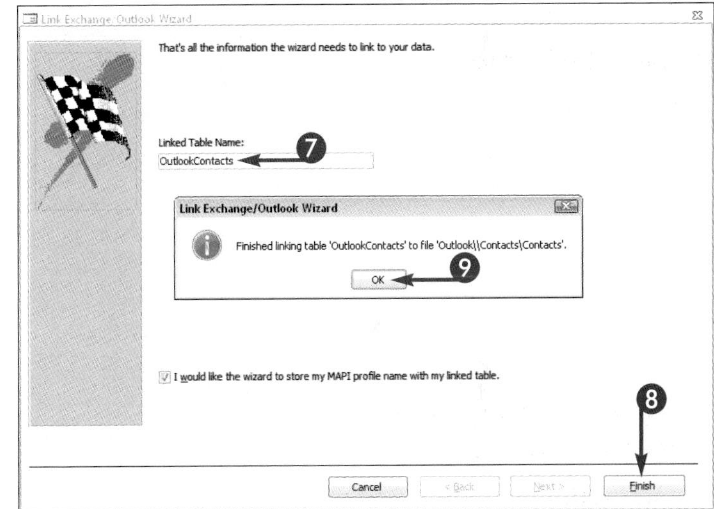

Can I import the data from Outlook rather than linking it?

Yes. It works very much like importing data from Excel. In step **3**, click the **Import the source data into a new table in the current database** radio button (◯ changes to ◉). Keep in mind, however, that if you import data, any future changes you make to the data in Outlook will not be reflected in Access.

What are the Address Books listed in the Outlook folders list in step 5?

Outlook has an Address Book utility that interfaces with your Contacts list and also optionally interfaces with other data sources, such as an employee directory on a file server or a mobile address book from a handheld device. You can link to one of these sources instead of Contacts if you prefer. Be cautious, though, about linking to an address book stored on a mobile device that might not always be available.

Manage Linked Tables

Linked tables are not updated automatically just by opening the database; they are updated only when you actually open the table. If you need to update all the linked tables at once without having to open each one, you can use the Linked Table Manager to accomplish that.

Manage Linked Tables

1. Right-click on one of the linked tables.
2. Click **Linked Table Manager**.

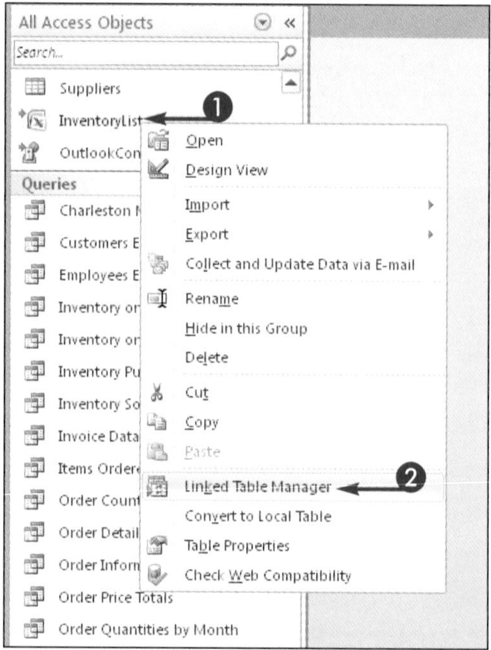

The Linked Table Manager opens.

3. Click the check box for each linked table that you want to update (☐ changes to ☑).

- You can also click **Select All**.

4. Click **OK**.

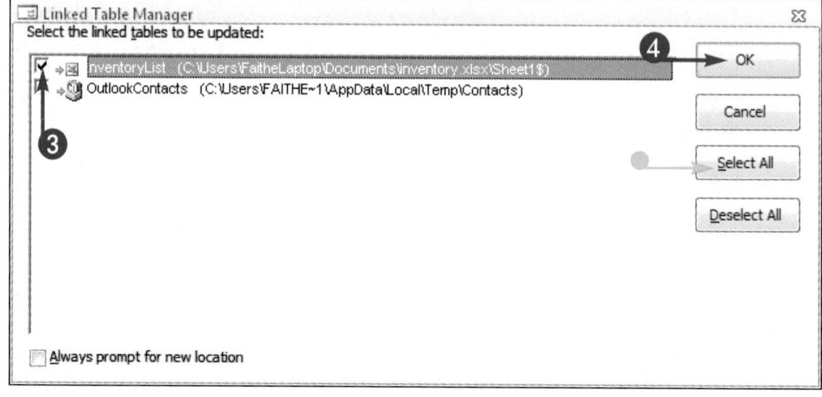

If a linked table cannot be located, a Select New Location dialog box opens.

If Access finds the linked table, you can skip to step **7**.

5 Browse to the new location to select the file.

6 Click **Open**.

You may have to repeat steps **5** and **6** for additional tables.

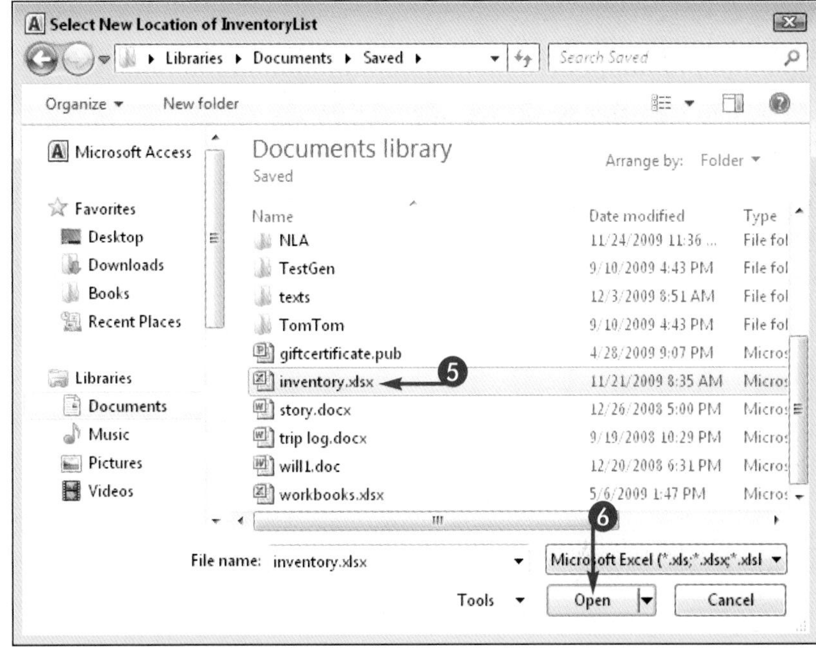

A message appears, stating that the tables were refreshed.

7 Click **OK**.

You are returned to the Linked Table Manager.

8 Click **Close**.

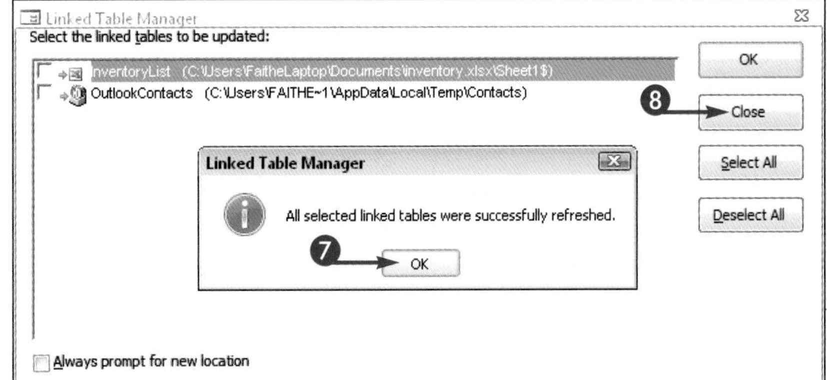

How can I change the location to which a link refers, even though the original location is still working?

Click the **Always prompt for new location** check box in the Linked Table Manager (☐ changes to ☑). It then prompts you for each table's location, even if the existing location is still working.

What if I get a #Num! error?

This error appears when a column contains mostly one type of value (text, date, or number) but a few entries of another type. Those other entries may not be imported correctly, and the #Num! error might appear. To minimize the instances of this error, try to clean up your data before importing, making sure that each column contains values of only one data type. Formatting the columns in the Excel file with a particular numeric type also helps.

Import a Table from Another Access Database

You can combine the data from multiple Access database files into a single database file by importing the tables from one file into another.

You can also import other objects, including queries, forms, reports, macros, and modules, but the destination database must have the needed tables and queries on which they are based.

Import a Table from Another Access Database

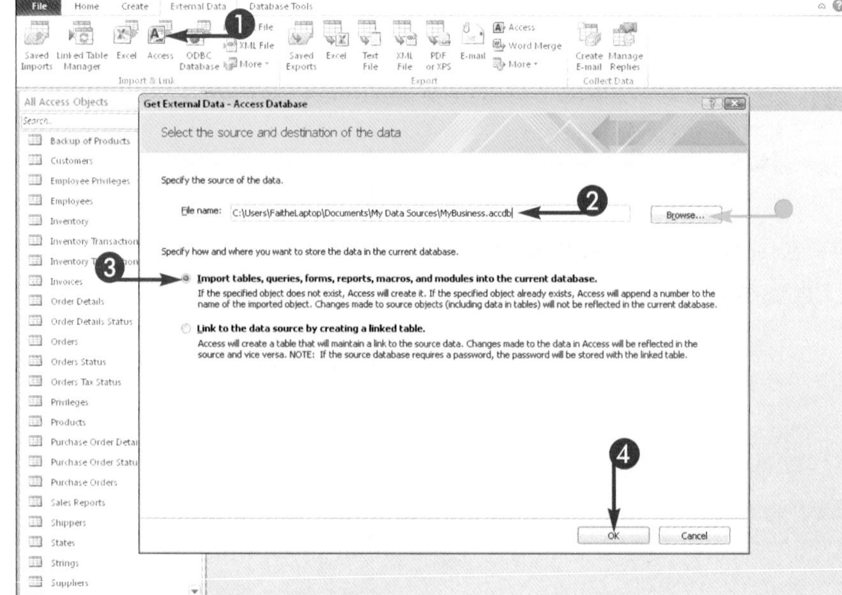

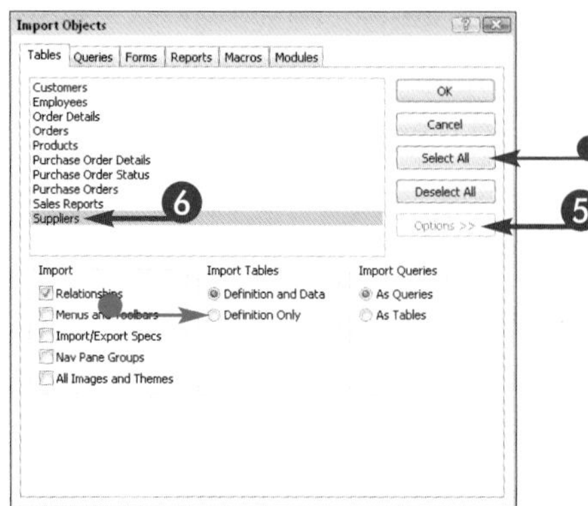

1. On the External Data tab in the Import & Link group, click **Access**.

   The Get External Data – Access Database dialog box opens.

2. In the File name field, type the path and file name for the Access file.

   - You can click **Browse** to browse for the file if you prefer.

3. Click the **Import tables, queries, forms, reports, macros, and modules into the current database** radio button (◎ changes to ◉).

4. Click **OK**.

   The Import Objects dialog box opens.

5. Click **Options**.

   The Import options appear at the bottom of the dialog box.

6. Click the tables you want to import.

   - You can click **Select All** to include all the tables.
   - For each table or query, you can optionally click the **Definition only** radio button (◎ changes to ◉) to import only the table structure, not the data.

7 Click the **Queries** tab.

8 Click any queries you want to import.

9 If you selected any queries, click how you want them to be imported.

You can click other tabs and select any other objects you want.

10 Click **OK**.

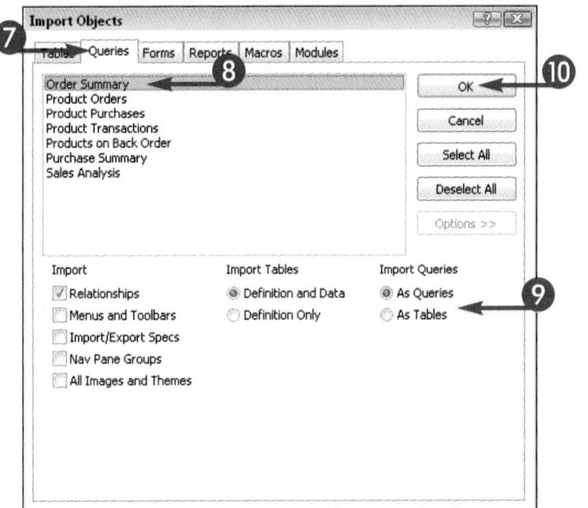

The Save Import Steps screen appears.

11 Click **Close**.

The objects are imported into the database.

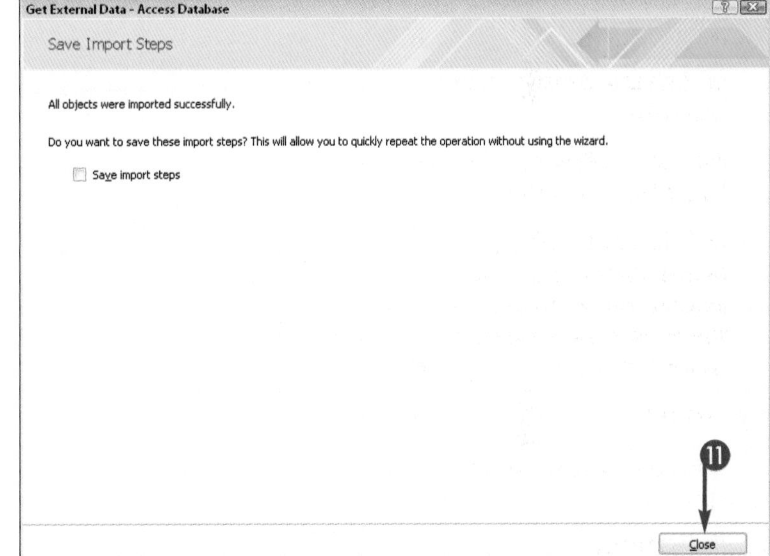

What is the difference between importing a query as a table and importing it as a query?

Importing a query as a table creates a new table with a datasheet that looks like the query's results. Any records or fields the query definition excludes are excluded. Importing a query as a query imports just the query definition. The database must have a table of the same name as the one the query uses, with compatible fields.

Can I link to content from another Access database?

Yes. In the Get External Data – Access Database dialog box, click the **Link to the data source by creating a linked table** radio button (◎ changes to ◉).

Import Data from a Delimited Text File

You can use a delimited text file to transfer database data from a database program that does not support Access as an export option.

From the other database program, you export in a comma-delimited or tab-delimited format. Then, you import that file into Access.

Import Data from a Delimited Text File

1. On the External Data tab in the Import & Link group, click **Text File**.

   The Get External Data – Text File dialog box opens.

2. In the File name field, type the path and file name of the text file.

- You can click **Browse** to browse for the file if you prefer.

3. Click the **Import the source data into a new table in the current database** radio button (◎ changes to ◉).

Note: *Alternatively, you can choose to link to the data source or append to an existing table.*

4. Click **OK**.

   The Import Text Wizard opens.

5. Click the **Delimited** radio button (◎ changes to ◉).

Note: *Fixed-width data files are rare; a fixed-width data file includes extra spaces after some entries, so the width of a field is defined by spaces rather than by a delimited character.*

6. Click **Next**.

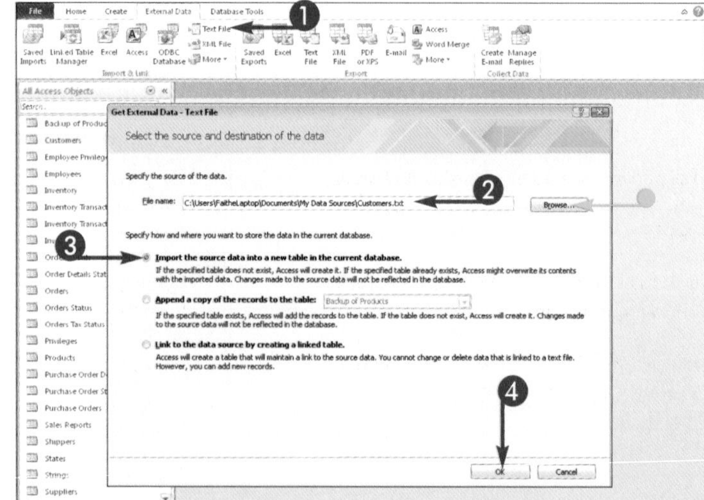

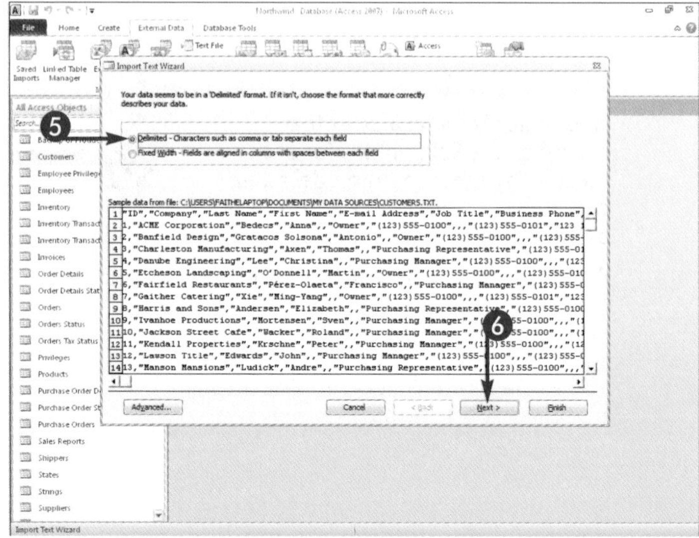

7. Click the delimiter character used in the file (◎ changes to ◉).
   - You know that you have chosen the correct delimiter when the data appears in orderly rows and columns in the sample area.

8. Click the **First Row Contains Field Names** check box (☐ changes to ☑) if the first row contains the field names.

9. Click **Next**.

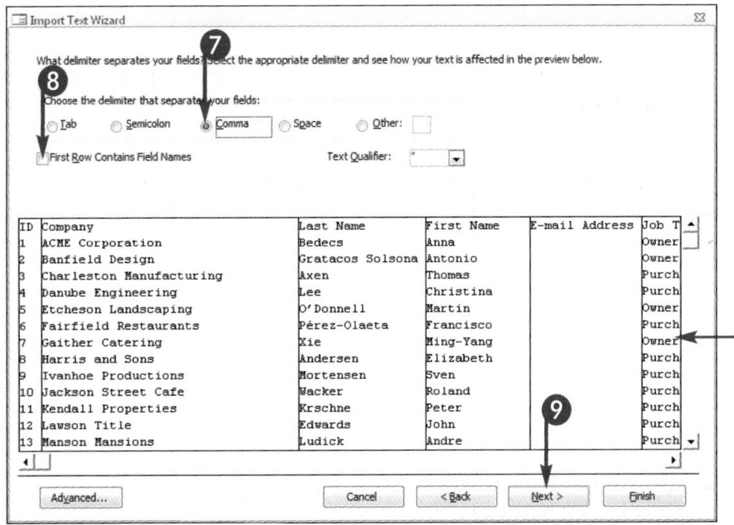

10. Click a field to select it.

11. Change the field name if needed.

Note: *If the first row does not contain field names, field names are generic and should be changed in step* ***11***.

12. Click here (▾) to change the data type if needed.

13. Repeat steps **10** to **12** for each field you want to change.

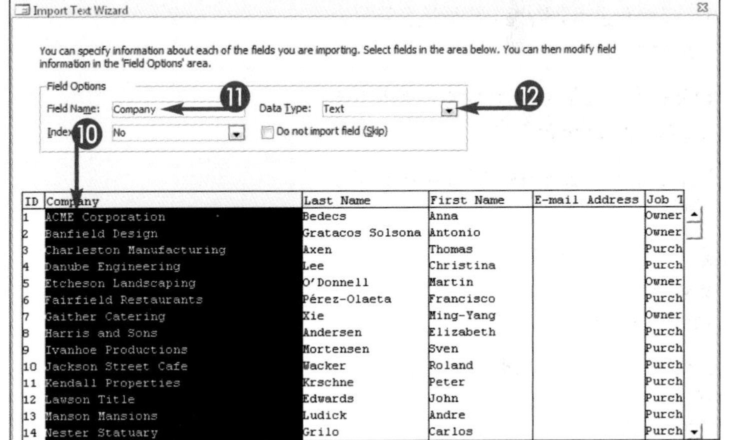

TIPS

What is a delimiter?

A *delimiter* is the character that separates the field entries for each record. The most common delimiters are tabs and commas. Each record is separated by a paragraph break (Enter)

An alternative that is sometimes (but rarely) used in database text files is fixed-width. For example, suppose a certain field is 20 characters wide. For each entry that is fewer that 20 characters, extra spaces are inserted between that field and the next one for that record.

How do I get data into a delimited text file from another database program?

That depends on the program. Nearly all database programs have some type of export feature that exports in a variety of formats. These almost always include tab-delimited and comma-delimited. Neither one is better than the other; they both work well. To find out the exact steps for exporting data from another database program, look up Exporting in that program's Help system.

continued

Import Data from a Delimited Text File *(continued)*

Except for the beginning part of the process, the steps for importing from a text file are nearly identical to those for importing from an Excel file. You can specify a primary key, choose which fields should be indexed, and even choose to skip certain fields, just as you can with an Excel file import.

Import Data from a Delimited Text File *(continued)*

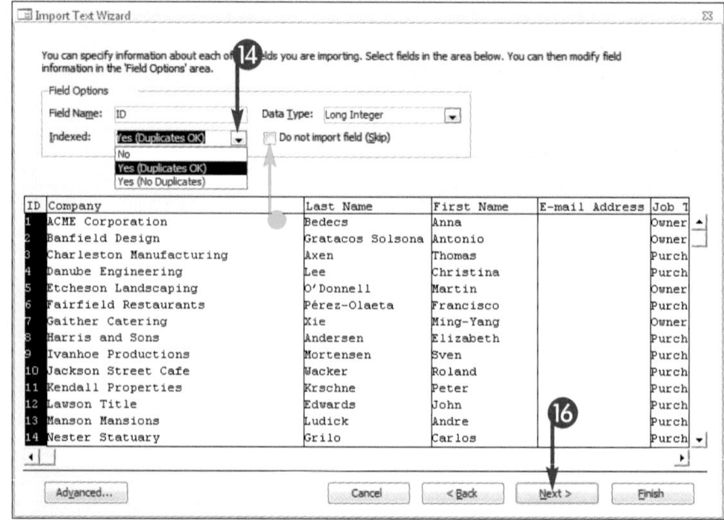

1. **14** Click here (▾) to change the indexing setting if needed.

***Note:** If you choose Yes (No Duplicates), make sure that each record has a unique entry for this field; otherwise, an error will occur at import.*

- You can click the **Do not import field (Skip)** check box (☐ changes to ☑) to skip a field.

15 Repeat steps **10** to **13** for each field.

16 Click **Next**.

17 If the imported data already contains a field that you want to use as the primary key, click the **Choose my own primary key** radio button (◎ changes to ◉) and then choose that field from the drop-down menu.

- You can also allow the wizard to create a new field to be used as a primary key by clicking the **Let Access add primary key** radio button (◎ changes to ◉).
- You can also decline to use a primary key in the table by clicking the **No primary key** radio button (◎ changes to ◉).

18 Click **Next**.

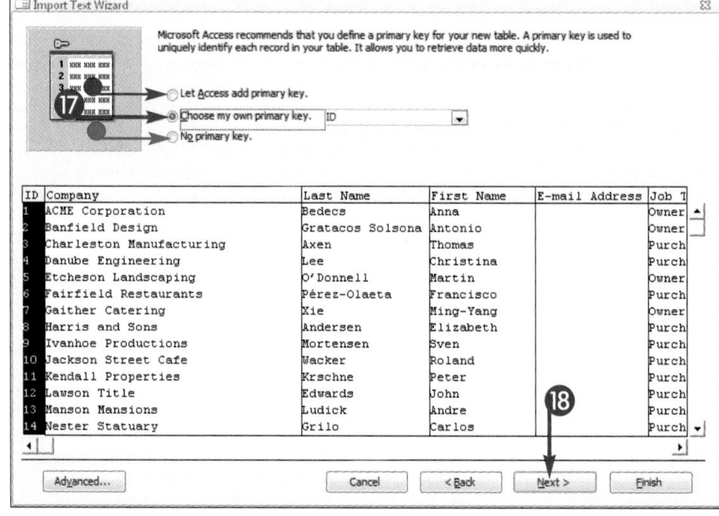

19 Type the name to use for the imported table.

20 Click **Finish**.

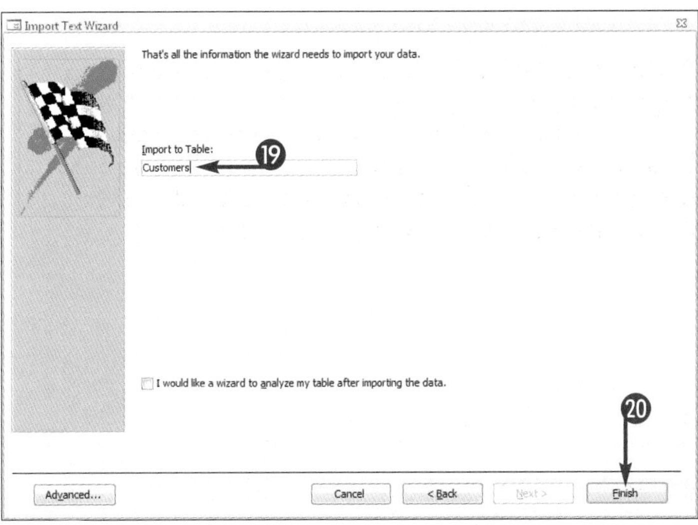

The Save Import Steps screen appears.

- You can click the **Save import steps** check box (☐ changes to ☑) to save the import, as described later in this chapter.

21 Click **Close**.

The data is imported into a new table with the name that you specified.

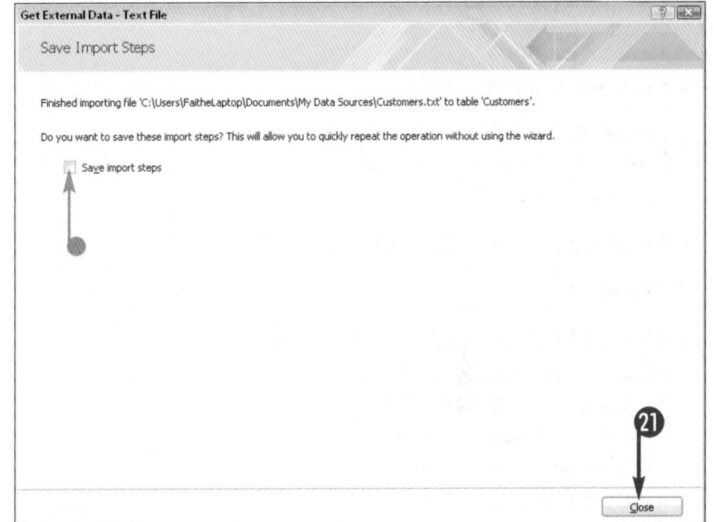

How can I append records to an existing table from a plain text file?

On the initial Get External Data – Text File screen, click the **Append a copy of the records to the table** radio button (◯ changes to ◉) and then select the table. For this to work, the table must have the same fields, with the same field types, as the data you are importing.

Do I have to specify field names in order to import data if the data file does not already have field names in the first row?

No. But generic field names will be used (Field1, Field2) in the imported table. You can then use Table Design view to modify the field names. Make sure that you change the field names to names that are more meaningful before you start using the imported table as the basis for other objects such as queries, forms, and reports.

Export Data to Excel

In addition to importing data from Excel, you can also export it from an Access table into the Excel format. As you are performing the export, you can choose to export in a variety of Excel formats, including Excel 2010 and earlier versions.

Export Data to Excel

1. Select the table to be exported.
2. On the External Data tab in the Export group, click **Excel**.

   The Export – Excel Spreadsheet dialog box opens.
3. In the File name field, type the path and file name for the file to be exported.

- You can click **Browse** to locate a file or folder if you prefer.

4. Click here (▾) to choose a file format.

- You can click the **Export data with formatting and layout** check box (☐ changes to ☑) to export formatting and layout as well as data.

5. Click **OK**.

- You can optionally click the **Save export steps** check box (☐ changes to ☑) to save these export steps for later use.

6. Click **Close**.

   The export is complete.

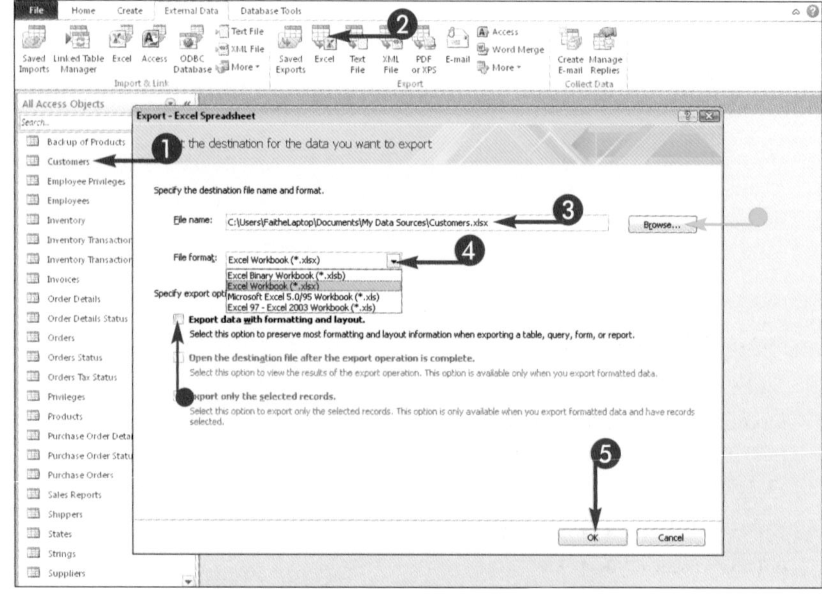

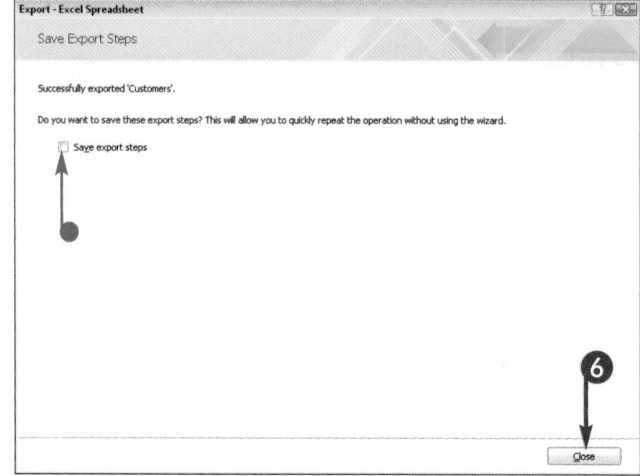

Export Data as HTML

One way to share data with others is to export it to a Web page — that is, to the HTML format.

There are more complex ways of making Access data available online, such as through data access pages, but for simple sharing where the data is fixed, an HTML page is the easiest way to go.

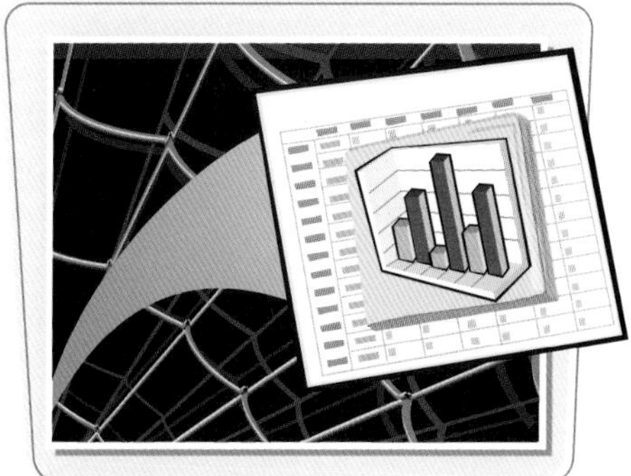

Export Data as HTML

1. Select the table to be exported.
2. On the External Data tab in the Export group, click **More**.
3. Click **HTML Document**.

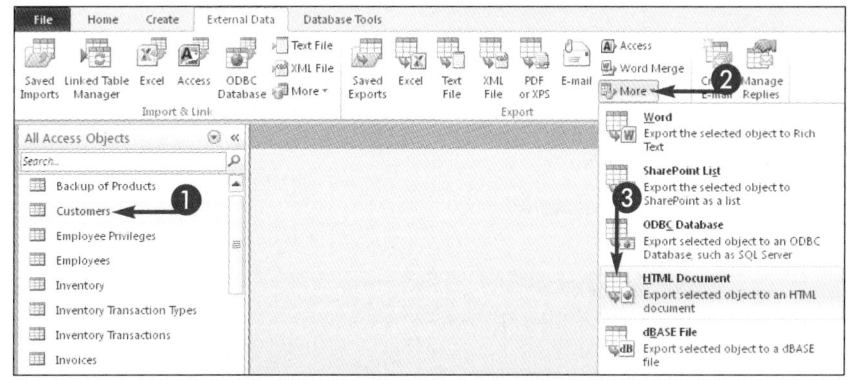

The Export – HTML Document dialog box opens.

4. In the File name field, type the path and file name for the file to be exported.

- You can click **Browse** to locate a file or folder if you prefer.

5. Click **OK**.

The Save Export Steps dialog box opens.

6. Click **Close**.

The export is complete.

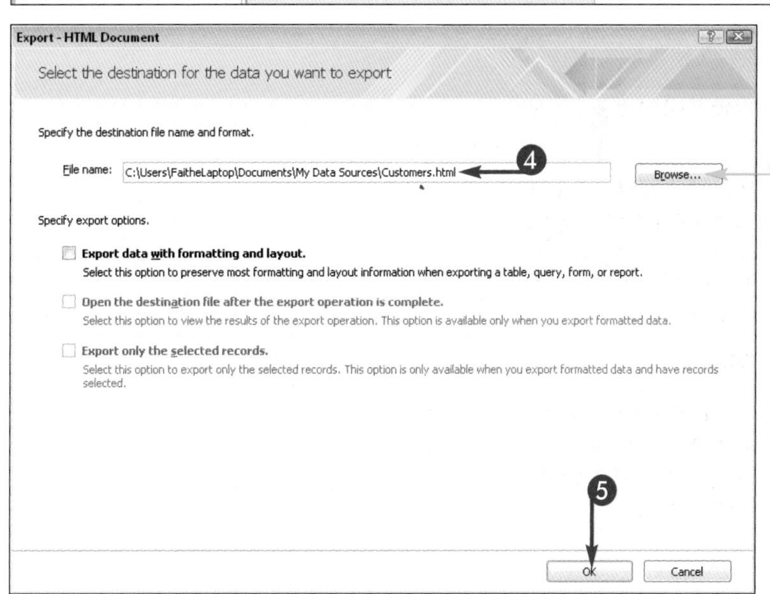

Export Data to a Plain Text File

When you need to import data from Access into some other database program that does not accept Excel or any of the other formats available to you, a plain text export may be your only option.

Plain text exports can be delimited by characters such as commas or tabs or, less frequently, they can be set to be fixed-width.

Export Data to a Plain Text File

1. Select the table to be exported.
2. On the External Data tab in the Export group, click **Text File**.

   The Export – Text File dialog box opens.

3. In the File name field, type the path and file name for the file to be exported.

- You can click **Browse** to locate a file or folder if you prefer.

4. Click **OK**.

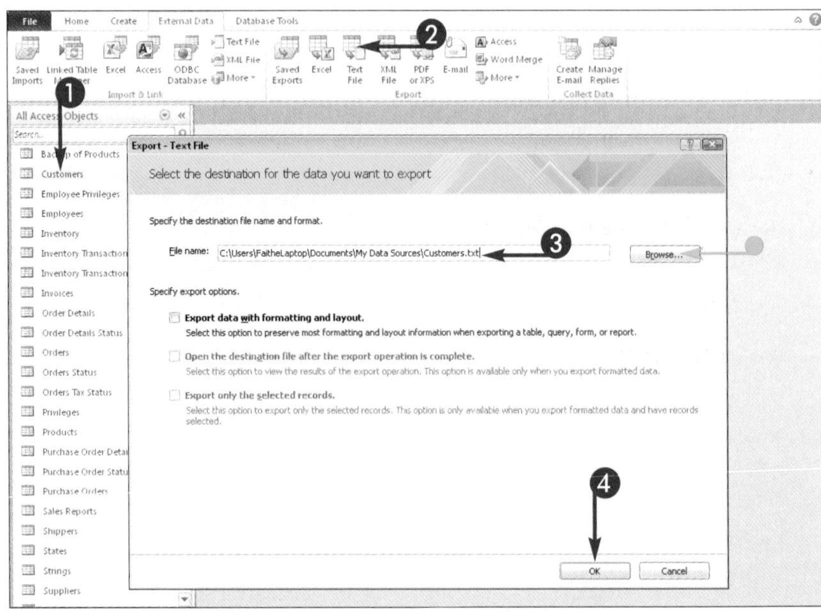

The Export Text Wizard opens.

5. Click the **Delimited** radio button (◯ changes to ◉).

Note: *It is unusual to do a Fixed Width export; most database programs can import delimited data.*

6. Click **Next**.

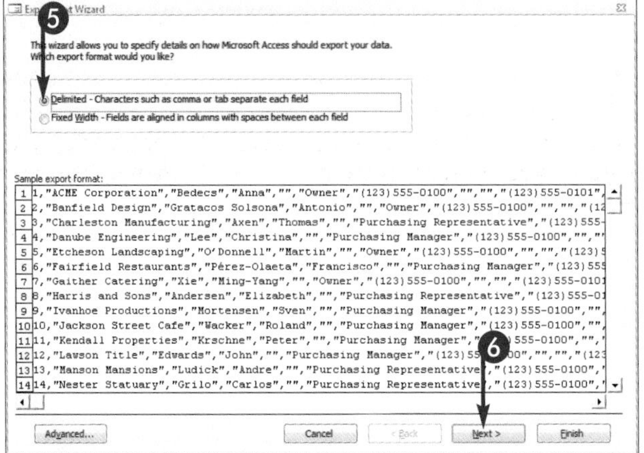

7 Click the delimiter character you want to use (◎ changes to ◉).

8 Click the **Include Field Names on First Row** check box (☐ changes to ☑) if you want to include the field names on the first row.

9 Click **Next**.

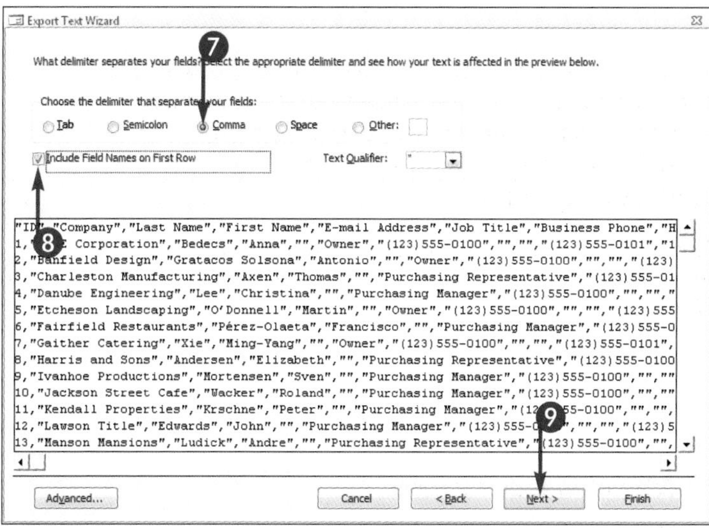

10 Confirm the path and file name for the file you want to export.

11 Click **Finish**.

The Save Export Steps dialog box opens.

12 Click **Close**.

The export is complete.

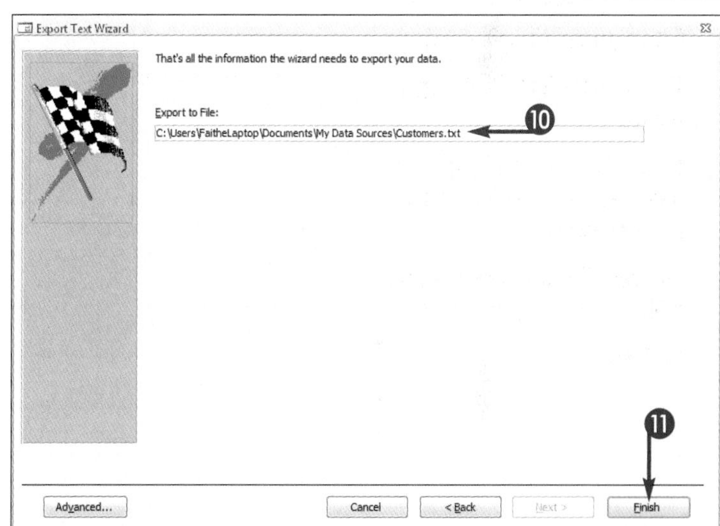

When should I use the Export data with formatting and layout feature?

Use this feature when you want to include helper characters in certain types of data, such as parentheses and dashes in phone numbers or dashes in a nine-digit ZIP code. If you choose this option, the rest of the steps in the process are different (just follow the prompts), and the result is a fixed-width file rather than a delimited one.

How can I change field names as I export?

After step **5**, click **Advanced** to open the Export Specification dialog box. From here, you can change field names, change the delimiter character, and more. To change one of the field names, double-click it in the Field Information area and then type a new name.

Save Import or Export Specifications

The last step of every import or export process is a dialog box in which you can optionally click a check box to save the import or export steps.

In these steps, you will look at what happens when you click that check box and where the settings are stored.

Save Import or Export Specifications

1. On the Save Export (or Import) Steps screen of an export or import operation, click the **Save export steps** (or **Save import steps**) check box (☐ changes to ☑).

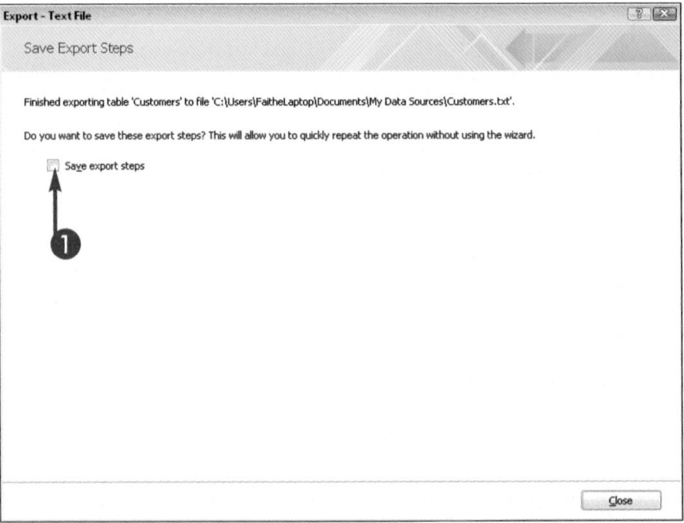

Additional text boxes appear in the dialog box.

2. Click here to type a name for the saved settings.
3. You can click here to type a description.
4. You can click the **Create Outlook Task** check box (☐ changes to ☑) to create an Outlook task to remind you of this activity.
5. Click **Save Export** (or **Save Import**).

The operation is saved.

If you chose to create an Outlook task, the task opens in Outlook.

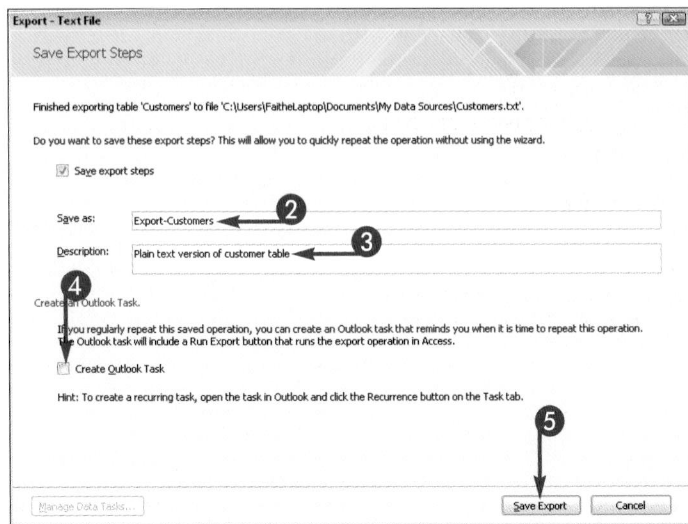

Using Saved Import or Export Specifications

After you have saved an import or export specification, you can easily recall it.

Saved settings perform an import or export by using the same source and the same destination, with all the same settings, file formats, and other specifications.

Using Saved Import or Export Specifications

1. On the External Data tab, click **Saved Exports**.
   - For an import, you would click **Saved Imports**.

   The Manage Data Tasks dialog box opens.
2. Click the export or import that you want to use.
3. Click **Run**.

   The export or import is run.

   If the file still exists from a previous export or import, a warning appears.
4. Click **Yes** to replace the previously exported or imported file.

   A message appears, saying that the file has been exported or imported.
5. Click **OK**.
6. Click **Close**.

Note: *The saved settings are saved in the Documents folder for the current user.*

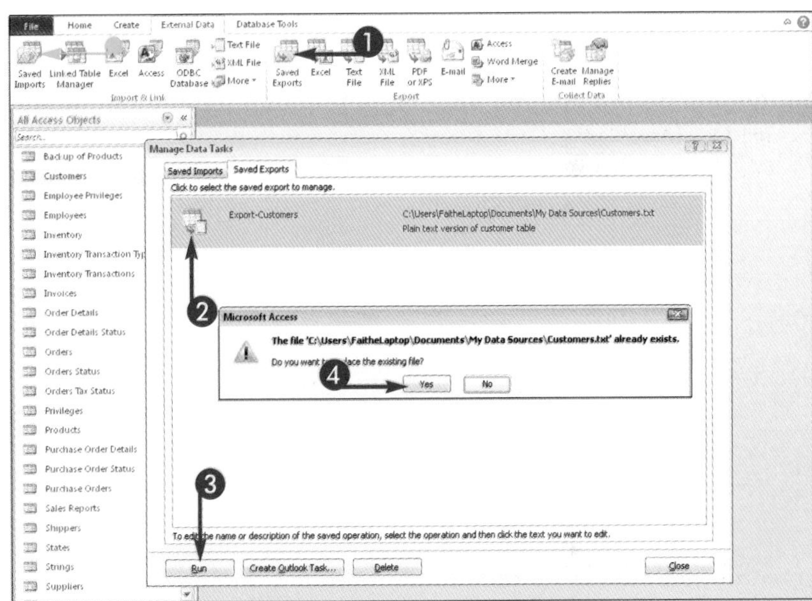

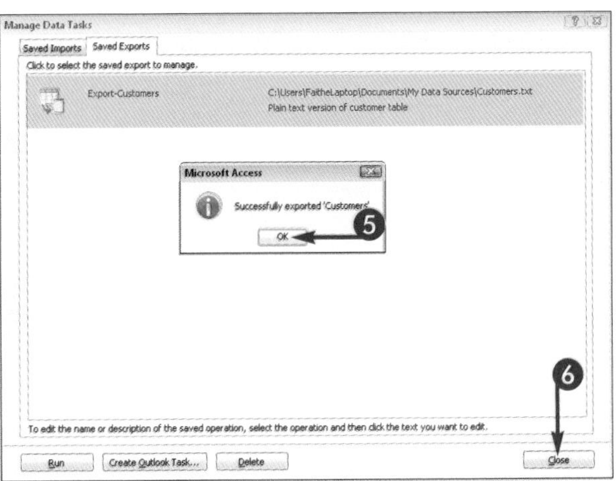

CHAPTER 16

Performing a Mail Merge with Microsoft Word

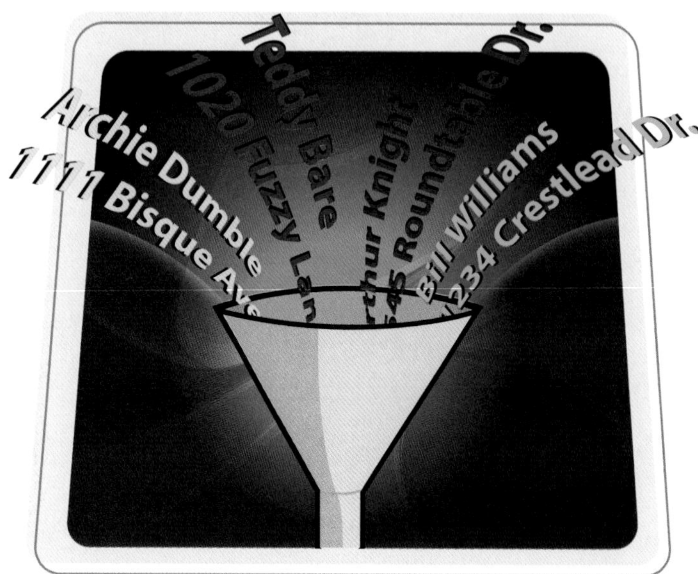

One common use for a database is to store names and addresses of people to whom you send written correspondence. That can be anything from a family holiday letter to a business mass-mailing to thousands of customers. You can combine the capabilities of Access with those of a word-processing program, such as Microsoft Word, to easily produce hundreds or even thousands of personalized copies of a letter with a few simple mouse clicks.

Begin a Mail Merge

You can begin a mail merge either from Access or from Word. In this chapter, you will learn how to do it from Access. Either way, you will work primarily from Microsoft Word because that is where you set up the main document. The Access database serves as a passive supplier of data when the actual merge occurs.

Running the Mail Merge Wizard in Access gives you the opportunity to create a new Word document to serve as the main document or to use an existing one. The steps in this chapter assume that you will create a new Word document as part of the mail merge process.

Begin a Mail Merge

1. Select the table you want to use as a data source for the merge.

Note: *Make sure that the table contains adequate fields to address a postal mailing. At the minimum, it should include the name, address, city, state, and ZIP code.*

2. On the External Data tab in the Export group, click **Word Merge**.

   The Microsoft Word Mail Merge Wizard opens.

3. Click the **Create a new document and then link the data to it** radio button (◎ changes to ◉).

4. Click OK.

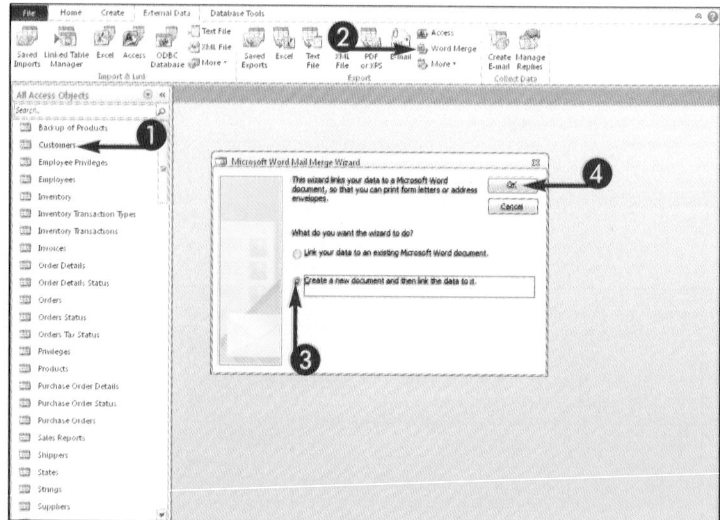

Microsoft Word opens a new document and then opens the Mail Merge task pane.

5. In Microsoft Word, under Select document type, click the **Letters** radio button (◎ changes to ◉).

- You can click other data types if you prefer.

6. Click **Next: Starting document**.

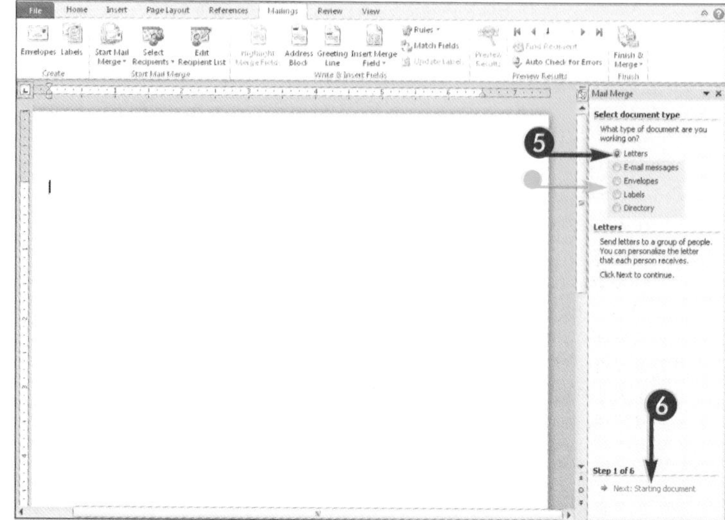

7. Make sure that the **Use the Current Document** radio button is selected (◎ changes to ◉).
8. Click **Next: Select recipients**.
9. Leave the data source settings as they are.

   Because you started the merge from Access, the correct Access table is already selected.
10. Click **Next: Write your letter**.

    The next set of options appear in the task pane.

Do I need to do anything special in Access to prepare the table to be used for mail merge?

If you are going to use the mail merge results for postal mailings, the table should include all the fields you need for that purpose: full name, address, city, state, and ZIP code. Otherwise, you won't be able to construct complete, useable addresses.

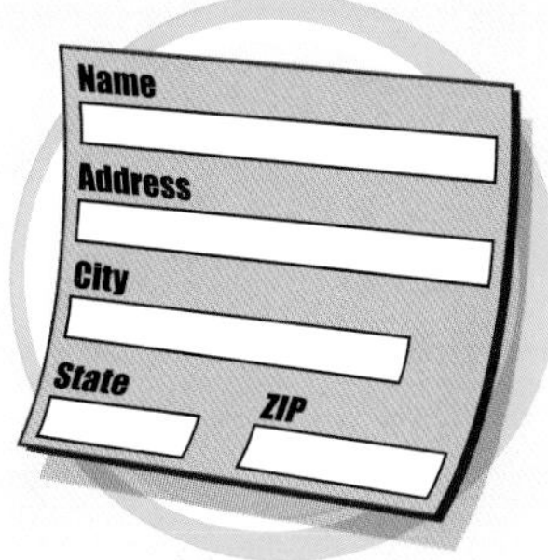

Do I have to use the Mail Merge Wizard?

No. You can use the commands on the Mailings tab in Word to manually set up a mail merge. This chapter does not cover those methods, but you can learn about them by using Help in Word.

Create the Main Document in Word

The main document is the one that contains all the parts of the letter that stay the same for each copy. For example, if you are writing a letter to customers, the main document will contain the current date, your return address, the message to the customers, and your signature line.

You can create all the text for the main document at once or you can insert fields in the letter. Inserting fields is covered later in this chapter.

Create the Main Document in Word

1. In Word, type all the parts of the letter except those that should be personalized.

- Leave blanks where you will put the fields, such as the address and the greeting.

The letter is now ready for you to insert merge fields, which you will learn to do in the following sections.

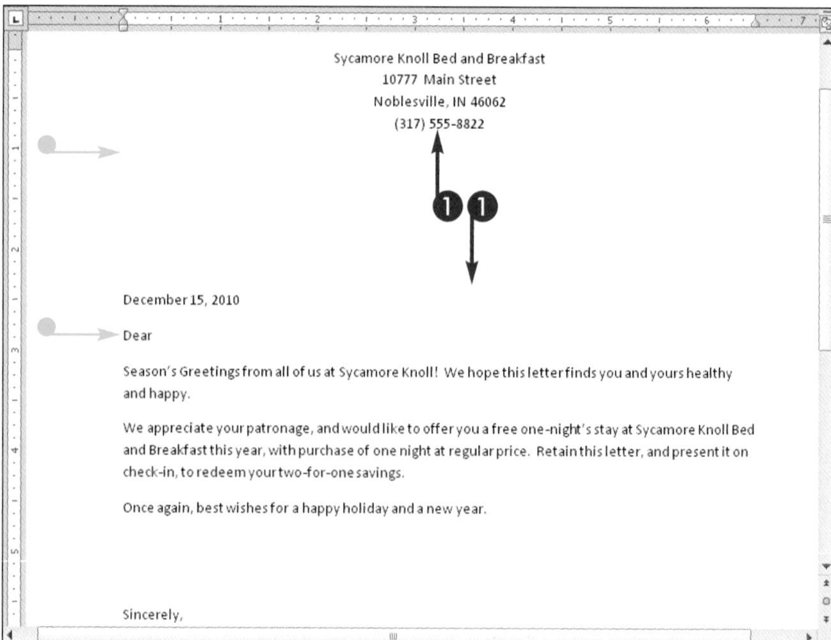

Insert an Address Block

If you have selected a table that contains all the elements needed to construct a mailing address block (name, address, city, state, and ZIP code), you can use the Address Block field code to automatically insert all the fields needed for the address in a single step. Word is able to determine which fields to use in most cases.

If the Address Block field code does not deliver the results you expect, you can instead insert the individual field codes, which are covered later in this chapter.

Insert an Address Block

1. In the main document, put the insertion point where the address block should be placed.
2. In the task pane, click **Address block**.

- Alternately, on the Mailings tab, you can click **Address Block**.

  The Insert Address Block dialog box opens.

- You can choose a different format for the recipient's name.
- You can choose to include or omit the company name.
- You can see how the records from your database will appear in the letter.

Note: *If the sample does not look right, see the section "Match Fields" for help.*

3. Click **OK**.

- An <<AddressBlock>> field code appears in the document.

Note: *Field names in a main document are surrounded by double arrow brackets.*

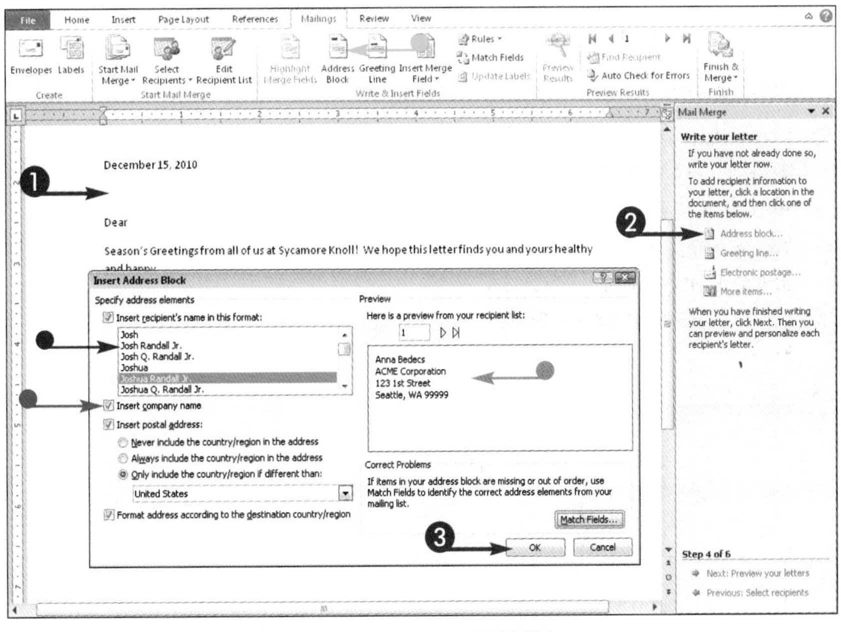

December 15, 2010

«AddressBlock»

Dear

Season's Greetings from all of us at Sycamore Knoll! We hope this letter finds you and yours healthy and happy.

Insert a Greeting Line

A greeting line field code inserts a greeting, such as "Dear," along with one or more fields. If you want to greet the letter recipient with multiple fields, such as Prefix, First Name, and Last Name, using a greeting line field code is more efficient than inserting the individual fields one by one.

If the greeting line field code does not deliver the results you expect, you can instead insert the individual field codes, which are covered later in this chapter.

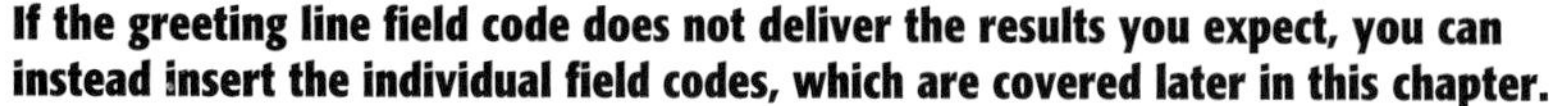

Insert a Greeting Line

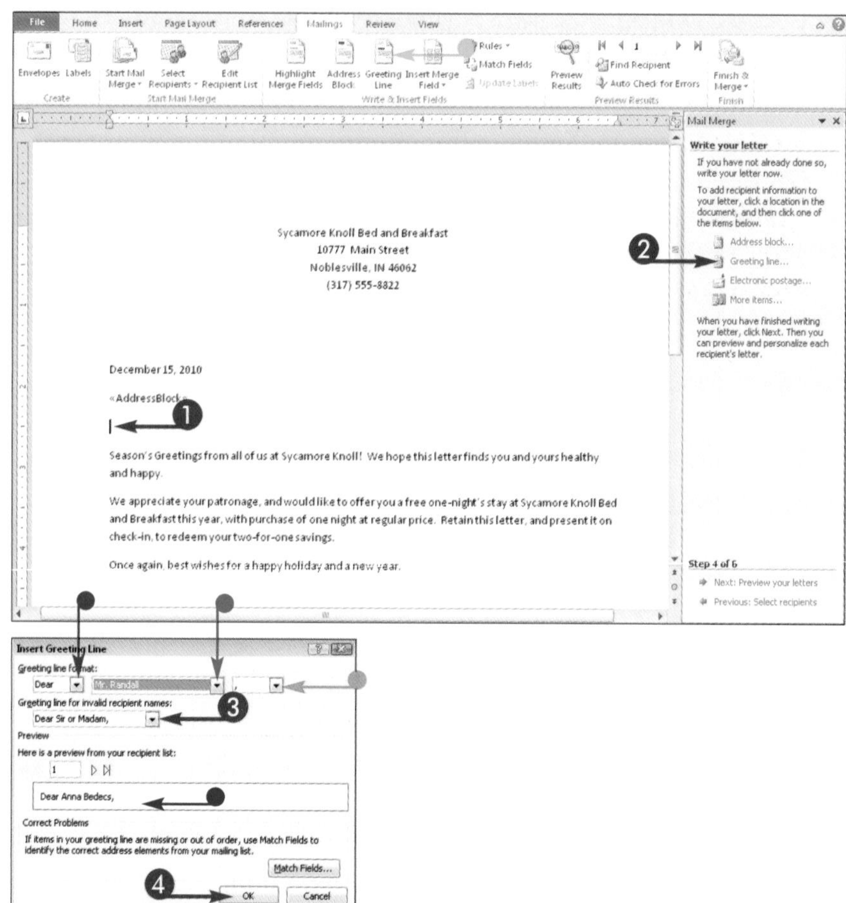

1. In the main document, put the insertion point where the greeting line should be placed.
2. In the task pane, click **Greeting line**.
   - Alternately, on the Mailings tab, you can click **Greeting Line**.

   The Insert Greeting Line dialog box opens.

   - You can click here (▾) to choose a different prefix type for the greeting.
   - You can click here (▾) to choose how the name will appear (for example, whether a prefix will be used and whether the first name, last name, or both will be included).
   - You can click here (▾) to choose what punctuation will follow the greeting.
3. Click here (▾) to choose a greeting to use if the record lacks the fields needed to construct a regular greeting.
   - You can preview the greeting line here.
4. Click **OK**.

Match Fields

If Word is not able to correctly match up the fields from the database table to the right spots in the address block when you are inserting a greeting line, you can manually match up the fields yourself.

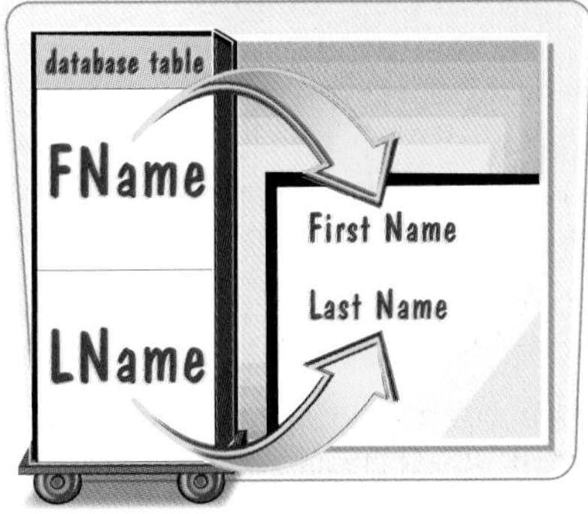

Match Fields

1. In the Insert address Block or Insert Greeting Line dialog box, click the **Match Fields** button.

   The Match Fields dialog box opens.

- Alternately, if neither of those dialog boxes is open, you can click **Match Fields** on the Mailings tab.

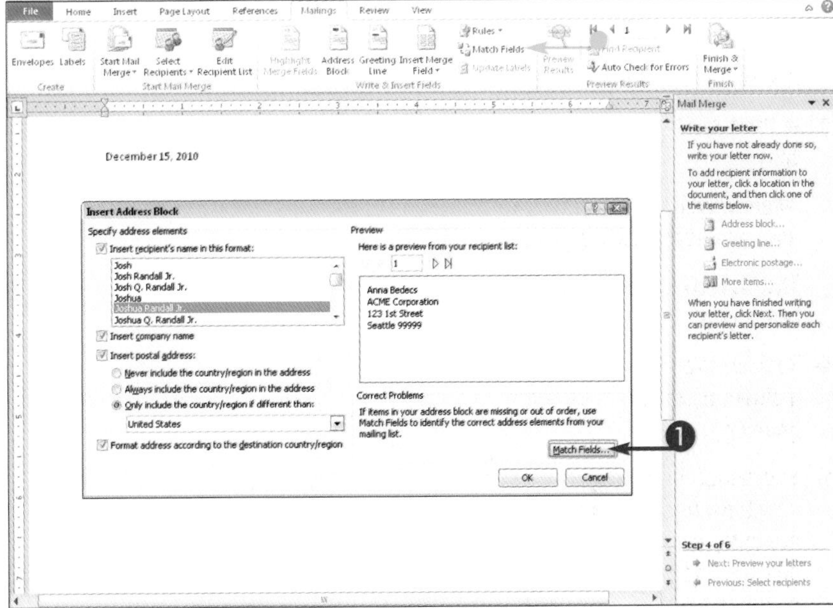

2. Click here (▾) to open the drop-down menu for a field placeholder and then select the corresponding field in the data source.
3. Repeat step **2** for each field.
4. Click **OK**.

   The fields are now matched as you have indicated.

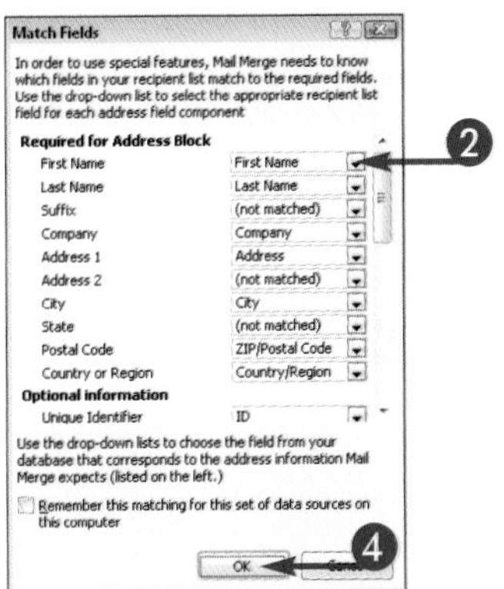

Insert Individual Fields

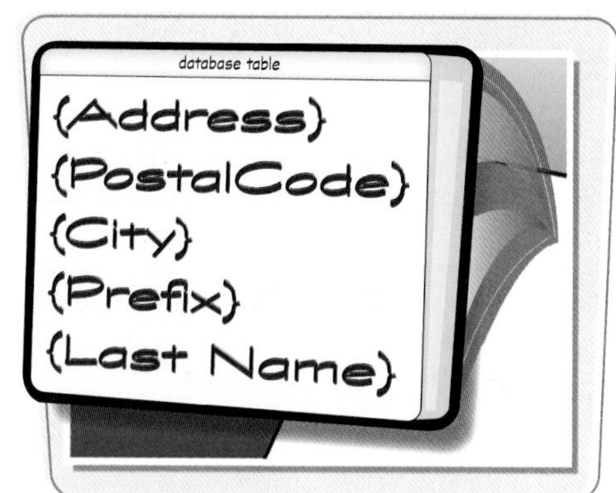

In addition to creating an address block, you may also want to insert other fields from the database table. For example, after "Dear," you might want to insert the person's first name.

You can also insert individual field codes to create your own version of the address block instead of using the <<AddressBlock>> code.

Insert Individual Fields

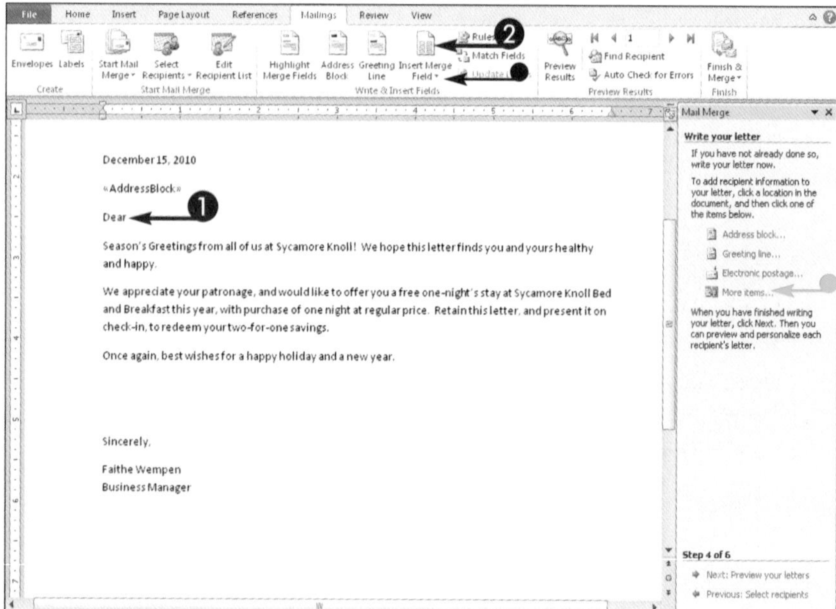

1. Put the insertion point where you want the field code to be placed.
2. On the Mailings tab, click **Insert Merge Field**.

- You can also click **More items** in the task pane.

  The Insert Merge Field dialog box opens.

- If you click the drop-down arrow (▾) under the Insert Merge Field button rather than the actual button, a menu of available fields opens; you can click one of the fields there instead of using the dialog box.

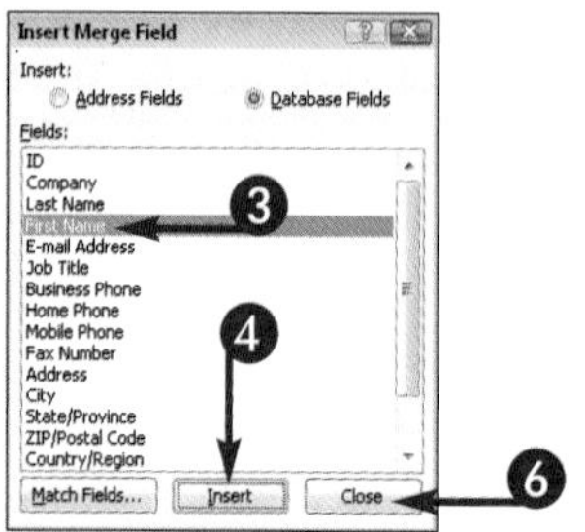

3. Select the field you want to insert.
4. Click **Insert**.
5. Repeat steps **3** and **4** to insert other fields if needed.

***Note:** You may want to type some punctuation between steps **4** and **5** to separate the fields, such as a space between the first and last names.*

6. Click **Close**.

   The field code(s) are inserted.

Preview the Merge Results

Before you print the mail merge, you might want to preview the merge on-screen to save paper in case there are problems that need correcting before printing.

Word enables you to page through the records one at a time, examining each one to make sure the addresses are valid and the fields are appropriately set up to display the right information.

Preview the Merge Results

1. In the Mail Merge task pane, click **Next: Preview your letters**.

- The document changes to show the first copy of the letter as it will appear when printed.

2. Click here (>>) to display the next record and then continue until you have checked all the records.

- You can click **Exclude this recipient** to exclude a record that you did not intend to include.

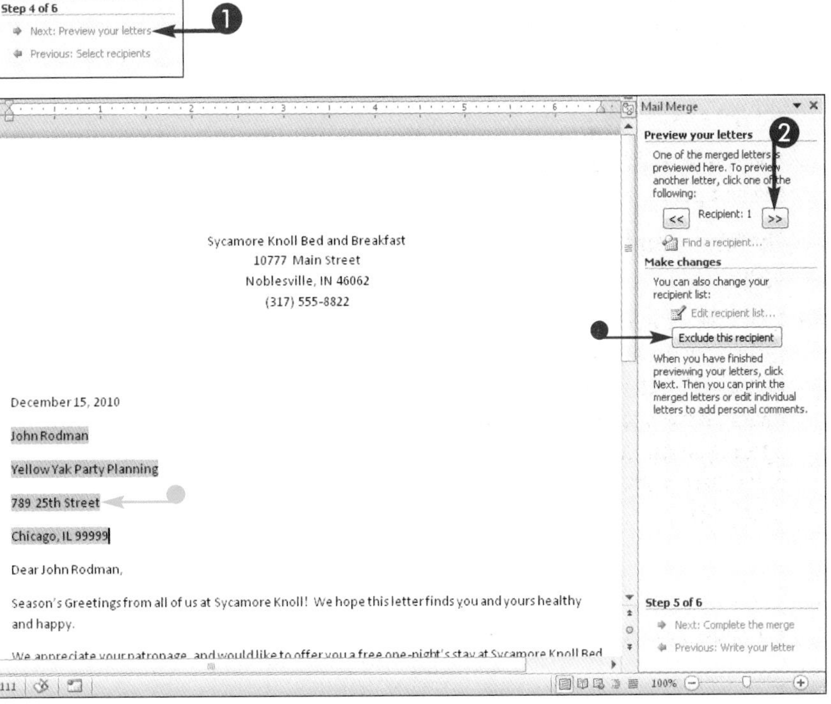

Filter the Recipient List

Besides excluding individual records, you can filter the recipient list more broadly by examining the entire list in a dialog box and then deselecting the ones you do not want or applying a filtering rule that automatically deselects certain ones.

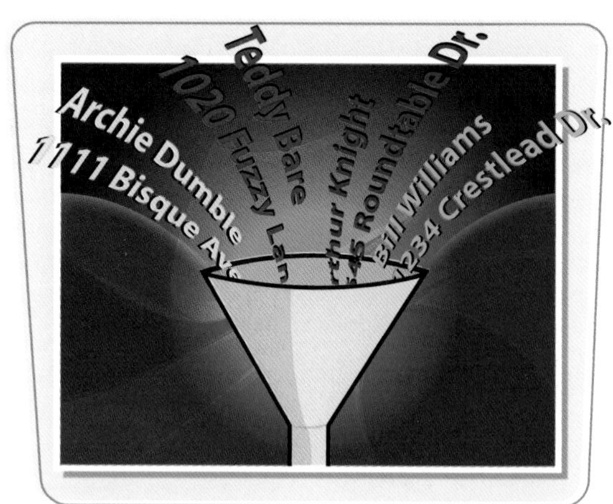

Filter the Recipient List

Filter the Recipient List to Exclude Certain Records

1. On the Mailings tab, click **Edit Recipient List**.

- You can also click **Edit recipient list** in the task pane.

The Mail Merge Recipients dialog box opens.

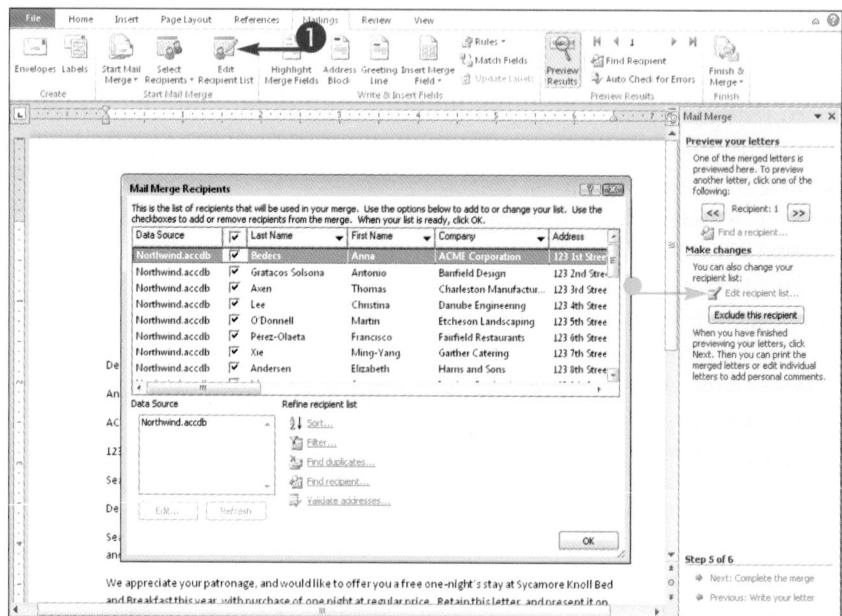

2. Deselect the check boxes for any records you do not want to include (☑ changes to ☐).

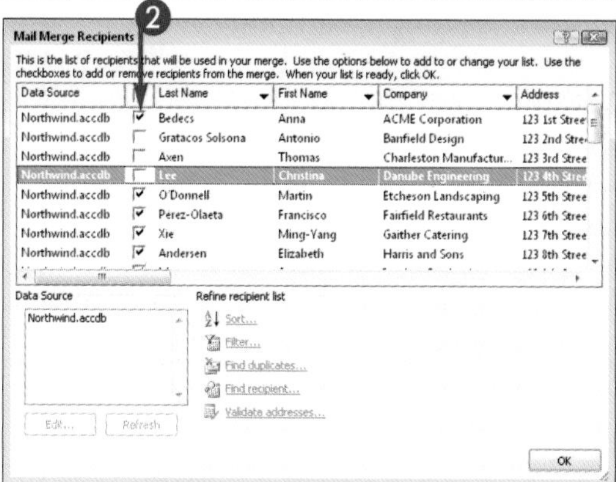

Filter the Recipient List Based on Criteria

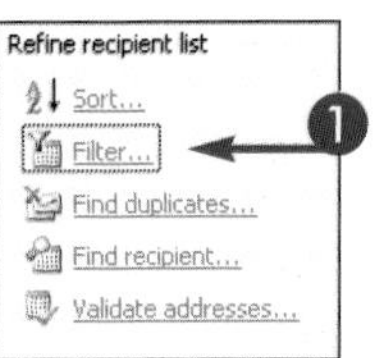

1. In the Mail Merge Recipients dialog box, click **Filter**.

   The Filter and Sort dialog box opens.

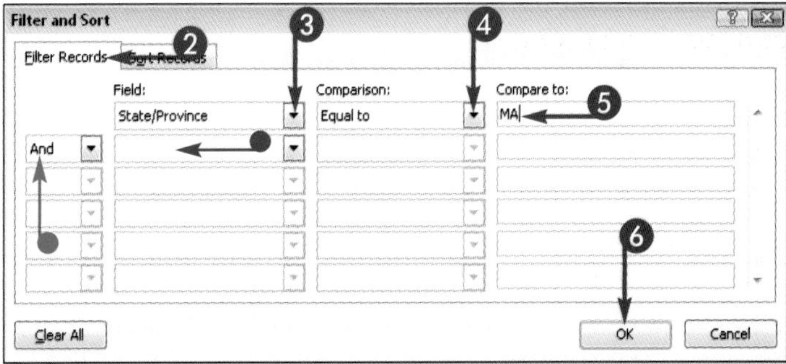

2. Click the **Filter Records** tab.
3. Click here (▾) to choose the field by which you want to filter.
4. Click here (▾) to choose the comparison operator.
5. Click here to type the value to which you want to compare.

- You can choose additional criteria on subsequent lines.
- Click here (▾) to choose **And** to require all criteria to be met in order for a record to be included or choose **Or** to allow records to be included that meet any of the criteria.

6. Click **OK**.

- The recipient list changes to show only records that match your criteria.

7. Click **OK** to accept the filtered list of recipients.

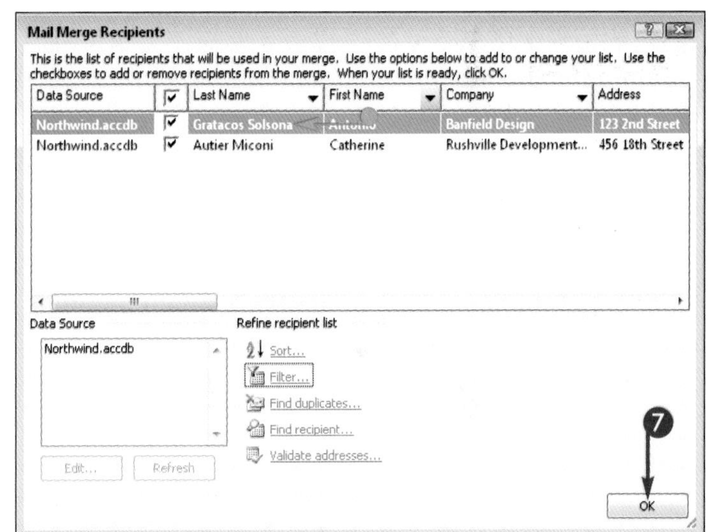

How do I clear a filter?

- To clear the filter, click **Filter** again in the Mail Merge Recipients dialog box (which reopens the Filter and Sort dialog box) and then click **Clear All**.

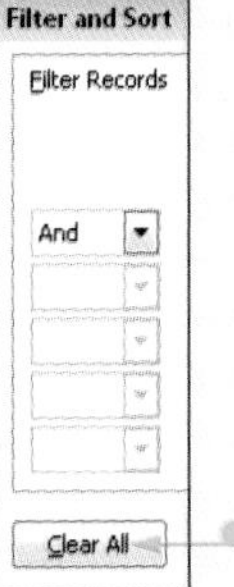

Can I filter based on whether a particular field is blank or nonblank?

Yes. In the Mail Merge Recipients dialog box, click the heading above the column by which you want to filter and then choose **(Blanks)** or **(Nonblanks)** from the menu that appears.

Company
Sort Ascending
Sort Descending
(All)
(Blanks)
(Nonblanks)
(Advanced...)

Sort the Recipient List

You might want the mail merge results to print in a certain order. For example, you might want them to be sorted by ZIP code, as is required for some mass-mailing services, or you might want them sorted by the recipient's last name to make it easier to file copies of the letters.

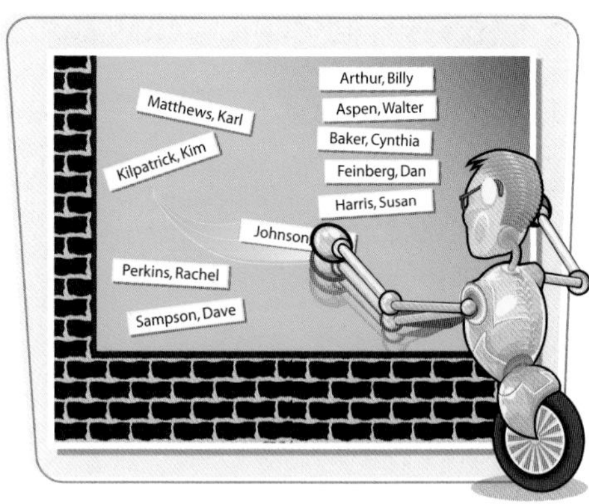

Sort the Recipient List

1. On the Mailings tab, click **Edit Recipient List**.

- You can also click **Edit recipient list** in the task pane.

The Mail Merge Recipients dialog box opens.

2. Click the heading of the field by which you want to sort.

The list is sorted by the field you chose.

If you want to sort in reverse order, click the column heading again.

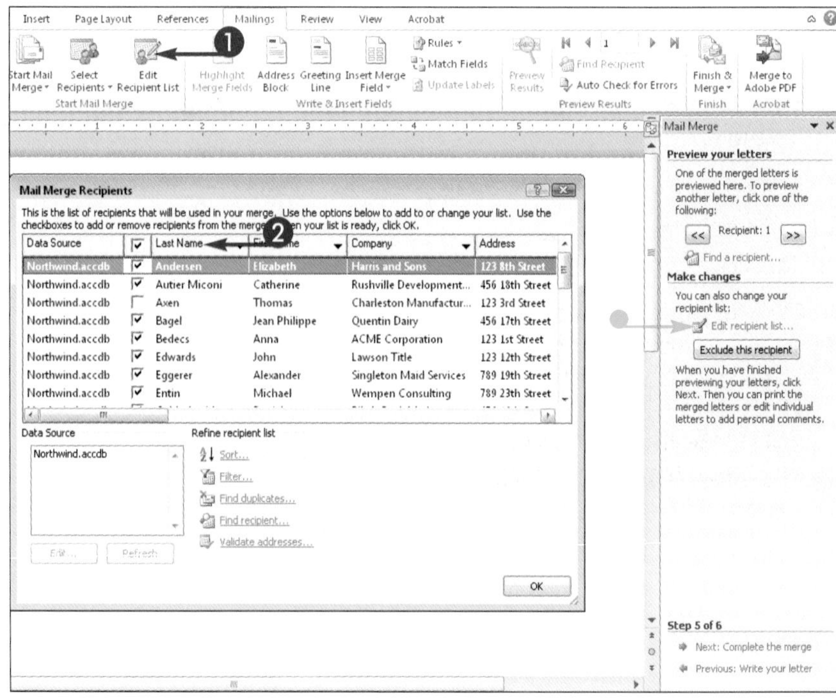

- You can also click here (▾) to open a menu and then click **Sort Ascending** or **Sort Descending**.

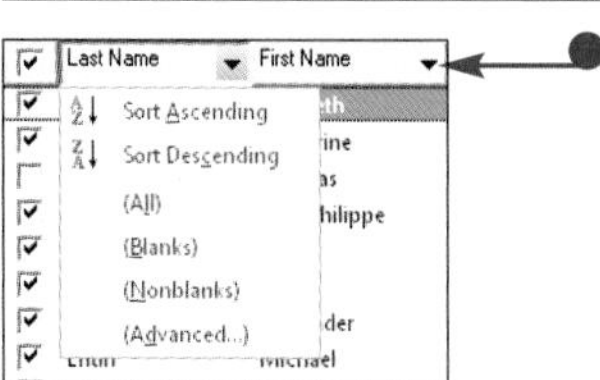

Merge to a New Document

Instead of merging directly to a printer, you might prefer to merge to a new Word document and then print the letters later. For example, you may not have the printer available that you want to use or you may want someone else to approve them before printing.

Merge to a New Document

1. On the Mailings tab, click **Finish & Merge**.
2. Click **Edit Individual Documents**.

   The Merge to New Document dialog box opens.
3. Click **OK**.

   The letters appear in a new Word document. You can save it, print it, or discard it by closing it without saving your changes. You can also make changes to individual letters before printing.

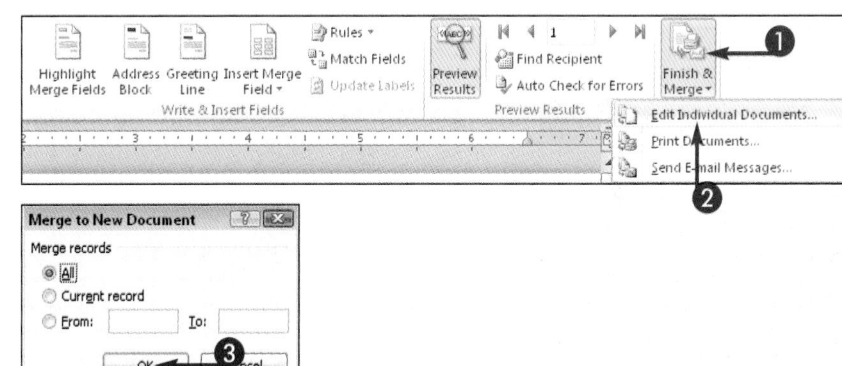

Merge Directly to a Printer

If you are confident in the results of your merge after having previewed it, you might want to merge directly to your printer. This is a good shortcut, especially for a previously created merge that you are simply reprinting.

Windows uses whatever printer you set as the default unless you specify a different printer.

Merge Directly to a Printer

1. On the Mailings tab, click **Finish & Merge**.
2. Click **Print Documents**.

   The Merge to Printer dialog box opens.
3. Click **OK**.

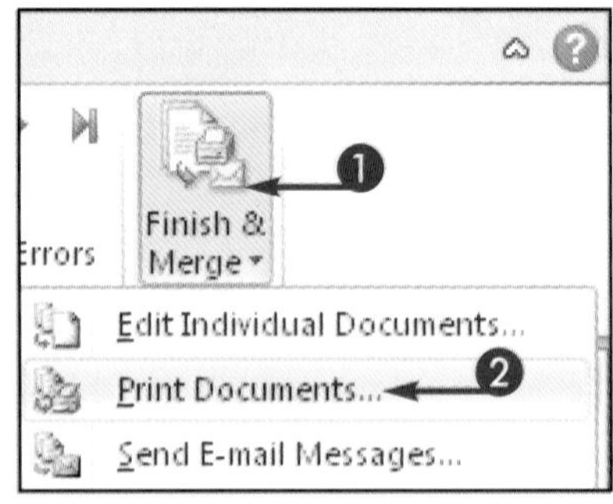

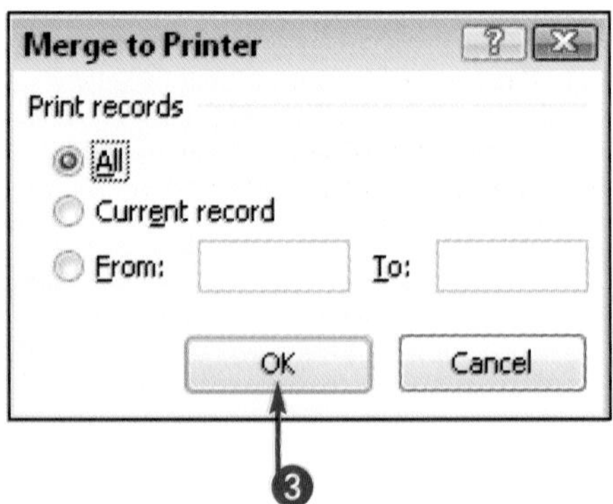

The Print dialog box opens.

4. Change any print settings if needed.

- You can change printers here.

5. Click **OK**.

   The letters print.

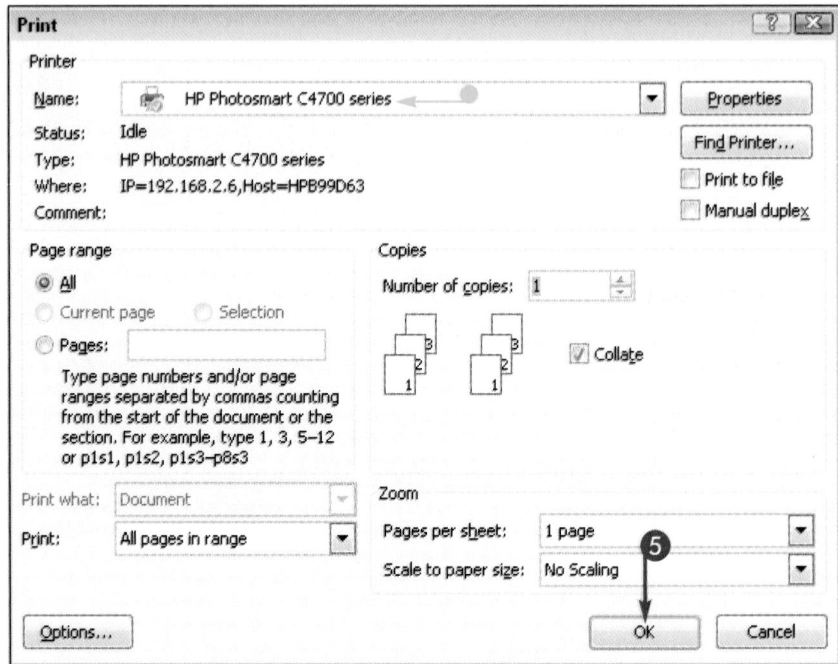

Save the Merge for Later Use

Saving the main document (that is, the merge document you have created in this chapter) is different from saving the results of a merge. When you save the main document, you can rerun the merge later. This might be useful if the records are likely to change. For example, you could have a mail merge for your Christmas letter and then rerun it every year based on your database of friends.

Save the Merge for Later Use

1. Click **File**.
2. Click **Save**.

   You can also click the **Save** button on the Quick Access Toolbar or press Ctrl + S.

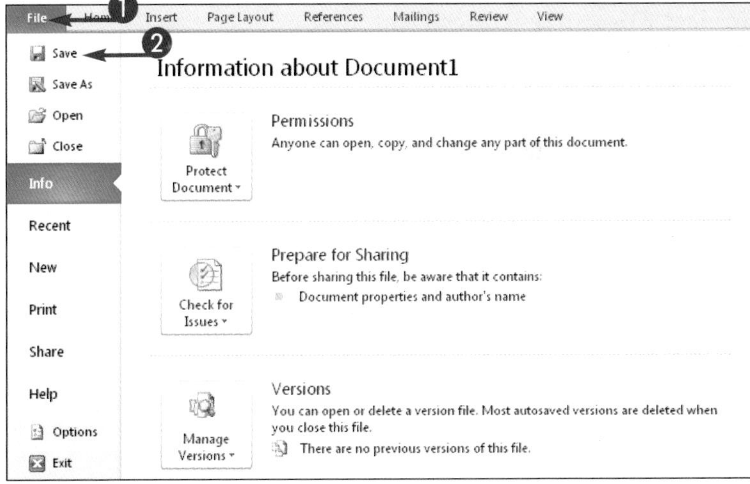

The Save As dialog box opens.

- You can change the save location here.
- You can change the file name here.

3. Click **Save**.

   The file is saved.

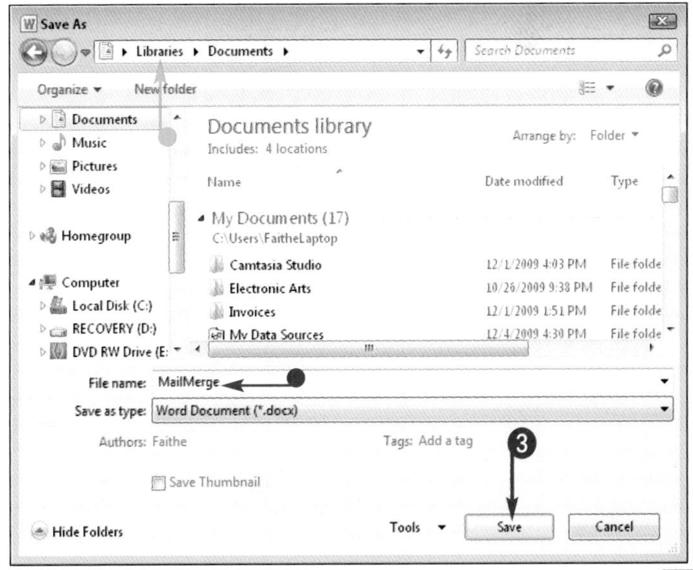

CHAPTER 17

Maintaining a Database

Access provides several tools for performing maintenance and administrative functions on a database. You can switch between file formats and back up, repair, and compact a database. You can also create an easy-to-use Switchboard system that makes your database more accessible to beginners.

Set a Trusted Location

When you open a file from an untrusted location, security warnings appear. One way to avoid this problem is to save your Access database files in a trusted location. By default, your Documents (or My Documents) folder is trusted; you can also set up other trusted locations.

Set a Trusted Location

1. Click **File**.
2. Click **Options**.

The Access Options dialog box opens.

3. Click **Trust Center**.
4. Click **Trust Center Settings**.

The Trust Center dialog box opens.

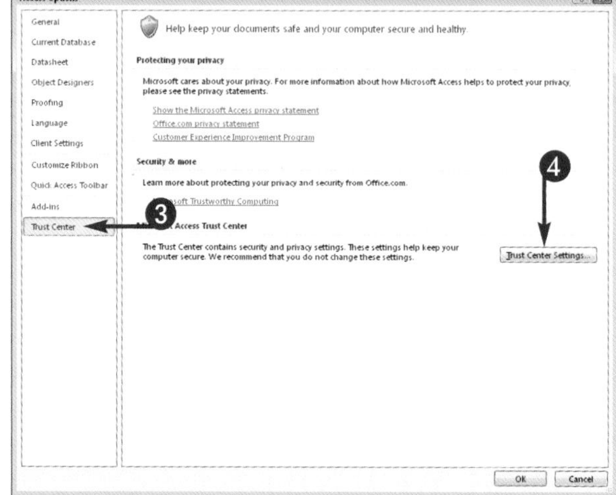

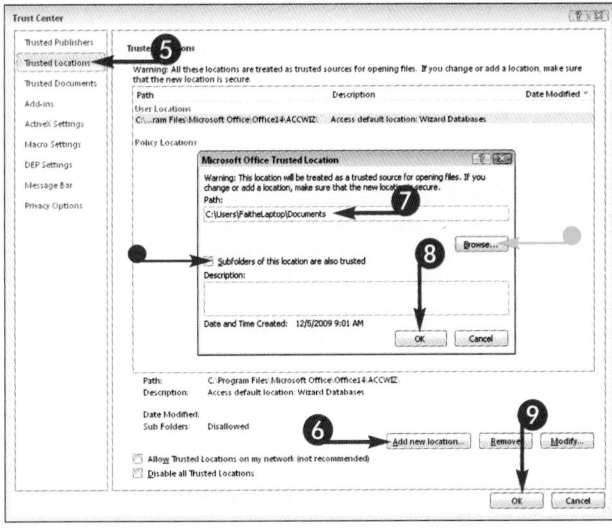

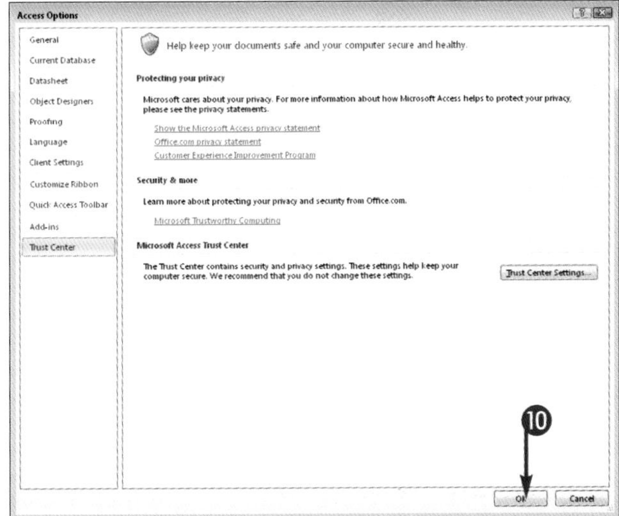

5. Click **Trusted Locations**.
6. Click **Add new location**.

   The Microsoft Office Trusted Location dialog box opens.
7. Type the path you want to set to be trusted.

- You can also click **Browse** to locate the path.
- You can click the **Subfolders of this location are also trusted** check box (☐ changes to ☑) to also trust subfolders of this location.

8. Click **OK**.

   The location is added to the Trusted Locations list.

   The Microsoft Office Trusted Location dialog box closes, and you are returned to the Trust Center dialog box.
9. Click **OK**.

   The Trust Center dialog box closes, and you are returned to the Access Options dialog box.
10. Click **OK**.

    The Access Options dialog box closes.

What is the Allow Trusted Locations on my network check box for?

- This option enables you to set up trusted locations that point to shared folders on your local area network. The reason it is marked "(not recommended)" is that you probably do not have control over what others put in those folders.

What is the Disable all Trusted Locations check box for?

- This option temporarily turns off all location-based trusting. It is quicker and easier than removing each trusted location from the list and then adding them to the list again later.

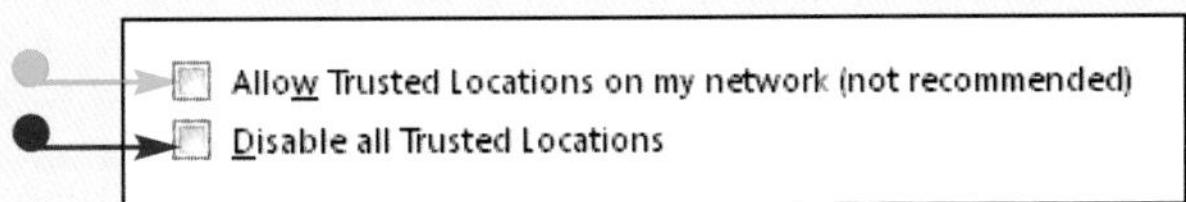

Save in a Previous Version Format

The file format used in Access 2007 and 2010 is not backward-compatible with earlier versions of Access. Therefore, if you need to share a data file with someone who uses an earlier version, you must save it in that earlier format.

If you will be sharing the file on an ongoing basis with others who use Access 2003 and earlier, you must continue using it in that format.

Save in a Previous Version Format

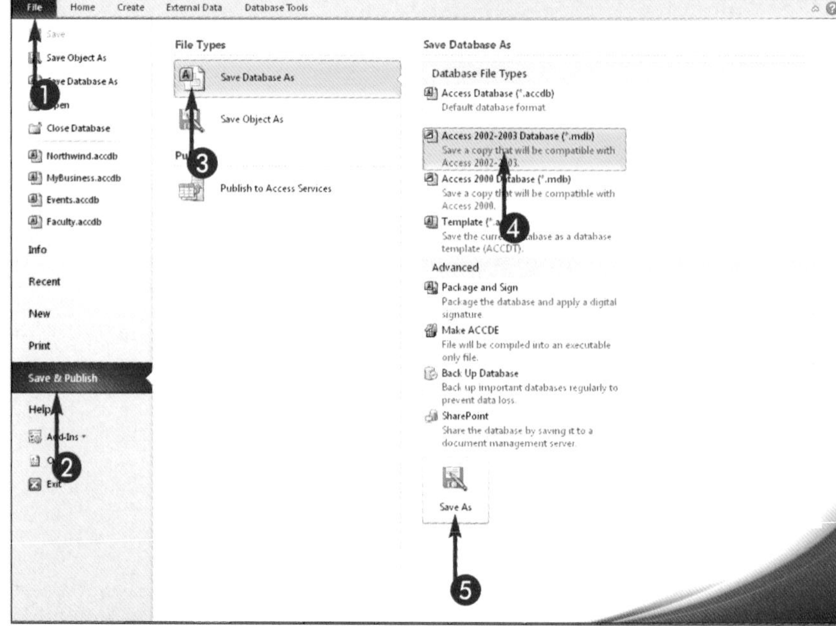

1. Click **File**.
2. Click **Save & Publish**.
3. Click **Save Database As**.
4. Click the older format you want to use.

Note: *Certain database features make it impossible to save the file in an earlier version, such as multivalued fields. If you have any such features in your database, an error will appear letting you know. At that point, you can edit the database to remove those features or you can decide not to save the older format.*

5. Click **Save As**.

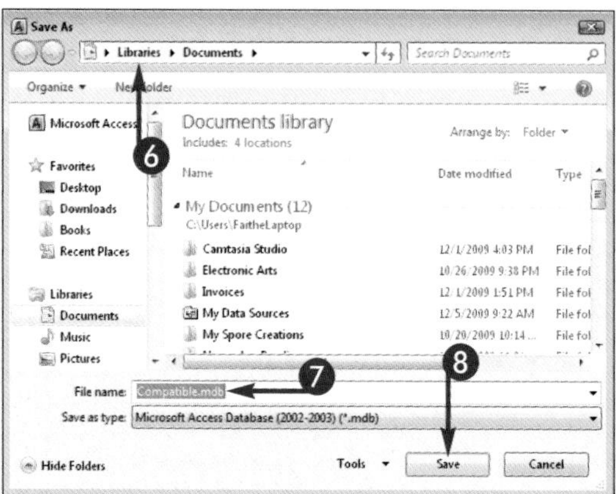

The Save As dialog box opens.

6. If needed, choose a different save location.
7. Type a file name here.
8. Click **Save**.

The file is saved in the older format to the location that you specified.

Convert to the Access 2007/2010 Format

If you have databases created in previous versions of Access, you can choose to update them to the Access 2007/2010 format. (Access 2007 and 2010 use the same format.) Doing so offers several advantages, including the ability to use multivalued fields and other features.

Convert to the Access 2007/2010 Format

1. Click **File**.
2. Click **Save & Publish**.
3. Click **Save Database As**.
4. Click **Access Database**.
5. Click **Save As**.

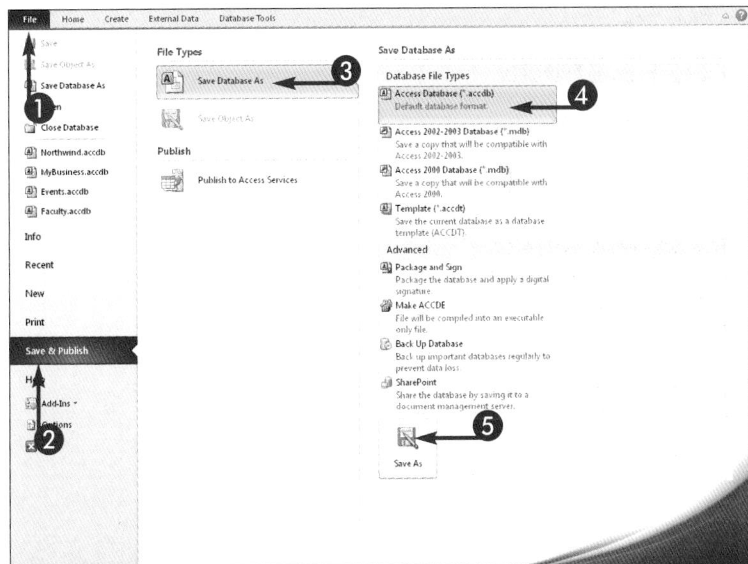

The Save As dialog box opens.

6. Change the save location if needed.
7. Type a different file name if needed.
8. Click **Save**.

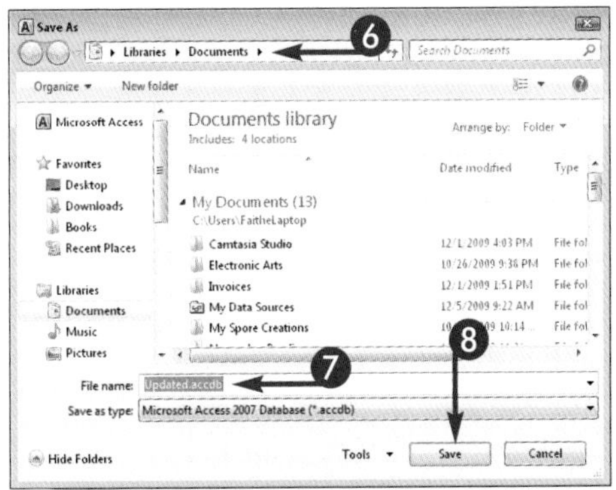

A confirmation box appears.

9. Click **OK**.

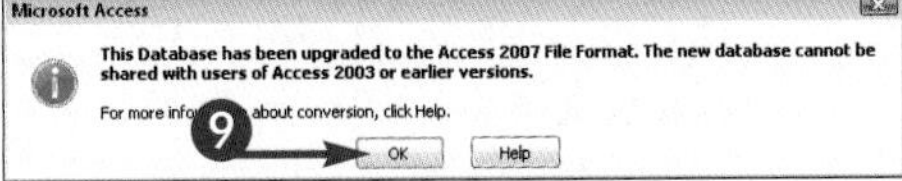

The database file remains open but is now in the latest Access format.

Back Up a Database

You will probably want to back up your database files periodically to ensure that your data is safe in the event of a system crash or file-corruption problem.

Backing up a database is similar to saving a copy of it; the main difference is that by default, the current date is appended to the file name.

Back Up a Database

1. Click **File**.
2. Click **Save & Publish**.
3. Click **Save Database As**.
4. Click **Back Up Database**.

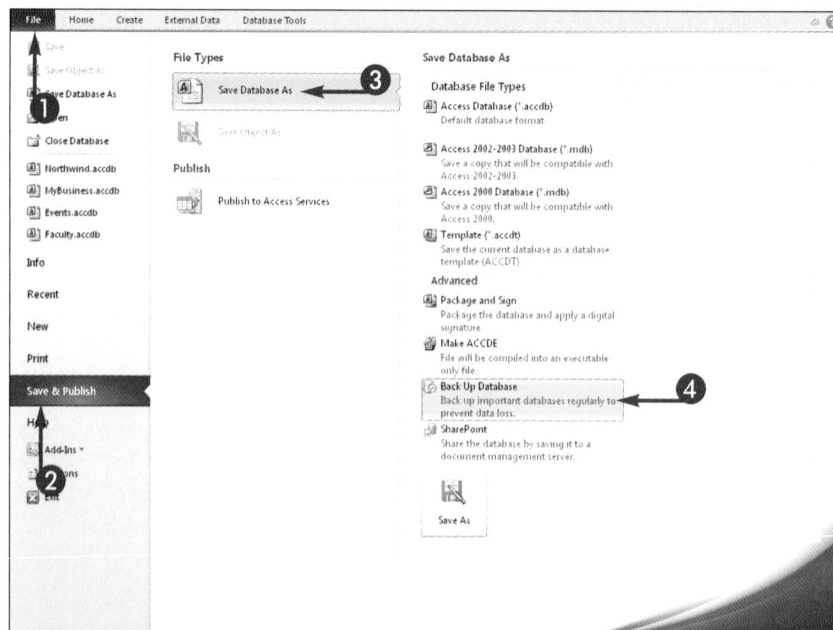

The Save As dialog box opens.

5. Change the save location if needed.
6. Change the file name if needed.
7. Click **Save**.

The backup is saved.

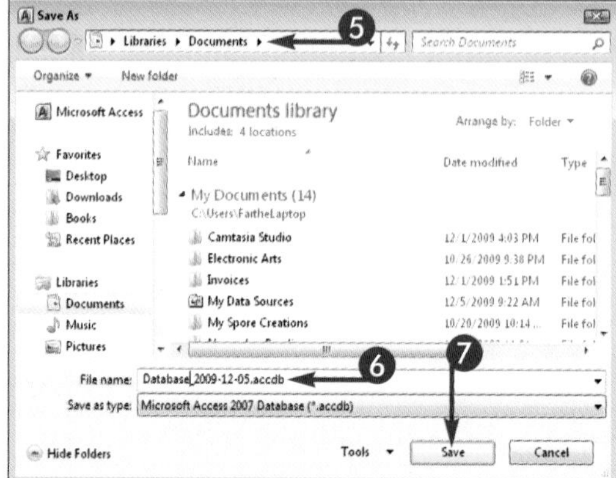

Often, a database designer is asked to create notes that explain to other designers the structure of his or her database. Access can automatically generate this documentation and put it in a report.

Document a Database

1. On the Database Tools tab, click **Database Documenter**.

   The Documenter dialog box opens.

2. On each tab, click the check box next to each object you want to include in the documentation.

Note: *You can include relationships and properties from the Current Database tab.*

3. Click **OK**.

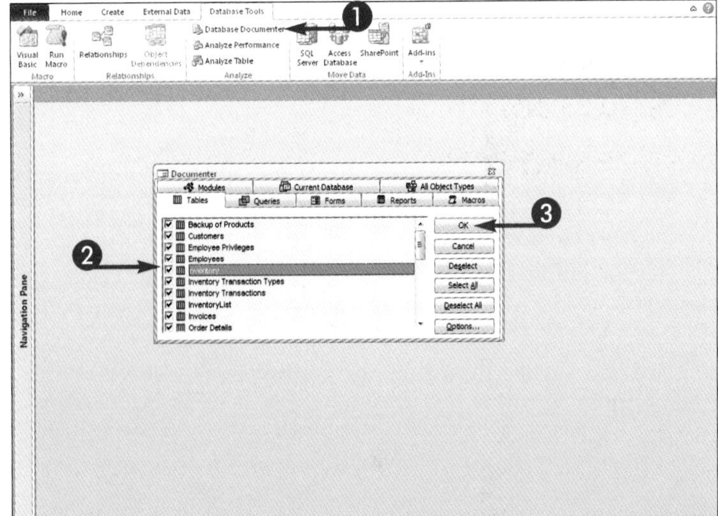

- The report appears in Print Preview. From here, you can save it and print it.

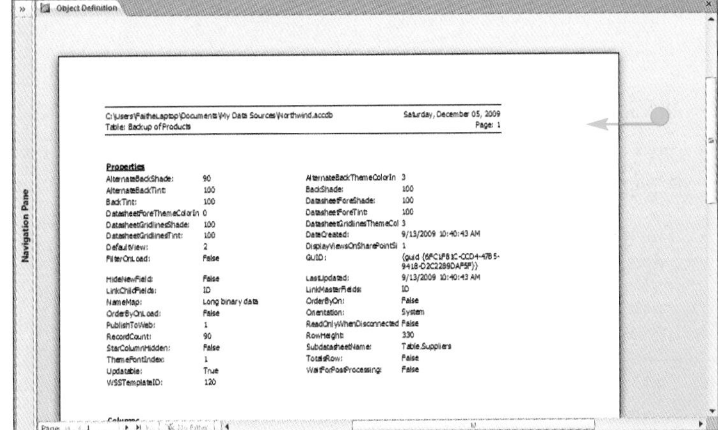

Compact and Repair a Database

Compacting a database reduces the file size by eliminating wasted blank space. Repairing a database checks it for storage errors and corrects any that it finds. You can optionally set up the database to compact itself automatically each time you close it.

Compacting and repairing are actually two separate functions, but they are performed by using the same command.

Compact and Repair a Database

Compact and Repair

1. Click **File**.
2. Click **Compact & Repair Database**.

   The file is compacted and repaired. No additional prompts appear.

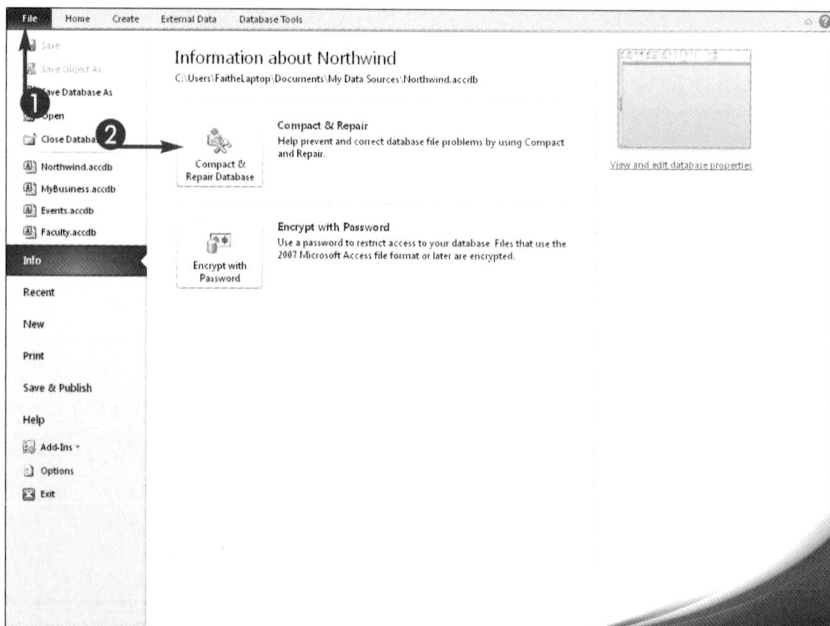

Automatically Compact on Close

1. Click **File**.
2. Click **Options**.

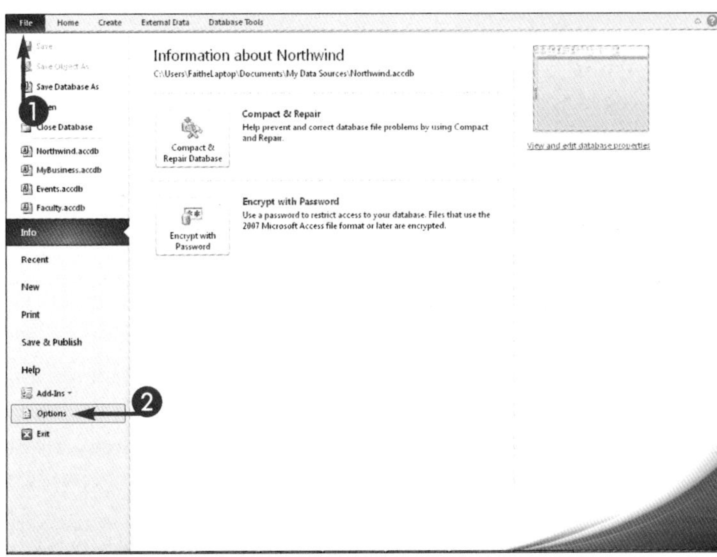

The Access Options dialog box opens.

3. Click **Current Database**.
4. Click the **Compact on Close** check box (☐ changes to ☑).
5. Click **OK**.

The database will now automatically compact whenever you close it.

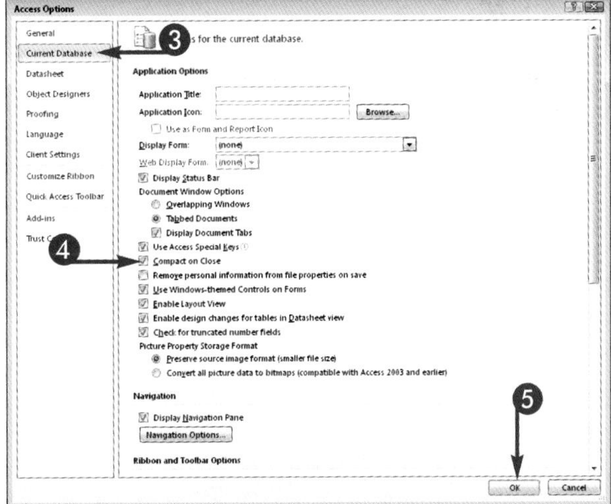

What does compacting do?

Compacting a database removes any blank space that it contains so that it takes up less space on disk. When you delete records, for example, the space that they occupied in the database remains as blank space until you compact the database.

What does repairing do?

Repairing fixes any logical or linkage problems in the database — anything that may cause the database to not open properly or any of its objects not to perform as expected. Periodic repairing of a database file can ensure that small problems do not escalate into large ones.

Password-Protect a Database

You can assign a password to a database so that only authorized users can open it.

Before you can set or change a password for the database, however, you must open it for exclusive use. This prevents others from using the database at the same time you are trying to put a password on it.

Password-Protect a Database

Open a Database for Exclusive Use

1. Click **File**.
2. Click **Close Database**.
3. Click **Open**.

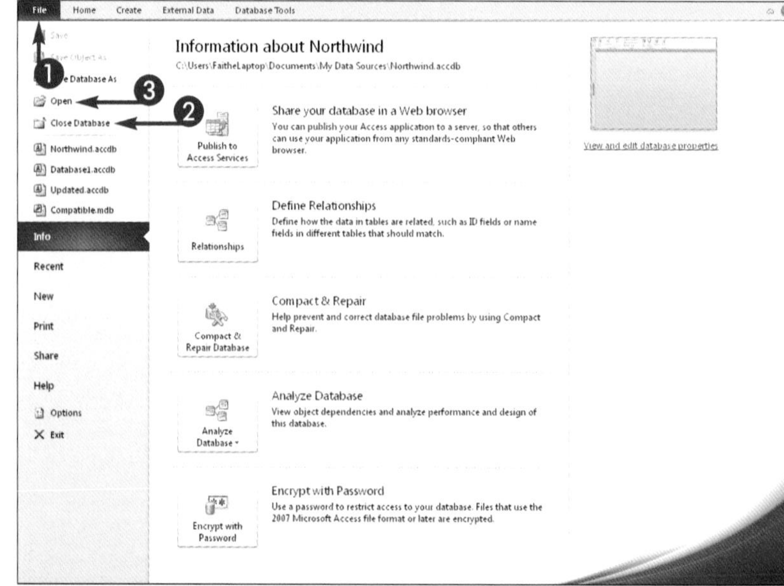

The Open dialog box opens.

4. Click the file that you want to open.
5. Click here (▾) to choose **Open Exclusive**.

The database opens for exclusive use.

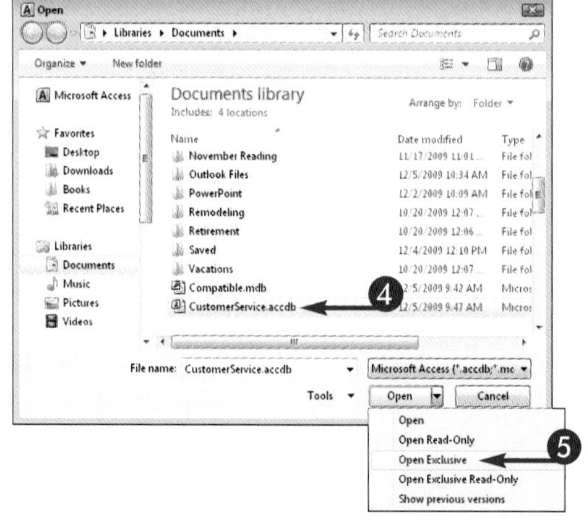

Password-Protect the Database

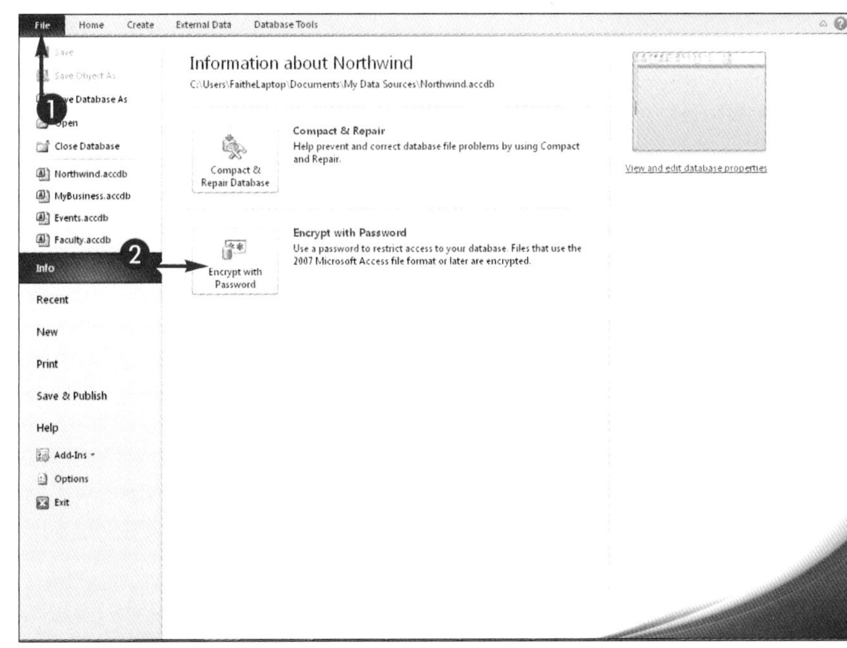

1. Click **File**.
2. Click **Encrypt with Password**.

The Set Database Password dialog box opens.

3. Type the password you want to use.
4. Click here to type the same password again.
5. Click **OK**.
6. If a warning appears, click **OK**.

The file is now password-protected.

The next time you open the file, you are prompted for a password.

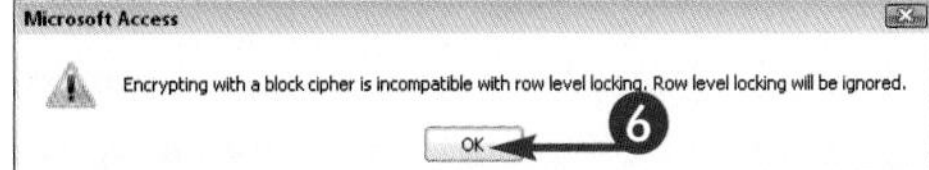

How does password protection actually work?

The password actually encrypts the entire database, so it cannot be browsed from outside of Access. This is good because then nobody can bypass the Access password protection to hack into the file with an editing utility.

How do I unset (remove) a password?

1. Open the database for exclusive use
2. Click **File**.
3. Click **Decrypt Database**.
4. Type the password.
5. Click **OK**.

You cannot unset the password if you do not know it.

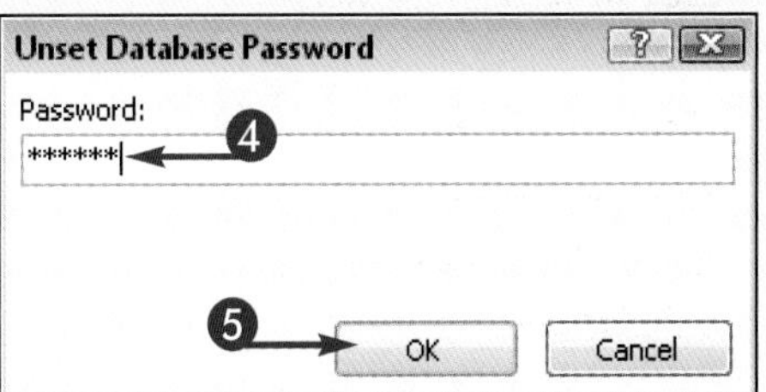

Create a Switchboard

A database with many objects can be intimidating for an end user to navigate. Many of the people who may use and benefit from your database may not have the same level of computer expertise as you and may find it easier to work with a simpler interface. You can create your own navigation forms one by one by creating and linking forms together, but there is an easier way: the Switchboard feature. A switchboard automatically creates and links the forms to provide an easy-to-navigate user interface.

The Switchboard Manager utility is not available on any of the default Ribbon tabs, so you must add it to the Quick Access Toolbar before you can use it.

Create a Switchboard

Add the Switchboard Manager to the Quick Access Toolbar

1. Click **File**.
2. Click **Options**.

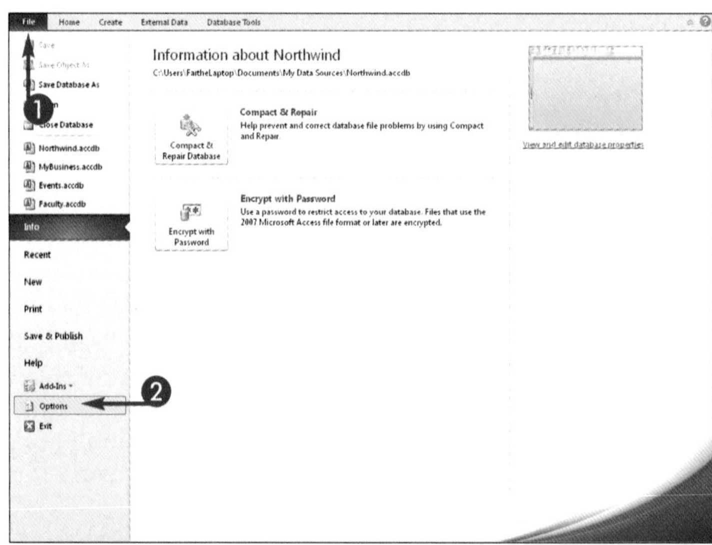

The Access Options dialog box opens.

3. Click **Quick Access Toolbar**.
4. Click here (▼) to choose **Commands Not in the Ribbon**.
5. Click **Switchboard Manager**.
6. Click **Add**.
7. Click **OK**.

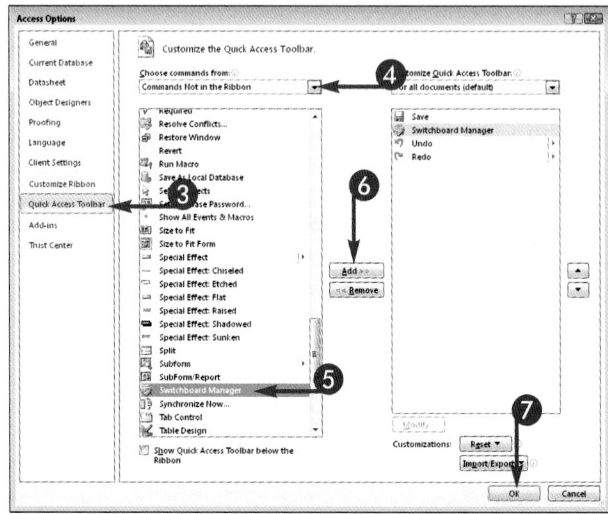

Start a New Switchboard

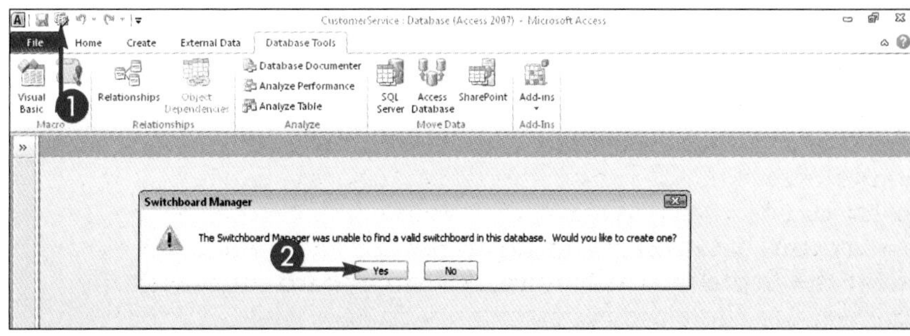

1. Click the **Switchboard Manager** (☐) button on the Quick Access Toolbar.

   A message appears that the Switchboard Manager was unable to find a valid switchboard and asks if you want to create one.

2. Click **Yes**.

- The Switchboard Manager opens with a default switchboard page created.

You can now create additional switchboard pages and add items to each page.

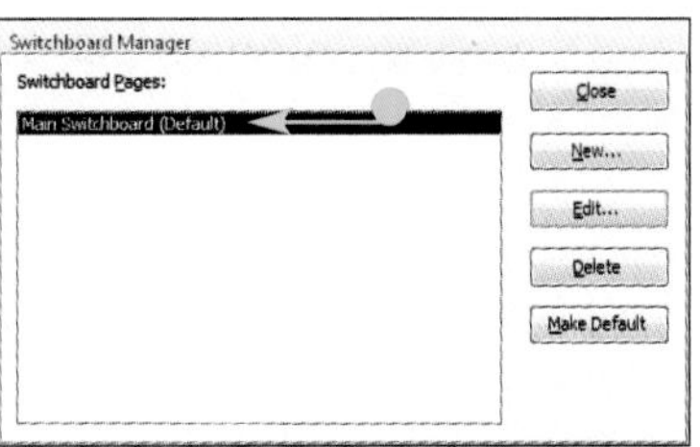

Can I format the switchboard?

Yes. The switchboard is a form and can be formatted like other forms.

- After closing the Switchboard Manager, you can open the Switchboard form in Design view and change the fonts, background, and other attributes. However, you should avoid making layout changes to the form or deleting the placeholders on it.

- The Switchboard form pulls its data from a table called Switchboard Items, and if you delete the ItemText placeholder on the form, it loses its connection to the data it needs.

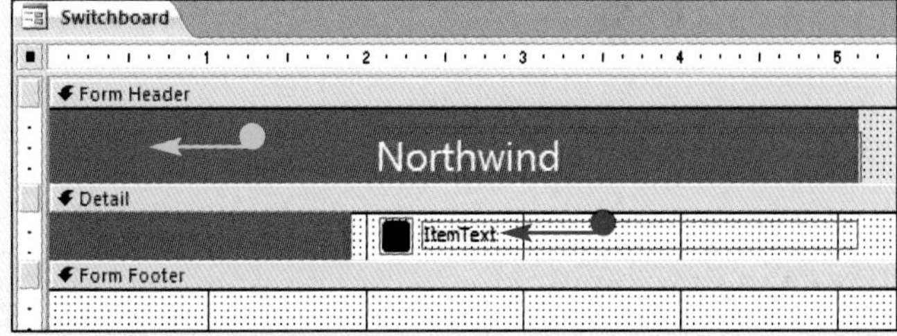

- You can open the Switchboard Items table in Datasheet view, the same as other tables. Examining that table can provide a behind-the-scenes view of how the switchboard works.

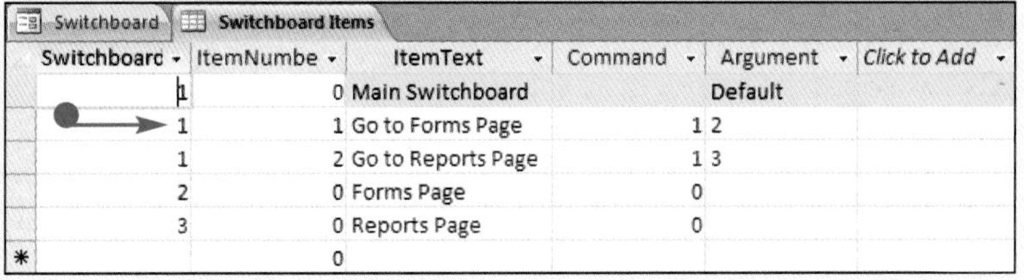

Switchboard	ItemNumbe	ItemText	Command	Argument	Click to Add
1	0	Main Switchboard		Default	
1	1	Go to Forms Page	1	2	
1	2	Go to Reports Page	1	3	
2	0	Forms Page	0		
3	0	Reports Page	0		
*	0				

continued

Create a Switchboard *(continued)*

The basic switchboard consists of a single page. You may want to create additional pages and link them to the main page rather than placing all your commands on that single main page. For example, on the main page, you might have links for Forms and Reports and then you might create two separate pages: Forms Page and Reports Page. On each of those pages, you would then create links that open various forms and reports, respectively.

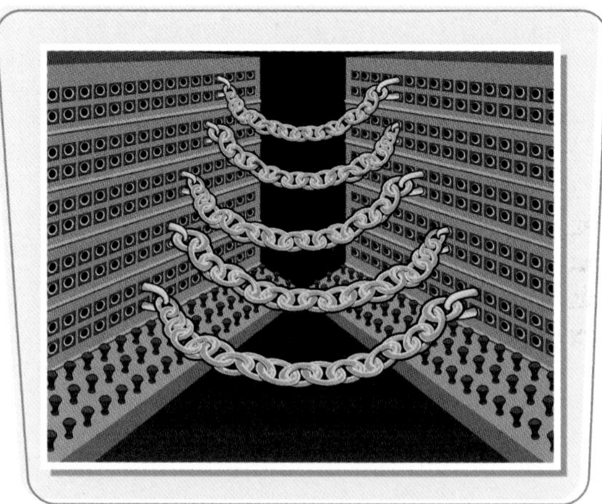

Create a Switchboard *(continued)*

Add a Switchboard Page

1. From the Switchboard Manager, click **New**.

   The Create New dialog box opens.

2. Type the name for the new page.
3. Click **OK**.

   Leave the Switchboard Manager open for further customization in the following section.

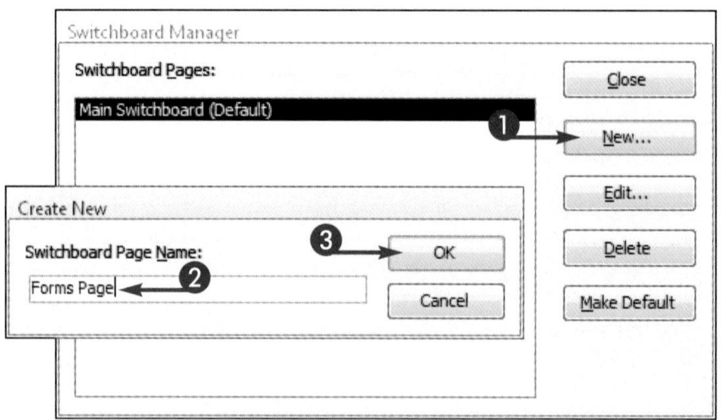

Add Commands to a Switchboard Page

1. From the Switchboard Manager, click the page you want to edit.
2. Click **Edit**.

   The Edit Switchboard Page dialog box opens.

3. Click **New**.

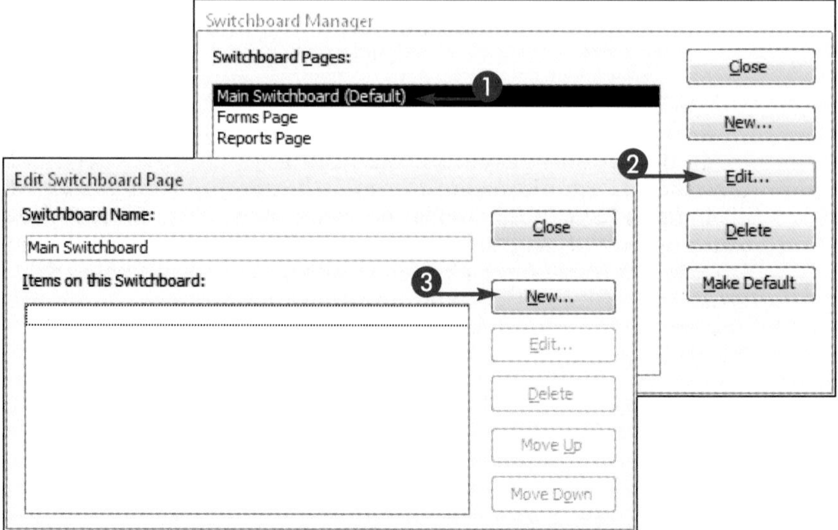

The Edit Switchboard Item dialog box opens.

4. Type the text that should appear for that item on the form.
5. Click here (▾) to choose an action for the item.

   In this example, a button is being created that will open up a different page of the switchboard.

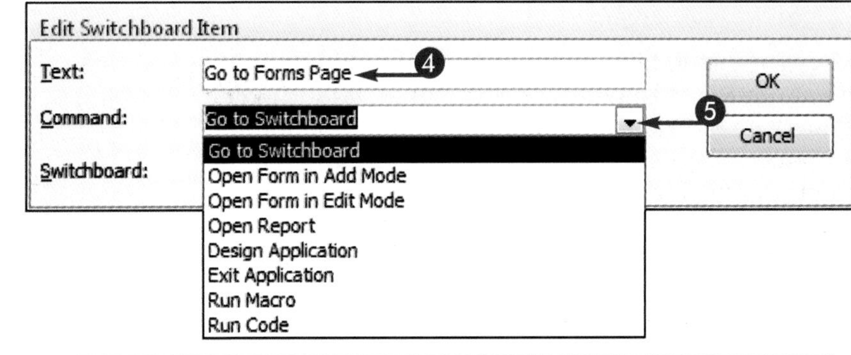

6. Click here (▾) to choose the item that the command will affect.

***Note:** The name of this command changes depending on what you chose in step **5**.*

7. Click **OK**.
8. Repeat steps **3** to **7** to create more commands as needed.
9. Click **Close** to close the Edit Switchboard Page dialog box.

   Your edits to the page are saved.

   You can close the Switchboard Manager window or leave it open for further editing.

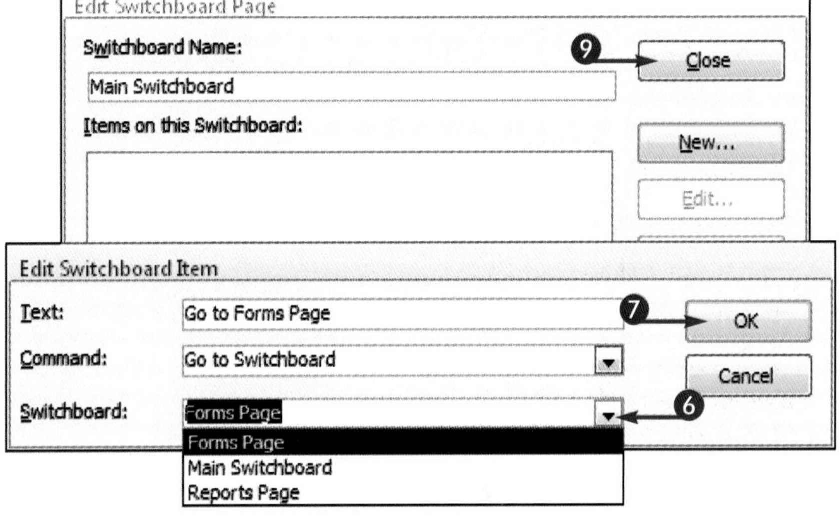

How do I create items that open forms or reports?

Follow the steps under "Add Commands to a Switchboard Page." For a form, in step **5**, choose either **Open Form in Add Mode** (opens the form with a new record started, for data entry) or **Open Form in Edit Mode** (opens the form with an existing record displayed). Then, choose the form name in step **6**. For a report, in step **5**, choose **Open Report** and then choose the report in step **6**.

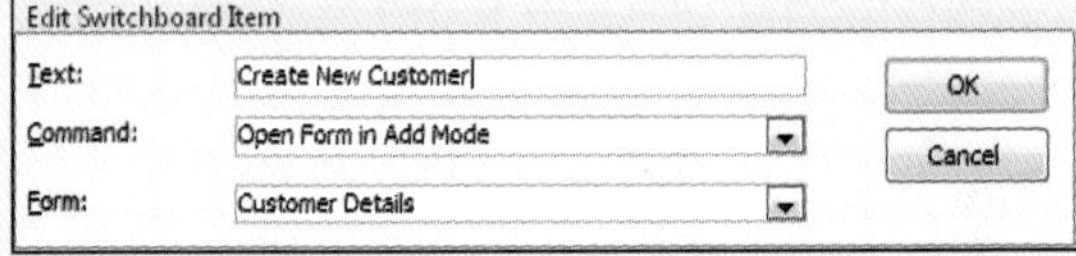

How do I return to the main switchboard from one of the other pages?

Create an item on each switchboard page called Return to Main Switchboard and set its command to **Go to Switchboard** (step **5**). Set the switchboard you want to go to as the **Main Switchboard**.

Set Switchboard Startup Options

The switchboard is most useful when it is set to appear automatically every time the database opens. That way, the user does not need to understand how to open a form by using the Navigation pane; the form simply appears.

You may also want to make the switchboard a pop-up form in a window rather than a tabbed form (the default). Users are more likely to be familiar with windows than with tabbed pages, so the windowed style may make them feel more comfortable.

Set Switchboard Startup Options

Set the Switchboard to Open Automatically at Startup

1. Click **File**.
2. Click **Options**.

The Access Options dialog box opens.

3. Click **Current Database**.
4. Click here (▾) to choose **Switchboard** from the Display Form drop-down menu.
5. Click **OK**.

   A message appears that you must close and reopen the database for the change to take effect.

6. Click **OK**.

   The form is now set to display automatically the next time you open the database.

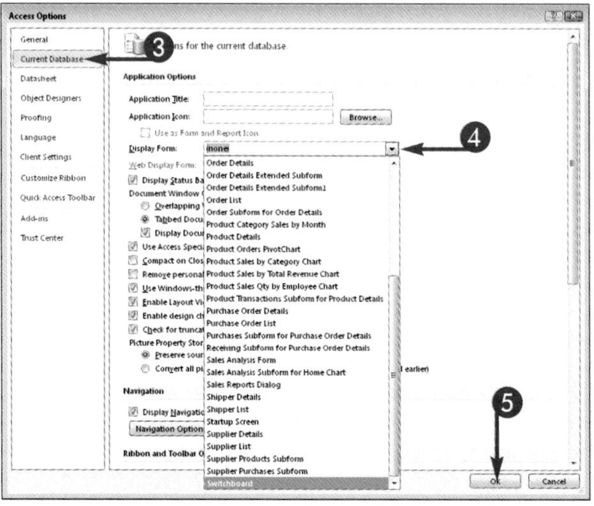

Set the Switchboard to Open as a Floating Pane

1. Right-click on the Switchboard form and then choose **Design View** from the shortcut menu.

   The form opens in Design view.

2. Click **Property Sheet**.

   The Property Sheet opens.

3. Click here (▾) to choose **Form** if it does not already appear.

4. Click the **All** tab.

5. Set the Pop Up setting to **Yes**.

6. Click here (💾) to save the form.

7. Click here to preview the form.

   The form appears as a pop-up window.

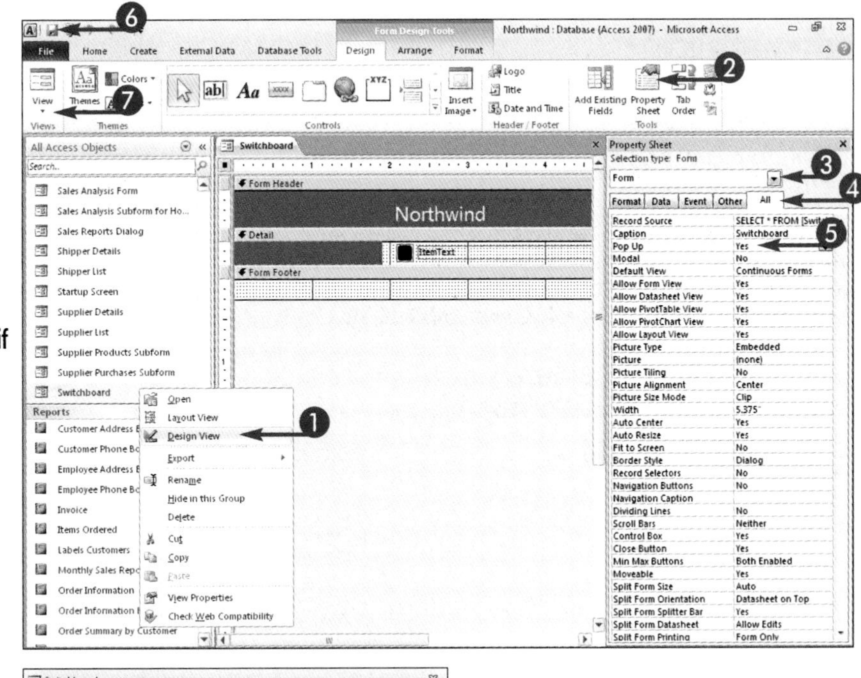

The Switchboard window has a lot of empty space at the bottom. How can I make it appear smaller?

This happens because by default, the Switchboard form is set to display as Continuous Forms. On the Property Sheet in Design view, set the Default View property to Single Form.

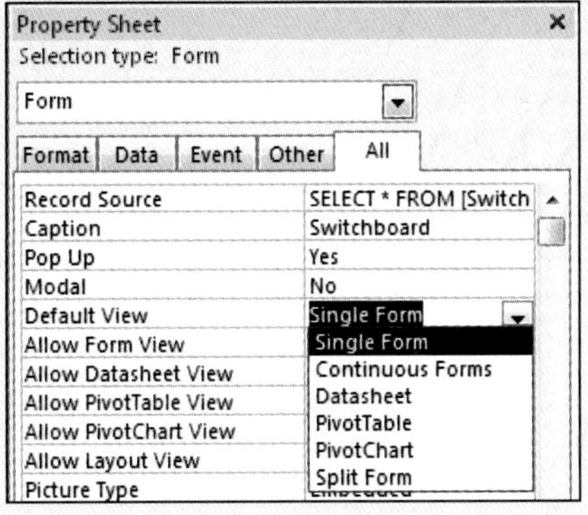

After I put the form in Pop-up mode, how can I get back to Design view to edit it some more?

Right-click on the Switchboard form in the Navigation pane and then choose **Design View** from the shortcut menu.

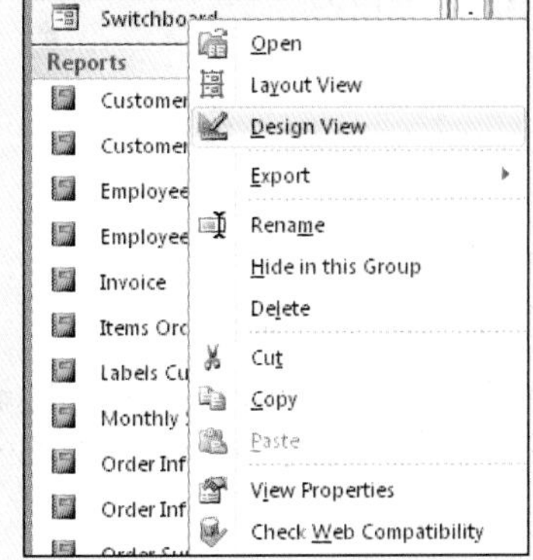

Index

E

Index

G

Index

N

O

P

Index

S

Index

V

W

X–Y–Z

...all designed for visual learners—just like you!

Master VISUALLY®

Your complete visual reference. Two-color interior.

- 3ds Max
- Creating Web Pages
- Dreamweaver and Flash
- Excel
- Excel VBA Programming
- iPod and iTunes
- Mac OS
- Office
- Optimizing PC Performance
- Photoshop Elements
- QuickBooks
- Quicken
- Windows
- Windows Mobile
- Windows Server

Visual Blueprint™

Where to go for professional-level programming instruction. Two-color interior.

- Ajax
- ASP.NET 2.0
- Excel Data Analysis
- Excel Pivot Tables
- Excel Programming
- HTML
- JavaScript
- Mambo
- PHP & MySQL
- SEO
- Ubuntu Linux
- Vista Sidebar
- Visual Basic
- XML

Visual Encyclopedia™

Your A to Z reference of tools and techniques. Full color.

- Dreamweaver
- Excel
- Mac OS
- Photoshop
- Windows

Visual Quick Tips

Shortcuts, tricks, and techniques for getting more done in less time. Full color.

- Crochet
- Digital Photography
- Excel
- Internet
- iPod & iTunes
- Knitting
- Mac OS
- MySpace
- Office
- PowerPoint
- Windows
- Wireless Networking

For a complete listing of Visual books, go to wiley.com/go/visual